Coordination of Large-Scale Multiagent Systems

Coordination of Large-Scale Multiagent Systems

Edited by

Paul Scerri
Carnegie Mellon University

Régis Vincent
SRI International

Roger Mailler
Cornell University

 Springer

Paul Scerri
Carnegie Mellon University

Régis Vincent
SRI International

Roger Mailler
Cornell University

Library of Congress Cataloging-in-Publication Data

Coordination of large-scale multiagent systems / edited by Paul Scerri, Régis Vincent,
  Roger Mailler.
     p. cm.
  Includes bibliographical references and index.
  ISBN 0-387-27972-5 (e-book)
    1. Intelligent agents (Computer software) 2. Electronic data processing--Distributed
  processing. 3. Distributed artificial intelligence. I. Scerri, Paul, 1974- II. Vincent, Régis.
  III. Mailler, Roger, 1971-

  QA76.76.I58C72 2005
  006.3--dc22

ISBN 978-1-4419-3872-5
ISBN 978-0-387-27972-5 (e-book)

2005050015

Printed in the United States of America

9 8 7 6 5 4 3 2 1

springeronline.com

Contents

Preface

The increased availability of low-cost, high-power computation has made it feasible to consider building distributed systems on a previously unimagined scale. For example, in domains such as space exploration, military planning and disaster response, groups with hundreds or thousands of intelligent agents, robots and people that work together can revolutionize the achievement of complex goals. To effectively and efficiently achieve their goals members of a group need to cohesively follow a joint course of action while remaining flexible to unforeseen developments in the environment. Such coordination entails a new set of challenges that have not been adequately addressed by previous coordination research.

It is becoming increasingly clear that many algorithms, theories and infrastructures developed for smaller groups of agents have serious limitations or weaknesses when the size of the group is scaled above 10-20 agents. For example, establishing and maintaining joint commitments between a thousand agents is infeasible, likewise existing multi-agent programming languages, e.g., Taems, do not provide an appropriate level of support for programming large groups. On the other hand, established techniques specifically designed for coordinating very large numbers of agents, primarily swarm based groups, do not provide developers with the required level of control needed to ensure coherent behavior of the group as a whole.

The key assumption drawing together the chapters in this book is that meeting the challenges of very large scale coordination will likely require new theories, abstractions, tools and algorithms. The goal of this book is to present some of the most recent insights and approaches used by researchers working or thinking about very large groups of coordinating agents. By bringing together key ideas, the field can progress towards establishing a sound theoretical and experimental basis for coordinating many agents. Eventually, we hope that methods for designing, implementing, and understanding large-scale coordination will have the same level of maturity that has been already achieved for smaller groups.

This book is broken down into four main parts. In Part I - "Effects of Scaling Coordination", we present work from various researchers who have developed systems that operate on a large scale. Each of these systems demonstrate behaviors which only occur when the systems are scaled beyond the size of a few or several. Part II - "Scaling Exisiting Coordination Approaches", presents a number of interesting attempts at scaling exisiting small-scale methods to operate on large volume problems. Part III - "New Approaches for Large Scale Coordination" presents algorithms specifically designed for large scale coordination. Finally, Part IV - "Robustness and Flexibility for Large Scale Coordination" presents novel methods for ensuring that large scale systems remain stable when faced with failures and changes that become increasingly common when large numbers of agents are involved.

We hope that this book represents the first step towards a science of large scale coordination that one day forms the basis for revolutionary systems that change the planet for the better.

Paul Scerri, Roger Mailler and Regis Vincent.

Part I

Effects of Scaling Coordination

The Effects of Locality and Asymmetry in Large-Scale Multiagent MDPs

Dmitri A Dolgov[1] and Edmund H Durfee[2]

[1] University of Michigan; Ann Arbor, MI 48109; ddolgov@umich.edu
[2] University of Michigan; Ann Arbor, MI 48109; durfee@umich.edu

Summary. As multiagent systems scale up, the complexity of interactions between agents (cooperative coordination in teams, or strategic reasoning in the case of self-interested agents) often increases exponentially. In particular, in multiagent MDPs, it is generally necessary to consider the joint state space of all agents, making the size of the problem and the solution exponential in the number of agents. However, often interactions between the agents are only local, which suggests a more compact problem representation. We consider a subclass of multiagent MDPs with local interactions where dependencies between agents are asymmetric, meaning that agents can affect others in a unidirectional manner. This asymmetry, which often occurs in large-scale domains with authority-driven relationships between agents, allows us to make better use of the locality of agents' interactions. We discuss a graphical model that exploits this form of problem structure and use it to analyze the effects of locality and asymmetry on the complexity and structure of optimal policies. For problems where the solutions retain some of the compactness of problem representation, we present computationally-efficient algorithms for constructing optimal multiagent policies.

1 Introduction

Markov decision processes [2, 17] are widely used for devising optimal control policies for agents in stochastic environments. Moreover, MDPs are also being applied to multiagent domains [3, 18, 19]. However, a weak spot of traditional MDPs that subjects them to "the curse of dimensionality" [1], and presents significant computational challenges, is the *flat* state space model, which enumerates all states the agent can be in. This is especially significant for large-scale multiagent MDPs, where, in general, it is necessary to consider the joint state and action spaces of all agents. Because of this, as the number of agent in a multiagent system increases, the size of the flat MDP representation increases exponentially, which means that very quickly it becomes impossible to even model the problem, let alone solve it.

Fortunately, there is often a significant amount of structure to MDPs, which can be exploited to devise more compact problem and solution representations, as well as efficient solution methods that take advantage of such representations. For example, a number of *factored* representations have been proposed [4, 5, 10] that model the state space as being factored into state variables, assume the reward function is additive, and use dynamic Bayesian network [8] representations of the transition function to exploit the locality of the relationships between variables.

In this work, we focus on multiagent MDPs and on a particular form of problem structure that is due to the locality of interactions between agents. Central to our problem representation are *dependency graphs* that describe the relationships between agents. The idea is very similar to other graphical models, e.g., *graphical games* [12], *coordination graphs* [10], and *multiagent influence diagrams* [13], where graphs are used to more compactly represent the interactions between agents to avoid the exponential explosion in problem size. Similarly, our representation of a multiagent MDP is exponential only in the degree of the dependency graph, and can be exponentially smaller than the size of the flat MDP defined on the joint state and action spaces of all agents. A distinguishing characteristic of the graphical representation that we study in this work is that it makes more fine-grained distinctions about how agents affect each other: we distinguish between agents' effects on other agents' reward functions from their effects on other agents' transition functions.

We focus on asymmetric dependency graphs, where the influences that agents exert on each other do not have to be mutual. Such interactions are characteristic of large-scale multiagent domains with authority-based relationships between agents, i.e., low-authority agents have no control over higher-authority ones. As we discuss below, there are problem classes where this asymmetry has important positive implications on the structure of optimal multiagent policies and the problem complexity.

For any compact problem representation, an important question is whether the compactness of problem representation can be maintained in the solutions, and if so, whether it can be exploited to devise more efficient solution methods. We must answer the same question for the graphical model discussed in this work. To that end, we analyze the effects of optimization criteria and shapes of dependency graphs on the structure of optimal policies, and for problems where the compactness can be maintained in the solution, we present algorithms that make use of the graphical representation. The main contribution of this work is that it answers, for several classes of multiagent MDPs, the question of whether optimal policies can be represented compactly. However, we analyze the structure and complexity of *optimal* solutions only, and the claims do not apply to approximation techniques that exploit compact MDP representations (e.g., [10, 6, 7, 20]). As such, this work provides complexity results and can serve as a guide to where it is necessary to resort to approximate algorithms for large-scale multiagent policy optimization problems.

The rest of the paper is organized as follows. Section 2 briefly discusses Markov decision processes and introduces the graphical MDP representation that is the basis of our study. Section 3 discusses the properties of the graphical model and establishes some results that facilitate the analysis of the following sections, where the properties of optimal policies and solution algorithms are discussed. In Section 4, we focus on cooperative agents that maximize the social welfare of the group, and in Section 5, we analyze the case of self-interested agents, each of whom maximizes its own payoff. Section 6 makes further assumptions about the structure of the agents' influence on each others' rewards and analyzes their effects on optimal policies. We conclude by summarizing our results and discussing some unanswered questions in Section 7.

2 Model and Background

In this section, we briefly review some background and introduce our compact representation of multiagent MDPs.

2.1 Markov Decision Processes

A single-agent fully-observable MDP can be defined as a n-tuple $\langle S, \mathcal{A}, P, R \rangle$, where:

- $S = \{i\}$ is a finite set of states an agent can be in.
- $\mathcal{A} = \{a\}$ is a finite sets of actions the agent can execute.
- $P : S \times \mathcal{A} \times S \mapsto [0, 1]$ defines the transition function; the probability that the agent goes to state j if it executes action a in state i is $P(i, a, j)$.
- $R : S \mapsto \mathbb{R}$ defines the rewards; the agent gets a reward of $R(i)$ in state i.[3]

A solution to a MDP is a policy defined as a procedure for selecting an action. It is known [17] that, for such fully-observable MDPs, there always exist policies that are *uniformly-optimal* (optimal for all initial conditions), stationary (time independent), deterministic (always select the same action for a given state), and Markov (history-independent); such policies (π) can be described as mappings of states to actions: $\pi : S \mapsto \mathcal{A}$.

Let us now consider a multiagent environment with a set of n agents $\mathcal{M} = \{m\}$ ($|\mathcal{M}| = n$), each of whom has its own set of states $S_m = \{i_m\}$ and actions $\mathcal{A}_m = \{a_m\}$. The most straightforward and also the most general way to extend the concept of a single-agent MDP to the fully-observable multiagent case is to assume that all agents affect the transitions and rewards of all other agents. Under these conditions, a multiagent MDP can be defined simply as a large MDP $\langle S_{\mathcal{M}}, \mathcal{A}_{\mathcal{M}}, P_{\mathcal{M}}, R_{\mathcal{M}} \rangle$, where the *joint* state space $S_{\mathcal{M}}$ is defined as the cross product of the state spaces of all agents: $S_{\mathcal{M}} = S_1 \times \ldots \times S_n$, and the joint action space is the cross product of the action spaces of all agents: $\mathcal{A}_{\mathcal{M}} = \mathcal{A}_1 \times \ldots \times \mathcal{A}_n$. The transition and the reward functions are defined on the joint state and action spaces of all agents in the standard way: $P_{\mathcal{M}} : S_{\mathcal{M}} \times \mathcal{A}_{\mathcal{M}} \times S_{\mathcal{M}} \mapsto [0, 1]$ and $R_{\mathcal{M}} : S_{\mathcal{M}} \mapsto \mathbb{R}$.

This representation, to which we refer as *flat*, is the most general one, in that, by considering the joint state and action spaces, it allows for arbitrary interactions between agents. However, the weak spot of this representation is that the problem (and solution) size grows exponentially with the number of agents, making it unacceptable for large-scale multiagent systems.

Let us note that, if the state space of each agent is defined on a set of world features, there can be some overlap in features between the agents, in which case

---

[3] Often, rewards are said to also depend on actions and future states. For simplicity, we define rewards as function of current state only, but our results can also be extended to the more general case.

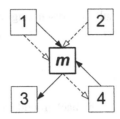

Fig. 1. Agent dependency graph

the joint state space would be smaller than the cross product of the state spaces of all agents, and would grow as a slower exponent. For simplicity, we ignore the possibility of overlapping features, but the results are directly applicable to that case as well.

2.2 Graphical Multiagent MDPs

In many multiagent domains, the interactions between agents are only local, meaning that the rewards and transitions of an agent are not directly influenced by all other agents, but rather only by a small subset of them. To exploit the sparseness in agents' interactions, we use a compact representation that is analogous to the Bayesian network representation of joint probability distributions of several random variables. Given its similarity to other graphical models (e.g., [11, 12]), we label the representation a *graphical multiagent MDP* (graphical MMDP).

Central to the definition of a graphical MMDP is a notion of a *dependency graph* (Figure 1), which shows how agents affect each other. The graph has a vertex for every agent in the multiagent MDP. There is a directed edge from vertex k to vertex m if agent k has an influence on agent m. The concept is very similar to *coordination graphs* [10], but we distinguish between two ways agents can influence each other: (1) an agent can affect another agent's transitions, in which case we use a solid arrow to depict this relationship in the dependency graph, and (2) an agent can affect another agent's rewards, in which case we use a dashed arrow in the dependency graph. For example, if an agent is trying to go through a doorway, and a second agent is controlling the state of the door, the transition probabilities of the first agent are affected by whether the door is open (state of the second agent), in which case we use a solid transition-related arrow from the second agent to the first. In a different scenario, if the door is always open, but the second agent sometimes rewards agents for going through the doorway, the transition probabilities of the first agent are not affected by the second one, but the reward that the first agent gets depends on the state of the second agent. In this case, we use a dashed reward-related arrow from the second agent to the first.

To simplify the following discussion of graphical multiagent MDPs, we also introduce some additional concepts and notation pertaining to the structure of the dependency graph. Consider an agent $m \in \mathcal{M}$ and its neighbors. Let us label all agents that directly affect m's transitions as $\mathcal{N}_m^-(P)$ (parents of m with respect to transition function P), and all agents whose transitions are directly affected by m as $\mathcal{N}_m^+(P)$ (children of m with respect to transition function P). Similarly, we use $\mathcal{N}_m^-(R)$ to refer to agents that directly affect m's rewards, and $\mathcal{N}_m^+(R)$ to refer to agents whose rewards are directly affected by m. Thus, in the graph shown in Figure 1, $\mathcal{N}_m^-(P) = \{1,4\}$, $\mathcal{N}_m^-(R) = \{1,2\}$, $\mathcal{N}_m^+(P) = \{3\}$, and $\mathcal{N}_m^+(R) = \{4\}$. We use the terms "transition-related" and "reward-related" parents and children to distinguish between the two categories. Sometimes, it will also be helpful to talk about the union of transition-related and reward-related parents or children, in which case we use $\mathcal{N}_m^- = \mathcal{N}_m^-(P) \cup \mathcal{N}_m^-(R)$ and $\mathcal{N}_m^+ = \mathcal{N}_m^+(P) \cup \mathcal{N}_m^+(R)$. Furthermore, let us label the set of all *ancestors* of m (all agents from which m is reachable) with respect to transition-related and reward-related dependencies as $O_m^-(P)$ and $O_m^-(R)$, respectively. Similarly, let us label the *descendants* of m (all agents reachable from m) as $O_m^+(P)$ and $O_m^+(R)$, with $O_m^- = O_m^-(P) \cup O_m^-(R)$ and $O_m^+ = O_m^+(P) \cup O_m^+(R)$ referring to the unions of all ancestors and descendants, respectively.

We define a graphical MMDP with a set of agents $\mathcal{M}$ as follows. Associated with each agent $m \in \mathcal{M}$ is a n-tuple $\langle S_m, \mathcal{A}_m, P_m, R_m \rangle$, where the state space S_m and the action space $\mathcal{A}_m$ are defined exactly as before, but the transition and the reward functions are defined as follows:

$$P_m : S_{\mathcal{N}_m^-(P)} \times S_m \times \mathcal{A}_m \times S_m \mapsto [0,1]$$
$$R_m : S_{\mathcal{N}_m^-(R)} \times S_m \mapsto \mathbb{R}, \tag{1}$$

where $S_{\mathcal{N}_m^-(P)}$ and $S_{\mathcal{N}_m^-(R)}$ are the joint state spaces of the transition-related and reward-related parents of m, respectively. In other words, the transition function of agent m specifies a probability distribution over its next states S_m as a function of its own current state S_m, the current states of all of its parents $S_{\mathcal{N}_m^-(P)}$, and its own action $\mathcal{A}_m$. That is $P(i_{\mathcal{N}_m^-(P)}, i_m, a_m, j_m)$ is the probability that agent m goes to state j_m if it executes action a_m when its current state is i_m and the states of its transition-related parents are $i_{\mathcal{N}_m^-(P)}$. The reward function is defined analogously on the current states of the agent itself and the reward-related parents (i.e., $R(i_{\mathcal{N}_m^-(R)}, i_m)$ is the reward that agent m gets when it is in state i_m and its parents are in states $i_{\mathcal{N}_m^-(R)}$).

Notice that, in (eq. 1), the transition function of m does not depend on actions of m's parents, but only on their current states. This is done for notational convenience and to simplify the discussion. It does not limit the generality of our model, as (eq. 1) can be used to model the more general case, by encoding the information about the last executed action in the state. Such an encoding might not be desirable for efficiency reasons, in which case the alternative is to modify our model, which should not present any fundamental difficulties.

Also notice that we allow cycles in the agent dependency graph, and moreover the same agent can both influence and be influenced by some other agent (e.g., agents 4 and m in Figure 1). We also allow for *asymmetric* influences between agents, i.e., it could be the case that one agent affects the other, but not *vice versa* (e.g., agent m in Figure 1 is influenced by agent 1, but the opposite is not true). This is often the case in domains where the relationships between agents are authority-based. It turns out that the existence of such asymmetry has important implications on the compactness of the solution and the complexity of the solution algorithms. We return to a discussion of the consequences of this asymmetry in the following sections.

It is important to note that, in this representation, each transition and reward function only specifies the rewards and transition probabilities of agent m, and contains no information about the rewards and transitions of other agents. This implies that the reward and next state of agent m are conditionally independent of the rewards and the next states of other agents, given the current action of m and the state of m and its parents $\mathcal{N}_m^-$. Therefore, this model does not allow for correlations between the rewards or the next states of different agents. For example, we cannot model the situation where two agents are trying to go through the same door and whether one agent makes it depends on whether the other one does; we can only represent, for each agent, the probability that it makes it, independently of the other. This is analogous to the commonly-made simplifying assumption that variables in a dynamic Bayesian network are independent of other variables within the same time slice. This limitation of the model can be overcome by "lumping together" groups of agents that are correlated in such ways into a single agent as in the flat multiagent MDP formulation. In fact, we could have allowed for such dependencies in our model, but it would have complicated the presentation. Instead, we assume that all such correlations have already been dealt with, and the resulting problem only consists of agents (perhaps composite ones) whose states and rewards have this conditional independence property.

It is easy to see that the size of a problem represented in this fashion is exponential in the maximum number of parents of any agent, but unlike the flat model, it does not depend on the total number of agents. Therefore, for large-scale multiagent problems where each agent has a small number of parents, space savings can be significant. In particular, this can lead to exponential (in terms of the number of agents) savings for domains where the number of parents of any agent is bounded by a constant.

3 Properties of Graphical Multiagent MDPs

Given the compact representation of multiagent MDPs described above, two important questions arise. First, can we compactly represent the solutions to these problems? And second, if so, can we exploit the compact representations of the problems and the solutions to improve the efficiency of the solution algorithms? Positive answers to these questions would be important indications of the value of this graphical problem representation. However, before we attempt to answer these questions and get into a more detailed analysis of the related issues, let us lay down some groundwork that will simplify the following discussion.

First of all, let us note that a graphical multiagent MDP is just a compact representation, and any graphical MMDP can be easily converted to a flat multiagent MDP, analogously to how a compact Bayesian network can be converted to a joint probability distribution. For example, for a problem where all agents in a graphical MDP are maximizing the social welfare of the team (sum of rewards of all agents), this graphical MMDP is equivalent to the following flat MDP:

$$S_{\mathcal{M}} = S_1 \times \ldots \times S_m,$$

$$\mathcal{A}_{\mathcal{M}} = \mathcal{A}_1 \times \ldots \times \mathcal{A}_m,$$

$$R_{\mathcal{M}}(i_{\mathcal{M}}) = \sum_{m \in \mathcal{M}} R_m(i_{\mathcal{N}_m^-(R)}, i_m), \tag{2}$$

$$P_{\mathcal{M}}(i_{\mathcal{M}}, a_{\mathcal{M}}, j_{\mathcal{M}}) = \prod_{m \in \mathcal{M}} P_m(i_{\mathcal{N}_m^-(P)}, i_m, a_m, j_m)$$

Therefore, all properties of solutions to flat multiagent MDPs (e.g., stationarity, history-independence, etc.) also hold for equivalent problems that are formulated as graphical MMDPs. However, in general, it is not possible to convert a flat multiagent MDP to a graphical MMDP without "lumping" together all agents into one by taking cross products of their state and action spaces. This suggests that it might be possible to more compactly represent the class of policies that are optimal for problems that are representable as graphical MMDPs.

Let us make the following simple observation that defines the notation and sets the stage for the following discussion.

Observation 1 *For a graphical MMDP* $\langle S_m, \mathcal{A}_m, P_m, R_m \rangle$, $m \in \mathcal{M}$, *with an optimization criterion for which optimal policies are Markov, stationary, and deterministic,*[4] *such policies can be represented as* $\pi_m : S_{X_m} \mapsto \mathcal{A}_m$, *where* S_{X_m} *is a cross product of the state spaces of some subset of all agents* $(X_m \subseteq \mathcal{M})$.

Clearly, this observation does not say much about the compactness of policies, since it allows $X_m = \mathcal{M}$, which corresponds to a solution where an agent has to consider the states of all other agents when deciding on an action. If that were always the case, using this compact graphical representation for the problem would not (by itself) be beneficial, because the solution would not retain the compactness and would be exponential in the number of agents. However, for some problems, X_m can be significantly smaller than $\mathcal{M}$. Thus we are interested in determining, for every agent m, the *minimal* set of agents whose states m's policy has to depend on:

Definition 1 *In a graphical MMDP, a set of agents* X_m *is a minimal domain of an optimal policy* $\pi_m : S_{X_m} \mapsto \mathcal{A}_m$ *of agent m if and only if, for any set of agents* $\mathcal{Y}$ *and any policy* $\pi'_m : S_{\mathcal{Y}} \mapsto \mathcal{A}_m$, *the following implications hold:*

$$\mathcal{Y} \subset X_m \implies U(\pi'_m) < U(\pi_m)$$

$$\mathcal{Y} \supseteq X_m \implies U(\pi'_m) \leq U(\pi_m),$$

where $U(\pi)$ *is the payoff that is being maximized.*

In words, any policy that is defined on the states of a subset of the minimal domain X_m will be strictly worse than π_m, and no policy defined on a superset of X_m can be better than π_m.

---

[4] We will implicitly assume that optimal policies are Markov, stationary, and deterministic from now on.

In essence, this definition allows us to talk about the sets of agents whose joint state space is necessary and sufficient for determining optimal actions of agent m. From now on, whenever we use the notation $\pi_m : S_{X_m} \mapsto \mathcal{A}_m$, we implicitly assume that X_m is the minimal domain of π_m.

3.1 Assumptions

As mentioned earlier, one of the main goals of the following sections will be to characterize the minimal domains of agents' policies under various conditions. We will be interested in analyzing the worst-case complexity of policies (i.e., the structure of policies for the most difficult examples from a given class of multiagent MDPs). One way to perform such an analysis is by studying examples of such worst-case scenarios. However, we take a different route which we believe is more illustrative: we first make some assumptions about properties of minimal domains that allow us to rule out some non-interesting degenerate special cases, and then rely on these assumptions to derive our complexity results. As such, these assumptions do not limit the general complexity results that follow, as the latter only require that there exist *some* problems for which the assumptions hold. In the rest of the paper, we implicitly assume that they hold.

Central to our future discussion will be an analysis of which random variables (rewards, states, etc.) depend on which others. It will be very useful to talk about the conditional independence of future values of some variables, given the current values of others.

Definition 2 *We say that a random variable X is* Markov *on the joint state space S_Y of some set of agents Y if, given the current values of all states in S_Y, the future values of X are independent of any past information. If that property does not hold, we say that X is non-Markov on S_Y.*

We make the following assumptions:

Assumption 1 *For a minimal domain X_m of agent m's optimal policy, and a set of agents Y, the following hold:*

    1. X_m *is unique*

    2. $m \in X_m$

    3. $l \in X_m \implies S_l$ *is Markov on S_{X_m}*

    4. S_m *is Markov on $S_Y \iff Y \supseteq X_m$*

The first assumption allows us to avoid some special cases where there are sets of agents whose states are 100% correlated, and equivalent policies can be constructed as functions of either of the sets.

The second assumption states that the domain of an optimal policy of an agent should include its own state, which is true for all but the most trivial cases.

The third assumption says that the state space of any agent l that is in the minimal domain of m must be Markov on the state space of the minimal domain. Since the state space of agent l is in the minimal domain of m, it must influence m's rewards in a non-trivial manner. Thus, if S_l is non-Markov on S_{X_m}, agent m will, in general, be able to increase its payoff by expanding the domain of its policy to make S_l Markov (since that will allow it to better predict future rewards).

The fourth assumption says that the agent's state is Markov only on supersets of its minimal domain. Indeed, if there exists a smaller domain $Z \subset X_m$ such that the agent's state space S_m is Markov on Z, the agent should be able to implement the same policy on Z, contradicting the definition of the minimal domain. Conversely, S_m must be Markov on the minimal domain, since if the opposite were true, the agent would, in general, benefit from expanding the domain of its policy to better predict future rewards. Clearly, if S_m is Markov on X_m, it must be Markov on any superset of X_m.

These assumptions are slightly redundant (e.g., 4 could be deduced from weaker conditions), but we use this form for brevity and clarity.

We can combine Assumptions 1.1 and 1.4 into the following useful result.

Corollary 1 *For a minimal domain X_m of agent m's optimal policy and a set of agents $\mathcal{Y}$, such that $\mathcal{Y} \not\supseteq X_m$, the following holds: S_m is non-Markov on $S_{\mathcal{Y}}$.*

Indeed, if the above did not hold, meaning that S_m were Markov on $S_{\mathcal{Y}}$, by Assumption 1.4, $\mathcal{Y}$ would be a superset of some minimal domain $X'_m \neq X_m$, which would violate the uniqueness assumption 1.1.

3.2 Transitivity

Using the assumptions of the previous sections, we can derive an important property of minimal domains that will significantly simplify the analysis that follows.

Proposition 1 *Consider two agents $m, l \in \mathcal{M}$, where the optimal policies of m and l have minimal domains of X_m and X_l, respectively ($\pi_m : S_{X_m} \mapsto \mathcal{A}_m$, $\pi_l : S_{X_l} \mapsto \mathcal{A}_l$). Then, under Assumption 1, the following holds:*

$$l \in X_m \implies X_l \subseteq X_m,$$

i.e., if the minimal domain X_m of agent m's policy includes agent l, then X_m must also include the minimal domain of l.

Proof: We will show this by contradiction. Let us consider an agent from l's minimal domain: $k \in X_l$. Let us assume (contradicting the statement of the proposition) that $l \in X_m$, but $k \notin X_m$. Consider the set of agents that consists of the union of the two minimal domains X_m and X_l, but with agent k removed:

$$\mathcal{Y}_m = X_m \bigcup (X_l \setminus k).$$

Then, since $\mathcal{Y}_m \not\supseteq X_l$, Assumption 1.4 implies that S_l is non-Markov on $S_{\mathcal{Y}_m}$. Thus, Assumption 1.3 implies $l \notin X_m$, which contradicts our earlier assumption. $\blacksquare$

Essentially, this proposition says that the minimal domains have a certain "transitive" property: if agent m needs to base its action choices on the state of agent l, then, in general, m also needs to base its actions on the states of all agents in the minimal domain of l. As such, this proposition will help us to establish lower bounds on policy sizes.

Intuitively, the proposition says that since m's policy depends on l's state, and the trajectory of l's state depends on X_l, it makes sense for agent m to base its actions on the states of all agents in X_l. Otherwise, the evolution of m's own state might not be Markov and agent m might not be able to predict the future as well as it could, leading to suboptimal policies. To illustrate, let us once again refer to our doorway example, where one agent, m, needs to go through a doorway that is being controlled by a second agent, l. Naturally, the optimal action of the first agent, m, depends on the state of the second agent, l, implying that $l \in X_m$ (second agent is in the minimal domain of the first one). Now, suppose that the door-opening policy of the second agent l depends on the state of a third agent k (perhaps the third agent controls the power to the building), which by definition means that $k \in X_l$. Under these conditions the first agent m should base its action choices on the state of agent k (e.g., no sense pursuing a policy that requires going through the door if there is no power and no chance of the door opening). Thus, agent m should expand its domain to include all the external factors which affect the policy of the door-controlling agent l.

In the rest of the paper, we analyze some classes of problems to see how large the minimal domains are under various conditions and assumptions, and for domains where minimal domains are not prohibitively large, we outline solution algorithms that exploit graphical structure. In what follows, we focus on two common scenarios: one, where the agents work as a team and aim to maximize the social welfare of the group (sum of individual payoffs), and the other, where each agent maximizes its own payoff.

4 Maximizing Social Welfare

The following proposition characterizes the structure of the optimal solutions to graphical multiagent MDPs under the social welfare optimization criterion, and as such serves as an indication of whether the compactness of this particular representation can be exploited to devise an efficient solution algorithm for such problems. We demonstrate that, in general, when the social welfare of the group is considered, the optimal actions of each agent depend on the states of all other agents (unless the dependency graph is disconnected). Let us point out that this scenario where all agents are maximizing the same objective function is equivalent to a single-agent factored MDP, and our results for this case are analogous to the fact that the value function in a single-agent factored MDP does not, in general, retain the structure of the problem [14].

The implication of these results is that for large-scale cooperative MDPs where all agents are maximizing the social welfare of the group, the complexity and size of optimal solutions very quickly becomes prohibitive. Therefore, for such problems it is necessary to resort to approximate solution methods [10, 6, 7, 20].

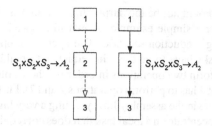

Fig. 2. Illustration for Proposition 2

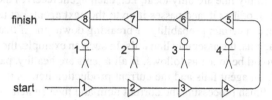

Fig. 3. Assembly line example.

Proposition 2 *For a graphical MMDP with a connected (ignoring edge direction-ality) dependency graph, under the optimization criterion that maximizes the social welfare of all agents, an optimal policy π_m of agent m, in general, depends on the states of all other agents, i.e., $\pi_m : S_{\mathcal{M}} \mapsto \mathcal{A}_m$.*

Proof (Sketch): Agent m must, at the minimum, base its action decisions on the states of its immediate (both transition- and reward-related) parents and children (as illustrated in Figure 2). Indeed, agent m should worry about the states of its transition-related parents, $\mathcal{N}_m^-(P)$, because their states affect the one-step transition probabili-ties of m, which certainly have a bearing on m's payoff. Agent m should also include in the domain of its policy the states of its reward-related parents, $\mathcal{N}_m^-(R)$, because they affect m's immediate rewards and agent m might need to adjust its behavior de-pending on the states of its parents. Similarly, since the agent cares about the social welfare of all agents, it will need to consider the effects of its actions on the states and rewards of its immediate children, and must thus base its policy on the states of its immediate children $\mathcal{N}_m^+(P)$ and $\mathcal{N}_m^+(R)$ to potentially "set them up" to get higher rewards.

Having established that the minimal domain of each agent must include the im-mediate children and parents of the agent, we can use the transitivity property from the previous section to extend this result. Although Proposition 1 only holds under the conditions of Assumption 1, for our purpose of determining the complexity of policies *in general*, it is sufficient that there exist problems for which Assumption 1 holds. It follows from Proposition 1 that the minimal domain of agent m must include all parents and children of m's parents and children, and so forth. For a connected dependency graph, this expands the minimal domain of each agent to all other agents in $\mathcal{M}$. ∎

The above result should not be too surprising, as it makes clear, intuitive sense. Indeed, let us consider a simple example, shown in Figure 3, that has a flavor of a commonly-occurring production scenario. The agents are operating an assembly line, where several tasks have to be done in sequence to build the output product. Each agent has to perform two operations in order for the whole process to succeed (e.g., in Figure 3, agent 2 has to perform operations 2 and 7). Furthermore, each agent can choose to participate in the assembly line, yielding a very high reward if all agent cooperate, or it can concentrate on a local task that does not require the cooperation of other agents, but which has a much lower social payoff. The interactions between the agents in the assembly line are only local, i.e., each agent receives the product from a previous agent, modifies it, and passes it on to the next agent. Let us now suppose that each agent has a certain probability of breaking down, and if that happens to at least one of the agents, the assembly line fails. In such an example, the optimal policy for the agents would be to act as follows. If all agents are healthy, participate in the assembly line. If an agent fails and the current production item is not "blocked" by the failed agent, finish processing the current item and then switch to the local task. If the agent that fails blocks the ongoing process, switch to local task immediately. Clearly, in this example, agents' policies are functions of the states of all other agents.

The take-home message of this section is that, when the agents care about the social welfare of the group, even when the interactions between the agents are only local, the agents' policies depend on the joint state space of all agents. The reason for this is that a state change of one agent might lead all other agents to want to immediately modify their behavior. Therefore, the compact problem representation (by itself and without additional restrictions) does not lead to compact solutions.

5 Maximizing Own Welfare

In this section, we analyze problems where each of the agents maximizes its own payoff. Under this assumption, unlike the discouraging scenario of the previous section, the complexity of agents' policies is slightly less frightening. The following result characterizes the sizes of the minimal domains of optimal policies for problems where each agent maximizes its own utility. It states that the policy of every agent depends on the states of all of its ancestors.

Proposition 3 *For a graphical MMDP with an optimization criterion where each agent maximizes its own reward, the minimal domain of m's policy consists of m itself and all of its transition- and reward-related ancestors: $X_m = \mathcal{E}_m^-$, where we use $\mathcal{E}_m^- = m \cup O_m^- = m \cup O_m^-(P) \cup O_m^-(R)$ to refer to m and all of its ancestors.*

Proof (Sketch): To show the correctness of the proposition, we need to prove that, (1) the minimal domain must include at least m itself and its ancestors ($X_m \supseteq \mathcal{E}_m^-$), and (2) that X_m does not include any other agents ($X_m \subseteq \mathcal{E}_m^-$).

We can show (1) by once again applying the transitivity property. Clearly, an agent's policy should be a function of the states of the agent's reward-related and transition-related parents, because they affect the one-step transition probabilities and rewards of the agent. Then, by Proposition 1, the minimal domain of the agent's policy must also include all of its ancestors.

We establish (2) as follows. We assume that it holds for all ancestors of m, and show that it must then hold for m. We then expand the statement to all agents by induction.

Let us fix the policies π_k of all agents except m. Then, consider the tuple $\langle S_{\mathcal{E}_m^-}, \mathcal{A}_m, \widetilde{P}_{\mathcal{E}_m^-}, \widetilde{R}_{\mathcal{E}_m^-} \rangle$, where $\widetilde{P}_{\mathcal{E}_m^-}$ and $\widetilde{R}_{\mathcal{E}_m^-}$ are functions with the following domains and ranges:

$$\widetilde{P}_{\mathcal{E}_m^-} : S_{\mathcal{E}_m^-} \times \mathcal{A}_m \times S_{\mathcal{E}_m^-} \mapsto [0,1]$$
$$\widetilde{R}_{\mathcal{E}_m^-} : S_{\mathcal{E}_m^-} \mapsto \mathbb{R} \tag{3}$$

and are defined as follows:

$$\widetilde{P}_{\mathcal{E}_m^-}(i_{\mathcal{E}_m^-}, a_m, j_{\mathcal{E}_m^-}) = P_m(i_{\mathcal{N}_m^-(P)}, i_m, a_m, j_m)$$
$$\prod_{k \in O_m^-} P_k\left(i_{\mathcal{N}_k^-(P)}, i_k, \pi_k(i_{\mathcal{E}_k^-}), j_k\right) \tag{4}$$

$$\widetilde{R}_{\mathcal{E}_m^-}(i_{\mathcal{E}_m^-}) = R_m(i_{\mathcal{N}_m^-(R)}, i_m)$$

The above constitutes a fully-observable MDP on $S_{\mathcal{E}_m^-}$ and $\mathcal{A}_m$ with transition function $\widetilde{P}_m$ and reward function $\widetilde{R}_m$. Let us label this decision process MDP_1. By properties of fully-observable MDPs, there exists an optimal stationary deterministic solution π_m^1 of the form $\pi_m^1 : S_{\mathcal{E}_m^-} \mapsto \mathcal{A}_m$.

Also consider the following MDP on an augmented state space that includes the joint state space of all the agents (and not just m's ancestors): $MDP_2 = \langle S_{\mathcal{M}}, \mathcal{A}_m, \widehat{P}_{\mathcal{M}}, \widehat{R}_{\mathcal{M}} \rangle$, where $\widehat{P}_{\mathcal{M}}$ and $\widehat{R}_{\mathcal{M}}$ are functions with the following domains and ranges:

$$\widehat{P} : S_{\mathcal{M}} \times \mathcal{A}_m \times S_{\mathcal{M}} \mapsto [0,1]$$
$$\widehat{R} : S_{\mathcal{M}} \mapsto \mathbb{R} \tag{5}$$

and are defined as follows:

$$\widehat{P}_{\mathcal{M}}(i_{\mathcal{M}}, a_m, j_{\mathcal{M}}) = P_m(i_{\mathcal{N}_m^-(P)}, i_m, a_m, j_m)$$
$$\prod_{k \in O_m^-} P_k\left(i_{\mathcal{N}_k^-(P)}, i_k, \pi_k(i_{\mathcal{E}_k^-}), j_k\right)$$
$$\prod_{k \in \mathcal{M} \backslash (m \cup O_m^-)} P_k\left(i_{\mathcal{N}_k^-(P)}, i_k, \pi_k(i_{\mathcal{M}}), j_k\right) \tag{6}$$
$$\widehat{R}_{\mathcal{M}}(i_{\mathcal{M}}) = R_m(i_{\mathcal{N}_m^-(R)}, i_m)$$

Basically, we have now constructed two fully-observable MDPs: MDP_1 that is defined on $S_{\mathcal{E}_m^-}$, and MDP_2 that is defined on $S_{\mathcal{M}}$, where MDP_1 is essentially a "projection" of MDP_2 onto $S_{\mathcal{E}_m^-}$. We need to show that no solution to MDP_2 can have a higher value[5] than the optimal solution to MDP_1. Let us refer to the optimal solution to MDP_1 as π_m^1. Suppose there exists a solution π_m^2 to MDP_2 that has a higher value than π_m^1. The policy π_m^2 defines a stochastic trajectory for the system over the state space S_M (for any fixed initial distribution over the state space). Let us label the distribution over the state space at time t as $\rho(i_M, t)$ and its projection onto $S_{\mathcal{E}_m^-}$ as $\rho(i_{\mathcal{E}_m^-}, t)$. Under our assumptions we can always construct a non-stationary randomized policy $\widetilde{\pi}_m^1(t) : S_{\mathcal{E}_m^-} \times \mathcal{A}_m \mapsto [0,1]$ for MDP_1 that yields the same distribution $\rho(i_{\mathcal{E}_m^-}, t)$ over the state space $S_{\mathcal{E}_m^-}$ as the one produced by π_m^2. Thus, there exists a randomized non-stationary solution to MDP_1 that has a higher payoff than π_m^1, which is a contradiction, since we assumed that π_m^1 was optimal for MDP_1.

We have therefore shown that, given that the policies of all ancestors of m depend only on their own states and the states of their ancestors, there always exists a policy that maps the state space of m and its ancestors ($S_{\mathcal{E}_m^-}$) to m's actions ($\mathcal{A}_m$) that is at least as good as any policy that maps the joint space of all agents (S_M) to m's actions. Then, by using induction, we can expand this statement to all agents (for acyclic graphs we use the root nodes as the base case, and for cyclic graphs, we use agents that do not have any ancestors that are not simultaneously their descendants). ∎

The intuition behind the above result is very simple: if an agent is maximizing its own welfare, it should not worry about the state of agents that have no bearing on its future rewards and transitions (the descendants). It does, however, need to worry about all of its reward and transition-related ancestors, because otherwise the agent's state or reward sequence might not be Markov on the state space of its minimal domain, in which case its policy will, in general, be suboptimal.

The implication of the above proposition is that, for situations where each agent maximizes its own utility, the optimal actions of each agent do not have to depend on the states of all other agents, but rather only on its own state and the states of its ancestors. In contrast to the conclusions of Section 4, this result is more encouraging. For example, for dependency graphs that are trees (typical of authority-driven organizational structures), the number of ancestors of any agent equals the depth of the tree, which is logarithmic in the number of agents. Therefore, if each agent maximizes its own welfare, the size of its policy will be exponential in the depth of the tree, but only linear in the number of agents.

5.1 Acyclic Dependency Graphs

Thus far we have shown that problems where agents optimize their own welfare can allow for more compact policy representations. We now describe an algorithm that exploits the compactness of the problem representation to more efficiently solve such policy optimization problems for domains with acyclic dependency graphs.

It is a distributed algorithm where the agents exchange information, and each one solves its own policy optimization problem. The algorithm is very straightfor-

---

[5] The proof does not rely on the actual type of optimization criterion used by each agent and holds for any criterion that is a function only of the agents' trajectories.

Algorithm 1: Solving acyclic multiagent MDPs.

Function SolveAcyclicMDP()
in : $\langle S_m, \mathcal{A}_m, P_m, R_m \rangle$ – MDP of agent m
   : $\mathcal{N}_m^-$ – parents of agent m
   : $\mathcal{N}_m^+$ – children of agent m
out: optimal policy π_m for agent m

wait for policies π_k of all ancestors ($k \in O_m^-$) from parents $\mathcal{N}_m^-$
form MDP M=$\langle S_{\mathcal{E}_m^-}, \mathcal{A}_m, \tilde{P}_{\mathcal{E}_m^-}, \tilde{R}_{\mathcal{E}_m^-} \rangle$ per (eq. 4)
$\pi_m \leftarrow$ solve MDP $\langle S_{\mathcal{E}_m^-}, \mathcal{A}_m, \tilde{P}_{\mathcal{E}_m^-}, \tilde{R}_{\mathcal{E}_m^-} \rangle$
send own policy π_m and π_k to children $\mathcal{N}_m^+$

---

ward and works as follows. First, the root nodes of the graph (the ones with no parents) compute their optimal policies that are simply mappings of their own states to their own actions. Once a root agent computes a policy that maximizes its welfare, it sends the policy to all of its children. Each child waits to receive the policies π_k, $k \in \mathcal{N}_m^-$ from its ancestors, then forms a MDP on the state space of itself and its ancestors as in (eq. 4). It then solves this MDP $\langle S_{\mathcal{E}_m^-}, \mathcal{A}_m, \tilde{P}_{\mathcal{E}_m^-}, \tilde{R}_{\mathcal{E}_m^-} \rangle$ to produce a policy $\pi_m : \mathcal{E}_m^- \mapsto \mathcal{A}_m$, at which point it sends the policy and the policies of its ancestors to its children. The process repeats until all agents compute their optimal policies. Essentially, this algorithm performs, in a distributed manner, a topological sort of the dependency graph, and computes a policy for every agent. Let us note that parents have no incentive to hide their policies from the children, since the children cannot influence the parents' utility, because of to the asymmetry.

5.2 Cyclic Dependency Graphs

We now turn our attention to the case of dependency graphs with cycles. Note that the complexity result of Proposition 3 still applies, because no assumptions about the cyclic or acyclic nature of dependency graphs were made in the statement or proof of the proposition. Thus, the minimal domain of an agent's policy is still the set of its ancestors.

The problem is, however, that the solution algorithm of the previous section is inappropriate for cyclic graphs, because it will deadlock on agents that are part of a cycle, since these agents will be waiting to receive policies from each other. Indeed, when self-interested agents mutually affect each other, it is not clear how they should go about constructing their policies. Moreover, in general, for such agents there might not even exist a set of stationary deterministic policies that are in equilibrium, i.e., since the agents mutually affect each other, the best responses of agents to each others' policies might not be in equilibrium.

A careful analysis of this case falls in the realm of Markov games (e.g., [21, 16, 15]), and is beyond the scope of this paper. However, if we assume that there exists an equilibrium in stationary deterministic policies, and that the agents in a cycle have some "black-box" way of constructing their policies, we can formulate

---
Algorithm 2: Solving cyclic multiagent MDPs.

Function SolveCyclicMDP()
in : $\langle S_m, \mathcal{A}_m, P_m, R_m \rangle$ – MDP of agent m
    : $\mathcal{N}_m^-$ – parents of agent m
    : $\mathcal{N}_m^+$ – children of agent m
out: optimal policy π_m for agent m

$G_m \leftarrow$ find all your peers
wait for policies π_k of all ancestors not in G_m
$P_m^0 \leftarrow$ local transition function from P_m and $\{\pi_k\}$
form a joint MDP $\langle S_{E_m^-}, \mathcal{A}_{G_m}, P_{G_m}, R_{G_m} \rangle$
$\pi_m \leftarrow$ solve joint MDP $\langle S_{G_m}, \mathcal{A}_{G_m}, P_{G_m}, R_{G_m} \rangle$
send own policy π_m to children $\mathcal{N}_m^+$

---

an algorithm for computing optimal policies, by modifying the algorithm from the previous section as follows. The agents begin by finding the largest cycle they are a part of, and then, after the agents receive policies from their parents who are not also their descendants, the agents proceed to devise an optimal joint policy for their cycle, which they then pass to their children.

Notice that the algorithm relies on a way for each agent m to find all other agents that are a part of a cycle that contains m. Since the set of agents that are in a cycle with m is the intersection of the ancestors and descendants of m, finding all peers of an agent can be done in polynomial time (in the number of agents) via a simple algorithm that performs a traversal of the dependency graph.

6 Additive Rewards

In our earlier analysis, a reward function R_m of an agent could depend in an arbitrary way on the current states of the agent and its parents (eq. 1). In fact, this is why agents, in general, needed to adjust their behavior depending on the states of their parents (and children in the social welfare case), which, in turn, was why the effects of reward-related dependencies propagated just as the transition-related ones did.

In this section, we consider a subclass of reward functions for which locality is better maintained. Namely, we focus on *additively-separable* reward functions:

$$R_m(i_{\mathcal{N}_m^-(R)}, i_m) = r_{mm}(i_m) + \sum_{k \in \mathcal{N}_m^-(R)} r_{mk}(i_k), \tag{7}$$

where r_{mk} is a function ($r_{mk} : S_k \mapsto \mathbb{R}$) that specifies the contribution of agent k to m's reward. In words, we assume that a reward of agent m can be expressed as a sum of several terms, each of which depends on the state of only one agent.

Furthermore, the results of this section are only valid under certain assumptions about the optimization criteria the agents use. Let us say that if an agent receives a history of rewards $\mathcal{H}(r) = \{r(t)\} = \{r(0), r(1), \ldots\}$, its payoff is $U(\mathcal{H}(r)) =$

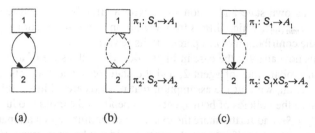

Fig. 4. Additive rewards. Two-agent problems.

$U(r(0), r(1), \ldots)$. Then, in order for our results to hold, U has to be *linear additive*:

$$U(\mathcal{H}(r_1 + r_2)) = U(\mathcal{H}(r_1)) + U(\mathcal{H}(r_2)) \qquad (8)$$

Notice that this assumption holds for the commonly-used risk-neutral MDP optimization criteria, such as expected total reward, expected total discounted reward, and average per-step reward, and is, therefore, not greatly limiting.

In the rest of this section we examine problems with reward functions that are subject to these conditions. We begin by analyzing some important special cases with only two agents (shown in Figure 4) and then discuss whether and how these results can be extended to problems with more than two agents.

First, let us observe that all problems in Figure 4 have cyclic dependency graphs. Therefore, if the reward functions of the agents were not additively-separable, per our earlier results of Section 5, there would be no guarantee that there would exist an equilibrium in stationary deterministic policies. The problem in Figure 4a has a cycle in transition-related dependencies, and our assumptions about the reward functions will not help us with the existence of equilibria. Therefore, in this section, we will only consider problems where there are no cycles due to transition-related dependencies. Under these conditions, as we show below, our assumption about the additivity of the reward functions ensures that an equilibrium always exists for problems such as the ones in 4b and 4c.

Let us consider the case in Figure 4b. Clearly, the policy of neither agent affects the transition function of the other. Thus, given our assumptions about additivity of rewards and utility functions, it is easy to see that the problem of maximizing the payoff is separable for each agent. For example, for agent 1 we have:

$$\max_{\pi_1, \pi_2} U_1\left(\mathcal{H}(R_1(i_1, i_2))\right) = \max_{\pi_1} U\left(\mathcal{H}(r_{11}(i_1))\right) + \max_{\pi_2} U\left(\mathcal{H}(r_{21}(i_2))\right) \qquad (9)$$

Thus, regardless of what policy agent 2 chooses, agent 1 should adopt a policy that maximizes the first term in (eq. 9). In game-theoretic terms, each of the agents has a (weakly) dominant strategy, and will adopt that strategy, regardless of what the other agent does. This is what guarantees the above-mentioned equilibrium.

Now that we have demonstrated that, for each agent, it suffices to optimize a function of only that agent's own states and actions, it is clear that each agent can construct its optimal policy independently. Indeed, each agent has to solve a standard

MDP on its own state and action space with a slightly modified reward function: $R'_m(i_m) = r_{mm}(i_m)$, which differs from the original reward function (eq. 7) in that it ignores the contribution of m's parents to its reward.

Let us now analyze the case in Figure 4c, where the state of agent 1 affects the transition probabilities of agent 2, and the state of agent 2 affects the rewards of agent 1. Again, without the assumption that rewards are additive, this cycle would have caused the policies of both agents to depend on the cross product of their state spaces $S_1 \times S_2$, and furthermore the existence of equilibria in stationary deterministic policies between self-interested agents would not be guaranteed. However, when rewards are additive, the problem is simpler. Indeed, due to our assumptions, we can write the optimization problems of the two agents as:

$$\max_{\pi_1,\pi_2} U_1(\ldots) = \max_{\pi_1} U_1(\mathcal{H}(r_{11})) + \max_{\pi_1,\pi_2} U_1(\mathcal{H}(r_{12}))$$
$$\max_{\pi_1,\pi_2} U_2(\ldots) = \max_{\pi_1} U_2(\mathcal{H}(r_{21})) + \max_{\pi_1,\pi_2} U_2(\mathcal{H}(r_{22}))$$
(10)

Notice that here the problems are no longer separable (as they were in the previous case of Figure 4b), so neither agent is guaranteed to have a dominant strategy.

However, we can make an additional assumption about the structure of agents' rewards that will guarantee an existence of a Nash equilibrium in stationary deterministic policies. Namely, let us assume that agents' reward functions are subject to the following condition:

$$r_{mk}(i_k) = l_{mk}(r_{kk}(i_k)),$$
(11)

where l_{mk} is a positive linear function ($l_{mk}(x) = \alpha x + \beta$, $\alpha > 0, \beta \geq 0$). This condition implies that agents' preferences over each other states are positively (and linearly) correlated, i.e., when an agent increases its local reward, its contribution to the rewards of its reward-related children also increases linearly.

Under that assumption, (eq. 10) will always have an equilibrium solution in stationary deterministic policies. This is due to the fact that a positive linear transformation of the reward function of a MDP does not change its optimal policy, as demonstrated below (for concreteness we show this for MDPs with the total expected discounted reward optimization criterion, but the statement is true more generally).

Observation 2 *Consider two MDPs:* $\Lambda = \langle S, \mathcal{A}, R, P \rangle$ *and* $\Lambda' = \langle S, \mathcal{A}, R', P \rangle$, $R'(i) = \alpha R(i) + \beta$, *where* $\alpha > 0$ *and* $\beta \geq 0$. *Then, a policy* π *is optimal for* Λ *under the total expected discounted optimization criterion if and only if it is optimal for* Λ'.

Proof: Let us consider how the linear transformation of the reward function will affect the Q function of the MDP. It is easy to see that the linear transformation $R'(i) = \alpha R(i) + \beta$ of the reward function will lead to a linear transformation of the Q function, where $Q'(i,a) = \alpha Q(i,a) + \beta(1-\gamma)^{-1}$, where γ is the discount factor.

Indeed, suppose that this is true. Then, the new Bellman equations for the transformed MDP Λ' will have the form:

$$Q'(i,a) = R'(i) + \gamma \sum_j P(i,a,j) \max_a Q'(j,a)$$

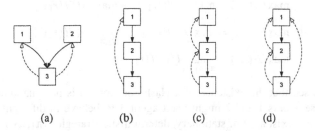

Fig. 5. Multiagent problems, additive rewards: existence of equilibrium strategies.

or, under our hypothesis about the transformation of the Q function:

$$\alpha Q(i,a) + \frac{\beta}{1-\gamma} = \alpha R(i) + \beta + \gamma \sum_j P(i,a,j) \max_a \left(\alpha Q(j,a) + \frac{\beta}{1-\gamma} \right)$$

After a trivial algebraic manipulation, the above can be expressed as

$$Q(i,a) = R(i) + \gamma \sum_j P(i,a,j) \max_a Q(j,a) + \frac{\beta}{\alpha} + \frac{\gamma\beta}{\alpha(1-\gamma)} - \frac{\beta}{\alpha(1-\gamma)},$$

where the last terms cancel out, yielding exactly the Bellman equation for the original MDP Λ:

$$Q(i,a) = R(i) + \gamma \sum_j P(i,a,j) \max_a Q(j,a)$$

Therefore, since the agent computes the optimal policy as

$$\pi(i) = \max_a Q'(i,a) = \max_a \alpha Q(i,a) + \beta(1-\gamma)^{-1} = \max_a Q(i,a),$$

a policy π is optimal for Λ if and only if it is optimal for Λ'. ∎

Observation 2 implies that, for any policy π_1, a policy π_2 that maximizes the second term of U_1 in (eq. 10) will be simultaneously maximizing (given π_1) the second term of U_2 in (eq. 10). In other words, given any π_1, both agents will agree on the choice of π_2. Therefore, agent 1 can find the pair $\langle \pi_1, \pi_2 \rangle$ that maximizes its payoff U_1 and adopt that π_1. Then, agent 2 will adopt the corresponding π_2, since deviating from it cannot increase its utility because π_2 is simultaneously maximizing the second terms in (eq. 10) for both agents.

Let us now consider whether these results carry over to problems with more than two agents. Unfortunately, there is no trivial extension of the analysis to problems with arbitrary numbers of agents and general dependency graphs, because the question of the existence of equilibria in stationary deterministic strategies becomes more complicated. To illustrate the issue, let us consider a few more special cases shown in Figure 5.

Consider the dependency graph in Figure 5a. The optimization problems the agents face are as follows.

$$\max U_1(\ldots) = \max_{\pi_1} U_1(\mathcal{H}(r_{11})) + \max_{\pi_1,\pi_3} U_1(\mathcal{H}(r_{13}))$$

$$\max U_2(\ldots) = \max_{\pi_2} U_2(\mathcal{H}(r_{22})) + \max_{\pi_2,\pi_3} U_2(\mathcal{H}(r_{23})) \qquad (12)$$

$$\max U_3(\ldots) = \max_{\pi_1,\pi_1,\pi_3} U_3(\mathcal{H}(r_{33}))$$

It is easy to see that the existence of a Nash equilibrium is not guaranteed in this case, because agents 1 and 2 might want agent 3 to behave in different ways and there might not exist a set of stationary, deterministic strategies $\langle \pi_1, \pi_2, \pi_3 \rangle$ that are in equilibrium (i.e., one of the agents might want to deviate). The problem with this example is due to the fact that agent 3 has multiple transition-related parents, which suggests that problems with tree-like transition dependency graphs might be better-behaved.

Let us, therefore, consider the example in Figure 5b, whose transition dependency graph is a tree. The optimization problems of the agents are:

$$\max U_1(\ldots) = \max_{\pi_1} U_1(\mathcal{H}(r_{11})) + \max_{\pi_1,\pi_2,\pi_3} U_1(\mathcal{H}(r_{13}))$$

$$\max U_2(\ldots) = \max_{\pi_1,\pi_2} U_2(\mathcal{H}(r_{22})) \qquad (13)$$

$$\max U_3(\ldots) = \max_{\pi_1,\pi_2,\pi_3} U_3(\mathcal{H}(r_{33}))$$

Here, the existence of an equilibrium is also not guaranteed because, even though agents 1 and 3 will always agree on π_3 (given any π_1), agents 1 and 2 might not have an equilibrium. In other words, given a π_1 (which defines the transition function and thus the optimization problem of agent 2) agent 2 can find its best policy $\pi_2^*(\pi_1) = \arg\max_{\pi_2} U_2(\mathcal{H}(r_{22}))$. However, given π_2^*, agent 1 might want to change its π_1 to improve its reward. Here, the problem is due to the fact that agent 2 has control of agent 3 who does not contribute to 2's rewards directly, but does effect the rewards of a parent of 2.

The above suggest that perhaps limiting reward loops to immediate transition-related children and parents (as in the case of two agents) might lead to equilibria. To investigate, let us consider the example from Figure 5c. The agents' optimization problems are:

$$\max U_1(\ldots) = \max_{\pi_1} U_1(\mathcal{H}(r_{11})) + \max_{\pi_1,\pi_2} U_1(\mathcal{H}(r_{12}))$$

$$\max U_2(\ldots) = \max_{\pi_1,\pi_2} U_2(\mathcal{H}(r_{22})) + \max_{\pi_1,\pi_2,\pi_3} U_2(\mathcal{H}(r_{23})) \qquad (14)$$

$$\max U_3(\ldots) = \max_{\pi_1,\pi_2,\pi_3} U_3(\mathcal{H}(r_{33}))$$

Alas, here a Nash is also not guaranteed, because once again the interests of agents 1 and 2 might conflict (for example, the term $U_1(\mathcal{H}(r_{12}))$ might be the most important for agent 1, whereas agent 2 might want to choose π_2 to increase $U_2(\mathcal{H}(r_{23}))$ above all else).

A condition that does ensure the existence of an equilibrium is illustrated by the example in Figure 5d, where the optimization problems of the agents are:

$$\max U_1(\ldots) = \max_{\pi_1} U_1(\mathcal{H}(r_{11})) + \max_{\pi_1,\pi_2} U_1(\mathcal{H}(r_{12})) + \max_{\pi_1,\pi_2,\pi_3} U_1(\mathcal{H}(r_{13}))$$

$$\max U_2(\ldots) = \max_{\pi_1,\pi_2} U_2(\mathcal{H}(r_{22})) + \max_{\pi_1,\pi_2,\pi_3} U_2(\mathcal{H}(r_{23})) \tag{15}$$

$$\max U_3(\ldots) = \max_{\pi_1,\pi_2,\pi_3} U_3(\mathcal{H}(r_{33}))$$

Here, an equilibrium exists, because each agent maximizes a subset of reward terms that its parent is maximizing, i.e., given any π_1 and π_2, all three agents will agree on the choice of π_3; similarly, given a π_1 the agents will agree on the choice of π_2 and π_3.

Thus, just like in the two-agent problems discussed earlier, if the contributions of agents to each other's rewards are aligned (as in (eq. 11)), and the maximization problem of each agent includes reward terms that are a subset of the terms of each of its parents, an equilibrium strategy profile exists. In this case, the agents can formulate their optimal policies via algorithms similar to the ones described in Section 5.1.

An interesting question is whether this is a necessary condition for the existence of equilibria in stationary deterministic strategies for problems with arbitrary dependency graphs and numbers of agents, or whether weaker assumptions would be sufficient. An analysis of this issue is one of the directions of our current and future work.

7 Conclusions

We have analyzed the use of a particular compact, graphical representation for a class of multiagent MDPs with local, asymmetric influences between agents. As is the case with other graphical models, the representation studied in this work can lead to exponential savings in problem representation. However, in general, because the effects of agents' influences on each other propagate with time, the compactness of the problem representation is not fully preserved in the solution. We have shown this for multiagent problems with the social welfare optimization criterion, which are equivalent to single-agent problems, and for which similar results are known [14]. Because optimal policies for such problems do not retain any of the structure of the original problem (agents' policies depend on the states of all other agents), exact solution methods are infeasible, and approximate solution techniques appear well-justified.

We have also analyzed multiagent problems with self-interested agents, and have shown the complexity of solutions to be less prohibitive in some cases (acyclic dependency graphs). We have demonstrated that under further restrictions on agents' effects on each others' rewards (additively-separable, positive linear functions), locality is preserved to a greater extent. Under these conditions, equilibria in stationary deterministic strategies can exist even for graphs with reward-related cycles.

Our future work will combine the graphical representation of multiagent MDPs with other forms of problem factorization, including constrained multiagent MDPs [9].

Another direction of our future work includes analyzing problems where re-distribution of rewards is possible, which might cause agents to negotiate policies with their children.

8 Acknowledgments

This work was supported, in part, by a grant from Honeywell Laboratories, and by DARPA/ITO and the Air Force Research Laboratory under contract F30602-00-C-0017 as a subcontractor through Honeywell Laboratories.

References

1. R. Bellman. *Adaptive Control Processes: A Guided Tour*. Princeton University Press, 1961.
2. Richard Bellman. *Dynamic Programming*. Princeton University Press, 1957.
3. Craig Boutilier. Sequential optimality and coordination in multiagent systems. In *Proceedings of the 1999 International Joint Conference on Artificial Intelligence*, pages 478–485, 1999.
4. Craig Boutilier, Thomas Dean, and Steve Hanks. Decision-theoretic planning: Structural assumptions and computational leverage. *Journal of Artificial Intelligence Research*, 11:1–94, 1999.
5. Craig Boutilier, Richard Dearden, and Moises Goldszmidt. Stochastic dynamic programming with factored representations. *Artificial Intelligence*, 121(1-2):49–107, 2000.
6. D. P. de Farias and B. Van Roy. The linear programming approach to approximate dynamic programming. *Operations Research*, 51(6), 2003.
7. Daniela de Farias and Benjamin Van Roy. On constraint sampling in the linear programming approach to approximate dynamic programming. *Mathematics of Operations Research*, 29(3):462–478, 2004.
8. Thomas Dean and Keiji Kanazawa. A model for reasoning about persistence and causation. *Computational Intelligence*, 5(3):142–150, 1989.
9. Dmitri A. Dolgov and Edmund H. Durfee. Optimal resource allocation and policy formulation in loosely-coupled Markov decision processes. In *Proceedings of the Fourteenth International Conference on Automated Planning and Scheduling (ICAPS 04)*, pages 315–324, June 2004.
10. C. Guestrin, D. Koller, R. Parr, and S Venkataraman. Efficient solution algorithms for factored MDPs. *Journal of Artificial Intelligence Research*, 19:399–468, 2003.
11. M. I. Jordan. Graphical models. *Statistical Science (Special Issue on Bayesian Statistics)*, 19:140–155, 2004.
12. Michael Kearns, Michael L. Littman, and Satinder Singh. Graphical models for game theory. In *Proceedings of the 17th Conference in Uncertainty in Artificial Intelligence (UAI01)*, pages 253–260, 2001.
13. Daphne Koller and Brian Milch. Multi-agent influence diagrams for representing and solving games. In *Proceedings of Seventeenth International Joint Conference on Artificial Intelligence*, pages 1027–1036, 2001.
14. Daphne Koller and Ronald Parr. Computing factored value functions for policies in structured MDPs. In *Proceedings of the Sixteenth International Conference on Artificial Intelligence IJCAI-99*, pages 1332–1339, 1999.

15. Michael L. Littman. Markov games as a framework for multi-agent reinforcement learning. In *Proceedings of the 11th International Conference on Machine Learning (ML-94)*, pages 157–163, New Brunswick, NJ, 1994. Morgan Kaufmann.
16. Guillermo Owen. *Game Theory: Second Edition*. Academic Press, Orlando, Florida, 1982.
17. M. L. Puterman. *Markov Decision Processes*. John Wiley & Sons, New York, 1994.
18. D. Pynadath and M. Tambe. Multiagent teamwork: Analyzing the optimality and complexity of key theories and models. In *In Proceedings of the First Conference on autonomous agents and multiagent systems (AAMAS-2002)*, 2002.
19. Satinder Singh and David Cohn. How to dynamically merge Markov decision processes. In Michael I. Jordan, Michael J. Kearns, and Sara A. Solla, editors, *Advances in Neural Information Processing Systems*, volume 10. The MIT Press, 1998.
20. Robert St-Aubin, Jesse Hoey, and Craig Boutilier. Apricodd: Approximate policy construction using decision diagrams. In *NIPS*, pages 1089–1095, 2000.
21. J. van der Wal. Stochastic dynamic programming. *Mathematical Centre Tracts*, 139, 1981.

A Study of Scalability Properties in Robotic Teams*

Avi Rosenfeld, Gal A Kaminka, Sarit Kraus

Bar Ilan University, Ramat Gan, Israel

Summary. In this chapter we describe how the productivity of homogeneous robots scales with group size. Economists found that the addition of workers into a group results in their contributing progressively less productivity; a concept called the Law of Marginal Returns. We study groups that differ in their coordination algorithms, and note that they display increasing marginal returns only until a certain group size. After this point the groups' productivity drops with the addition of robots. Interestingly, the group size where this phenomenon occurs varies between groups using differing coordination methods. We define a measure of *interference* that enables comparison, and find a high negative correlation between interference and productivity within these groups. Effective coordination algorithms maintain increasing productivity over larger groups by reducing the team's interference levels. Using this result we are able to examine the productivity of robotic groups in several simulated domains in thousands of trials. We find that in theory groups should always add productivity during size scale-up, but spatial limitations within domains cause robots to fail to achieve this ideal. We believe that coordination methods can be developed that improve a group's performance by minimizing interference. We present our findings of composite coordination methods that provide evidence of this claim.

1 Introduction

Teams of robots are likely to accomplish certain tasks more quickly and effectively than single robots [9, 12, 23]. To date, only limited work has been performed on studying how performance scales with the addition of robots to such groups. Should one expect linear, exponential, or decreasing changes in productivity as the group size grows? Previous work by Rybski et al. [23] demonstrated that groups of identical robots do at times demonstrate marginal decreasing returns. As such, their productivity curves resembled logarithmic functions; the first several robots within their group added the most productivity per robot and each additional robot added successively less. In contrast, Fontan and Matarić [26] found that robotic groups reached

---

* This material is based upon work supported in part by the NSF under grant #0222914 and ISF grant #1211/04 . Sarit Kraus is also affiliated with UMIACS.

a certain group size, a point they call "critical mass", after which the net productivity of the group dropped. Similarly, Vaughan et al. [29] wrote that the rule of "too many cooks" applies to their groups and adding robots decreases performance after a certain group size.

Economists have studied the gains in productivity within human groups. According to their Law of Marginal Returns, if one factor of production is increased while the others remain constant, the overall returns will relatively decrease after a certain point [4]. As the size of the group becomes larger, the added productivity by each successive worker is likely to become negligible, but never negative. This classical model contains no reference to a concept similar to a "critical mass" group size after which the added worker decreases the total productivity of the group.

Our research goal is to understand when the marginal returns predicted by the economic model would be consistently realized as work by Rybski [23] found they were, and when adding robots would decrease performance as Fontan and Vaughan [26, 29] described. Towards this goal, we first analyze several existing group coordination algorithms and empirically observe the different groups' productivity with the addition of robots. We observe that the different coordination techniques affect the productivity graphs of these groups during scale up.

To determine the cause for the differences between coordination algorithms, we define a measure of interference that facilitates comparison, and find a high negative correlation between group interference and productivity. Effective coordination algorithms maintain marginal productivity over larger groups by reducing interference levels. Using this result we are able to examine robotic group productivity in several simulated domains in thousands of trials. We find that groups in theory always produce marginally, but that competition over space causes robots to deviate from this ideal.

We believe this result can aid in studying the scalability qualities of robots. First, our interference metric is useful post-facto, for understanding the scalability qualities within robotic groups. The effectiveness of a coordination method can be judged based on its ability to minimize interference. A team's ability to scale will be hampered if interference is not kept in check. Additionally, we believe interference can be used in an online fashion to increase the group's productivity and scalability. We present preliminary results of composite coordination methods that indicate that our interference metric can be used to adapt a group's coordination activities to the needs of the domain. For future work, we plan to further study the use of this metric in improving the scalability, and performance qualities of robotic groups.

2 Related Work

The study of robotic groups is quite important for several reasons. Certain tasks require groups of robots. For example, a large hazardous item might require the combined strength of several robots to physically move it. Other tasks can be accomplished through groups of robots more quickly and robustly. Rybski et al. [23] demonstrated that groups of robots are likely to finish certain collection tasks faster than one robot. Groups of inexpensive robots are also useful in certain domains where there is a high probability damage will be incurred by any single robot. Thus, tasks such as mine clearing are well suited for groups of inexpensive robots. In this work we study the scalability qualities of these type of robotic tasks, but many of our results are likely to be useful for other categories of robotic activity as well.

We study methods for improving upon the productivity of robotic groups through improving the coordination methods in these groups. At the logical level, various formal frameworks for teamwork have been proposed such as the joint intentions theory of Cohen and Levesque [5], Grosz and Kraus' SharedPlans [11], and Joint Intentions [14] have been presented for creating a cohesive team unit. Several practical teamwork implementations have been proposed for dynamic environments based on these models. The GRATE* teamwork method [14] is based on creating Joint Recipes based on the needs of a specific domain. The STEAM [28] teamwork engine is based on creating a set of domain independent team rules. All of these frameworks revolve around having the members of the group agreeing to and maintaining a mutual beliefs among all members of the group. These beliefs are often explicitly communicated, and team members require robust sensing and communication capabilities. Finally, a behavior based approach, Alliance [20], operates through members of a robot team using impatience and acquiescence behaviors to create teamwork. This approach does not explicitly model teamwork and relies on using team behaviors within each robot to create team cohesion.

A second model of group behavior revolves around swarm group behaviors, instead of formalized teamwork. Swarm behaviors typically involve homogeneous groups of members with limited processing and operating ability. Often these models are inspired from group activity of animals [17, 21]. Such approaches are typically best suited for domains where large groups are available, the task does not require tight cooperation between group members, and robust sensing and communication abilities do not exist in group members. Dudek et al. [6] present a taxonomy of these and other possible categories.

Between these extremes lies numerous possibilities. Swarms could be created with high level reasoning and sensing abilities. These large groups could use high level team reasoning skills. For example, Scerri et al. [25] presents a scalable approach where large teams are based on dynamically evolving subteams. This work presents the challange of creating effective coordination methods that can scale. Novel coordination approaches are needed in addressing this issue.

Our research goal in this work is to understand how to increase the effectiveness of robotic groups' coordination during scale-up. Previous work by Fontan and Matarić [26] noted that proper coordination lies at the root of effective group behavior. As such, the creation of effective coordination is critical for achieving high productivity within a group. Our first step was to study how adding robots effects the groups' productivity. We wished to ascertain when adding foraging homogeneous robots hurt group performance as [26] and [29] predict they will after a certain team size, and when these robots continuously adds to the team's performance as Rybski et al. found [23].

Several coordination methods have been developed for use within the foraging domain. This domain is formally defined as locating target items from a search region S, and delivering them to a goal region G [10]. We began by studying this domain because of the wealth of existing research conducted within this environment [9, 10, 19, 23, 26, 29].

The foraging domain is characterized by a limited field of operation where spatial conflicts between group members are likely to arise. Many other robotic domains such as waste cleanup, search and rescue, planetary exploration and area coverage share this trait. In fact, this paper demonstrates that our foraging results were equally applicable within a second search domain.

We first studied the interplay between the success of group's coordination and the corresponding productivity during group scale up. Several coordination methods have been developed for use within the foraging domain. For the sake of simplifying the comparison, we initially only contrasted methods that operate on homogeneous robots, do not require prior knowledge of the domain, and do no require any communication. Arkin and Balch [1] describe a system of using repulsion schema any time a robot projects it is in danger of colliding. It additionally adds a noise element into its direction vector to prevent becoming stuck at a local minima. Vaughan et al. [29] describe an algorithm that uses *Aggression* to resolve possible collisions by pushing its teammate(s) out of the way. They posit that possible collisions can best be resolved by having the robots compete and having only one robot gain access to the resource in question. A third approach, is a dynamic *Bucket Brigade* mechanism [19]. In this method, a robot drops the item it is carrying when it detects another robot nearby. In theory, the next closest robot should retrieve the recently dropped object and carry it closer to the goal. While this last method may be effective in foraging, it is limited to certain domains. This coordination method is not appropriate for certain tasks such as searching. It also requires the robot to drop and retrieve its target without cost - an assumption that is not necessarily true in domains such as toxic cleanup.

Other foraging coordination algorithms exist that require advance knowledge of physical details of the operating domain and/or use groups of heterogeneous robots. Examples of these algorithms include the territorial allocation method developed by Fontan and Matarić [26] and the territorial arbitration scheme in Goldberg and Matarić [9]. Both methods limit each foraging robot to a specific area or zone and thus prevent collisions. Thus, these methods assume that improved performance can be achieved by specializing the robots to operate only within portions of the field. Another group of algorithms preassigns values so that certain robots inherently have a greater priority to resources than others. This group of coordination methods is similar to the Aggression method mentioned [29], but it preassigns robots to be aggressive or meek. The fixed hierarchy system within Vaughan et al. [29] and the caste arbitration algorithm in Goldberg and Matarić [9] implemented variations of this idea on foraging robots.

Other variations of these coordination methods exist within other domains. For example, Jäger and Nebel [12] presented an algorithm that can dynamically create limiting areas of operation for robots in a vacuuming domain, but require the robots to communicate locally. Within the robotic soccer domain, various groups have been created that rely on allocating each group member to a role. Communication is then needed to allocate and reallocate these roles. One example of this idea is within Marsella et. al. [18].

Because the first group of algorithms require no communication, they seem more suitable to scale to larger groups of robots. As they do not require prior knowledge of the domain, they seem better suited for working with unknown or dynamic environments. More generally, a survey work done by Kraus [16] presented various multi-agent coordination schemes and states that those requiring large overheads are typically unable to scale beyond small groups. Similarly, Jones and Mataric [15] point out that *minimal* robots, or those with low requirements for communication or sensor input from teammates are more suited to scale to large swarms of robots. Minimalistic methods have been used in collection tasks [10] and formation control [8].

To date, only limited work exists on improving robot group scalability. The work by Fontan and Matarić [26] found that groups of 3 robots performed best within their foraging domain. Adding more robots only hurt performance when using their territorial coordination method. Jäger and Nebel [13] presented a collision avoidance technique for use in trajectory planning among robot groups that requires local communication. They noted that their coordination method will not scale beyond groups of 4 robots. Rybski et al. [23] found increasing marginal productivity up to groups of 5 foraging robots, but did not study larger sizes.

Within the general agent community, Shehory et al. [27] presented a scalable algorithm for a package delivery domain suitable for groups of thousands of agents. He based his algorithm on concepts borrowed from physics. Later work by Sander et al. [24] studied how computational geometry techniques could be applied to groups in the same domain. Both found that group productivity did scale marginally with the addition of agents and that a point existed where adding agents did not significantly improve the productivity of their system. Their agents did not compete over physical space, and they never found that adding agents hurt group performance. Specific to the search domain, work by Felner et al. [7] studied the scalability qualities of their PHA* algorithm, and found that their algorithm yields marginally better results with the addition of agents. Our research goal is to understand when robotic teams would similarly scale.

The Law of Marginal Returns, also often called the Law of Diminishing Returns, is well entrenched as a central theory within economics. Most economic domains have spatial limitations and other finite production resources. These limiting factors cause the groups' performance to typically increase marginally with the addition of labor. Brue [4] demonstrated that economists from the Enlightenment Period until modern times often did not provide empirical evidence for their theories. He concluded, "more empirical investigation is needed on whether this law is operational" within new domains, and "conjectures by 19th century economists about input and outputs ... simply won't do!" The first goal of this paper was to provide this robust study for robotic groups.

3 Comparing Group Coordination Methods

In this section we present our initial study of scalability within groups of foraging robots. In order to minimize the factors involved in this experiment, we limited
our study to groups of homogeneous robots without communication where only the
coordination methods differed between groups. We were surprised to find that the
coordination method strongly impacted the scalability qualities of the group. While
every group demonstrated diminishing positive marginal gains up to a certain group
size, the shape of this graph varied greatly between groups.

3.1 Initial Experiment Setup

We implemented a total of eight coordination methods for use on foraging robots.
The Noise, Bucket Brigade and Aggression methods were based on previously published methods described in the previous section. Our implementation for the *Noise*
team was included as the default team in the Teambots distribution [3]. The *Bucket
Brigade* coordination behavior was initiated once a robot detected a teammate within
2 robot radii. Then, these robots would drop the target being carried, move backwards
for 25 cycles, and finally revert to the random walk behavior. The *Aggression* group
was based on the random function of aggressive behaviors described in Vaughan et
al. [29]. For every cycle a robot found themselves within 2 robot radii of a teammate,
it selected either an aggressive or timid behavior. In order to decide, we had each
robot choose a random number between 1 and 100. If the random number was lower
than fifty, it became timid and back away for 100 cycles. Otherwise it proceeded
forward, mimicking the aggressive behavior. As all robots within two radii choose
whether to continue being aggressive every cycle, one or both of the robots assumed
the timid behavior before a collision occurred.

Our remaining five methods were based on variations of existing methods. Similar to the Aggression group, the *Repel Fix* group backtracked for 100 cycles but
mutually repelled like the Noise group. The *Repel Rand* group moved backwards
for a random interval uniform over 1 – 200 and also mutually repelled. The *Gothru*
and *Stuck* groups both removed all coordination behaviors. The *Gothru* group was
allowed to ignore all obstacles, and as such spent no time engaged in coordination
behaviors. This "robot" could only exist in simulation as it simply passes through
obstacles such as other robots. However, this group was still not allowed to exit the
boundaries of the field. We used this group to benchmark ideal performance without productivity lost because of teammates. At the other extreme, the *Stuck* group
also contained no coordination behaviors but simulated a real robot. As such, this
group was likely to become stuck when another robot blocked its path. Like the
Stuck group, the *Timeout* group contained no repulsion vector to prevent collisions.
However, these robots did add noise to the direction vector after a certain threshold
had been exceeded where their position did not significantly change. The *Timeout*
group moved with a random walk for 150 cycles once these robots did not significantly move for 100 cycles. If the timeout threshold was set too low, the robot may
consider itself inactive while approaching a target or its home base. However, if this

value was set too high, it did not successfully resolve possible collisions in a timely fashion. We experimented with various values until we found that this combination seemed to work well.

We used a well-tested robotic simulator, Teambots [3], to collect data on groups of these foraging robots. We strongly preferred using a simulator as it allowed us the ability to perform thousands of trials of various team sizes and compositions. The sheer volume of this data allowed us to make statistical conclusions that would be hard to duplicate with manually setup trials of physical robots. Using a simulator also allows us to research behaviors, such as Gothru's, that cannot exist with physical robots.

In this experiment, Teambots [3] simulated the activity of groups of Nomad N150 robots. The field measured approximately 5 by 5 meters. Our implementation of foraging followed Balch's [2] multi-foraging task in which the robots attempt to retrieve two or more types of objects. There were a total of 40 such target pucks, 20 of which where stationary within the search area, and 20 moved randomly. Each trial measured how many pucks were delivered by groups of 1 – 30 robots within 9 minutes. For statistical significance, we averaged the results of 100 trials with the robots being placed at random initial positions for each run. Thus, this experiment simulated a total of 24,000 trials of 9 minute intervals.

The simulated robots we studied were based on the same behaviors. The only software differences between the robots lay within their implementation of the previously described teamwork coordination behaviors. Each robot had three common behaviors: wander, acquire, and deliver. In the *wander* phase, the robots originated from a random initial position, and proceeded in a random walk until they detected a resource targeted for collection. This triggered the *acquire* behavior. While performing this second behavior, the robots prepared to collect the puck by slowing down and opening up their grippers to take the item. Assuming they successfully took hold of the object, the deliver behavior was triggered. At times the puck moved, or was moved by another robot, before the robot was able to take it. Once this target resource moved out of sensor range, the robot reverted once again to the wander behavior. The *deliver* behavior consisted of taking the target resource to the goal location which was in the center of the field.

3.2 Initial Results

Figure 1 graphically represents the results from this experiment. Our X-axis represents the various group sizes ranging from 1 to 30 robots. The Y-axis depicts the corresponding average number of pucks the group collected over its 100 trials.

According to the economic Law of Marginal Returns, marginal returns will be achieved when one or more items of production are held in fixed supply while the quantity of homogeneous labor increases. In this domain, the fixed number of pucks acted as this limiting factor of production. Consequently, one would expect to find production graphs consistent with marginal returns. However, only the Gothru group demonstrated this quality over the full range of group sizes. All other groups contained a critical point (CP1) where maximal productivity was reached. After the

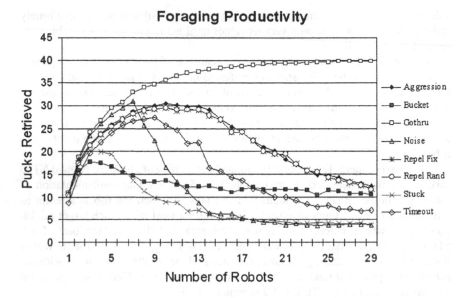

Fig. 1. Comparing Foraging Productivity Results during Group Size Scale-Up

group size exceeded this point, productivity often dropped precipitously. Eventually, the groups reached a level (CP2) where the addition of more robots ceased to significantly negatively effect the groups' performance.

With the exception of the Aggression, Repel Fix, and Repel Rand groups, all groups' productivity graphs differed significantly. For example, the Stuck group reached its CP1 point with an average of only 20.94 pucks collected with groups of 3 robots. The Aggression group reached a maximum of 30.84 pucks collected in groups of 10 robots. Even among equally sized groups, the differences were large. When comparing foraging groups of 10 robots, the Stuck group gathered only 8.58 pucks - far fewer than Gothru's 35.62 pucks, while the Aggression group collected 30.52 pucks, only 5.2 fewer than Gothru. Large differences between the level of CP2 also existed between groups. Notice how the Bucket Brigade group maintained a CP2 level near 12 pucks, while the Stuck and Noise group's CP2 level was near 4 pucks. The Bucket Brigade mechanism was more effective even in large group sizes.

Our resulting research was motivated by these results. The Gothru group was the only group capable of realizing marginal gains throughout the entire range of 30 robots. However, many groups demonstrated the positive quality of maintaining increasing productivity over a larger range of robots. For example, the Noise group only kept marginal gains until groups of seven robots, while the Aggression group kept this quality through groups of 10 robots. We also found that the positive qualities of improved performance and maintaining marginal performance over larger groups are not always synonymous. The Noise group kept positive marginal performance over a smaller range than the Aggression group, yet performed better in groups sized seven or less. A closer look at the various coordination models was needed to draw lessons about how to create groups with both properties.

4 Why does Performance Drop?

We needed a mechanism for understanding why certain coordination methods were more effective than others during size scale-up. We posited that differences among robotic groups were often sparked from clashes in spatial constraints. Specific to foraging, conflicts arose over which robot in the group had the right to go to the home base first. As the group size grew, this problem became more common. This caused the groups to deviate from the ideal marginal productivity, depicted by the Gothru group, by greater amounts. The length of time robots clashed with their teammates because of joint resources, such as the home base location, served as the basis in comparing coordination models within any domain.

Previous work by Goldberg and Matarić [9] found a connection between the level of interference a group demonstrated and its corresponding performance. They defined interference as the length of time robots collide, and we began by using this definition to equate between our coordination algorithms. This measure sufficed for some robots, such as those simulated by the Stuck group, because they did not engage in any other coordination behaviors. However, this metric of interference could not explain the differences between all groups. Many robots, such as those simulated by the Aggression group, never collided. If one takes the position that only collisions constitute interference within robotic groups, these robots do not interfere. Yet we clearly observed how the addition of robots detracted from the groups' productivity after its maximal productivity point.

In this section we present our measure of interference. We describe scale up experiments in foraging and search domains that are characterized by resources that lend themselves to group conflicts. We find that interference and productivity are strongly negatively correlated in such domains, and use this metric to explain differences in productivity between all teams. We posit that in the absence of spatial conflicts, all teams should consistently demonstrate marginal gains during scale up. We confirm this idea by easing the "space crunch" in our domains and notice how all groups consistently demonstrate marginal returns. We conclude that any domain with group spatial conflicts will suffer from deviations in marginal performance once the causes of interference cannot be resolved.

4.1 Interference: Measure of Coordination

We define interference as the length of time an agent is involved with, either physically or computationally, projected collisions, real or imaginary, from other robots and obstacles. This period of involvement often extends well beyond the actual collision between two robots. Any time spent before a supposed collision in replanning and avoidance activities must also be recorded. Similarly, all post-collision resolution activity must be included as well. Thus, according to our definition, the Gothru group has zero interference because it never engages in any interference resolution behaviors and represents idealized group performance. The Aggression group engages in interference resolution behaviors before a collision ever happens. Its various timid and aggressive behaviors to avoid collisions all constitute interference by our definition. The Bucket Brigade group demonstrates that interference can exist after a collision is prevented. For this group, one needs to measure the productivity lost by handing off the resource from one robot to the next. Many times this group lost productivity during this process because the second robot never properly took the dropped target. Only this measure takes into the account the total interference resolution process.

According to our hypothesis, we expected to see a negative correlation between levels of interference and productivity in three respects. We reasoned that the degree to which a group deviates from the idealized marginal gains is proportional to the amount of average interference within the group. This can impact where the group hits maximal performance. Those groups which reached CP1 with a small number of robots spiked high levels of interference much faster than those where this point was delayed. Second, even before groups hit their maximum productivity point, we hypothesized that the more productive groups have lower levels of interference than their peers. Finally, we expected that differences in where the productivity of the groups eventually plateau can be attributed to the group's saturation level of interference. Those robots that more effectively deal with interference even in large groups will have CP2 values at higher levels.

In order to confirm this hypothesis, we reran our eight foraging groups and logged their interference levels according to our definition. The Gothru group never registered any interference. For all remaining groups, we used the simulator to measure the number of cycles the robots in the groups collided. For all groups other than the Stuck and Gothru groups, we additionally measured the number of cycles the robots triggered interference resolution behaviors when they were not colliding. In the Noise and repulsion groups, this represented the number of cycles spent in repelling activities. In the Aggression group, it was the number of cycles spent in timid and aggressive behaviors. In the Timeout group, this was the cycles spent trying to resolve a collision once the robot timed out. In the Bucket Brigade group, internal behaviors alone did not suffice to measure interference by our definition. We only recorded cycles spent when the robots came close to another and consequently dropped the resource they were carrying. However, we could not measure the time lost when the second robot did not effectively take that resource as we did not have omnipotent knowledge of such events. As a result, our measurement for interference for this group did not necessarily represent an exact measurement, but an underestimate.

Figure 2 represents the result from this trial. The X-axis once again represents the group size, and the Y-axis represents the average number of interference cycles that each robot within the group registered over the 100 trials.

Foraging Interference Comparison

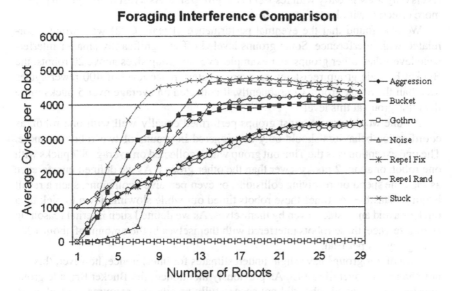

Fig. 2. Interference Levels in Foraging Domain

We found that CP1 typically occurred for all groups when the average inter-ference level within each robot of the group reached a level between 1500 and 2500 cycles. The longer the group was able to maintain classically diminishing returns, the more cycles of interference were needed to cause the critical point. This is because CP1 will only be reached once the productivity lost due to interference is larger than the total marginal productivity of the group. Before this point, the total production of the group increases, albeit marginally. For example, the Stuck group, which reached its critical point with only four robots, needed closer to only 1500 cycles to cause this critical point. The Aggression group hit CP1 with 10 robots, and consequently needed approximately 2200 cycles to counter the productivity of more robots.

Even when viewing the differences between productivity among equally sized groups, interference differences were significant. We found a very strong average negative correlation of -0.94 between the groups' performance and their interfer-ence level over the entire range of 1 to 30 robots. For example, the Noise group most closely followed the idealized Gothru productivity graph for groups up until 7 robots, and registered significantly less interference than the other groups. This interference resolution mechanism had little overhead, and needed fewer cycles to resolve a pos-sible collision. However, this method didn't scale well beyond this point. When the group size became larger than seven, its interference levels grew exponentially and the group's performance quickly decayed. In contrast, the Aggression and other re-pelling groups had significant levels of interference from the onset, but interference levels only grew linearly with respect to the group size. As a result, this group proved more effective with larger group sizes.

We also found that the eventual performance plateau (CP2) was strongly correlated with interference. Some groups leveled off at significantly smaller interference levels than other groups. For example, even in group sizes above 20 robots, the Bucket Brigade group registered an average interference level of 400 fewer cycles less than the Stuck group. Consequently, it collected on average over 5 pucks more than this group at this level.

As one would expect, most groups performed equally well with one robot, as coordination behaviors should only be triggered in groups of two robots or more. The one exception was the Timeout group which collected on average 8.7 pucks with one robot, or about 2 pucks fewer than the other groups. As we defined interference as the time spend on resolving collisions, or even perceived collisions, such a result is quite plausible. At times these robots timed out while slowing down to pick up a puck or avoid an obstacle even by themselves. As we defined such internal reasoning as interference, these robots interfered with themselves in the amount of about 1000 average cycles per trial.

Two of our groups have slight underestimates for interference; however, this did not change our overall results. As previously mentioned, the Bucket Brigade group interfered if a second robot did not successfully receive the resource handed off to it. We found that this did occur at times when there were relatively small groups of these robots. Thus, the correlation between their productivity and that of other groups' among groups of 2–6 robots dropped to -0.80. By discounting this range, the average overall correlation reached almost -0.97. However, after 6 robots we found that there were enough robots in the area to ensure a second robot would quickly take the resource, and the amount of this underestimate was less significant. The Noise group also registered an underestimate for interference. These robots actually used two repulsion fields for collision resolution. They triggered a strong repulsion field when they sensed another robot or obstacle 0.1 meters away. We only measured the number of times this repulsion field was triggered. However, a second, much weaker repulsion field was triggered from 1.5 meters away. In this instance, our underestimate did not seem to significantly statistically detract from our results. With or without the data from this group, the average correlation between groups was -0.94.

4.2 Competing over Spatial Resources

We proceeded to study if our results were limited to foraging or were a general phenomenon seen when robotic groups are faced with restriction production resources. We created a new spatially limited search domain where the task goal was to find the exit out of the room as quickly as possible. We placed groups of robots within a room of 1.5 by 1.5 meters with one exit 0.6 meters wide. We reasoned a critical productivity point would once again form in this domain. Too few robots would result in a long search time until the exit was found. However, too many robots would cause interference as the exit was only physically wide enough for one robot.

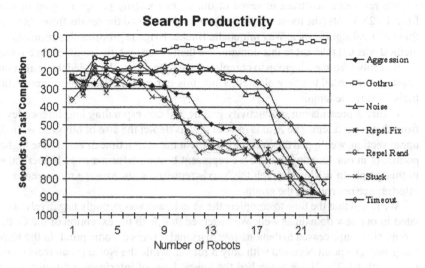

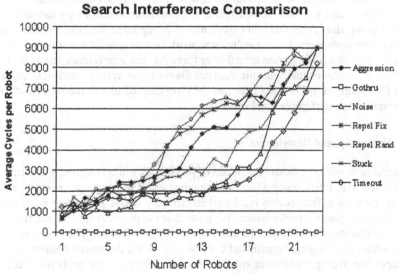

Fig. 3. Search Time and Interference Measurements during Group Size Scale-Up

We ran simulated trials of seven of our eight foraging groups ranging in sizes from 1 - 23 robots (the room holds 23 robots) and averaged the results from 100 trials for statistical significance. We omitted the Bucket Brigade group as this coordination method was not relevant to this domain. We then measured the length of time it took the first robot from each group to completely exit the room. We ended the trial at that point and recorded the time elapsed. Thus, this experiment constitutes over 16,000 trials of variable length.

Figure 3 presents our productivity graphs and corresponding interference levels from this experiment. The X-axis in both graphs depict the size of our groups. In the upper section, we flipped the Y-axis to represent the search time of zero as the highest point. As in our foraging graphs, we represent better performance as higher values in this graph. In the lower graph the Y-axis represents our average measurement of interference per robot in the group.

We found that the time to complete the search task was strongly negatively correlated in our new domain as well. We observed that with the exception of the Gothru group, all groups ceased to demonstrate marginal returns at some point. In the Repel Fix group this point occurred with only 5 robots, while the Noise group reached this point with 10. The Noise group had the lowest level of interference through groups of 13 robots, and was able to most closely approximate Gothru's performance until this group size. After this point the Timeout group fared the best. We found that certain interference resolution mechanisms work best in specific domains. While the repulsion methods were quite effective in foraging, the interference levels in these groups grew exponentially in this domain. Overall, the average statistical correlation for groups of 1-23 robots between the time elapsed to exit the room and their corresponding interference level was -0.94.

4.3 Easing Spatial Restrictions

According to our hypothesis, deviations of productivity in robot groups are strongly correlated with interference. Once our foraging and search groups ceased to effectively resolve interference they reached their critical group sizes. Adding more robots only hurt the groups' performance. We posit that the physical space limitations existent within many robotic groups often cause this interference. The one home base area within the foraging domain and the one exit within the search domain create a competition over space between robots that cannot always be properly resolved.

We were able to confirm that our robotic groups always demonstrated marginal returns once restrictions over physical space were eased. We changed the foraging group requirement of returning the pucks to one centralized home base location. Instead, they were allowed to consider the pucks to be in the home base immediately. With the exception of the Bucket Brigade group, we reused all 8 previously studied foraging groups. Once again, we omitted this method because it was not applicable to our new domain. We left all other environmental factors such as the number of trials, the size and shape of the field and the targets to be delivered identical. Thus, Teambots [3] simulated 21,000 trials of 9 minute intervals in this experiment.

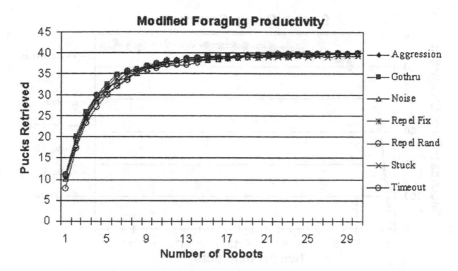

Fig. 4. Productivity of Groups in Modified Foraging Domain during Size Scale-Up

As figure 4 shows, all groups did indeed always achieve marginal returns in the modified foraging domain. While Gothru still performed the best, the differences between it and other groups' coordination methods were not as pronounced. The level of interference all groups demonstrated was also minimal, and thus not displayed. We concluded that not every foraging domain needed to have a critical point for productivity where marginal gains during scale up ceased.

Within the search domain, we hypothesized that limitations in the room size and width of the exits created the large amounts of interference during scale up. In order to ease this restriction, we doubled the size of the room to become approximately 3 by 3 meters, and widened the exit to allow free passage out of the room by more than one robot. Once again, we measured the time elapsed (in seconds) until the first robot left the room and averaged 100 trials for each point. This experiment also constituted over 16,000 trials of varying lengths. Figure 5 graphically shows that our modified domain consistently realized marginal increases in faster search times with respect to group size. Once again, interference levels were also negligible in our new domain. Thus, we concluded that achieving marginal productivity gains was always possible once competition over spatial resources was removed.

5 Improved Scalability through Coordination Combination

Our next step was to apply lessons based on our understanding of the coordination methods we studied towards creating methods with improved productivity and scalability properties. In this section we present our *Composite Coordination Methods*. We found that it was possible to combine methods with different scalability prop-

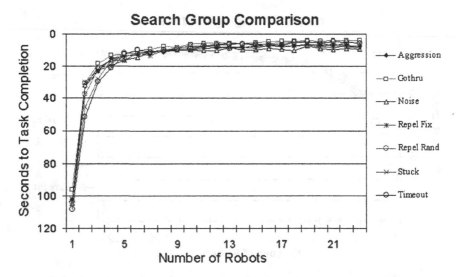

Fig. 5. Productivity of Groups in Modified Search Domain during Size Scale-Up

erties to create a new composite method. This method achieved higher productivity levels in the foraging and search domains we studied. Surprisingly, we found that our new composite method at times far exceeded the productivity levels of even the that highest levels of productivity from the groups they were based on. We believe that using multiple methods in tandem allowed robots to more effectively deal with the spatial limitations that characterized their operating domain. This allowed for the gains we found in these groups' scalability properties.

5.1 Composite Coordination Methods

Our composite coordination methods combined the two best coordination methods for any given domain. Our previous study demonstrated that it possible to order coordination methods based on groups sizes where they are most effective. In the foraging domain, the Noise group had the highest productivity in small groups, while the Aggression group had higher productivity in larger groups. In the search domain, the Noise group again had the highest productivity in the small groups with the Timeout group faring better in larger group sizes. In both domains, our implementation for the composite method was based on allowing these two simpler methods to be triggered under different domain conditions.

Our implementation of the composite method in the foraging domain revolved around using two different methods to attempt to prevent collisions. Robots first used the Noise method, but if this method proved insufficient opted for the more robust Aggression method. Once a robot detected that another teammate came within two robot radii away, it attempted to resolve a possible collision by inserting a slight repulsion and noise element into its trajectory. In cases when the probability of collisions was low, as was the case in small group sizes, this behavior alone sufficed. However, at times the spatial conflicts in the domain could not be resolved through this simple coordination behavior. For example, in large group sizes, the probability that two or more robots mutually blocked became substantial. In these cases, the robots continued to move closer despite the use of this method. Once the robots came within a second, closer threshold, which we set to one robot radii, the second, more robust Aggression method was triggered. The timid and aggressive behaviors in this method were more successful in resolving spatial conflicts than the simpler behaviors in the Noise method. However, the interference overhead in the Aggression behavior was higher, and not justified in situations where the simpler behavior sufficed. Thus, by two different thresholds we attempted to match the correct collision prevention behavior to the domain conditions.

We found this approach to be very effective within our foraging domain. Figure 6 displays the productivity of the composite foraging group, Noise + Aggression, compared to the two methods it is based on. In the top portion of the graph we display the average number of pucks retrieved (Y-axis) over different group sizes (X-axis). The bottom graph displays the varying interference levels (Y-axis) as a function of the group size. Notice how the composite group significantly outperformed the two groups it was based on. We performed the two-tailed t-test between our composite group and the two static ones it was based on. Both p-scores were well below 0.05 needed to establish the statistical significance, with the higher score of 0.003 found between the Aggression group and the composite one. We also found that the relationship between interference and productivity applies to this new group with a strong negative correlation of -0.92 between all three group's productivity and the corresponding interference level averaged over the interval of 1 – 30 robots.

Our motivation in the search domain was similar, but our composite coordination method was implemented slightly differently. In this domain we also created our composite method between two methods – Noise and Timeout. These two methods resolve collisions with different mechanisms. The Noise method attempts to prevent collisions before they occur through repulsion. In contrast, the Timeout behavior was purely reactive in nature and its behavior only was triggered after collisions already occurred. Thus, a composite coordination method between these two methods was able to created without two different distance thresholds. The Noise method behavior was fully implemented to attempt to prevent collisions. The Timeout behavior was also fully implemented. In cases when the Noise behavior did not prevent a collision, this second behavior was effective in then resolving the conflict.

We also found that this approach yielded marked improvement in performance and scalability properties for our search domain. Figure 7 displays the productivity of the composite foraging group, Noise + Timeout, compared to the two methods it is based on. In the top portion of the graph we display the average time to complete the search task (Y-axis) over the different group sizes (X-axis). The bottom graph displays the varying interference levels (Y-axis) as a function of the group size. Notice how the composite group again significantly outperformed the two groups it was based on, especially in larger group sizes. We performed the two-tailed t-test between

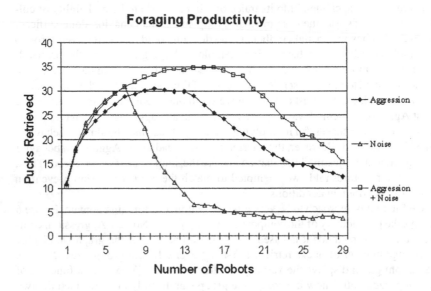

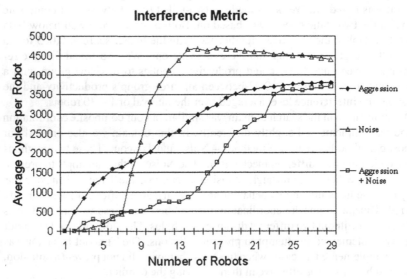

Fig. 6. Comparing a Composite Foraging Method to its Two Base Methods

our composite group and the two static ones it was based on. Both p-scores were well below 0.05 needed to establish the statistical significance, with the higher score of 0.004 found between the Noise group and the composite one. We also confirmed that the relationship between interference and productivity applies to this new group with a strong negative correlation of -0.98 between the three groups' productivity levels and their corresponding interference levels over the interval of 1 – 23 robots. It is important to note that the composite method in the search domain was able to eliminate the critical group size that existed in every group we studied except for the theoretical Gothru group. As such, this group demonstrated the best scalability quality from all methods we studied – the group's average productivity never significantly dropped with the addition of robots. Further study was needed to understand why these composite groups had significantly better productivity and scalability qualities than the methods they were based on.

5.2 Studying How to Improve Scalability

Our interference metric was useful for understanding why the composite methods we created were able to significantly outperform the simpler methods they were based on. These composite methods had significantly lower levels of interference, allowing marginal gains and larger productivity over larger groups. However, we believe that coordination methods can be developed to improve the scalability capabilities of robots. It is possible that our interference metric is not only useful post-facto, but can facilitate online adaptation to improve performance even in dynamic and changing environments. We have begun to study how to create adaptive methods based on interference and have presented our initial results in [22].

We believe coordination methods that respond to the triggers of interference can minimize the time spent resolving those instances. Throughout the course of one trial, many spatial conflicts are likely to occur. The speed with which the robots resolve these conflicts will determine the success of the robots to achieve higher productivity and scalability properties. As such, we posit that a causal relationship exists between a robot's interference level and the corresponding productivity that robot is able to contribute to its group. The more time spent on resolving coordination conflicts, the less time will be left to perform the desired action. Thus, if robots could reduce their interference levels, they will consequently be able to achieve higher productivity.

Our working hypothesis is that groups that effectively deal with interference episodes are going to improve their productivity levels. While coordination behaviors themselves constitute interference, at times they are needed for achieving cohesive group behavior. Effective behaviors cannot realistically eliminate interference. Optimal coordination methods behaviors can only minimize interference levels given domain conditions. For example, in the foraging domain we studied, the Noise method's simpler coordination method contained little overhead. However, as collisions within the domain became frequent, this method did not suffice, and robots were not capable of successfully resolving space conflicts and thus loss productivity. The Aggression method had an overhead that made it more effective in larger group

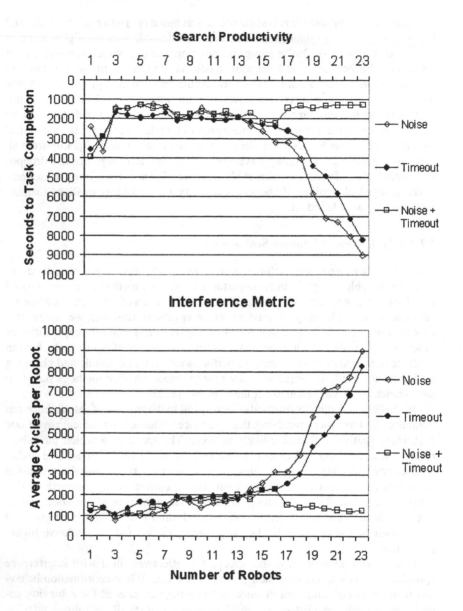

Fig. 7. Comparing a Composite Search Method to its Two Base Methods

sizes, but the larger interference overhead in this method made it less effective in smaller group sizes.

We believe that our composite methods outperformed the static method because of their improved ability to effectively match their coordination efforts to the needs of their domain. This allowed these robots to change the time spent on resolving coordination conflicts based on the needs of the domain. Figure 8 demonstrates the ability of our composite method to resolve conflicts in a more timely fashion. The graph represents the percentage of foraging robots that on average collided throughout the course of three trials (540 simulated seconds) in groups of 20 robots. The X-axis in this graph represents the number of seconds that elapsed in the trial (measured in ten second intervals), while the Y-axis measures the percentage of robots colliding at that time in the Noise, Aggression, and Noise + Aggression methods. Notice that the Noise group was ineffective in resolving collision instances in this group size and thus throughout the trial nearly all robots were exclusively engaged in collision resolution behaviors. As a result, this group had the highest interference levels and the poorest productivity. The Aggression group was able to more effectively deal with collisions, but on average consistently spent more than half of their time resolving spatial conflicts. In contrast, robots in the composite group were able, on average, to resolve conflicts and thus reduce their interference levels. This resulted in the significantly higher productivity levels in this group over the two static ones it was based upon.

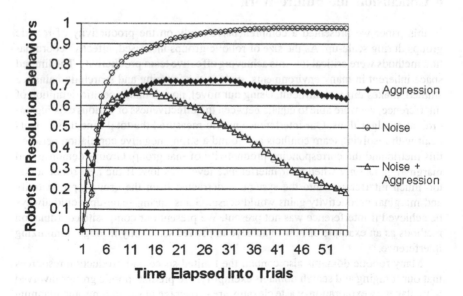

Fig. 8. Average Percentage of Robots Colliding as a Function of Time

When viewing spatial conflicts on a per trial basis, the fluctuations in the instances of interference and the robot's ability to react to those fluctuations are even more pronounced. We posit that the composite method used the Aggression method in reaction to collisions becoming more frequent within the domain. To support this claim we viewed the internal state of these robots over the course of our trials. Figure 9 displays three individual foraging trials of the composite group, again in groups of 20 robots. In the upper graph we mapped the percentage of robots that were engaged in resolution behaviors (Y-axis) over the course of the trials (the Y-axis). The bottom graph represents the internal coordination state of these robots as a number between 1 and 2. A value of 1 represents all robots being engaged in the Noise behavior, and a value of 2 corresponds to all robots in the Aggression behavior. Groups on average typically have a value between these extremes with robots autonomously choosing different states based on how close its closest teammate is at that moment. Notice the relationship between these two graphs with the composite robots using the Aggression behavior (an average state closer to 2) when collisions are more frequent. On average over the entire time period, we found a strong negative correlation of -0.90 between these two graphs. This supports our claim that changes in interference can be sensed autonomously by robots. We believe this allowed the composite groups to achieve such a strong improvement in the productivity and scalability qualities of these teams.

6 Conclusion and Future Work

In this paper we presented a comprehensive study on the productivity of robotic groups during scale-up. As the size of robotic groups increased, effective coordination methods were critical towards achieving effective team productivity. The limited space inherent in many environments, such as the foraging and search domains we studied, makes this task difficult. Using our novel, non-domain specific definition of interference, we were able to equate between the effectiveness of various existing coordination algorithms. Our interference metric measured the total time these robots dealt with resolving team conflicts and found a strong negative correlation between this metric and the corresponding productivity of that group. Groups demonstrated marginal gains only when their interference level was low. If the new robot added too much interference into the system, it detracted from the group's productivity and marginal productivity gains would cease. Gains during scale-up would always be achieved if interference was not present. We present our composite coordination methods as an example of how to achieve improved scalability through minimizing interference.

Many robotic domains also contain the limited space and production resources that our foraging and search domains exemplify. We predict robotic groups involved with planetary exploration, waste cleanup, area coverage in vacuuming, and planning collision-free trajectories in restricted spaces will all benefit from use of our interference metric. We plan to implement teams of real robots in these and other domains in the future.

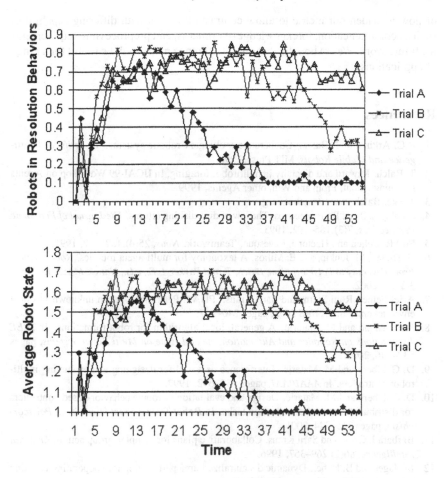

Fig. 9. Fluctuations in Collisions over Time and the Corresponding Foraging Method

We demonstrated in our paper that the spatial restrictions within robotic domains often prevented marginal gains from being realized as group sizes grew. The corollary of this hypothesis is that marginal returns will always be achieved in domains that do not clash over resources. It is not surprising that groups of agents should therefore always realize marginal returns during scale up once group interference issues have be resolved or are not applicable.

Many applications and extensions to our interference metric are possible. For future work, we hope to address several directions for possibly extending our metric. This paper limited its study to homogeneous robots without communication. Additionally, we did not study coordination methods which require pre-knowledge of their domain or algorithms that use other forms of preprocessing. We leave the study of how to widen our metric to allow contrasting robots with differing capabilities such as communication, foreknowledge of domains, and preprocessing requirements for future work. We are hopeful that our interference metric will be useful for a range of applications.

References

1. R.C. Arkin and T. Balch. Cooperative multiagent robotic systems. In *Artificial Intelligence and Mobile Robots*. MIT Press, 1998.
2. T. Balch. Reward and diversity in multirobot foraging, In IJCAI-99 Workshop on Agents Learning About, From and With other Agents, 1999.
3. Tucker Balch. www.teambots.org.
4. Stanley L. Brue. Retrospectives: The law of diminishing returns. *The Journal of Economic Perspectives*, 7(3):185–192, 1993.
5. Phil R. Cohen and Hector J. Levesque. Teamwork. *Nous*, 25(4):487–512, 1991.
6. G. Dudek, M. Jenkin, and E. Milios. A taxonomy for multi-agent robotics. *Robot Teams: From Diversity to Polymorphism, Balch, T. and Parker, L.E., eds., Natick, MA: A K Peters*, 3:3–22, 2002.
7. Ariel Felner, Roni Stern, and Sarit Kraus. PHA*: Performing A* in unknown physical environments. In *AAMAS 2002*, pages 240–247.
8. J. Fredslund and M. Matarić. A general, local algorithm for robot formations. In *IEEE Transactions on Robotics and Automation, special issue on Multi Robot Systems*, pages 837–846, 2002.
9. D. Goldberg and M. Matarić. Interference as a tool for designing and evaluating multi-robot controllers. In *AAAI/IAAI*, pages 637–642, 1997.
10. D. Goldberg and M. Matarić. Design and evaluation of robust behavior-based controllers for distributed multi-robot collection tasks. In *Robot Teams: From Diversity to Polymorphism*, pages 315–344, 2001.
11. Barbara J. Grosz and Sarit Kraus. Collaborative plans for complex group action. *Artificial Intelligence*, 86(2):269–357, 1996.
12. M. Jager and B. Nebel. Dynamic decentralized area partitioning for cooperating cleaning robots. In *ICRA 2002*, pages 3577–3582.
13. Markus Jager and Bernhard Nebel. Decentralized collision avoidance, deadlock detection, and deadlock resolution for multiple mobile robots. In *IROS*, 2001.
14. Nicholas R. Jennings. Controlling cooperative problem solving in industrial multi-agent systems using joint intentions. *Artificial Intelligence*, 75(2):195–240, 1995.
15. C. Jones and M. Matarić. Adaptive division of labor in large-scale minimalist multi-robot systems. In *Proceedings of the IEEE/RSJ International Conference on Robotics and Intelligent Systems (IROS)*, pages 1969–1974, 2003.
16. Sarit Kraus. Negotiation and cooperation in multi-agent environments. *Artificial Intelligence*, 94(1-2):79–97, 1997.
17. C. Ronald Kube and Hong Zhang. Collective robotic intelligence. pages 460–468, 1992.
18. Stacy Marsella, Jafar Adibi, Yaser Al-Onaizan, Gal A. Kaminka, Ion Muslea, and Milind Tambe. On being a teammate: experiences acquired in the design of RoboCop teams. In Oren Etzioni, Jörg P. Müller, and Jeffrey M. Bradshaw, editors, *Proceedings of the Third International Conference on Autonomous Agents (Agents'99)*, pages 221–227, Seattle, WA, USA, 1999. ACM Press.

19. E. Ostergaard, G. Sukhatme, and M. Matari. Emergent bucket brigading - a simple mechanism for improving performance in multi-robot constrainedspace foraging tasks. In *Proceedings of the 5th International Conference on Autonomous Agents*, 2001.
20. L. Parker. Alliance: An architecture for fault-tolerant multi-robot cooperation. *IEEE Transactions on Robotics and Automation*, 14(2):220–240, 1998.
21. Craig W. Reynolds. Flocks, herds, and schools: A distributed behavioral model. *Computer Graphics*, 21(4):25–34, 1987.
22. A. Rosenfeld, G. Kaminka, and S. Kraus. Adaptive robot coordination using interference metrics. In *The Sixteenth European Conference on Artificial Intelligence*, Valencia, Spain, August 2004.
23. P. Rybski, A. Larson, M. Lindahl, and M. Gini. Performance evaluation of multiple robots in a search and retrieval task, In Workshop on Artificial Intelligence and Manufacturing, 1998.
24. Pedro Sander, Denis Peleshcuk, and Barbara Grosz. A scalable, distributed algorithm for efficient task allocation. In *AAMAS 2002*, pages 1191–1198.
25. Paul Scerri, Yang Xu, Elizabeth Liao, Justin Lai, and Katia Sycara. Scaling teamwork to very large teams. In *AAMAS '04: Proceedings of the Third International Joint Conference on Autonomous Agents and Multiagent Systems*, pages 888–895. IEEE Computer Society, 2004.
26. M. Schneider-Fontan and M. Mataric. A study of territoriality: The role of critical mass in adaptive task division. 1996.
27. O. Shehory, S. Kraus, and O. Yadgar. Emergent cooperative goal-satisfaction in large scale automated-agent systems. *Artificial Intelligence journal*, 110(1):1–55, 1999.
28. M. Tambe. Towards flexible teamwork. *Journal of Artificial Intelligence Research*, 7:83–124, 1997.
29. R.T. Vaughan, K. Støy, G.S. Sukhatme, and M.J. Matarić. Go ahead, make my day: robot conflict resolution by aggressive competition. In *Proceedings of the 6th int. conf. on the Simulation of Adaptive Behavior*, 2000.

Comparing Three Approaches to Large-Scale Coordination

Paul Scerri[1], Régis Vincent[2], Roger Mailler[3]

[1] Carnegie Mellon University
[2] SRI International
[3] Cornell University

Summary. Coordination of large groups of agents or robots is starting to reach a level of maturity where prototype systems can be built and tested in realistic environments. These more realistic systems require that both algorithmic and practical issues are addressed in an integrated solution. In this chapter, we look at three implementations of large-scale coordination examining common issues, approaches, and open problems. The key result of the comparison is that there is a surprising degree of commonality between the independently developed approaches, in particular the use of partial, dynamic centralization. Conversely, open issues and problems encountered varied greatly with the notable exception that debugging was a major issue for each approach.

1 Introduction

Coordinating large groups of intelligent robots to perform a complex task in a complex environment requires meeting a range of challenges in an integrated solution. These challenges range from well-known algorithmic issues, e.g., managing the computational complexity of task and resource allocation, to more practical issues, e.g., initialization and deployment of a large number of robots. In the past few years, a small number of systems have been developed that are capable of demonstrating real coordination between large numbers of robots in realistic domains. While extensively leveraging the large body of previous work, these systems required new techniques to deal with the practical complexity of coordinating a large group of robots. In this chapter, we look at three successful approaches to coordination to find commonalities and differences in the techniques used. The aim is to identify ideas that generalize across approaches as well as issues that appear to come up regardless of the approach used.

Each of the applications and approaches described in this chapter involves at least 100 completely unselfish and cooperative group members. One application required coordination of simulated agents for a complex task, one involved 100 robots on an exploration and, tracking task and another involved hundreds of sensors for a montoring task. The group members are relatively homogeneous, although there is always some heterogeneity due to location. Thus despite being relatively homogeneous in design, the agents were not always easily interchangeable. The complex tasks on which the teams were working were relatively decomposable, although constraints (either resource or spatial or both) existed between the decomposed subtasks. In all cases, the coordination algorithms had to deal with many of the issues faced by any multi-agent system, as well as complications due to scale. Since the applications involve at least somewhat realistic environments, the approaches were required to address a full spectrum of issues, including many practical challenges often ignored in the multiagent literature. Some of these practical challenges are well known, e.g., dealing with lossy communication or building reliable software, while others were more novel, e.g., working out how 100 robots can enter a building in a reasonable amount of time.

While the approach to each application was developed independently of the others and was underpinned by a diverse set of philosophies and constraints, there was a surprising amount of commonality in both the solutions and the open problems. Two specific, major commonalities were of particular interest. The first was that each approach used some form of *dynamic, partial centralization* to reduce the overall complexity. In particular, some decision-making responsibility for a small group of agents was dynamically assigned to an agent particularly able to make those decisions. The form of the centralization varied greatly, from dynamic subteams to dispatchers to mediation. In each case, only a small subset of the team was involved in the centralization, and the agents involved, as well as the "center", were not chosen in advance. The reason for this commonality appears to stem from a need to balance the complexity of key algorithms and the practical limitations of time and communication resources. In situations where coordinated decision making involved a large percentage of the group, developers resorted to various heuristics for controlling resource requirements, and when a small percentage of the group was involved, partial centralization was used. Although the reason for it is unclear, it is noteworthy that no optimal completely distributed algorithms were used, perhaps because in cases where they were applicable partial centralization was more efficient.

Most likely related to the dynamic localized centralization, the second notable commonality between the three approaches was that the coordination was neither simple and relying on emergent properties nor highly structured with top-down guidance. While the lack of top-down structure was at least partially due to the decomposibility of the task, there was more structure to the coordination than the task, indicating that the coordination was not simply designed to mirror the task. Interestingly, none of the approaches were inspired by any particular organizational theory, human or biological. Structure limited the decisions that could be made by an individual, including who that individual could communicate with about what, what tasks the individual could perform, and protocols for making coordinated decisions. For example, in one of the approaches, the notion of a subteam was strictly defined and carried certain responsibilities that were often not required for best coordinated behavior, but simplified the possible organizations that could occur. Although not explicit in any of the designs, it appears that each approach carefully balanced imposed structure for making the coordination intelligible to a human and flexibility for allowing the group to find the best way to complete a task. The need for intelligibility was key when programming, testing, deploying and improving the system, but the additional structure limited the potential of the team. Future development tools may open the possibility to decrease the amount of structure and, thus, increase the potential of the group.

In contrast to the high degree of commonality between the approaches used, the problems encountered and the major open problems were varied. In two of the approaches, determining appropriate parameters for heuristics was identified as a problem. In two approaches, there was unwanted emergent behavior. In one approach, sharing information was a problem. It does not appear that any of the approaches are immune to the problems encountered by the others, only that the specific problems were not induced by the specific applications. This diversity of problems and open issues is especially interesting since the approaches had so much in common. However, it is unclear what to conclude from this, since one might come to the mutually exclusive conclusions that the basic approach was poor and problems manifested themselves in different ways or that the approach was fundamentally good and time was spent on more detailed issues. More applications are required for a definitive conclusion. In each approach, debugging was found to be a major difficulty with only the most rudimentary support available for debugging extremely complex, distributed applications. The most stunning evidence of this problem is that all approaches reported that major bugs went unnoticed for extended periods of time, before being discovered by chance. The bugs went unnoticed because the overall behavior was not accurately predicted in advance, so disappointing performance was attributed to causes other than faulty software.

In the remainder of this chapter, we briefly describe the way each of the three approaches addresses a variety of problems. By showing in detail the commonalities and differences, we provide a fair comparison of the approaches. Finally, open, important problems, identified in the development of the systems, are described to help shape the research agenda for large-scale coordination.

2 Applications and Assumptions

Each of the applications involves at least 100 cooperative entities and has been tested either in hardware or realistic simulation of hardware. Although specific communication restrictions differ, communication is identified as a much bigger limitation than computation. None of the applications requires optimal performance; instead, the focus is on doing a large task robustly.

2.1 Teamwork and Machinetta

Machinetta software proxies are used to develop teams where the members are assumed to be completely cooperative and willing to incur costs for the overall good of the team [20]. Typically, team members will be highly heterogeneous, ranging from simple agents and robots to humans. When a group of agents coordinates via *team-work* they can flexibly and robustly achieve joint goals in a distributed, dynamic and potentially hostile environment [7, 9]. Key teamwork algorithms have evolved from an extensive body of work on both the theory and practice of teamwork [23, 8, 3]. Teams of heterogeneous actors have potential applications in a wide variety of fields, ranging from supporting human collaboration [1, 22] to disaster response [16] to manufacturing [9] to training [23] to games [10]. To date we have demonstrated teams of 500 software agents [21], in both a UAV simulation [19] and a disaster response simulation, but teams of as many as 200,000 agents are envisioned.

Given the complexity of the domains, tasks, and heterogeneity of the team, we typically assume that optimality is not an option. Instead, we look for satisficing solutions, that can achieve the goals rapidly and robustly. The assumption is that doing something reasonable is a very good start. For example, in a disaster response domain, we assume that it is better to have fire trucks on reasonable routes to fires, than to delay departure with computationally expensive optimization. While the team will be able to leverage reasonably high bandwidth communication channels, we assume that the bandwidth is not sufficiently high to allow centralized control. The team will need to achieve complex goals in a complex, dynamic domain. We assume that some decomposition of the complex task into relatively independent subtasks can take place.

2.2 Centibots Dispatching

Funded by DARPA, the CENTIBOTS project is aimed at designing, implementing, and demonstrating a computational framework for the coordination of very large robot teams, consisting of at least 100 small, resource-limited mobile robots (CEN-TIBOTS, see Figure 1), on an indoor search-and-rescue task. In this project, communication was limited and unreliable, and any coordination mechanisms had to deal with the limitations. There are two types of agents in the Centibots system; hence, heterogeneity is not an issue. Similarly, optimality is infeasible, so having a reactive, "good enough" system was the primary aim.

In the scenario, the CENTIBOTS are deployed as a search-and-rescue team for indoor missions. A first set of mapping-capable CENTIBOTS surveys the area of interest to build and share a distributed map highlighting hazards, humans, and hiding places. A second wave of robots, with the capability of detecting an object of interest (e.g. biochemical agents, computers, victims), is then sent. The key goal of the second wave is to *reliably* search *everywhere* and report any findings to the command center. These robots are then joined by a third wave (possibly the same robots used during the second wave) of tracking robots that deploy into the area, configuring themselves to effectively sense intruders and share the information among themselves and a command center [11].

Communication is done using an ad-hoc wireless network, which has a maximum *shared* bandwidth of 1 Mpbs. Communication is not guaranteed because as the robots move to achieve their own missions, links between the agents are created and lost. Because the robots fail, break, and get lost, planning the entire mission ahead of

Fig. 1. 100 Robots used during the January 2004 evaluation.

time is not possible. Essentially, there is no chance that all the robots will finish the mission. In addition, resources (i.e. robots) and goals can be added, removed, or disabled at any time, making an adaptable system crucial.

2.3 Cooperative Mediation

Scalable, Periodic, Anytime Mediation (SPAM) [12] is a *cooperative-mediation*-based algorithm that was designed to solve real-time, distributed resource allocation problems (RTDRAP). SPAM was developed to coordinate the activities of hundreds to thousands of agents that controlled sensors within a large sensor network as part of the DARPA Autonomous Negotiating Teams (ANTS) program (see figure 2).

In this project, sensors were randomly placed in the environment and had to co-ordinate their internal schedules in order to discover and track moving targets. Each of the sensor platforms had three Doppler-radar-based sensor heads capable of re-turning amplitude and frequency shift information for objects within their 20-foot range and 120-degree viewable arc. Because of this, multiple, temporally coordi-nated measurements from different sensors within the network were needed in order to triangulate the precise position of a target at any given time. In addition, each of the sensor platforms was controlled by a Basic stamp micro-controller that was ca-pable of processing the incoming sensor data from only one head at a time. These two factors when combined together formed the basis of a difficult, distributed re-source allocation problem that was further complicated by dynamics created by the movement of the targets.

Adding to the complexity of this problem, communications varied from 100 Mbps TCP-based wired networks to 14.4 kbps half duplex, RF-based, multichannel wireless communications. In the latter, message passing was very unreliable and loss rates of 50% were not uncommon. The communication restrictions combined with

Fig. 2. Researchers work on a demonstration involving 36 sensors and 3 mobile targets.

the real-time coordination needs made complete centralization out of the question and traditional distributed techniques inadequate.

SPAM has been tested in real-world hardware environments with 36 sensors and in simulated environments with more than 500 sensors.

3 Key Algorithms and Principles

Although distinct approaches are used, i.e., teamwork, hierarchical dispatching and cooperative mediation, each approach imposes some limited, flexible structure on the overall group. Notice that a central aim of each approach is to efficiently, robustly, and heuristically allocate and reallocate tasks and resources.

3.1 Machinetta and Teamwork

A key principle in teamwork is that agents have both models of teamwork and models of other team members [21]. The models are used to reason about which actions to take to achieve team goals. Having explicit models with which the agents can reason leads to more robustness and flexibility than fixed protocols. The key abstraction in our implementation of teamwork is a Team Oriented Plan, which breaks a complex joint activity down into individual *roles*, with constraints between the roles [18]. Typically, a large team will be executing many team-oriented plans at any time. Dynamically changing subteams form to execute each of the plans. Small amounts of communication occur across subteams, to ensure that sub-teams do not act at cross purposes or duplicate efforts.

Scalable algorithms required to perform the teamwork were designed with two key ideas in mind. First, we use probabilistic models of team activity and state to inform key algorithms. This actually leverages the size of the team because the probabilistic models tend to be more accurate with a large number of agents, since local variation gets canceled out more effectively. The teamwork algorithms are designed to leverage the probabilistic models to make very rapid decisions that are likely to be at least "reasonable". Second, we note that when there are very many team members, Murphy's Law[4] applies, simply because everything happens so many times. Creating efficient, lightweight software that is simple enough to be implemented reasonably quickly, yet robust enough to be used in teams with thousands of agents, is as much a function of the algorithms as it is of the actual code. Significant emphasis must be placed on designing algorithms that are sufficiently simple to be straightforward to implement in a very robust manner. Specifically, most key algorithms use *tokens* to encapsulate "chunks" of coordination reasoning [19]. A good example of these principles is in our algorithm for ensuring that the team is not working on conflicting plans. That algorithm uses tokens, for robustness, and the associates network to ensure, *with high probability*, that the team is not working at cross purposes.

These two principles are embodied in the role allocation process that uses a probabilistic model of the current capabilities and tasks of the team to calculate a threshold capability level that a team member performing a role would have in a good overall allocation, and then uses a *token* that moves around the team until an available team member is found with capability above the threshold [5].

3.2 Centibots Dispatching

Once the Centibots have produced a map as a bitmap image, an abstraction is needed so search goals can be created to ensure that all space is searched. The abstraction is done by building a Voronoi diagram from the map, and then the Voronoi skeleton is abstracted into a graph. This abstraction is solely based on the sensor capabilities of a robot. Once we have all the goals generated, coordination is required to allocate them to a pool of robots.

To coordinate the robots' activities, we use a hierarchical dispatching system, where robots can register with multiple *dispatching agents*, one of which is considered "preferred". Teams of robots are formed by a *commander*, and for each team, a manager or dispatcher is selected. The manager selection is unimportant as known solutions can be used. The commander assigns a set of goals to each team and the teams' dispatchers assign these to individual robots. When a robot has finished its assigned goals, it notifies the dispatcher, making itself available, and asks for a new goal.

A key problem for Centibots was the strategy used by a dispatcher to assign goals to robots. Since all robots started from the same position, the problem is to minimize the search time. This allocation is in theory similar to a multiple traveling salesman problem except that there is no a priori notion of how many salesmen you might have, and a salesman can fail at any time during the traveling. Given these constraints, we found, after trying several techniques, that the best strategy for the dispatcher is to send the robot the farthest away for the first goal and then minimize its movement by taking the closest goals after the first one.

---

[4] Anything that can go wrong will go wrong.

3.3 Cooperative Mediation

SPAM works by having one or more agents concurrently take on the role of mediator. An agent decides to become a mediator whenever it identifies a conflict with a neighbor (both scheduled a sensor for use at the same time) or it recognizes a suboptimality in its allocation (it could achieve higher utility if it changed its sensor assignment). As a mediator, an agent solves a localized portion (or subproblem) of the overall global problem. In SPAM, this subproblem entails the agents with which the mediator shares sensor resources. As the problem solving unfolds, the mediator gathers preference information, from the agents within the session, which updates and extends its view and overlaps the context that it uses for making its local decisions with that of the other agents. By overlapping their context, agents understand why the agents within the session have chosen a particular value that allows the system to converge on mutually beneficial assignments.

This technique represents a new paradigm in distributed problem solving. Unlike current techniques that attempt to limit the information the agents use to make decisions in order to maintain distribution [28, 27], SPAM and more generally cooperative mediation centralize portions of the problem in order to exploit the speed of centralized algorithms.

4 Key Novel Ideas

New ideas were required to overcome weaknesses in the principles as approaches were scaled from small numbers of agents to the large numbers needed for the coordination.

4.1 Machinetta and Teamwork

There are a variety of novel ideas in the Machinetta proxies. To maintain cohesion and minimize conflicted effort, the whole team is connected via a static, scale free *associates network* [21]. As well as the obligation to communicate information to members of its dynamically changing subteam, as required by teamwork, an agent must keep its neighbors in the associates network appraised of key information. The network allows most conflicted or duplicated efforts to be quickly and easily detected and resolved. Movement of information around the team, when team member(s) requiring the information are not known in advance, also leverages the associates network. Every time information is communicated, the agent receiving the information updates a model of where it might send other information, based on information received to date [26]. Because of a phenomenon known as *small worlds networks*, information passed around a network in this manner can be efficiently sent to the agent(s) requiring the information.

Allocating roles in team-oriented plans to best leverage the current skill set of the team is accomplished by a novel algorithm called LA-DCOP [5]. LA-DCOP extends distributed constraint optimization techniques in several ways to make it appropriate for large, dynamic teams. Most important, LA-DCOP uses probabilistic models of the skills of the team and the current roles to be filled to estimate the likely skill of an agent filling a role in a "good" allocation. To take advantage of human coordination reasoning, when it is available, we represent all coordination tasks explicitly as *coordination roles* and allow the proxy to meta-reason about the coordination role [20]. For example, in a disaster response domain, there may be a role for fighting some particular fire that no firefighter is able to fill. The proxies can recognize this and send the role to some person and allow that person to determine what action to take.

4.2 Centibots

The hierarchical dispatching model offers two key interesting qualities. The communication is minimal since the dispatcher is eavesdropping on the status message. Assuming the status message is required, then using a centralized dispatching will outperform any distributed methods. The drawback is the need of communication between the team of robots and the dispatcher. We assume that the dispatcher is a network service that resides physically anywhere on the network. The dispatcher can be running on any team member, and would require only local communication. The second quality is a natural hierarchy can be created to handle a large number of robots. In this configuration, we could have a hierarchy of dispatchers, each responsible for an area of the map, using a subteam of robots. Each robot can already subscribe to several dispatchers. If a dispatcher has completed all its goals, then it can release its assets for other dispatchers to use, achieving a load-balancing system. Like the SPAM system, the Centibots architecture leverage the power of the mediation by centralizing a sub portion of the problem.

4.3 Cooperative Mediation

The key principle that allows SPAM to be scalable is the heuristic restriction of the size of the subproblem that the mediators are able to centralize. Mediators in SPAM are only allowed to conduct sessions including agents with which they directly share resources. Although this prevents the search from being complete, in all but the most tightly constrained problem instances, this technique limits the amount of communication and computation that must occur within any single mediator. The downside to this heuristic approach, however, is that the mediators have less information and are often unaware of the consequences of their actions on other agents. To combat this effect, SPAM incorporates the use of *conflict propagation* and *conflict dampening*.

As the name implies, conflict propagation occurs whenever a mediator causes conflicts for agents that are outside of one of its sessions. It easy to envision this as the mediator pushing the conflicts onto agents over which it has no control (or responsibility). The key goal of the propagation is to find regions within the global resource problem that are under-constrained and can absorb the conflict. The actual propagation occurs when one the agents that has the newly introduced conflict takes

over the role of mediator. These agents can then either absorb the conflict (by finding a satisfying assignment to their subproblem) or can push the conflict onto other
agents, which may push it even further.

It is easy to see that conflict propagation alone would have disastrous consequences if it were not for conflict dampening. Conflict dampening is very similar
to the min-conflict heuristic presented in [13]. When an agent mediates, it gathers
information about the impact of particular assignments from each of the agents involved in the session. This allows the mediator to choose solutions that minimize the
impact on agents outside of its view. Overall the effects of conflict propagation and
dampening can be visualized as ripples in a pond that eventually die down because
of the effects of friction and gravity.

SPAM also incorporates a number of resource-aware mechanisms that prevent
it over-utilizing communication. In particular, SPAM monitors the state of the communications links between itself and other agents and when it notices that one of
the agents in the session has become overburdened, it is dropped from the session.
In addition, if an agent notices that it has become a communication hotspot, then it
avoids taking the role of mediator until the situation resolves itself. Overall, these
mechanisms allow SPAM to tradeoff utility for scalability of communications.

5 Software

We describe the major pieces of technology, specifically software, that are used for
the coordination in each of the approaches.

5.1 Machinetta and Teamwork

The teamwork algorithms are encapsulated in domain-independent *software proxies*
[17]. Each member of the team works closely with its own proxy. The proxy handles
all the routine coordination tasks, freeing the agent to focus on specific domain-level
tasks. The proxy communicates with the domain-level agent (or robot or person) via
an agent-specific, high-level protocol. Adjustable autonomy reasoning is applied to
each decision, allowing either the agent or the proxy to make each coordination decision [20]. Typically, all decisions are made by the proxy on behalf of agents or robots,
but when the proxy is working with a person, key decisions can be transferred to that
person. The current version of the proxies is called Machinetta and is a lightweight
Java implementation of the successful SOAR-based TEAMCORE proxies [21]. The
proxies have been successfully tested in several domains including coordination of
UAVs, disaster response, distributed sensor recharge, and personal assistant teams.
The proxy code can be freely downloaded from the Web. The application-dependent
aspects of the proxies, specifically the communication code and the interface to the
agents, are implemented as "pluggable" modules that can be easily changed for new
domains, thus improving the applicability of the proxies. The proxy software is freely
available on the Internet.

5.2 Centibots

The Centibots software makes an extensive use of the Jini [24] architecture. Each robot and each key algorithm is a network service that registers, advertises and interacts independently of its physical location. We have services like the map publisher that aggregates data from the mappers and publishes a map for the other robots, and like the dispatcher that allocates tasks to robots or even the user interface. The result is a very modular, scalable infrastructure. Each robot has its own computer where it runs localization, navigation, path planning, and vision processing algorithms.

5.3 Cooperative Mediation

The SPAM protocol is implemented both within simulation and as part of more complex agents designed to work on sensor hardware. The protocol itself is composed of several finite state machines (FSMs) that are written in Java. Each state in the FSM encapsulates a nondecomposable decision point within the protocol. Transitions between states are event driven and allow the protocol to specify state transitions based on time-outs, message traffic, specific execution conditions, and so on. This allows the protocol to be time and resource aware, modifying its behavior based on the current environmental conditions. SPAM is currently being considered for use in a number of domains, including real-time airspace deconfliction and the control of sensors for severe weather tracking.

6 Key Unexpected Challenges

Challenges were encountered during development that were not expected at the outset. Each approach ran into different, unexpected problems, ranging from sharing information to controlling oscillations.

6.1 Machinetta and Teamwork

Two main unexpected challenges occurred during the development of large teams. First, it was often the case that some team member had information that could be relevant to some other member of the team, but did not know to which other team member the information was relevant. For example, in a disaster response domain, an agent may get information about chemicals stored in a particular factory, but not know which firefighters will be attending that fire. Restricting knowledge of current activities to within a subteam provides scalability but reduces the ability of other team members to provide potentially relevant information. Previous approaches, including blackboards, advertisement mechanisms and hierarchies, do not immediately solve this problem in a manner that can effectively scale. To address this problem we made use of the fact that the associates network connecting team members had a small worlds property and allowed an agent to *push* information to its neighbor most likely to be able to make use of that information or know who would [26].

The second unexpected problem encountered was that there were many algorithm parameters that interact with one another in highly nonlinear ways. Moreover, slightly different situations on the ground require substantially different configuration of the algorithm parameters. Determining appropriate values for all parameters for a given domain is as much art as science and typically requires extensive experimentation. When the situation changes significantly at runtime, an initially appropriate configuration of algorithm parameters can end up being poor. We are currently developing techniques that use neural networks to model the relationships between parameters and assist the user in finding optimal settings for specific performance requirements and tradeoffs.

6.2 Centibots Challenges

The two main challenges we had to face are the instability of the communications and the number of goals to be assigned per agent. In this project, the communication was coordinated assuming a very conservative range for the wireless network. Unfortunately, we have encountered more than once parts of buildings where this conservative distance was not working. In this case, any robot that enters this communication dead zone will not be able to contact the centralized dispatcher. Our solution was to have the dispatcher living on close-by robots , which was a good improvement but did not completely solve the problem. As a result, we had to implement a low-level behavior where the robot, after waiting a known timeout, will return to its original starting position if it could not contact the dispatcher. In this case, at least we would retrieve it.

The second challenge was to determine the number of goals to assign to a robot. There was no way to know a priori how many robots would be part of the mission; therefore, a fair division of the number of goals was not possible. In section 5.2 we have shown that the most effective dispatching would require an assignment of several close-by goals; the key question is how many. Since the number of robots assigned to the mission is unknown (robots assigned will break and the commander may reassign others in the middle of the mission), the solution we use is an empirical function. The number of goals assigned varies (one to seven) depending on the number of goals left to be assigned. At the end of each run we collect the number of goals fulfilled by each robot and we collect each ending time; if there is a large variation (meaning some robots were under-utilized and others were overutilized) we vary the total number of goals to be assigned.

6.3 Cooperative Mediation

Because the SPAM protocol operates in a local manner, a condition known as *oscillation* can occur. Oscillation is caused by repeated searching of the same parts of the search space because of the limited view that the agents maintain throughout the problem solving process.

During the development of the SPAM protocol, we explored a method in which each mediator maintained a history of the sensor schedules that were being mediated whenever a session terminated. By doing this, mediators were able determine if they previously may have been in a state that caused them to propagate in the past. To stop the oscillation, the propagating mediator lowered its solution quality to force itself to explore different areas of the solution space. It should be noted that in certain cases oscillation was incorrectly detected by this technique, which resulted in having the mediator unnecessarily accept a lower-quality solution.

This technique is similar to that applied in [14], where a *nogood* is annotated with the state of the agent storing it. Unfortunately, this technique does not work well when complex interrelationships exist and are dynamically changing. Because the problem changes continuously, previously explored parts of the search space need to be constantly revisited to ensure that an invalid solution has not recently become valid.

In the final implementation of the SPAM protocol, we allowed the agents to enter into potential oscillation, maintaining almost no prior state from session to session and relied on the environment to break oscillations through the movement of the targets, asynchrony of the communications, timeouts, and so on.

7 Open Problems

As with the unexpected problems, each approach has different open problems. Even though most of the problems appear to be reasonably approach independent, e.g., traffic control in Centibots, neither of the other approaches has specific solutions to that problem, suggesting that the problems may be general.

7.1 Machinetta and Teamwork

Despite its successes, Machinetta has some critical limitations. Most critically, Machinetta relies on a library of predefined team-oriented plan templates. While some constructs exist for expressing very limited structure in the plans, these constructs are hard to use. In practice, to write successful Machinetta plans, the domain must be easily decomposable into simple, relatively independent tasks. The ability to write and execute more complex plans is a pressing problem.

While the probabilistic heuristics used by Machinetta are typically effective and efficient, occasionally an unfortunate situation happens and the resulting coordination is very poor. Sometimes the coordination will be unsuccessful or expensive because the situation is particularly hard to handle, but sometimes it will be that the particular heuristic being used is unsuited to the specific situation. Critically, the agents themselves cannot distinguish between a domain situation that is difficult to handle and a case where the coordination is failing. For example, it is difficult for a team to distinguish between reasonable role allocation due to a dynamic and changing domain and "thrashing" due to a heuristic not being suited to the problem. While individual problems, such as thrashing, can be solved on an ad hoc basis, the general problem of having the team detect that the coordination is failing is important before deploying teams. If such a problem is detected, the agents may be able to re-configure their algorithms to overcome the problem. However, as mentioned above, determining how to configure the algorithms for a specific situation is also an open problem.

7.2 Traffic Control in Centibots

Linked to the goal assignment, traffic control for several dozen robots in a small environment is a huge challenge. The assignment should take into consideration the schedule in which each robot will do its tasks to prevent deadlocks. For a robot, a doorway is a very narrow choke point, and only one robot can go through at one time. When more than two robots try to enter and exit the same room at the same time, you have a conflict. Currently we are not managing this problem; luck and local avoidance is how we solve it. We have seen in our dozens of real-life experiments some conflicts becoming literally traffic jams and blocking permanently one access of an area. The only way to reason about the choke point is as resource and solve the conflict during the assignment by using a method such as SPAM.

7.3 Cooperative Mediation

The most interesting open questions for the SPAM protocol deal with the when, why, and whom for extending the view of the mediators given different levels of en-vironmental dynamics and interdependency structures. Because the optimality and scalability of the protocol are strongly tied not only to the size, but to the charac-teristics of the subproblem that the mediators centralize, a detailed study needs to be conducted to determine the relationship between these two competing factors. Some work has already been done that preliminarily addresses these questions. For example, the whom and why to link questions were in part addressed in the *texture measures* work of Fox, Sadeh, and Baycan [6]. In addition, recent work on phase transitions in CSPs [2, 4, 15] in part addresses the question of when. It is clear that a great deal of work still needs to be done.

8 Evaluation and Metrics

We agree that evaluating the algorithms and the metrics used to measure performance is an immature and difficult science. Clearly, useful and comparable metrics will need to be developed, if sensible comparison is to be performed.

8.1 Machinetta and Teamwork

Evaluating teamwork is very difficult. While success at some particular domain-level task is clearly a good sign, it is a very coarse measure of coordination ability, and thus it is only one aspect of our evaluation. To ensure that we are not exploiting some feature of the domain when evaluating the algorithms, we have endeavored to use at least two distinct domains for testing. Moreover, typically it is infeasible to test head to head against another approach; hence, we are limited to varying parameters in the proxies. For the larger teams, a single experiment takes on the order of an hour, severely limiting the number of runs that can be performed. Unfortunately, because of the sheer size of the environment and the number of agents, there tends to be high variation in performance, implying that many runs must be performed to get statistically significant results. Even determining what to measure in an experiment is a difficult decision. We measure things like number of messages, number of plans created, roles executed and scalability, although it is not clear how some of these numbers might be compared to other algorithms. Typically, we measure global values, such as the overall number of messages rather than local values such as the number of messages sent by a particular agent.

Since there are no modeling techniques available for mathematically analyzing the algorithms' performance, we have developed a series of simple simulators that allow specific algorithms to be tested in isolation and very quickly. These simulators typically also allow comparison against some other algorithms. Currently, we have simple simulators for role allocation, subteam formation, and information sharing. Performing very large numbers of experiments with these simulators, we are able to understand enough about the behavior of the algorithms to perform much more focused experimentation with the complete Machinetta software.

8.2 Centibots Evaluation

This project was driven by the challenge problem set by DARPA and in this sense the evaluation was independently done by a DARPA team that has measured the behaviors of the Centibots software to solve the search-and-rescue mission, not purely the coordination. For a week in January 2004, the Centibots were tested at a $650m^2$ building in Ft. A.P. Hill, Virginia. They were tested under controlled conditions, with a single operator in charge of the robot team.

For searching, the evaluation criteria were time to locate object of interests (OOIs), positional accuracy, and false detections. There were four evaluation runs, and the results, in the Table 1, show that the team was highly effective in finding the object and setting up a guard perimeter. Note that we used very simple visual detection hardware and algorithms, since we had limited computational resources on the robots – false and missed detections were a failure of these algorithms, rather than the spatial reasoning and dispatching processes.

The results were not focused on the coordination portion but measured the overall performance of the system to solve the search-and-rescue mission. As explained in the next section, extracting meaningful data from such a system is not an easy task.

8.3 Cooperative Mediation

The SPAM protocol was implemented and tested within a working sensor network, but most of the development and analysis of the protocol was done in simulation.

Run	Mapping Time	Map Area	Search Robots	Search Time False Pos	Position Error / Topo Error
1	22 min	96%	66	34 min / 0	11 cm / none
2	26 min	97%	55	76 min / 1	24 cm / none
3	17 min (2 robots)	95%	43	16 min / 0	20 cm / none
4	19 min (2 robots)	96%	42	Missed / 2	NA
Avg.	21 min	96%	51	30 min / 0.75	14 cm / none

Table 1. Results of the four evaluation runs.

The primary metrics used to measure SPAM were the number of targets being effectively tracked during a fixed period of time, the number of messages being used per agent, and the social utility being obtained. For this problem, *social utility* is defined as the sum of the individual utilities for each target with penalties assigned for ignoring objects.

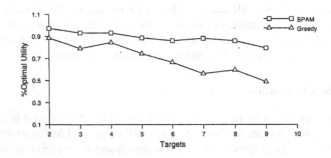

Fig. 3. Percentage of optimal utility for SPAM and greedy solutions.

We implemented two alternative methods for comparison. The first, which are called *greedy*, involved having each agent request all possible sensing resources to track its target, potentially overlapping with the requests of other agents. The utility calculation treated these overlaps as subdivided sensor time for each of the tracks. We also implemented algorithms to calculate the optimal utility and optimal number of tracks. Because these algorithms took so long to find the optimal solution however, we were forced to restrict the size of the problems to less than 10 targets. Overall, SPAM performed nearly optimally under various amounts of resource contention (see Figure 3). Independent analysis of the protocol was also conducted in [25], which verified these findings.

9 Testing and Debugging

Testing and debugging of the approaches is perhaps the most unexpectedly difficult area. Despite the sophisticated basic approaches and the relatively straightforward algorithms used, debugging always degenerated into a process of pouring over logfiles, which is clearly inappropriate if such systems are to be widely used.

9.1 Machinetta and Teamwork

Testing and debugging Machinetta teams is extremely difficult. Probabilistic reasoning and complex, dynamic domains lead to occasional errors that are very hard to reproduce or track down. We have extensive logging facilities that record all the decisions the proxies make, but without tool support determining why something failed can be extremely difficult and time-consuming. Simple simulators play a role in allowing extensive debugging of protocols in a simplified environment, but the benefit is limited. We believe that development tools in general, and testing and debugging support specifically, may be the biggest impediment to the deployment of even larger teams.

9.2 Centibots

Debugging is especially difficult because overall the system is behaving correctly. In one experiment, we had 66 robots in use at one time, producing over 1 MB of logs and debugging information per minute. We ran our experiment for more than 2 hours. In Centibots, we have a very sophisticated logging mechanism that writes every event, every message and information in an SQL database. By using the database, it is possible to replay an entire experiment. We also built SQL scripts that can extract statistics such as average running time per robot, average traveling time per robot, and number of goals fulfilled per robot that are very useful to the debugging process. Unless the system is performing very strangely, noticing the presence of bugs is extremely hard. In fact, one bug persisted for more than a year before being detected and fixed, leading to a dramatic improvement in performance.

9.3 Cooperative Mediation

Even with specialized simulation environments, testing and debugging coordination protocols that operate in the large is very difficult. On reasonably small problems involving tens of agents, noncritical problems often went unnoticed for long periods of time. We encountered a number of problems in trying to debug and test SPAM.

In the end, countless hours were spent pouring over many large log files, adding additional debugging text, rerunning, and so on. We did develop several graphical displays that helped to identify pathologies (or emergent behaviors) that could be witnessed only by viewing the system's performance from a bird's eye perspective. It is clear that a combination of macro and micro debugging methods is essential to developing systems of this type.

10 Conclusion

We have presented three initial attempts at performing large-scale coordination among robots or agents. We have shown striking similarities between the approaches that raise interesting scientific questions that must be addressed in a principled way. Critically, design of the coordination seems to be driven more by the difficult challenge of developing the software to implement it than by principles or theory. It will be important, for the field to move forward, to balance (or mitigate) development complexity with algorithmic performance in a better way than has been done so far. If these challenges can be met, the promise of large-scale coordinating is very exciting.

References

1. Hans Chalupsky, Yolanda Gil, Craig A. Knoblock, Kristina Lerman, Jean Oh, David V. Pynadath, Thomas A. Russ, and Milind Tambe. Electric Elves: Agent technology for supporting human organizations. *AI Magazine*, 23(2):11–24, 2002.
2. P. Cheeseman, B. Kanefsky, and W. Taylor. Where the really hard problems are. In *Proceedings of the 12th International Joint Conference on Artificial Intelligence (IJCAI-91)*, pages 331–337, 1991.
3. Philip R. Cohen and Hector J. Levesque. Teamwork. *Nous*, 25(4):487–512, 1991.
4. Joseph Culberson and Ian Gent. Frozen development in graph coloring. *Theoretical Computer Science*, 265(1–2):227–264, 2001.
5. Alessandro Farinelli, Paul Scerri, and Milind Tambe. Building large-scale robot systems: Distributed role assignment in dynamic, uncertain domains. In *Proceedings of Workshop on Representations and Approaches for Time-Critical Decentralized Resource, Role and Task Allocation*, 2003.
6. Mark S. Fox, Norman Sadeh, and Can Baycan. Constrained heuristic search. In *Proceedings of the 11th International Joint Conference on Artificial Intelligence (IJCAI-89)*, volume 1, pages 309–316, Detroit, MI, August 1989. Morgan Kaufmann.
7. J. Giampapa and K. Sycara. Conversational case-based planning for agent team coordination. In *Proceedings of the Fourth International Conference on Case-Based Reasoning*, 2001.
8. Barbara Grosz and Sarit Kraus. Collaborative plans for complex group actions. *Artificial Intelligence*, 86:269–358, 1996".
9. Nick Jennings. Controlling cooperative problem solving in industrial multi-agent systems using joint intentions. *Artificial Intelligence*, 75:195–240, 1995.
10. Hiroaki Kitano, Minoru Asada, Yasuo Kuniyoshi, Itsuki Noda, Eiichi Osawa, , and Hitoshi Matsubara. RoboCup: A challenge problem for AI. *AI Magazine*, 18(1):73–85, Spring 1997.
11. Kurt Konolige, Dieter Fox, Charlie Ortiz, Andrew Agno, Michael Eriksen, Benson Limketkai, Jonathan Ko, Benoit Morisset, Dirk Schulz, Benjamin Stewart, and Regis Vincent. Centibots: Very large scale distributed robotic teams. In *Proc. of the International Symposium on Experimental Robotics*, 2004.
12. Roger Mailler, Victor Lesser, and Bryan Horling. Cooperative Negotiation for Soft Real-Time Distributed Resource Allocation. In *Proceedings of Second International Joint Conference on Autonomous Agents and MultiAgent Systems (AAMAS 2003)*, pages 576–583, Melbourne, July 2003. ACM Press.

13. Steven Minton, Mark D. Johnston, Andrew B. Philips, and Philip Laird. Minimizing conflicts: A heuristic repair method for constraint satisfaction and scheduling problems. *Artificial Intelligence*, 58(1-3):161–205, 1992.

14. Pragnesh Jay Modi, Hyuckchul Jung, Milind Tambe, Wei-Min Shen, and Shriniwas Kulkarni. Dynamic distributed resource allocation: A distributed constraint satisfaction approach. In John-Jules Meyer and Milind Tambe, editors, *Pre-proceedings of the Eighth International Workshop on Agent Theories, Architectures, and Languages (ATAL-2001)*, pages 181–193, 2001.

15. Remi Monasson, Riccardo Zecchina, Scott Kirkpatrick, Bart Selman, and Lidror Troyansky. Determining computational complexity from characteristic 'phase transitions'. *Nature*, 400:133–137, 1999.

16. R. Nair, T. Ito, M. Tambe, and S. Marsella. Task allocation in robocup rescue simulation domain. In *Proceedings of the International Symposium on RoboCup*, 2002.

17. David V. Pynadath and Milind Tambe. An automated teamwork infrastructure for heterogeneous software agents and humans. *Journal of Autonomous Agents and Multi-Agent Systems, Special Issue on Infrastructure and Requirements for Building Research Grade Multi-Agent Systems*, page to appear, 2002.

18. D.V. Pynadath, M. Tambe, N. Chauvat, and L. Cavedon. Toward team-oriented programming. In *Intelligent Agents VI: Agent Theories, Architectures, and Languages*, pages 233–247, 1999.

19. P. Scerri, E. Liao, Yang. Xu, M. Lewis, G. Lai, and K. Sycara. *Theory and Algorithms for Cooperative Systems*, chapter Coordinating very large groups of wide area search munitions. World Scientific Publishing, 2004.

20. P. Scerri, D. V. Pynadath, L. Johnson, P. Rosenbloom, N. Schurr, M Si, and M. Tambe. A prototype infrastructure for distributed robot-agent-person teams. In *The Second International Joint Conference on Autonomous Agents and Multiagent Systems*, 2003.

21. P. Scerri, Yang. Xu, E. Liao, J. Lai, and K. Sycara. Scaling teamwork to very large teams. In *Proceedings of AAMAS'04*, 2004.

22. K. Sycara and M. Lewis. *Team Cognition*, chapter Integrating Agents into Human Teams. Erlbaum Publishers, 2003.

23. Milind Tambe. Agent architectures for flexible, practical teamwork. *National Conference on AI (AAAI97)*, pages 22–28, 1997.

24. Jim Waldo. The Jini architecture for network-centric computing. *Communications of the ACM*, 42(7):76–82, 1999.

25. Guandong Wang, Weixiong Zhang, Roger Mailler, and Victor Lesser. *Analysis of Negotiation Protocols by Distributed Search*, pages 339–361. Kluwer Academic Publishers, 2003.

26. Y. Xu, M. Lewis, K. Sycara, and P. Scerri. Information sharing in very large teams. In *In AAMAS'04 Workshop on Challenges in Coordination of Large Scale MultiAgent Systems*, 2004.

27. Makoto Yokoo. Asynchronous weak-commitment search for solving distributed constraint satisfaction problems. In *Proceedings of the First International Conference on Principles and Practice of Constraint Programming (CP-95)*, Lecture Notes in Computer Science 976, pages 88–102. Springer-Verlag, 1995.

28. Makoto Yokoo, Edmund H. Durfee, Toru Ishida, and Kazuhiro Kuwabara. Distributed constraint satisfaction for formalizing distributed problem solving. In *International Conference on Distributed Computing Systems*, pages 614–621, 1992.

Part II

Scaling Existing Coordination Approaches

Decentralized Partner Finding in Multi-Agent Systems

Marcelo M. Vanzin and K. S. Barber

The Laboratory for Intelligent Processes and Systems
Electrical and Computer Engineering Department
The University of Texas at Austin
Austin, TX 78712
vanzin@lips.utexas.edu and barber@mail.utexas.edu

One of the most compelling characteristics of multi agent systems is the ability to form coalitions to share their resources, create plans, share execution of tasks, etc. The work presented in this article offers scalable methods for finding potential coalition partners when not all agents in a large multi-agent system are known to the agents in need of help to achieve their goals. A new algorithm for finding partners in a MAS, based on concepts inspired by peer-to-peer networks, is described. The proposed algorithm design aims to provide a new, completely decentralized scheme that can be used by agents to gather information needed to make decisions about potential partners. The proposed algorithm is competitive with centralized approaches in smaller multi-agent systems and provides better scalability for larger systems.

1 Introduction

Multi-Agent Systems (MAS) are a particular field of distributed systems research, where nodes that comprise the system, termed Agents [20], have characteristics such as reactivity, autonomy, pro-activeness and social ability. These systems are sometimes referred to as Distributed Artificial Intelligence [8], since the agents in these systems often borrow ideas from the field of artificial intelligence to achieve their goals.

Among the characteristics of an agent system is the ability of different agents to work together to solve problems. Often when working on a goal, agents will discover that they lack the needed resources to accomplish that goal, or that work could be done more efficiently if other agents were helping by providing access to the resources they have available. By forming partnerships, agents can make use of the new resources provided by the partners to more efficiently work towards their objectives. There are several ways in which agents can cooperate [16]. These include but are not restricted to load-balancing (distributing the task of working on large computations), resource sharing (allowing other agents to use your resources if they need them to accomplish their objectives) and action coordination (agents planning together and deciding on a set of actions, aiming at maximizing the outcome of some effort).

There is no single solution to the problem of how to find information about these other agents in the system, and which resources they have. Different approaches have been proposed for forming coalitions [1, 14, 15]. The work presented in this article provides a method and algorithm for finding and evaluating information about agents in open, large, distributed systems where knowledge about or connectivity to potential information sources may not be available. This research aims to improve on the qualities of existing approaches while avoiding some of the shortcomings these approaches, such as having a single point of failure or depending on some specific network functionality that may not be available to the agents.

Finding partners is only the first part in the process of forming a coalition. After or as a part of the coalition formation process, there are a number of issues regarding the scope of the coalition and the organizational structure of the members. For this research, coalition scope is defined by the goals the members will seek to achieve jointly. Organizationally, it must be determined which coalition members are making decisions about which goals and which members are taking actions to accomplish these goals. Therefore, we need a representation to identify decision-making responsibility and execution authority within the coalition organization, giving agents a means to find and establish a coalition to best meet their goals. The representation used to capture a coalition's organizational structure is based on the concept of Decision-Making Frameworks (DMF) developed by Martin [7], which will be introduced briefly in a later section.

2 Motivation

The problem of coalition formation can be viewed as a composition of two separate problems:

1. Finding partners: agents must determine what are their needs regarding their current goals, and, when not able to accomplish the goals by themselves, decide on a group of agents with whom they are interested in working.
2. Forming the coalition: once enough knowledge exists about possible partners to form a coalition, the agent communicates its desires to those possible partners and starts a negotiation that leads to having all the agents agree on some coordination protocol to carry out the different tasks.

This research assesses the first step of the coalition formation process, finding partners in a MAS. In the scope of this research, the term "partners" will be used to refer to any agent in the system that can provide needed information or resources to an agent trying to achieve its goals.

When looking for potential coalition partners, an agent must have enough information about other agents in the system to be able to identify which agents contain the resources needed to complete the tasks leading to the accomplishment of the agent's goals. This information is not available to the agent a priori: the agent's knowledge base has to be built in some manner. In an information rich environment, it is crucial for an agent to have the ability to search for and evaluate potential partners quickly and efficiently.

Multi-Agent systems present several challenges for the agents in this respect. These include, but are not limited to:

Openness: agents may enter and leave the system at any time, changing the distribution of resources in the system.

Scale: as more agents enter the system, agents looking for partners are faced with a huge amount of information about potential partners.

Distribution: agents working in these systems are independent of each other. The implications of this are that agents make their own decisions when working to achieve their goals and do not have direct influence on the actions other agents take.

Partial knowledge: related to the scale problem, this means that it is unfeasible for the agents to hold data about everything in the environment, for several reasons that will be discussed in more detail below.

Partial connectivity: agents will only be able to talk directly to a small subset of the agents currently in the system. This also means that communicating with different agents incurs different costs in terms of latency and number of hops needed to reach a respective agent.

Addressing these challenges is important as agent systems become more complex. Below the concept of Decision-Making Frameworks used to represent coalitions in the scope of this research is briefly introduced. Also, an analysis of current methods applied to solve the problem at hand is presented, showing the advantages and shortcomings of each approach and providing some examples of systems that employ these techniques.

2.1 Decision-Making Frameworks

Agents in a coalition need some representation to capture the organizational structure of the coalition. One possible representation is a Decision-Making Framework (DMF) [7]. A DMF is represented by a tuple, defined as:

DMF $= \langle D, G, C \rangle$, where:

D : The set listing the agents acting as decision makers for the goals in G.

G : A non-empty set of goals to which the coalition is committed.

C : The set of agents that perform actions based on the decisions made by agents in the set D.

Regardless of how the process of reaching agreements with the resulting members of D and C is conducted, it is assumed that the agents already have enough knowledge about the system to be able to choose a set of partners for a new coalition. While it is important to separate the process of finding the possible partners and the process of negotiating and establishing partnerships in order to enhance the system's flexibility, finding the potential partners is an important step in the process of forming the coalitions. The need for a scalable algorithm for finding this information about potential partners in an open, dynamic multi-agent environment is the main incentive for this research.

2.2 The Problem of Finding Partners

Looking for the potential partners for a coalition requires the agent to have enough information about other agents in the system to be able to identify which ones provide the resources required for its tasks. This information is not available to the agent a priori: the agent's knowledge base has to be built in some manner.

Information about other agents in the system can come from many different sources. Some approaches to retrieving information about the environment are presented next.

Broadcasting

When searching for potential partners, agents could broadcast a request for a partner. Broadcasting involves sending a message that can be received by many, and possibly all, agents in the system. This may be done by using a communication infrastructure that allows broadcasting, or by sending the same message to several destinations, emulating the effect of a real broadcast domain. Once having received a message, the agents may choose to reply or not to the requests made in the message. The requesting agent then analyzes all the replies to form its internal model of the other agents and decide on possible partnerships. The main advantage of a system based on broadcasting messages is its simplicity in the case where a network infra-structure that supports broadcasting exists. On the other hand, its simplicity is also its disadvantage.

The first problem is that it becomes non-trivial to emulate a broadcast domain over networks that do not support broadcast messages. Especially when considering wireless ad-hoc networks, broadcasting is not trivial and can be very expensive [19]. This is unfortunate, since this kind of setup is very interesting for the deployment of agents, as it does not require any existing network infra-structure to be available.

Also, broadcasting makes it more difficult to protect the content of the messages, since all agents within reach of the message can read its contents. Cryptography may be used to allow only a subset of agents to read the message, but using this approach would require a complex key management scheme.

Contract Nets [17] employ a protocol that uses broadcasting to find potential partners for possible partnerships.

Environment Modeling

The agents may maintain information about other agents in the system based on their interactions with those agents.

The main advantage of this approach is reusing the information created by working with other agents in the system. The downside is that such information may not form an accurate and up-to-date model: the models will be dated by the date of the interactions, which will vary depending on the agent.

Also, requiring an agent to model the whole environment may be infeasible when the system is large or changes too quickly. In many cases, agents will have only limited memory and computational resources, limiting the amount of data they can hold and process at any time. Quickly changing systems pose a different challenge in this case: the changes may be occurring faster than the agent can notice these changes and update its model of the system, resulting in incorrect models that can negatively impact the work of the agent.

Centralized Directory

Using a central directory for information retrieval is common practice in several applications, due to its simplicity. Agents publish their information to a directory, and send a request to the directory when they need information about other agents, keeping the agent implementation very trivial. Centralized systems also make scalability rather easy, by simply adding more directories to the system to handle the larger number of requests that might be made by the agents.

The problems with the directory approach are the same as with other centralized systems. First of all, the system becomes reliant on a single entity, or a small number of nodes that act as a directory, allowing agents with malicious intent to easily attack the system and interfere with the work of other agents. Also, as the system grows, maintaining up-to-date information in the directory becomes harder, a problem that is even more difficult to solve when several directories are employed. In the case of multiple directories, there is also the problem of synchronizing information stored in the various directories.

Another concern related to agent operations is trust. In a heterogeneous environment it may be the case that a single directory is not trusted by all the agents in the system. In such a case, agents may not be willing to release information about themselves to a directory, or may not want to use a particular directory to retrieve information they need. This is a concern that exists for every approach that might be chosen, but a centralized system makes it especially harder to solve: the agents have no other information source to rely on aside from the directories.

An example of a centralized system would be one that uses the CoABS Grid [5] to find services. The CoABS Grid, while using more than one directory to hold information, is still based on requiring agents to publish their information to a directory and retrieve information from agents designed to be directories in the system, thus still suffering from the shortcomings discussed above.

Decentralized Information Exchange

A different approach is a system where explicit communication between the agents is used to exchange information such as resource availability, coalitions or any other information that may be useful for the agents.

Some work has been done in the area of finding partners using a peer-to-peer approach, such as the Distributed Matchmaking (DM) work conducted by Ogston [9, 10, 11]. The work described herein, while sharing some characteristics with DM, has some fundamental differences. First, this research will not rely on a central authority to maintain any kind of information, while DM still uses a central agent to hold information about the coalitions that are formed in the MAS. This research also expands the problem of finding partners in a MAS into the area of coalition formation, an area that is not explored by DM currently.

In the next section we examine how the agents can efficiently model the environment and how they can collaborate with each other when constructing those models, leading to a decentralized solution for the problem of finding partners in a large MAS.

3 Modeling Agents

The first step towards having an efficient partner finding algorithm is to maintain a consistent model of the other agents in the system, creating an Environment Model. This model must capture enough information about the agents to allow the holder to decide on trying to form a partnership or not, given its purposes. Also, the environment model needs to be regularly updated, since working with out-of-date information in a dynamic environment may lead to wasted time, such as agents trying to form coalitions with other agents that may not anymore be suitable for the tasks for which they were wanted.

To better understand how the modeling is done in the scope of this research, some clarification about how the agents represent their goals in the scope of this research is needed. A goal is defined as being a top-level task, comprised of a list of tasks that need to be executed by one agent. Tasks can be of two kinds: they can be atomic, meaning they cannot be decomposed and thus have to be executed by a single agent, or they can be decomposable, consisting of a list of other tasks (of either kind), meaning that if an agent cannot execute the task on its own, the task can be broken down and a group of agents can work to accomplish the respective task.

Tasks require certain resources to be executed. It is assumed that the resources cannot be used remotely. Instead, the task requiring a set of resources needs to be assigned to an agent that has those resources. If the agent does not have all resources needed to accomplish the task, and the task is not decomposable, then it is said that the agent cannot execute the task. If the task is decomposable, each sub-task is analyzed individually, recursively. One assumption is made about the nature of decomposable tasks, though. Let's say that a decomposable task t_1 needs a set of resources, $R = \{r_1, r_2, ..., r_n\}$. It is assumed that for any task $t_i (i \neq 1)$ that is a subtask of t_1, the set of resources needed by t_i is a subset of R, and is not equal to R, and the union of all sets of resources needed by the subtasks of t_1 is equal to R. In summary:

$$S = \{t_1^k, t_2^k, \ldots, t_n^k\} : \text{set of subtasks of task } t_k$$
$$R_i = \{r_1, r_2, \ldots, r_n\} : \text{set of resources needed by } t_i$$
$$\bigcup_{i=1\ldots n} (R_i) = R_k \text{ and } R_i \subset R_k$$

Agents build models of other agents in the MAS based on interactions. Generally, the agent will explicitly ask another agent for information, updating its internal model with the information received in return. But other kinds of interactions may also contribute to update the state of the internal model; for example, when trying to form a partnership, the agent being contacted may realize that it cannot execute some task anymore (e.g., because some resource it once had is not available anymore), so it may choose to send updated information about itself to the agent requesting the partnership and indicate another agent it knows about who can help with that particular problem.

As discussed before, having the agent hold information about every other agent and the resources thos agents currently hold can lead to scalability issues and lots of wasted resources, from memory space to communication needed to maintain those models. In this research, agents can work with a limited amount of models and communicate with each other in case some needed information is not in their local knowledge base.

The approach taken for modeling other agents in the system is to maintain a mapping between the resources the agent knows about in the system and the agent(s) that provide those resources. Building from this, two other features have been built into the model allowing an agent to easily manage information about a group of agents that share some commonality: Similar Agent Groups and Complementary Agent Groups.

Similar Agent Groups model a group of agents that provide similar resources. An agent orders similar agents internally according to an utility function. Similar agents can be used interchangeably for tasks that require the resources they share in common. This model can greatly simplify the work of searching for partners that provide a resource: a whole list of agents is readily available, in an arbitrary order defined by the agent. If the first agent in the list denies a partnership for some reason, it is easy for the agent to just choose the next one on the list, using the list as a "queue" of possible partners.

Complementary Agent Groups (CAGs) define agents that, together, can work on solving a set of tasks.An agent can use the CAG information when it cannot work alone on a goal, and needs some way to keep track of which agents can help accomplish the tasks that comprise that goal. CAGs are flexible with regard to matching of agents to tasks. Depending on the needs of the agent building the model, the choice of which agent will be assigned to which task may be done in different ways, such as:

- Minimize the number of agents in a coalition, in which case preference will be given to the agent that can execute a larger number of different tasks when choosing among assignees for a task.

- Reduce the total cost of communication among the members in the partnership, thus giving preference to agents with which it can communicate more efficiently when looking for coalition partners.

The experiments performed during this research used the "minimize coalition size" approach, meaning that the agents will choose the partners that can execute the most tasks, even if that incurs higher communication costs.

4 Searching for Partners

This section introduces an algorithm than can be used by agents to find partners in a large MAS. This algorithm has the following characteristics:

1. It is completely decentralized, meaning that there is no need for a central authority in the system during any part of the partner finding process of looking for partners.
2. It allows an agent to have only limited information about its environment, and assures that any information available in the environment can be reached.

It is assumed that the agents know enough information about the environment to at least maintain communication with one or more other agents, and use this capability to build a more complete environment model.

The algorithm is heavily influenced by peer-to-peer networks, so a brief introduction of such systems is presented next.

4.1 Brief overview of peer-to-peer systems

Peer-to-peer (P2P) systems have grown in popularity in the last few years, particularly because of their ability to easily provide to their users access to lots of information. The big advantage of P2P systems, though, is its decentralized nature: a desirable feature is that there is no central server where information resides. Every peer connected to the network can aid other peers in the process of searching for information and retrieving it.

P2P systems are sometimes also called "content addressable networks", since instead of providing a server from which information will be taken, the users provide the information they are looking for and the network provides facilities for discovering where the requested information is available. There are two main functions a P2P system provides for its nodes. The first one is discovery of other peers in the network, so that the node joining the network can have an initial set of information about how to connect to other nodes and start to look for and retrieve information. This is generally done using servers that cache node addresses (called "GWebCaches" [3] in the Gnutella network, for example), which send subsets of the information they hold to newly connected nodes, which then use that information to bootstrap their set of neighbors in the network.

This research is interested in content location, since this functionality can enable agents to discover the location of the resources they need to achieve their goals. In P2P networks, users will generally provide some keywords and receive a list of possible matches containing that keyword. The method used to retrieve this information varies from network to network: Gnutella, for example, floods the query to all known peers, which in their turn propagate the messages even further by re-sending the requests to their neighbors up to a certain time-to-live value for the request. This approach can make the search quite slow in a very large network but is acceptable for the purposes for which the system was developed. Other systems provide better algorithms for searching, in exchange for more complex protocols for maintaining the network in a consistent state.

A system that provides an interesting way of addressing content is the Chord [18] lookup protocol. Chord works by having nodes in the network choose an identifier, and mapping content to nodes based on a hash value (or key), which is used as the information's identifier in the network. Both nodes and information share the same identifier namespace, and information is assigned to the first node in the network whose identifier is equal to or higher than the information's computed hash value. Nodes can enter and leave the network at any time, triggering a reassignment of the information that was mapped to the leaving node, or the assignment of some information currently mapped to a neighboring node to the new node joining the network.

Chord uses what it calls a "finger table" to create links between nodes in the network. In this table, an entry at position i in node n's table means that the node is the first one that succeeds n by at least $2i - 1$ on the identifier circle. This property makes searching for a key in the circle an $O(log\ n)$ operation, where n is the number of nodes in the ring. This is possible because each step in the querying process will, at least, halve the distance from the node making the query to the node containing the sought information. Figure 1 illustrates one query in a Chord ring.

The query depicted in Figure 1 works as follows: node n_1 is looking for information $i_1 9$, and the only other node it knows in the network is node $n_1 0$. This causes n_1 to send a request for $i_1 9$ to $n_1 0$, even though $i_1 9$ would not be assigned to $n_1 0$ in this ring, since its identifier is higher than the node's identifier. Node $n_1 0$ knows about node $n_2 5$ (but not about node $n_2 0$), and according to its view of the system, information $i_1 9$ should be assigned to node $n_2 5$, so it sends the request to this node. Node $n_2 5$, however, knows about $n_2 0$, which means that $i_1 9$ should be assigned to it, and redirects the query to $n_2 0$. Node $n_2 0$ then replies to node n_1 with the requested information, causing n_1 to update its finger table to contain the new node $n_2 0$.

Chord's main benefit is enabling efficient searching with only limited amounts of information stored locally in each node. On the other hand, Chord does not support keyword queries, although such a system could be built using Chord at the expense of efficiency. Chord also has a more robust protocol for updating the ring state when peers join and leave the network.

Many other algorithms have been created to enable efficient lookups in peer-to-peer networks, many of them inspired by Chord. One of these algorithms is the one by Plaxton et al [13], referred to as PRR (after the names of the authors: Plax-

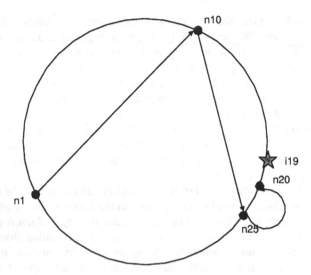

Fig. 1. Request propagation for a lookup of information i19

ton, Rajaraman and Richa) or Plaxton Mesh in some papers. PRR has a more complex structure when compared to Chord, dependent on the topology of the network and distances between nodes, but has more predictable behavior when performing a search, leading to tighter bounds for the needed number of messages and cost to find some information in the network. The Simplified PRR (SPRR) [6] algorithm is an enhancement of PRR, and very similar to Chord in the complexity of queries. The main advantage introduced by SPRR is that at the cost of more complexity to construct the identifier rings (SPRR can have many overlapping rings), the queries are guaranteed to follow a shortest path (relating to cost of communication) to the node holding information about the key.

Koorde [4] is another distributed hash table and lookup protocol, based on Chord, which provides degree-optimality (i.e., optimal number of hops to find the needed information given the degree of the hash table - the number of neighbors with which each node has to maintain contact). This is achieved by using de Bruijn graphs [2] instead of the standard Chord finger table to propagate requests in the ring.

4.2 Distributed Partner Finding (DPF)

Analyzing the different algorithms commonly used in P2P networks, some of which were presented in the previous section, it is not hard to notice that none of the approaches exactly matches the needs of a multi-agent system.

Keyword-based P2P networks generally are targeted at finding the information, with minimum regard to efficiency. Flooding the network with requests is a common technique, creating large numbers of messages going around the network. This works acceptably when you have fixed nodes with reliable, fast communication channels, which is generally the case in these networks. Such an approach would not work well in a MAS that does not have this kind of communication infra-structure in place, though.

Lookup algorithms such as Chord and Koorde work well when the agents know exactly what information they seek. This may not be the case in a MAS: agents may be looking for resources or combinations of different resources, making it impractical to create a distributed index of what are all the possible resource combinations available and where those resources are located. Even more importantly, keeping this distributed index up-to-date in an open, dynamic environment is a very difficult task, not to say impractical.

The proposed solution is to make a compromise between the two approaches: improving the efficiency of keyword-based queries by using concepts from systems that use indexing. The following sections described how the characteristics of different peer-to-peer systems were used to create a new Distributed Partner Finding algorithm for finding partners in a MAS.

Finding Partners

Given that the agents will not always have enough information available in their knowledge base to be able to find all the necessary partners to accomplish their tasks, an algorithm to find this information in the MAS is necessary. The algorithm must define how the agents will create these requests for information and propagate them to the other known agents, until the sought information can be found or the agent gives up finding the information.

The DPF algorithm works by using the current list of an agent's models describing other agents in the system as a finger table for requests, in the same manner that nodes in a Chord ring maintain a finger table of other nodes in the network. As we have discussed, the agent can not make the request based on the hash value of the information it is searching, so a more conservative request propagation strategy is necessary.

Some assumptions about the way communication works in the system are made:

- It is assumed that every agent in the system can communicate with at least one other agent.
- Communication is assumed to be asynchronous, meaning that the agent will send a message and not wait for an immediate reply. It will keep on working on its tasks until the other agent replies to its message. It may be the case also that no reply will ever come, due for example to an agent having problems and not being able to reply to a message that was received, so the algorithm must plan for this possibility.

The following is a description of the algorithm run by the agent issuing a request:

1. Send the request to the closest known agent in the system.
2. If nt reply arrives within a certain timeout period, re-send the request to a known agent further away than the previous, doubling the timeout period.

3. Repeat 2 until all of the agent's known peers are queried.
4. When the list of known agents is exhausted, the agent may choose to issue an error or restart the algorithm.

Agents receiving requests from other agents must also perform some operations, which are described next:

1. If an agent that fulfills the request is known, return information about that agent to the requesting agent.
2. If no agent is found to fulfill the requirements of the request, check if the time-to-live for the message has not expired.
3. If the time-to-live has not expired, decrease the time-to-live counter, then determine the set of agents that are closest. Propagate the request to one chosen agent from that set, or to the whole set of agents depending on the operation mode of the algorithm.

The algorithm relies on timeouts and time-to-live of messages to operate. These concepts and how each is implemented in the algorithm are described in the next section.

Timeouts and Time-to-Live

Timeouts and time-to-live are the main features used by the agents to determine how and when the requests should be re-sent. Basically, every time an agent sends a request, it determines the time it thinks it will take other agents to reply to that request. The agent then sets up a timer to execute after this period and re-process the request. Each request also has a maximum lifetime inside the MAS, the time-to-live value, so that it is not propagated forever if no one is able to respond to it.

The two concepts are borrowed from TCP/IP networks. The TCP protocol defines a timeout mechanism in which if a node does not receive an acknowledgement of a packet within a certain time period, it will re-send the packet and double the time it will wait for the acknowledgement. This is meant to allow the nodes to adapt to changing conditions in the network, such as routes changing during the lifetime of a connection, or congestion occurring in the network.

The IP protocol defines a property called time-to-live, or TTL, for packets. This property is an integer number that defines how many devices the packet can traverse in the network before being dropped. Each device that processes the packet in the IP routing process to the destination decreases the TTL counter, and if it ever reaches zero, the packet is discarded even if it has not reached the destination. TTL values are used mainly for ICMP (Internet Control Message Protocol) messages, since they are useful for discovering the topography of the network.

While TTL values are not used in regular IP traffic, the timeouts are one of the basic features of TCP connections. Timeout estimates are kept on a per-connection basis, meaning that they provide an estimate of the expected round-trip time of a message to its destination. To calculate this estimate, the Jacobson/Karels algorithm [12] is used. The algorithm works by maintaining two variables: the timeout estimate and a measure of the deviation of the sample round-trip times measured by the node. The following operations are then performed on the values when a new sample is obtained:

$$Difference = SampleRTT - EstimatedRTT$$
$$EstimatedRTT = EstimatedRTT + (\delta \times Difference)$$
$$Deviation = Deviation + \delta(|Difference| - Deviation)$$

Having the estimated round-trip time and the deviation updated, the timeout value to be used is calculated as follows:

$$Timeout = \mu \times EstimatedRTT + \Phi \times Deviation$$

For the DPF algorithm, the values used for μ and Φ are 1 and 4, respectively. These are the values typically used in TCP implementations, based on experience acquired by the implementors of the different versions of the protocol. δ is a number between 0 and 1, and 0.125 is used by the DPF implementation of the algorithm. The design of the algorithm is such that if large variations in the sampled round-trip time are measured, these variations will have more influence on the new value of the timeout. For lower variations, the estimated value for the timeout has larger impact on the timeout value.

While using the same algorithm for timeout calculations, the value of the estimate does not hold the same meaning in the DPF algorithm. The timeout estimate is not maintained per connection in DPF, since there is no notion of a long-lived connection between two agents as in the case of TCP. Consequently, only one estimate is maintained by each agent for all communication, providing a measurement of the expected time for a request to be replied to in the system regardless of the recipients of the request.

The management of the TTL value is simpler: the value is incremented by a certain amount at every timeout and decremented by the same amount when a reply is received. This means that if the agent needed several retransmissions to receive a reply, the TLL will grow, and if no retransmissions were needed it will shrink a little, until a minimum is reached. The minimum value for the TTL is one of the parameters than can be used to tune the algorithm.

The intent of maintaining a good estimate of the timeout and TTL values is to pursue a balance between the time needed to find the information that is being sought and the number of messages that are sent in the network. A low timeout value means that the agent will be re-sending requests too early, increasing the work load of other agents unnecessarily. A value that is too large means the agent will be waiting for a long time before considering a request as lost, and may miss the opportunity to re-send the request and receive a reply earlier.

The same reasoning can be applied to the TTL values: low values mean that the request will not be propagated much further into the MAS, meaning less probability of reaching an agent that has the wanted information. Large TTL values would incur in requests having a long lifetime in the system, meaning that the requests would still be alive and wasting agents' resources even after being successfully replied by some agent in the system.

Operation Modes

Having introduced the Distributed Partner Finding (DPF) algorithm, there can be different ways for the agent to route requests in the MAS. Three different modes of operation of the algorithm are described next. These modes only dictate the behavior of the agents creating requests - the propagation of received requests still follows the rules described in section 4.2 regardless of the mode of operation. The three different modes of operation are the Single Message Request Mode (DPF1), the Multiple Message Request Mode (DPF2) and the Flooding Mode (DPF3).

The Single Message Request Mode (DPF1)

This is the mode that exactly matches the description of the algorithm provided in section 4.2. In this mode of operation, the agent will choose the closest agent from the list of known agents and send the request to it. When a timeout occurs, the agent will look for one agent that is further away than the agent previously chosen, and re-send the request one more time.

This mode of operation is the most conservative in terms of the number of messages used by the algorithm: only one message is sent by the agent that created the request at every timeout. Figure 2 shows an example of a request using this mode, where t_0 means the time when the request process was initiated by the source (SRC), and to means the initial timeout value used for that request. "Local networks" define how far away agents are from each other. If a group of agents is in the same "local network", they are perceived to be at the same distance from some other agent in the system. This means that, in Figure 2, agents $A4$, $A5$, $A6$ and $A7$ are all at the same distance from agent $A1$, for example.

The Multiple Message Request Mode (DPF2)

The Multiple Message Request Mode is an extension of the Single Message Request Mode described above. When operating in this mode, the agent will send the request to every known agent at the chosen distance threshold at the same time. Thus, the first requests will be sent to all agents that are deemed by the agent as its "closest neighbors". After a timeout occurs, the agent will look for agents at a greater distance threshold, and send the same request to every agent at that threshold, and so forth. Figure 3 shows the message flow of a request using this mode of operation.

In Figure 3 it can be seen that since the source agent (SRC) knows agents $A1$ and $A2$ already, it will send the request to both at the same time. $A3$, which is not known to the source, will only receive the request after $A1$ checks that it can not answer it and decides to propagate it. The same behavior can be seen regarding agents $A4$ and $A7$, after the first timeout occurs.

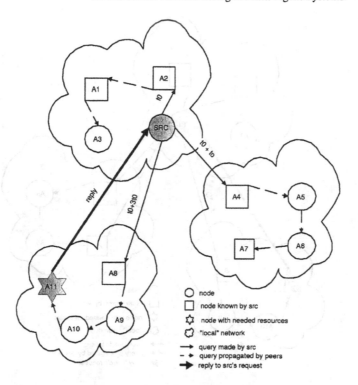

Fig. 2. Example of request using DPF1 - Single Message Request Mode

The goal of this mode is to send the request to more agents more quickly, avoiding the extra latency caused by waiting for other agents to propagate the request to their neighbors, at the cost of an increase in the number of sent messages.

The Flooding Mode (DPF3)

In this mode of operation, agents do not care about the distances to other agents. Requests are sent to every known agent when they are created, and re-sent to every known agent at every timeout.

This is the less conservative mode in terms of number of messages. Agents are expected to send a lot more messages than when using the other two modes until they find the information they are seeking.

This mode is intended to be used as a way to analyze the performance of the other two modes: how the timeout / time-to-live mechanism and the propagation of requests by the agents receiving the requests affect the efficiency of the algorithm.

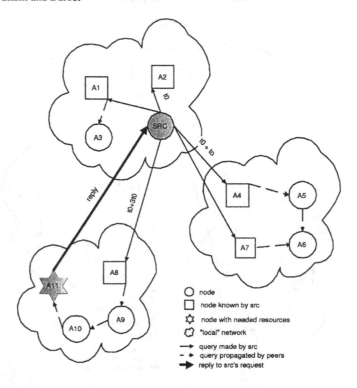

Fig. 3. Example of request using DPF2 - Multiple Message Request Mode

5 The DPF Experiment

The domain chosen for the experiment is a distributed sensing problem using Unmanned Aerial Vehicles (UAVs). The UAVs are small flying devices that have limited capabilities and various constraints on what kind of work they can do. The UAVs may carry a limited number of sensors, which might not be suitable to analyze their targets under every possible situation encountered. For example, if light conditions change, the UAVs that do not carry an infra-red sensor might not be able to analyze their targets correctly. In these cases, they must search in the system for other UAVs that have the appropriate sensors and can perform the necessary tasks to collect information about the targets.

The UAVs also cannot hold a lot of information at one time, and have limited processing capabilities. Sensors in the UAVs may fail during the operation of the vehicle, and it may not be possible to notify other UAVs of these problems. Thus, the UAVs must be able to locate other UAVs that are carrying the necessary sensors on demand, without the need to hold information about all the UAVs currently in the environment.

Relying on a central server to provide information is not a desirable solution, since the server may be out of the range of communication from the UAV, and also would provide a single location for an opponent to attack and try to sabotage the work of the UAVs. Having a limited range for communication also discards the possibility of using simple broadcast messages, since a request might not reach an agent that contains the requested resources unless a more complicated broadcast scheme is used.

The agents are distributed in several different "local networks" based on communication range. Within the same network, communication between the nodes has the same cost. Traffic leaving the local network needs to be routed in some way (which is not relevant to this research at this point), incurring a cost penalty and leading to longer delays for the arrival of messages.

Each UAV aims to achieve one goal, "Target Analysis", once a target is detected. Before working on its goals, the UAV is required to find the other UAVs that hold the necessary resources for performing the different tasks required by each goal.

5.1 Network Model

In the experiments, communication between agents is handled by the simulation environment using a simple network layer. This communication layer does not implement all the different layers that are generally part of the network stack in a real application, such as the physical layer and logical link layer. This means that there is no simulation of the possible issues that can occur in these other layers, such as congestion or delays caused by detecting a carrier signal in the physical layer.

The only feature provided by the communication layer is message delay. This delay is based on the distance between the agents in the system, and does not change over time. Similarly, there is no simulated message loss.

The goal of having such a simple network layer is to study the performance of the algorithm in a "best case" scenario, so that it is easier to detect shortcomings in the DPF algorithm without having to worry about issues in the other layers affecting the performance of the algorithm.

There are four types of messages exchanged among the agents during the simulation. Messages are stored in a priority queue in each agent until each is processed. For example, messages related to current goals of the agents are given higher priority, to speed up the process of working on goals. Table 1 shows the message types used in the experiment and their respective priorities.

ModelUpdate messages are given medium priority if those messages are replies to queries made by other agents. Otherwise, they are given low priority. Agents may choose to send un-requested model updates to other agents in the system in some circumstances, such as a change in the availability of resources.

5.2 Controlling Agent Execution

The experiment is run in discrete time, so it is important to define how much work an agent can do during one time step. Some assumptions are made here: mainly,

Table 1. Message Types

Message Type	Priority
ModelRequest	LOW
ModelUpdate	LOW or MEDIUM
TaskAssignment	HIGH
TaskCompleted	HIGH

the assumption that receiving messages and adding messages to the agent's message queue is cheap compared to processing the information the message contains. The same assumption is made for queuing messages for delivery to other agents.

The agents are allowed to do one unit of work each time step. A unit of work is defined as one unit of work for a task (the tasks have costs defined in "units of work") or processing one message from the waiting queue. The agents also make use of a timer facility to execute tasks at certain time steps or after some interval of time; the implementation is careful not to break the "unit of work" restriction by using the timers only to send new messages to other agents, and not for doing work or performing model updates.

A configuration option allows the central agent directory to have the number of units of work at each time step specified. This allows the agent directory to have an advantage over the other agents. This feature also tries to compensate for the fact that the directory will have to process messages from all the agents, while this work is distributed when the agents are working using DPF. Allowing more units of work per time step also serves as emulation of a "load-balancing" directory structure, although in this experiment the directory is still only one agent, meaning that agents will not be able to direct their queries to different directories based, for example, on distance.

5.3 Metrics

During each execution of the simulation scenario, the following metrics were observed and used to compare the different approaches:

Average number of messages sent : the average number of messages, of any kind, that an agent will send in the system during the simulation. This is intended to measure the overhead created by the use of the DPF algorithm instead of using a central directory.

Average time to start of goal execution : time elapsed between the assignment of a goal to an agent and the time the agent has found all partners that will help it achieve its goal. The average is weighed based on the number of tasks associated with the goal. The more tasks the goal has, the higher the probability the agent will need more requests for partners before the goals tasks can be executed, thus having a larger weight. This measures how fast an agent can find the partners to accomplish its tasks in the various tested configurations.

Average goal execution time : the time between the start of the execution of the goal, after finding all partners, and the time the goal has been accomplished (all tasks finished). The measurements are weighed based on the total cost of the goal. This is intended to measure how much the overhead the DPF algorithm imposes on the agents affects their ability to work on their goals.

The goals are always created and assigned randomly during the simulation. To reduce the effects of the randomness in the results, each different configuration was run five times. The average of these five runs was then taken to create the results presented below.

5.4 Experimental Setup

The experiment described above was partially implemented, with the goal of analyzing the characteristics of the proposed communication model for finding partners. The peer-to-peer approach was tested against the central directory approach, and some metrics were analyzed in the process.

Table 2 shows the different MAS configurations used by the research experiments. Each configuration tries to capture the characteristics of a real world scenario, where a large MAS would mean having more agents actively working on goals at the same time.

Table 2. MAS Configurations

1. Agents	2. Concurrent Goals	3. Max. held models	4. Dir. Work	5. Initial Msgs
10000	1000	45	{4, 8}	20
7500	750	43	{4, 8}	19
5000	500	44	{4, 8}	18
2500	250	36	{3, 6}	17
1000	100	30	{3, 6}	15
100	10	15	{2, 4}	10

Column 3 (maximum number of models) and column 5 (number of initial messages) only refer to the peer-to-peer simulations, since in the central directory simulations agents do not need to keep information unrelated to their current working goals. Column 5 shows the number of messages sent by each agent at the start of the simulation, trying to build an initial environment model.

Column 4 (directory work per time step) applies only to the central directory simulations, and shows the number of messages that the directory is allowed to process during a single time step. A total of five different simulations were run for each MAS configuration: one for each P2P mode, and two for the central directory mode.

Some simulations were also run to verify the scalability of the system with regard only to the number of concurrent goals in the system. These experiments have the same configuration as the 1000-agent MAS described in Table 2, but also use 50, 150 and 500 for the number of concurrent goals in the system.

The simulations were allowed to run until all goals were accomplished, or up to 50000 time steps, whichever occurred first. The measured time averages are weighted based on the total cost of the goals (for the execution time) and the number of tasks per goal (for the average time for the start of execution), and the results are the average of five runs. The results are presented next.

5.5 Experimental Results

Below we present several graphs showing the results obtained from the different simulations. The legend in the graphs refer to the following configurations:

DPF1 : agents using the DPF1 mode of the Distributed Partner Finding algorithm.
DPF2 : agents using the DPF2 mode of the Distributed Partner Finding algorithm.
DPF3 : agents using the DPF3 mode of the Distributed Partner Finding algorithm.
Dir:Base : system using a central directory with the low value for the directory work parameter as shown in Table 2, e.g., 2 for the system with 100 agents.
Dir:2x : system using a central directory with the high value for the directory work parameter as shown in Table 2, e.g., 4 for the system with 100 agents.

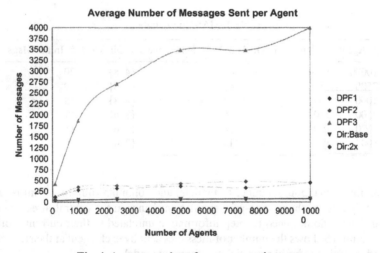

Fig. 4. Average number of message sent by agents

Figure 4 shows the communication overhead caused by the use of the Distributed Partner Finding algorithm instead of a central directory solution. For the DPF1 and DPF2 modes, the average number of messages an agent sends is larger, but still reasonable. DPF3 (flooding) shows a large increase in the number of messages with the growth of the system.

The information presented on Figure 4 related to the configurations that use a central directory needs to be analyzed more closely, since the data presented here is a little bit misleading. In these cases, a significant portion of the total number of messages is created by a single agent - the directory. The average number of messages sent by the other agents is much lower than in the simulations using DPF, at the cost of an overload of the directory agent, which must analyze a large number of incoming messages and reply to them.

Figure 5 shows how quickly agents can find partners to execute a goal using the different approaches. As the system grows, the number of concurrent queries sent to the directories results in a large message queue, leading to delays in the replies, while peer-to-peer configurations show more consistent performance.

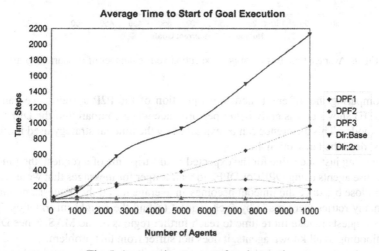

Fig. 5. Average time to start of goal execution

Although the data is not presented here, analysis of the quality of the solution shows that there is not a significant difference among the different approaches. The use of the priority queue to deliver messages allows mode DPF3 to perform as well as the others, in spite of the larger number of messages that must be processed by the agents.

It is interesting to notice that the central directory simulation has an "optimal" result in this case, at least in terms of communication cost, since the directory will find the nearest partner that can help the agent. However, the directory does not check how much work that agent is doing, so the solution cannot be considered optimal since the agent may be doing work for lots of coalitions.

Figure 6 shows results with varying numbers of concurrent goals for a fixed number of agents (1000). The configurations using DPF show better scalability, and all modes are able to surpass the performance of all directory-based approaches as the number of concurrent goals increase.

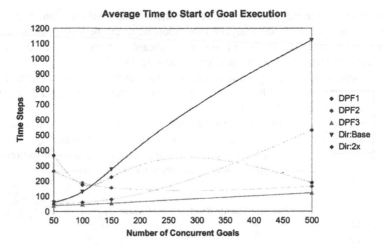

Fig. 6. Average time to start of goal execution versus number of concurrent goals

Comparing the different modes of operation of the P2P systems, we can see that DPF3 shows consistently better performance when compared to the DPF1 and DPF2 modes. This difference can be explained by the timeout strategy used for these modes, described in section 4.2.

By using just one value for the expected round-trip time of a request, the timeout may cause agents using DPF1 or DPF2 to wait longer for messages that were sent to agents close by, since the timeout becomes an average for all the requests, no matter how many retries were made by each request to find the sought information. This causes requests to take more time to reach further regions of the MAS. Since DPF3 does flooding to all known agents, it does not suffer from this problem.

To solve this issue, a different timeout mechanism should be used, taking into account the factors cited above. Nonetheless, the performance measured for DPF1 and DPF2 is still acceptable, and the system scales well even with the shortcomings identified above.

6 Conclusions and Future Work

Being able to efficiently find information about other agents in a multi-agent system is one of the main requirements in any modern agent system. The ability to find partners to form coalitions means that agents can more easily and/or efficiently achieve their goals when they do not have the appropriate resources or time to accomplish all the tasks related to their goals.

No single solution to this problem exists, and different solutions provide different compromises from which the system designer must choose. Different systems may benefit from different characteristics of these approaches.

The Distributed Partner Finding (DPF) algorithm was presented, leveraging peer-to-peer network research to create a new, completely decentralized scheme that can be used by agents to efficiently find information about potential coalition partners. It is the first step towards a revised scheme for explicit coalition formation, explicitly determining coalition membership as well as the coalition organizational structure, given by the allocation of decision-making responsibility and execution authority of the coalition's goals.

The experimental results show that it is feasible to use the DPF algrithm in place of a directory-based approach with reasonable performance penalties and better scalability.

However, more work is needed to analyze the robustness of the algorithm and its responsiveness to several different environmental characteristics. Testing larger agent systems and using a different network models are initial steps to be taken in this regard.

References

1. N. David, J. S. Sichman, and H. Coelho. Extending social reasoning to cope with multiple partner coalitions. In *Proceedings of the 9th European Workshop on Modelling Autonomous Agents in a Multi-Agent World (MAAMAW'99)*, pages 175–187, Valencia, Spain, 1999. Springer.

2. N. G. de Bruijn. A combinatorial problem. In *Koninklijke Nederlandse Akademie van Wetenschappen*, pages 758–764, Netherlands, 1946.

3. H. Dmpfling. Gnutella web caching system, 2003. Last updated: June 18th, 2003, last accessed: August 10th, 2004.

4. M. Kaashoek and D. R. Karger. Koorde: A simple degree-optimal distributed hash table. In *Proceedings of the 2nd International Workshop on Peer-to-Peer Systems (IPTPS '03)*, Berkeley, CA, 2003.

5. M. L. Kahn and C. D. T. Cicalese. The coabs grid. In *Proceedings of the Goddard / JPL Workshop on Radical Agent Concepts*, Tysons Corner, VA, 2002.

6. X. Li and C. G. Plaxton. On name resolution in peer-to-peer networks. In *Proceedings of the International Symposium on Distributed Computing (DISC 2002), Workshop on Principles of Mobile Computing*, Toulouse, France, 2002.

7. C. E. Martin. Representing autonomy in sensible agent-based systems. Master's thesis, The University of Texas at Austin, 1997.

8. B. Moulin and B. Chaib-draa. *An Overview of Distributed Artificial Intelligence*, chapter 1, pages 3–55. John Wiley & Sons, 1996.

9. E. Ogston and S. Vassiliadis. Local distributed agent matchmaking. In *Proceedings of the 9th International Conference on Cooperative Information Systems*, pages 67–79, Trento, Italy, 2001.

10. E. Ogston and S. Vassiliadis. Matchmaking among minimal agents without a facilitator. In *Proceedings of the 5th International Conference on Autonomous Agents*, pages 608–615, Montral, QC, Canada, 2001.

11. E. Ogston and S. Vassiliadis. Unstructured agent matchmaking: Experiments in timing and fuzzy matching. In *Proceedings of the Languages And Applications Special Track of the 17th ACM Symposium on Applied Computing*, pages 300–305, Madrid, Spain, 2002.

12. L. A. Peterson and B. S. Davie. *Computer Networks: A Systems Approach*. Morgan Kaufmann, 1999.
13. C. G. Plaxton, R. Rajaraman, and A. W. Richa. Accessing nearby copies of replicated objects in a distributed environment. In *Proceedings of the 9th Annual ACM Symposium on Parallel Algorithms and Architectures*, pages 311–320, Newport, RI, 1997.
14. T. W. Sandholm and V. R. Lesser. Coalitions among computationally bounded agents. *Artificial Intelligence*, 1(94):99–137, 1999.
15. S. Sen and P. S. Dutta. Searching for optimal coalition structures. In *Proceedings of the Fourth International Conference on MultiAgent Systems (ICMAS-2000)*, pages 287–292, Boston, MA, 2000.
16. O. Shehory and S. Kraus. Task allocation via coalition formation among autonomous agents. In *Proceedings of the Fourteenth International Joint Conference on Artificial Intelligence*, pages 655–661, Montral, QC, Canada, 1995.
17. R. G. Smith. The contract net protocol: High-level communication and control in a distributed problem-solver. *IEEE Transactions on Computers*, pages 1104–1113, 1980.
18. I. Stoica, R. Morris, D. Liben-Nowell, D. R. Karger, M. F. Kaashoek, F. Dabek, and H. Balakrishnan. Chord: A scalable peer-to-peer lookup protocol for internet applications. In *Proceedings of the ACM SIGCOMM '01 Conference*, San Diego, CA, 2001.
19. B. Williams and T. Camp. Comparison of broadcasting techniques for mobile ad hoc networks. In *Proceedings of the ACM International Symposium on Mobile Ad Hoc Networking and Computing (MOBIHOC '02)*, pages 194–205, 2002.
20. Michael Wooldridge and Nicholas R. Jennings. Intelligent agents: Theory and practice. HTTP://www.doc.mmu.ac.uk/STAFF/mike/ker95/ker95-html.h (Hypertext version of Knowledge Engineering Review paper), 1995.

Distributed Coordination of an Agent Society Based on Obligations and Commitments to Negotiated Agreements

Jiangbo Dang, Devendra Shrotri, and Michael N. Huhns

University of South Carolina
Department of Computer Science and Engineering
Columbia, SC 29208 USA
{dangj,shrotri,huhns}@engr.sc.edu

Summary. This chapter discusses coordination from a commitment basis. Typically, commitments are established via a process of negotiation between the parties—the debtor and creditor—involved in the commitment. We define obligations to be those commitments, sometimes termed norms or social commitments, without a clearly identifiable creditor. The establishment of a commitment occurs in response to the adoption of a goal or the acceptance and performance of a task. Using a service-oriented computing (SOC) context, we describe an efficient negotiation process for establishing commitments. We then show how commitments and obligations can be used to monitor and control the aggregate behavior of a group of agents to yield coordinated progress towards the agents' overall objective.

1 Introduction

In service-oriented multiagent environments, the participating agents are distinguished by the services they provide, the services they seek and the negotiated service agreements to which they commit. As an example, participants in typical real-world business environments interact by exchanging goods and providing services to each other. In seeking and providing services, they form associations by negotiating on service agreements, make promises, commit to products, quality, and service levels, fulfill what they promised, and attempt to achieve their intended goals.

The coherent behavior of systems in such an environment is governed by interactions among the agents, and we believe that commitments and obligations are the proper abstraction to characterize the interactions for monitoring and control of the systems. We hypothesize that a commitment is an appropriate abstraction for managing, monitoring, and assuring large-scale distributed coordination.

1.1 The Coordination Problem

Coordination is a ubiquitous problem for distributed systems, where the objective is to achieve coherent and efficient operation while making rapid progress toward system-wide goals. The problem can appear in many forms, ranging from managing access to shared resources to engaging the expertise of multiple participants in reaching an overall goal.

In this chapter, we make several assumptions to limit the scope of the coordination problem that we are considering. First, we assume that the problem can be cast in terms of a known set of agents performing a dynamic set of tasks to reach a globally known goal. Second, we assume that there might be thousands of individual tasks that need to be coordinated, but not millions and not just a few. Third, we assume that the time and resources needed to perform an individual task are generally available (not scarce). Fourth, we assume that the time needed to perform an individual task is much less than the time needed to reach the goal, allowing time for tasks to be created, modified, redone, cancelled, or reassigned. The individual tasks might be discrete (e.g., the task to remove an obstacle) or continuous (e.g., the task to prevent the introduction of an obstacle). Fifth, we assume that the tasks are organized into a workflow, which may evolve as commitments are made, resources are expended, and tasks are decomposed and performed. Sixth, we assume that the agents are each aware of and have accepted the global goal, but are otherwise self-interested and autonomous. (Sen [21] has shown that societies of purely selfless agents are inefficient.) Finally, we assume that the environment where the coordinated behavior takes place has the following characteristics.

1.2 A Service-Oriented Computing Environment

A typical real-world multiagent service-oriented environment is partially observable, stochastic, sequential, dynamic, and continuous. This environment consists of two classes of agents: participating agents and non-participating agents.

The participating agents either play the role of a service provider or that of a service seeker. These service providers and service seekers negotiate and reach a service agreement. Negotiation is a process by which agents communicate and compromise to reach an agreement on matters of mutual interest while maximizing their utilities. We believe that these negotiated agreements associate or bind these participating agents with each other and that this association can be best represented as the binary relationship of commitments.

In addition to this class of participating agents, there is another class of non-participating agents in this environment; these are agents that act more like impartial arbiters. The nonparticipating agents provide the context to a commitment relationship, termed a Sphere of Commitment (SoCom) [25]. Every agent in the environment is autonomous, hence at any point in time any agent may choose to either abide by its commitment or stray from it. The nonparticipating arbiters can be used to capture a participating agent's behavior with regard to its commitments. Historical information about a participating agent's behavior can be utilized to measure its commitment adherence for future interactions.

We assume that the service providers and service seekers have already identified each other. How service seekers and service providers locate each other, how they identify compatible providers or seekers and what structure of communication and protocol they use are questions beyond the scope of this chapter.

It is further assumed that in this commitment-driven service-oriented environment the partial view that an agent has is governed solely by the commitment relationships in which it participates. In other words, agents have knowledge of other agents with whom they are associated via commitment relationships. Furthermore, it is assumed that the knowledge about a commitment relationship is governed by commitment operations, i.e., an agent has knowledge about a commitment association only through operations that affect that commitment. For example, when a service-seeking agent and a service-providing agent participate in a commitment relationship, each will have knowledge of the other agent's commitment actions and each will have knowledge of when the commitment gets created, fulfilled, revoked, etc. However, knowledge such as how that commitment is fulfilled, why it was not fulfilled, or why it was canceled is not available to the participating agents.

The typical environment for commitments is dynamic and nondeterministic; hence its temporal dimension is best represented as branching time. The underlying temporal parameter moves forward and branches out like a tree. Also, an agent's beliefs, desires and intentions define its internal state of mind. We use Rao and Georgeff's BDI framework [19], Emerson's CTL framework [5], Singh and Huhns's definitions for commitments and operations on them [24], and Shrotri and Huhns's definitions of commitments in terms of BDI [22].

2 Modeling and Representation

Goals are achieved via interleaved phases of planning and execution. Planning, which may be done by humans or by the agents responsible for goal achievement, yields sets of executable tasks and the dependencies among them. The dependencies will be primarily temporal, e.g., one task must be performed before another, but they also might be conditional, e.g., one task must be performed only if another fails. The resultant ordering of the tasks is a workflow, which can exist at several levels of generality as tasks are either aggregated into composite tasks or decomposed into subtasks.

Each task has associated with it a number of attributes that are used by an agent to perform the coordination. Each task will have a latest finish time (deadline) by which the task must be completed, earliest start time, expected duration, priority, and worth. Temporal values allow the agent to reason about when a task can be performed. A task's priority and worth represent the value of the task to the goal. Task assignment to a particular agent leads to determination of values of several additional attributes: expected quality of a result, expected cost, and expected risk.

Tasks are associated with agents via a process of negotiation as described in Section 4. The resultant assignments, especially when dependent tasks are assigned to different agents, are monitored via commitments. A commitment is a well-defined data structure with an algebra of operations that have a formal semantics. A commitment has the form $C(a; b; p; G)$, where a is its creditor, b is its debtor, p the condition the debtor will bring about, and G the organizational context for the given commitment. The operations on commitments are *create*, *discharge*, *delegate*, *assign*, *cancel*, and *release*. Commitments capture the dependencies among the agents with regard to the tasks.

Note that tasks, interactions, and commitments are not completely known a priori, but can enter the system dynamically. We do not assume that each agent knows a priori all the possible tasks that it might be asked to perform. When it has been assigned and authorized to perform a task, then its commitment is formed. The dynamic nature of task assignment necessitates the ability of the system to reason about commitments in a principled way, thus enabling the agents to have optimized ways of dynamically forming and breaking commitments as new tasks enter the system.

Explicit representation of commitments helps coordination in the following two ways:

1. Commitment is an abstraction that explicitly refers to inter-agent dependencies, either through task temporal dependencies, task preconditions, or through contingencies (i.e., alternative ways of performing a task), thus allowing agents to recognize focus points in the revision process where coordination with other agents is needed; focusing the distributed search this way benefits the efficiency of coordination.
2. During the process of revising its local plan, an agent first tries to revise task timings that do not involve commitments; this heuristic modularizes the revision as much as possible, making it more scalable.

The following structures for tasks, goals, and task performers (agents) are consistent with the above assumptions, and also consistent with the TAEMS formulation [9]:

Task: a unit of work to be performed in furtherance of an overall goal
- duration (time needed to perform)
- effort required
- deadline (when task must be finished)
- resources required (consumable and non-consumable)
- utility, including cost and quality
- revocable?
- compensation (if result of task must be revoked and it is not revocable)

Agent: a performer of one or more tasks
- capabilities, including access to resources
- limitations

Goal: an overall mission or objective to be achieved
- workflow or goal decomposition

3 Negotiated Commitments

In supply chains, e-commerce, and Web services, the participants negotiate contracts and enter into binding agreements with each other by agreeing on functional and quality metrics of the services they request and provide. The functionality of a service is the most important factor, especially for discovering services. Once discovered, however, services are engaged, composed, and executed by the participants' negotiating over QoS metrics to maximize their profits.

Negotiation is a process by which agents communicate and compromise to reach agreement on matters of mutual interest while maximizing their individual utilities. Negotiation for QoS-aware services is currently limited to primitive QoS verification methods or sorting and matching algorithms. We extend current techniques by presenting an optimal negotiation procedure that considers the cost to reach an agreement for QoS-aware service engagement and contracting.

3.1 Research Issues

Semantic Web services, as envisioned by Berners-Lee, are intended to be applied not statically by developers, but dynamically by the services themselves through automatic and autonomous selection, composition, and execution. Dynamic selection and composition first require service requestors to discover service providers that satisfy the requestors' functional requirements. Second, the requestors and providers negotiate non-functional requirements (QoS), including cost and qualities such as response time, accuracy, and availability.

In general, negotiation is the technique for reaching mutually beneficial agreement through communication among agents. Negotiation in QoS-aware services involves a sequence of information exchanges between parties to establish a formal agreement among them, whereby one or more parties will provide services to one or more other parties. The agreement typically involves QoS issues [26]. By QoS, we refer to the non-functional properties of services, such as performance, cost, reliability, and security. To meet the requirements of service requestors, multiple issues, including both functional and non-functional, need to be taken into account during service advertisement, discovery, composition, and delivery. Preist [17] discussed how negotiation plays an important role in reaching a service agreement for a service.

Current standards for Web services do not support QoS negotiations. As a result, several researchers have attempted to merge negotiation from the MAS domain into QoS-aware Web services. Ran [18] proposes to enrich current UDDI registries by extending the SOAP message format and the UDDI data structures to describe QoS information. Petrone [16] proposed a conversation model to enrich the communication and coordination capabilities of Web services by adapting agent-based concepts to the communications among services and users. In [18, 8] researchers extend the Web service model by introducing a third party broker, certifier, or QoS manager for QoS enactment and enforcement. Their work includes simple QoS verification or match algorithms and permission for the broker to negotiate and make decisions on behalf of the requestors. This is problematic, especially in situations where price and payment issues are involved.

Maximilien and Singh [13] propose a Web service agent framework (WSAF) with a QoS ontology. When a service consumer needs to use a service, WSAF will create a service agent that can capture a consumer's QoS preference and select the most suitable service.

Negotiating for services involves both functional and non-functional issues. We can not apply existing multiple-issue negotiation models to service negotiation and contracting directly, because existing models often make the limiting assumption that agents know the private information of their opponents, and their theoretic models do not take computational cost into consideration. Therefore, these models do not fit the environment of on-line QoS negotiation for services.

Many researchers have investigated multiple-issue negotiation [10, 14, 6]. Fatima et al. [6] presented an optimal agenda and procedure for two-issue negotiation by introducing two negotiation procedures: *issue-by-issue negotiation* and *package deal*. For *n*-issue negotiation where $n > 2$, which is common in negotiation over QoS issues, the computational cost to reach a package deal might exceed the benefits obtained by optimizing the participants' utilities. By considering both utility optimization and computational efficiency, Dang and Huhns [2] propose the *coalition deal* that is suitable for multiple-issue negotiation, especially in the case of QoS negotiation for services.

In [10] agents know the incomplete preference information about their opponents and exploit this information to reach negotiation efficiency. This work is thus limited to cooperative negotiation, where agents care about not only their own utilities, but also equity and social welfare, which is not common in most application environments.

The outcome of multiple-issue negotiation depends on not only strategies, but also the procedure by which issues will be negotiated. Different procedures yield different outcomes. Based on an incomplete information assumption, Fatima et al. [6] discussed two procedures for multiple issue negotiation: *issue-by-issue* and *package deal*. For two-issue negotiation, they determined the equilibrium strategy for these procedures and analyzed the optimal agenda and procedure. Since their analysis is limited to two-issue negotiation, they concluded that the package deal is the procedure that provides agents with optimal utilities; they did not address the computational cost. However, the computational cost becomes crucial when more issues are involved. We focus on the optimal strategy of efficiently negotiating multiple QoS issues to reach an agreement that gives both the requestor and the provider their maximum utilities.

We hypothesize that a coalition deal negotiation can overcome these limitations. As shown in [2], this is the optimal strategy for service negotiation over multiple issues when computation cost is considered. The coalition deal mitigates the computational cost problem by making a trade-off between optimal utility and computational efficiency. This chapter makes four contributions to the advancement of QoS-aware service negotiation and contracting. First, it describes the coalition deal negotiation for reaching utility optimization and computational efficiency. Second, it generalizes the analysis of an optimal negotiation procedure to multiple-issue negotiation over more than two issues. Third, it tailors negotiation components to fit QoS-aware negotiation. Fourth, it focuses on agents' own information; no agent has any information, such as reserve price, about its opponent.

3.2 QoS Scenario for Negotiation

In order to illustrate the coalition deal for n-issue negotiation over the QoS metrics of a service, we present a motivating scenario. Consider how one site, a requestor, might arrange to get a stock quote from a service provider. In this scenario, a service requestor a (a.k.a. the creditor if a commitment is established) locates a *GetStock-Quote* Web service provided by b (a.k.a. the debtor if a commitment is established) that meets its functionality requirements. The *GetStockQuote* service takes the requestor's inquiring stock number as an input and a currency symbol as an argument, and provides a stock quote.

During the procedure of service selection, QoS becomes an important factor to both a and b. Before reaching a service contract, they need to negotiate over (1) **payment method** indicates the way a user pays for inquiries (e.g., pay per inquiry and pay for bundle); (2) **inquiry cost** indicates the cost per inquiry; (3) **update interval** represents how often the stock quote information is updated; (4) **response time** is the round-trip time between sending an inquiry and receiving the response; (5) **availability** represents the probability that this service is available and ready for immediate use; (6) **service plan cost** is the plan cost for service with agreed-upon quality.

Agents a and b could negotiate each issue individually using issue-by-issue negotiation, but some issues are related to each other and isolating them will degrade the utility and increase the risk of a conflict deal. A package deal allows both a and b to make trade-offs among all six issues, but the computation is intractable with exponential cost. By using a coalition deal, we can partition six issues into two partitions where strongly related issues are in the same partition. For example, payment method, inquiry cost and update interval belong to partition one, while response time, availability, and service plan cost belong to partition two. a and b can negotiate two partitions in parallel, where each partition is settled as a package deal and independently of other partitions. By pursuing a coalition deal, agents can reach a service agreement while optimizing their utilities with efficient computation. The coalition deal is explored in the next section.

4 Coalition Deal Negotiation

A service is what an agent performs when it works on and completes a task. Negotiating for tasks has four components: (1) a negotiation set, which represents the possible proposal space for both functionality and QoS metrics of a service; (2) a protocol, which defines the legal proposals that an agent can make, as defined in a service description and constrained by negotiation history; (3) a strategy, which determines what proposals the agents will make, decided by an agent's private preference and affected by the service discovery result; and (4) a rule enforced by a mediator to determine when a deal has been struck and what the agreement is. We focus on the negotiation procedure of multiple-issue negotiation for services, which adopts Rubinstein's alternating offers protocol.

As described in our motivating scenario, let a denote the service requestor and b the service provider. From a service viewpoint, a has a task and tries to find a service to perform it. From a task viewpoint, b has a service and is capable of fulfiling certain tasks, so b tries to find a task to work on. We assume that each agent only has complete information about its own negotiation parameters. For some private information, such as the opponent's deadline, we can use the negotiation protocol in [20] to make truth-telling about a negotiation deadline the dominant strategy. We use S_a (S_b) to denote the set of negotiation parameters for agent a (b) and describe the negotiation model similarly to that in [6].

4.1 Single-Issue Negotiation

Consider a and b negotiating over an issue set I, where $I = A$ and A is one issue, say, the inquiry price. The agents' parameter sets are defined as

$$S_a = \langle P_a^A, U_a^A, T_a^A, \delta_a^A \rangle$$
$$S_b = \langle P_b^A, U_a^A, T_b^A, \delta_b^A \rangle \tag{1}$$

where P_a^A, U_a^A, T_a^A, and δ_a^A denote agent a's reserve price over issue A, utility function over issue A, bargaining deadline, and time discounting factor, respectively. Agent b's negotiation parameters are defined analogously. The agents' utilities at price p and at time t are defined as in [6]:

$$U_a^A(p,t) = \begin{cases} (P_a^A - p)(\delta_a^A)^t & \text{if } t \leq T_a \\ 0 & \text{if } t > T_a \end{cases}$$
$$U_b^A(p,t) = \begin{cases} (P_b^A - p)(\delta_b^A)^t & \text{if } t \leq T_b \\ 0 & \text{if } t > T_b \end{cases} \tag{2}$$

The value for δ_a^A is > 1 when agent a is patient and gains utility with time, < 1 when a is impatient and loses utility with time, and $= 1$ when a's utility is independent of time. The same holds for agent b. We only consider $\delta_a^A \leq 1$, which is common in a service-oriented environment.

In single-issue negotiation, the preferences of the agents are symmetric, in that a deal which is more preferred from one agent's point of view is guaranteed to be less preferred from the other's point of view. At the beginning of the negotiation, an agent makes an offer that gives it the highest utility and then incrementally concedes as the negotiation progresses by offering its opponent a proposal that gives it lower utility. Because of the symmetric preference of agents, agents have to concede to offer deals that are more likely to be accepted by their opponents if they prefer reaching an agreement to the conflict deal. An outcome is *individual rational* if it gives an agent a utility that is no less than its utility from the conflict outcome. The maximum possible utility that agent a (b) can get from an outcome over issue A is denoted $U^A_{max,a}$ ($U^A_{max,b}$) and it is individual rational to both agents.

Agent a's strategy (denoted σ_a) is a mapping from the previous negotiation proposals $p_{a,t'<t}$ and S_a to the action $Ac_{a,t}$ that it takes at time t: $\sigma_a : p_{a,t'<t} \times S_a \rightarrow Ac_{a,t}$ is defined as:

$$Ac_{a,t} = \begin{cases} \text{Quit} & \text{if } t \geq T_a \\ \text{Accept} & \text{if } U^A_a(p^A_{b,t},t) \geq U^A_a(p^A_{a,t+1},t+1) \\ \text{Offer } p^A_{a,t+1} \text{ at t+1, otherwise.} \end{cases} \quad (3)$$

where $p^A_{b,t}$ is the offer made by agent b over issue A at time t. $p^A_{a,t+1}$ is defined analogously. Let $P^A_{a,t}$ denotes the offer that agent a makes at time t in equilibrium, drawn from agent a's equilibrium strategy. $P^A_{a,t}$ is determined by:

$$P^A_{a,t} = (U^{-1})^A_a((1 - y^A_{a,t}) \times U^A_{max,A}) \quad (4)$$

where $y^A_{a,t}$ is agent a's yield-factor [6] at time t.

4.2 Multiple-Issue Negotiation

We next consider multiple-issue negotiation over issue set I of k issues, where $I = \{I_1, I_2, \ldots, I_k\}$. The agents' parameter sets can then be defined as follows:

$$S_a = \langle P^I_a, U^I_a, T_a, \delta_a \rangle$$
$$S_b = \langle P^I_b, U^I_b, T_b, \delta_b \rangle \quad (5)$$

where $P^I_a = \{P^i_a \mid i \in I\}$ denotes agent a's reserve prices over I and P^i_a denotes a's reserve price over issue i, $U^I_a = \{U^i_a \mid i \in I\}$ denotes agent a's utility functions over I, T_a, and δ_a denote agent a's bargain deadline and discount factor. Agent b's negotiation parameters are defined analogously. We assume that an agent's utility from issue set I is the sum of its utilities from all issues, then we have:

$$U^I_{a,t} = \sum_{i \in I} U^i_{a,t}, \quad U^I_{max,a} = \sum_{i \in I} U^i_{max,a} \quad (6)$$

Two procedures for multiple-issue negotiation have been discussed [6]: *package deal* and *issue-by-issue negotiation*. For a package deal, an offer includes a value for each issue under negotiation. Thus for k issues an offer is a package of k values, one for each issue. This allows trade-offs to be made between issues. Agents can either accept a complete offer or reject a complete offer. For issue-by-issue negotiation, each issue is settled separately and an agreement can take place either on a subset of issues or on all of them.

We first describe the procedure for a package deal. Assume that the agents use the same protocol as described in the previous section for single issue negotiation, but instead of making an offer on a single issue, an agent offers a set of offers (an offer consists of a set of values for issues from I, all of which give it equal utility). This is because when there is more than one issue, an agent can make trade-offs across issues, resulting in a set of offer sets, all of which give it equal utility. As an example, Figure 1(a) illustrates the utility for 4-issue negotiation with two package deals of two issues each. Here, we focus on the utility frontiers for the issue set $I = \{A, B\}$. In this figure the agents' utilities are measured along two axes, and the origin represents the conflict outcome. The segment AA' is the utility frontier for issue A and BB' that for issue B. The utility frontier for I is $A''B''C''D''$ (i.e., the sum of all possible utilities from issue A and issue B). The points along LL' are pairs of values for issue A and issue B that give equal utility to agent a, but different utilities to agent b. L is Pareto-optimal since it is the only one, from all possible pairs along LL', that lies on the segment $A''B''C''D''$. Because an agent does not know its opponent's utility function, it does not know which of the possible pairs along LL' is Pareto-optimal. Therefore, agent a makes trade-offs across A and B, and then offers a set of pairs that correspond to points along LL'. The slopes of segments AA' and BB' represent how the agents value the issues A and B. Agent a is said to value issue A more (less) than b if the increase in a's utility for a unit change for issue A is higher (lower) than the increase in b's utility for a unit change for issue A. Therefore, the slope of the segment represents the agents' utility preference for a issue, and is named comparative interest in [6].

We define $P_{a,t}^I = \left\langle P_{a,t}^{I_1}, P_{a,t}^{I_2}, \ldots, P_{a,t}^{I_k} \right\rangle$ as agent a's current optimal utility offer for agent b that satisfies $U_b^I(P_{a,t}^I) = \mathbf{argmax}\ U_b^I(p_{a,t}^I)$ where $p_{a,t}^I \in P_t(U_{a,t}^{I\,'})$ and $P_t(U_{a,t}^{I\,'}) = \left\{ \left\langle p_{a,t}^{I_1}, \ldots, p_{a,t}^{I_k} \right\rangle \mid U_a^I(p_{a,t}^{I_1}, \ldots, p_{a,t}^{I_k}, t) = U_{a,t}^{I\,'} \right\}$. Therefore, agent a's action $Ac_{a,t}$ for the package deal procedure is defined as

$$Ac_{a,t} = \begin{cases} \text{Quit} & \text{if } t \geq T_a \\ \text{Accept} & \text{if } U_a^I(P_{b,t}^I, t) \geq U_{a,t+1}^{I\,'} \\ \text{Offer } P_{t+1}(U_{a,t+1}^{I\,'}) \text{ at t+1, otherwise.} \end{cases} \tag{7}$$

Agent a is playing its equilibrium strategy if $U_{a,t+1}^{I\,'} = (1 - y_{a,t+1}^I)U_{max,a}^I$, where $U_{max,a}^I$ is the maximum possible utility agent a can get from issue set I [6]. The equilibrium strategy for agent b is defined analogously. We now turn to the issue-by-issue procedure. Agent a's action $Ac_{a,t}$ is defined as follows and proved in [6]:

$$Ac_{a,t} = \begin{cases} \text{Quit} & \text{if } t \geq T_a \\ \text{for issue } i \in I & \begin{cases} \text{Accept if} & U_{a,t}^i(p_{b,t}^i) \geq U_{a,t}^i(p_{a,t+1}^i) \\ \text{Offer } p_{a,t+1}^i \text{ otherwise.} \end{cases} \end{cases} \tag{8}$$

where $p_{a,t}^i$ satisfies the constraints for the equilibrium strategy described in Section 4.1.

4.3 Coalition Deal Negotiation

We discussed two negotiation procedures: issue-by-issue negotiation and package deal. The outcome of negotiation depends on different negotiation strategies and procedures. For our example *GetStockQuote*, issue-by-issue negotiation and package deal may produce different negotiation outcomes and give agents different utilities. We assume that both a and b prefer agreement to the conflict deal for every issue. In issue-by-issue negotiation, for example, agents agree on the issue of payment method with pay for bundle, and they also reach agreement that p is the inquiry cost. Since agents negotiate these issues independently, it is possible that p is too high to a if a chooses to pay for the bundle as its payment method. That means issue-by-issue negotiation may degrade agents' utilities. In package deal negotiation, agents can make a set of values over six issues and propose offers and counter offers by crossing over issues. Agents may combine different payment methods with different inquiry costs to reach mutually beneficial agreement over the two issues. However, the package deal also leads to an exponential growth in the computation cost to generate the offer sets. Most tasks (services), of course, are more complex than our example, and when they are composed this computation problem is significant. To make negotiating for tasks both optimum and efficient, we introduce the coalition deal.

Definition and Negotiation Model

We define coalition deal negotiation, which makes a better trade-off between issue-by-issue negotiation and the package deal procedure, to provide agents approximately optimized utilities with minimized computation costs.

Definition 1. *For a coalition deal, all negotiation issues are partitioned into disjoint partitions and each partition is negotiated independently of other partitions. Like the package deal, issues inside the same partition are negotiated as a whole and an offer includes a value for each issue in this partition. Furthermore, there is more than one partition in a coalition deal and at least one partition that has more than one issue.*

From this definition, we can see that issue-by-issue negotiation is a specific case of a coalition deal where one issue per partition. The package deal is also a coalition deal, where there is only one partition for all issues. Coalition deal negotiation provides (a) better utility, (b) less computational cost, (c) more flexible negotiation, and (d) better management of QoS metrics for services.

Consider multiple-issue negotiation with issue set I of k issues, where $I = \{I_1, I_2, \ldots, I_k\}$. From the definition, we know that there exists a partition IP of size s over I, where $IP = \{IP_j \mid 1 \le j \le s\}$. IP satisfies the constraint: $\forall 1 \le m \le s, 1 \le n \le s, m \ne n$, we have $IP_m \cap IP_n = \emptyset$ and $\cup_{j \in IP} \cup_{i \in j} i = I$. Similarly, agents' parameter sets can be defined as follows:

$$S_a = \langle P_a^{IP}, U_a^{IP}, T_a, \delta_a \rangle$$

$$S_b = \langle P_b^{IP}, U_b^{IP}, T_b, \delta_b \rangle \tag{9}$$

where $P_a^{IP} = \{p_a^i \mid i \in j, j \in IP\}$ denotes agent a's reserve prices set over partitions of issue set I and p_a^i denotes a's reserve price over issue i, which belongs to partition j, $U_a^{IP} = \{U_a^i \mid i \in IP\}$ denotes agent a's utility functions over partition IP where

U_a^i denotes agent a's utility function over one partition i from IP, T_a and δ_a denotes agent a's bargaining deadline and discount factor. Agent b's negotiation parameters are defined similarly. An agent's utility from partition IP of issue set I is the sum of its utilities from all partitions, so then we have

$$U_a^{IP} = \sum_{j \in IP} U_a^j = \sum_{j \in IP} \sum_{i \in j} U_a^i, \quad U_{max,a}^I = \sum_{j \in IP} \sum_{i \in j} U_{max,a}^i \tag{10}$$

For a coalition deal, each partition is negotiated independently of other partitions. An agreement can take place either on some or all of the partitions. For each partition, an offer includes a value for each issue inside the partition that would be the same as the package deal for this partition. This allows trade-offs to be made between issues inside the partition. An agreement has to take place either on all or none of the issues inside the partition.

For each partition, we assume the agents use the same protocol as for the package deal, but instead of making a set of offers over issue set I, an agent makes a set of offers over issues from this partition. An agent can make trade-offs only across issues in the same partition, resulting in a set of offer sets, all of which give it equal utility. As an example, Figure 1(a) illustrates the utility frontiers for issue set I where $I = \{A, B, C, D\}$. There exists a partition IP for I where $IP = \{\{A, B\}, \{C, D\}\}$. Let $IP_1 = \{A, B\}$, and $IP_2 = \{C, D\}$. The utility frontier for IP_1 is $A''B''C''D''$ and the utility frontier for IP_2 is $S''T''V''U''$. For IP_1, the points along LL' are pairs of values for IP_1 that give equal utilities to agent a but different utilities to agent b. The points along RR'' are pairs of values for IP_1 that give equal utilities to agent b but different utilities to agent a. The utility for IP is the sum of the utilities from IP_1 and IP_2 after these partitions are negotiated independently. If we only consider the optimal outcome from both negotiations over IP_1 and IP_2, All optimal outcomes for IP_1 lie on the segment $MB''K$, and all optimal outcomes for IP_2 lie on the segment $XT''Y$ as we described for the package deal. Therefore, the possible utility frontier for IP is represented by region $OM''P''QQ'P$ in Figure 1(b). For a partition IP_i of k_i issues, we define $P_{a,t}^{IP_i} = \left\langle P_{a,t}^{IP_i(1)}, \ldots, P_{a,t}^{IP_i(k_i)} \right\rangle$ as agent a's current optimal utility offer for agent b that satisfies $U_b^{IP_i}(P_{a,t}^{IP_i}) = \mathbf{argmax}\, U_b^{IP_i}(p_{a,t}^{IP_i})$, where $p_{a,t}^{IP_i} \in P_t(U_{a,t}^{IP_i})$ and $P_t(U_{a,t}^{IP_i\,'}) = \left\{ \left\langle p_{a,t}^{IP_i(1)}, \ldots, p_{a,t}^{IP_i(k_i)} \right\rangle \mid U_a^{IP_i}(p_{a,t}^{IP_i(1)}, \ldots, p_{a,t}^{IP_i(k_i)}) = U_{a,t}^{IP_i\,'} \right\}$.

$P_{t+1}(U_{a,t+1}^{IP_i\,'})$ is defined analogously. For a coalition deal, each partition is considered using the package deal negotiation protocol. Agent a's action $Ac_{a,t}$ for the coalition deal procedure is defined as follows:

$$Ac_{a,t} = \begin{cases} \text{Quit} & \text{if } t \geq T_a \\ \text{Accept package deal for } IP_i & \text{if } U_a^{IP_i}(P_{b,t}^{IP_i}) \geq U_{a,t+1}^{IP_i\,'} \\ \text{Offer } P_{t+1}(U_{a,t+1}^{IP_i\,'}) \text{ for } IP_i \text{ at t+1, otherwise.} \end{cases} \tag{11}$$

Similarly, we define agent a as playing its equilibrium strategy for the package deal over a partition if $U_{a,t+1}^{IP_i\,'} = (1 - y_{a,t+1}^{IP_i})U_{max,a}^{IP_i}$, where $U_{max,a}^{IP_i}$ is the maximum possible cumulative utility agent a can get from partition IP_i. The equilibrium strategy for agent a and agent b over other partitions is defined analogously.

Coalition Deal Utility

In previous sections, we discussed three different negotiation procedures: issue-by-issue, package deal, and coalition deal. These three procedures can generate different outcomes, and consequently give different utilities to the agents. To decide the optimal procedure that gives the agents highest utilities, we need to compare agents' utilities from these procedures for n-issue negotiation. Fatima et al. [6] introduced the zone of agreement for individual issues where both agents prefer agreement over no deal. An issue has a zone of agreement if its utility frontier lies in quadrant $Q1$. We discuss the common scenario of service-oriented computing (SOC) in which both agents are *individual rational* (i.e., all issues have a zone of agreement ensured by the service description and the discovery procedure).

Lemma 1. *each agent's utility from the package deal is no worse than its utility from issue-by-issue negotiation for two-issue negotiation.*

Lemma 1 has been proven in [6]. In a service-oriented environment, there are many issues concerning functionality and quality that need to be negotiated during service engagement. Can we generalize Lemma 1 to cover more than two? Here, we compare agents' utilities from package deal and issue-by-issue negotiation for n-issue negotiation.

Theorem 1. *Each agent's utility from the package deal is no worse than its utility from issue-by-issue negotiation for n-issue negotiation, where $n > 2$.*

Theorem 1 has been proven in [2] by induction. From this theorem, we know that a package deal gives agents better utilities than issue-by-issue negotiation does. As stated in the previous section, a coalition deal provides approximately optimized utilities to agents. Then we prove that a coalition deal give agents utilities better than issue-by-issue negotiation does.

Theorem 2. *Each agent's utility from a coalition deal is no worse than its utility from issue-by-issue negotiation for n-issue negotiation, where $n > 2$.*

Theorem 2 has been proved by combining Theorem 1 and our assumption of additive utilities [2]. Both package deal and coalition deal give agents utilities better than issue-by-issue negotiation does. The remaining question is which procedure, package deal or coalition deal, gives agents better utilities. To answer this question, we first prove that the package deal gives agents utilities better than a coalition deal of two partitions.

Lemma 2. *Each agent's utility from the package deal is no worse than its utility from i-by-j negotiation for n-issue negotiation, where $i \geq 1, j \geq 1, n > 2$, and $i + j = n$.*

We have proven that the package deal gives agents utilities better than a coalition deal of two partitions for n-issue negotiation in [2]. For QoS negotiation for tasks, we need to extend Lemma 2 to the coalition deal with more than two partitions.

Theorem 3. *Each agent's utility from a coalition deal is no better than its utility from the package deal for n-issue negotiation, where $n > 2$ [2].*

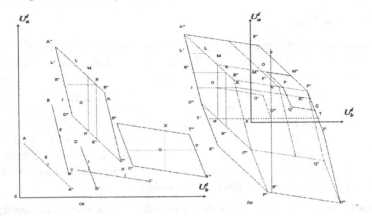

Fig. 1. Agents' utilities for 4-issue negotiation

Coalition Deal Efficiency

From Theorems 1, 2 and 3, we know that each agent's utility from the package deal is better than its utility from a coalition deal and issue-by-issue negotiation. Therefore, we should choose the package deal negotiation to maximize agents' utilities. However, we need to consider the computational costs, which can be the primary factor when negotiating for tasks.

Given an issue set $I = \{I_1, I_2, \ldots, I_n\}$ and a partition $IP = \{IP_1, IP_2, \ldots, IP_k\}$ over I, we define the unit computational cost for generating a price value for one issue as a constant. We assume that every issue in issue-by-issue negotiation can be negotiated in parallel and every partition in a coalition deal can also be negotiated in parallel. To compare the computational efficiency, we only need to compare the computational cost of generating an offer in each round of three different procedures. If we suppose agents need almost the same rounds of negotiation to reach an agreement in these three negotiation procedures, we can compare their computational costs by comparing the cost of generating an offer in each round.

An n-issue negotiation can be viewed as a distributed search through an n-dimensional space, where each issue has a separate dimension associated with it. In issue-by-issue negotiation, each issue is negotiated separately, Based on the above equilibrium strategy, agents will compute a value for each issue. Therefore, the computational cost in one round is $O(n)$, where n is the size of the issue set. In the package deal, an offer is a set including a value for each issue under negotiation. In each round, an agent can make trade-offs across all n issues to offer a set of offers that give it the same utilities. In the worst case, the computational cost in one round is $O(m^n)$, where we assume each issue may have m possible values.

The computation problem of generating an offer set is equivalent to searching in an n-dimensional space for all combinations of possible distributions of given utility value among all n issues with a utility constraint. This problem is intractable and takes $O(m^n)$ time in the worst case. Even worse, we have to solve this problem every round during the package deal negotiation procedure. It means that it will be infeasible for an agent to consider every possible offer given a utility constraint. In coalition deal negotiation, issues are partitioned into k disjoint partitions and each partition is settled independently of the other partitions. Like the package deal, issues inside the same partition are negotiated as a whole and an offer includes a value for each issue in this partition. Therefore, the computation problem is reduced to the sum of k searches where the i-th search is in an n_i-dimension space, where $n_i << n$ and $\sum_{i=1}^{k} n_i = n$. This problem takes $O(km^{n_s})$ time in the worst case, where $n_s =$ **argmax** n_i. Moreover, we can limit the maximum size of a partition to a constant C. Therefore, the computational cost of a coalition deal reduces to $O(nm^C)$. The time complexity will be $O(m^C)$ if we have several agents, one for each partition, work together to generate a coalition deal.

In our GetStockQuote service scenario, we divide six issues into two partitions. The computational cost is 6 in each round for issue-by-issue negotiation. In package deal, agents need to search through all possible offers in a 6-dimensional space to meet the given utility constraint. The computational cost is $O(a^6)$ in the worst case, where a is the size of possible value per issue. In a coalition deal, the computational cost is $O(a^3)$ in the worst case.

Coalition Deal Negotiation for Services

With much lower computational cost than that for the package deal, agents earn greater utilities from the coalition deal than from issue-by-issue negotiation. Besides computational cost and agent utility, another advantage of the coalition deal is that it is natural to partition issues into different categories and deal with each category separately. For example, in bilateral negotiation of a labor dispute, it would be easier if money issues such as salary and bonus are negotiated in a partition separately from issues such as working condition and healthcare. Of course, it is possible that both sides would benefit if they could deal with all issues as a package, but the negotiation might become infeasible.

In QoS-aware service contracting, self-interested service agents negotiate with each other over multiple issues besides QoS attributes to reach an agreement while maximizing their utilities. The optimal negotiation strategy for the coalition deal is: (1) Agents reveal their deadlines; honesty about their real deadline is enforced by the negotiation protocol. For example, the agent that has the latest deadline will receive better payoff at the time right before its deadline. (2) Each agent estimates individually the rounds this negotiation should have before the earliest deadline. (3) Agents are identified by their time discount factors (≤ 1) from their own utility functions. Agents choose either the *Boulware* or *conceder* discount functions by mapping their discount factor to different parameters. (4) Agents compute the expected cumulative utility by their Boulware/conceder functions and generate a set of offers, all of which give them equal utility, by crossing over multiple issues inside one partition.

Since all partitions can be negotiated in parallel and independently, the fourth steps can be executed in parallel for each partition. A service agent can breed several negotiation agents, each for one partition. These negotiation agents cooperate to reach a service agreement with distributed computation. The coalition among these negotiation agents provides the framework for a possibly more flexible negotiation procedure in the future.

5 Commitments and Obligations

Now that we have described efficient multiple-issue negotiation, in this section we define commitments and obligations and describe various operations that the participating agents can perform on them. We briefly revisit earlier formalisms of commitments and their operations [24, 22], and then define an extension useful for coordination.

5.1 Commitments

Social commitments are legal abstractions associating one entity with another. These commitments are accessible publicly and represent an interaction between two participating entities. Commitments are binary relationships that bind two agents: a "debtor agent" that promises to provide a particular service for a "creditor agent." For example, service level agreements, QoS agreements, online purchases, and service contracts are all real-world instances of commitments.

Earlier works have treated all the information about a commitment as publicly available or accessible. It is more realistic to treat some of the information as partially accessible and some as private. To do this, we refine the commitment structure in [24, 22] with the key properties of accessibility.

First, the commitment properties that are publicly accessible are

Multiagency: Commitments associate one agent with another. The agent that promises or commits to satisfying a condition is called the debtor agent and the agent that wants the condition to be fulfilled by the debtor is called the creditor agent. Each commitment is directed from its debtor to its creditor.

Scope: Commitments have a well-defined scope, also known as a Sphere of Commitment (SoCom), which gives context to the commitment.

Manipulability: Commitments are modifiable. They can become fulfilled, breached, active, suspended, or revoked, which is public information about their current status.

The following two additional parameters are not properties of a commitment per se, but represent an agent's attitude towards its commitments. These are also public.

Commitment Adherence Rating: Agents may choose to respect or ignore their commitments. For effective coordination, fulfilling promises is critical and determines an agent's reputation. A participating agent's history of commitment adherence can be captured and translated into a this rating, which represents the agent's reputation in a domain. Nonparticipating arbiters can be used to measure and maintain this parameter.

Utility Weighting: This is a numerical coefficient in the range $(0, 1]$ that represents the relative importance of the committed promise on the overall utility that is desired by the creditor agent. This commitment property is used for multiple-issue commitments. For single-issue commitments, the value is always 1. It cannot be 0, as that would represent an issue on which the creditor agent is completely agnostic.

The next (partially-accessible) property is accessible to the debtor of the commitment and to the nonparticipating arbiters, defined as follows:

Utility Coefficient: Imagine a scenario where a debtor agent makes false promises to many service seekers and then does nothing to fulfill the promises. In the real world there are checks and measures in place to discourage such behavior. The Utility Coefficient, which represents the affect of debtor's behavior on its utility, provides similar discouragement. Its value in the range $[0, 1]$ captures whether a debtor receives all of the utility associated with a commitment (value 1) or none of the utility (value 0).

Lastly, we revisit two key commitment properties [22] and redefine them as properties that represent an agent's private or internal information.

Life: Commitments have a life cycle; they are created, remain active, and at some point cease to exist. Continuous commitments are beyond the scope of this formalism and are a subject of future research.

Degree: We believe that when active, commitments do not necessarily remain in one constant state; they might age by becoming more or less important. This notion of commitment aging is captured by what we define as the degree of commitment. We believe that for a service-oriented coordination environment, the degree of commitment changes with changing beliefs, desires, and intentions. Also, specifically in the case of commitment cancellation or revocation, the commitment might not go from an active state to an inactive state instantaneously, but gradually decrease its degree until it becomes inactive.

Commitments are represented by a predicate C. The partially accessible commitment properties are represented inside angle brackets "$\langle \ldots \rangle$" and the private properties are represented inside square brackets "$[\ldots]$". Commitments have the form $C(i, a, b, p, S, W, \langle \mu \rangle, [d])$, where

i: is a unique identifier,
a: is the creditor agent,
b: is the debtor agent,
p: is the promise or the condition that the debtor will bring about,
S: is the context, also known as the *sphere of commitment*,
W: is the utility weighting,
μ: is the utility coefficient,
d: is the age or degree of commitment.

In this chapter, we do not use all of these properties, but mention them wherever pertinent. Throughout the rest of this chapter we refer to the creditor entity as a and the debtor entity as b.

5.2 Obligations

We believe that obligations are closely tied to the notions of duty and responsibility. An obligation is a promise that one makes to oneself; it is driven by the demand of ones own conscience or custom or socially accepted norms and it binds one to a specific course of action. We believe that obligations may also exist between a debtor agent and an abstract creditor agent, which cannot be represented as one concrete creditor, for instance society or say one's country. In this chapter however, we will consider only those obligations that represent promises one makes to oneself.

We believe that obligations can be represented as a special case of commitments. Obligations, unlike commitments, are best described as unitary and private in nature. In the described service-oriented environment, obligations are the abstractions of bindings that an agent imposes on itself. These obligations or internal bindings are visible only to the agent and are driven solely by agent's internal state of mind i.e. beliefs, desires and intentions. We believe that commitments' claim over a promise is stronger than that of obligations.

As we are dealing only with unitary obligations, the Multiagency and Utility Weighting properties are inapplicable. R and μ have special values set by the debtor agent itself. The other properties of Scope, Manipulability, Life, and Degree are treated the same as they are for commitments.

Obligations are represented by a predicate O, with their private properties inside square brackets "[. . .]". Obligations have the form: $O(i, b, p, S, \mu, [d])$, where

i: is a unique identifier,
b: is the debtor agent,
p: is the promise or the condition that the debtor will bring about,
S: is the context, also known as the *sphere of commitment*,
μ: is the utility coefficient,
d: is the age or degree of obligation.

5.3 Operations on Commitments and Obligations

As described above, our service-oriented environment is commitment-driven and participating agents' knowledge is governed solely by commitment operations. In this section, we describe commitment operations [23, 12] and their extension [22]. Commitments are treated as abstract data types that associate debtor, creditor, promise, and context. The seven fundamental commitment operations are

1. *Create (b, C(i, a, b, p, S))*: This operation establishes a commitment C in the situation S. This operation can only be performed by C's debtor.

2. *Discharge(b, C(i, a, b, p, S))*: This operation indicates that the inherent promise in the commitment C has been fulfilled; hence the commitment C has been satisfied.
3. *Revoke(b, C(i, a, b, p, S))*: This operation cancels the commitment C and can only be performed by C's debtor. This operation also reflects the autonomy of the participating entity.
4. *Release(a, C(i, a, b, p, S))*: This operation captures the situation where a creditor no longer wishes its debtor to fulfill its committed promise and releases it of its commitment. It can only be performed by C's creditor.
5. *Assign(a, z, C(i, a, b, p, S))*: This operation enables a commitment's creditor to designate another entity as the creditor. It can only be performed by C's creditor and replaces a with z as C's creditor.
6. *Delegate(b, z, C(i, a, b, p, S))*: This operation enables C's debtor to transfer its commitment promise to another agent. This operation can only be performed by C's debtor and replaces b with z as C's debtor.
7. *Suspend(b, C(i, a, b, p, S))*: This operation can only be performed by C's debtor, and describes a situation where the debtor has put its promised commitment on hold.

We use predicates to describe whether the commitment C has been satisfied, revoked, breached, or still holds, written as *satisfied(C)*, *revoked(C)*, *breached(C)*, and *active(C)*, respectively.

For obligations, only the following four of the above operations are applicable: *Create(b, C (i, b, p, S))*, *Discharge(b, C (i, b, p, S))*, *Revoke(b, C (i, b, p, S))*, and *Suspend(b, C (i, b, p, S))*. Obligations are unitary, internal, and private in nature; hence, assignment and delegation is not applicable. Because obligations can be treated as a special case of commitments, in the remainder of this chapter we use commitments as the basic abstraction for both binary and unitary agent bindings.

5.4 Negotiated Agreements as Commitment Promises

As described in Section 1, in service-oriented environments the participating agents, which play the roles of a service provider and a service seeker, negotiate and commit to a service agreement about the execution and completion of a task. During the negotiation, the agents communicate and compromise to reach an agreement on matters of mutual interest while maximizing their utilities. In this section we will describe how the negotiated agreements, which associate or bind these participating agents with each other, can be best encapsulated as commitment promises.

Let b denote the service provider or the debtor agent and a denote the service seeker or the creditor agent as described in Section 4.3. Both a and b negotiate on issues related to the service and come to an agreement. How they communicate and their particular negotiation strategy is beyond the scope of this section.

We first consider agreements over a single issue. Specifically, a and b have negotiated and agreed upon an issue set $I = A$, where A represents one issue, such as the product price in an e-commerce transaction.

Expanding on the agents' negotiation parameters as defined in Section 4, we define the agents' agreement parameters as

$$S_a = \langle P_a, U_a \rangle_A$$
$$S_b = \langle P_a, U_b \rangle_A \tag{12}$$

where, $P_a = P_b = P_{agreed}$ is the agreed price or the agreed parameter over issue A. This is public information.

U_a and U_b are utilities of the respective participating agents. The utilities are associated with the negotiated agreement on A. It is partially accessible information known to the owner agent and the non-participating arbiters. Note that the actual utility, $U_{actual} = \mu \times U$, is awarded to the agent once the commitment C reaches finality.

The negotiated agreement between agents a and b over issue A is a commitment in which the agreed parameter over A is the commitment promise. From section 5.1, and because this is a single-issue agreement so that $W = 1$, the commitment is represented as $C(i, a, b, P_{agreed}, S, 1, \langle \mu \rangle, [degree, age])$.

We now consider multiple-issue negotiated agreements. As an example, an online transaction between an online bookseller and a buyer would involve agreement from both sides on the multiple issues of book price, book condition (new or used), delivery method, etc. All these are sub-issues of the main issue of "buying a book."

Let there be an issue set I of k issues, where $I = \{I_1, I_2, \ldots, I_k\}$. Expanding on the agents' negotiation parameters as defined in Section 4, the agents' agreement parameter sets are defined as:

$$S_a = \langle P_a, U_a \rangle_I$$
$$S_b = \langle P_b, U_b \rangle_I \tag{13}$$

where, $P_a = \sum_{i \in I} P_a^i$, and similarly, $P_b = \sum_{i \in I} P_b^i$

This means that the overall agreed price or agreed parameter over issue I, which comprises k sub-issues, is the summation of the agreed price or the agreed parameter of all the sub-issues. Since a and b are in agreement, $P_a = P_b = P_{agreed}$, it is the overall agreed price or the overall agreed parameter over the issue A. This is public information, which is available to all the participants and the non-participating arbiters.

U_a and U_b are overall utilities of the respective participating agents. This utility is associated with the negotiated agreement on the issue I. This is partially accessible information, which means that it is known to the owner agent and the non-participating arbiters. Note that the actual utility, $U_{actual} = \mu \times U$ and will be awarded to the agent once the commitment C reaches some kind of finality. We know that $U_a = \sum_{i \in I} U_a^i$. Similarly, $U_b = \sum_{i \in I} U_b^i$. Which means that the overall utility for an agent to have an agreement on a parameter over issue set I, which comprises k sub-issues is the summation of utilities it gains on having an agreement on all the sub-issues.

Now we describe the concept of W in greater detail. As described above, the overall utility of the debtor agent b over the issue set I is the sum all the utilities ("sub-utilities") it gains over all the k sub-issues that make up the issue set I. We theorize that in the issue set I all of the sub-issues do not necessarily have an equally significant effect on its overall utility. In our book-selling example, let us assume that a service provider b and a service seeker a enter into a commitment relationship in which b promises to deliver a book to a. Of the many sub-issues that make up the complete transaction, the "color of the book cover" may not have as significant an impact on b's overall utility as does the "condition of the book" or the "delivery time". W represents the relative significance of sub-issues that make up an issue set.

Considering the negotiated agreement between agents a and b over the issue set I as a commitment relationship, the relationship between a and b can be represented as: $C_{ab} = \sum_{i \in I} C_{ab}^i$, which means that the commitment relationship between a and b over negotiated agreements on the issue set I, which comprises k sub-issues, is the summation of all the commitments on all the k sub-issues. Note that $\sum_{i \in I} W_b^i = 1$. Thus, service-oriented environments where participating agents are involved in negotiated agreements over single or multiple issues can be modeled by our commitment-driven approach.

6 Commitment-Based Coordination Protocol

Organizational control is needed to ensure that the appropriate information is communicated among the coordinating agents, so that they can make effective decisions to advance the overall objective. The key information being communicated is of three types:

1. Static information, such as authority relationships
2. Dynamic information, such as policies, standard operating procedures, and communication protocols
3. Contextual information, such as the current state of the overall workflow or plan and the states of the relevant agents.

An important aspect of our approach is that it treats organizational control as an integral aspect of planning, particularly for coordinating in the face of exceptions. This is a reasonable approach, because the flexibility of an organization reflects the complexity of its plans, the dynamism of its environment, and the risks faced by its plans. Thus heuristic techniques for encoding and using coordination strategies are naturally extended into strategies that accommodate organizational structure and control.

Moreover, organizational structure can be used to control the complexity both of the design and configuration of agent systems and of the execution by individual agents. This improves scalability. Well-designed organizations naturally yield narrow interfaces so that changes are not unnecessarily propagated and the right information flows at the right time. We cast the problem of organization design as a natural next step to the representation and design of agent heuristics, where the heuristics are selected so as to capture and exploit organizational structure. For example, we could have heuristics to report exceptions or anticipated exceptions to a supervisory role;

to delegate a commitment to a subordinate; to request a peer to accept a delegate; to assign a resource not needed to a peer; and so on. In this manner, the general approach for verifying correctness could be made more elaborate to take advantage of organizational structure. Moreover, a model of the agents' organization, policies, and authority can be integrated with coordinated decision making to ensure the compliance of decisions to organizational policies.

To make this discussion concrete, let's outline how inter-agent control and intra-agent control mesh:

1. One or more agents perceive or are notified of an event.
2. Each agent perceiving the event decides (a) whether the event changes its local plan, and (b) whether to communicate the change (by itself or along with additional results of its reasoning) to another agent.
3. If an agent decides the event does not affect it or any one of its dependent agents, then it filters out the event and continues on its prior execution path. If an agent decides that the event does not affect its own plan, but could possibly affect plans of its dependent agents, then it communicates the event to the affected agents.
4. If an agent decides that the change affects its own plan, it reconsiders its commitments and begins a renegotiation of those that cannot be met.
5. The actions proposed to meet commitments are subjected to a "filter" that detects any that are in opposition to policies. All agents have an obligation to act in accordance with appropriate and applicable policies.
6. If the coordinated commitment-revision process encounters difficulties, the agent who has the most severe difficulty is given its preference and the coordination continues.

The above process can be captured in a general and flexible manner through the use of commitments. As explained in Section 5, commitments provide a natural abstraction to encode relationships among autonomous, heterogeneous parties. Commitments are important for organizational control, because they provide a layer that mediates across the declarative semantics of organizations from the operational behavior of the team members. Organizational control based on commitments by a reasoner in an agent has the advantages that:

1. Commitments can be assigned to roles, so that any unit that fills the role of "transport troops" will, e.g., inherit a commitment assigned to the role to move troops from location A to location B.
2. Commitments can be delegated, so that a captain who has the commitment to "transport troops" can delegate the commitment to Helicopter Unit 1.
3. Commitments can be reassigned. For example, if Helicopter Unit 1 fails to meet its commitment (the helicopters break down) then the captain can release Unit 1 from the commitment and delegate it to Unit 2.
4. Commitments can be negotiated. The captain might ask another captain (a peer) to take over a commitment that could not otherwise be met.
5. Commitments can fail to be met, in which case the failure can be communicated to an agent with the authority to release the original commitment and reassign it.

Commitments to follow required policies are a kind of obligation, and are managed by a deontic reasoner. An organizational model based on obligations and rights can enable agents to represent and reason about the relationship between the responsibilities of the agent or group being coordinated and applicable policies, decision-making constraints, authorities, and overall objectives. This feature decides which organizational policies apply for the current situation and marks as unacceptable any intended actions that are inappropriate.

7 Commitments in Plan Revision

It is clear from the above that coordination is not a one-shot effort that can be satisfied through one round of planning, but must be carried out repeatedly. Further, coordination includes challenges such as unexpected events and changing situations, and must respect not only physical constraints, but also organizational challenges.

One aspect of commitments involves scheduling algorithms so that an agent can manage multiple commitments in the face of external events. Each agent applies classification to identify the general class of an event, then the classification is used to choose heuristics most likely to lead to effective coordinated behavior. Each agent maintains the consistency of formally represented commitments leading to robust, yet flexible coordination reasoning.

This relies upon a temporal semantics for commitments, which naturally leads to heuristics for ensuring that tasks that can be scheduled are satisfactorily scheduled given the emerging constraints. Another aspect involves reasoning about commitments more directly at the level of coordination as it relates to communication. To this end, it helps to develop additional representations based on commitments. Such representations can be thought of as patterns of coordination relationships.

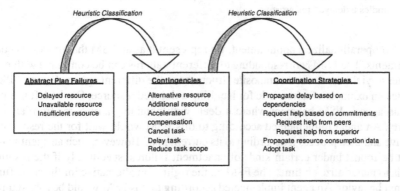

Fig. 2. Elements of a simple domain-independent mechanism for coordinating a response to conflicts and failures in plans

Commitments provide us with a basis for creating techniques that are generic and reusable. It is helpful to frame these as first-order patterns of interaction as well as second-order patterns of how other patterns are modified. These patterns would be indexed according to different situations and potential threats such as lost communications, ineffective participants, and so on. Figure 2 illustrates examples of how certain coordination strategies can be associated with potential plan failures. This is an example of heuristic classification in the sense of [1]. In our approach, this heuristic classification is supported by our semantics for commitments. Commitments are formally modeled via temporal logic; each agent's behavior is modeled via a simple finite-state machine (FSM).

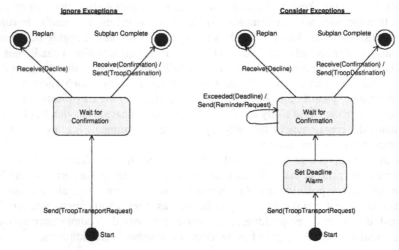

Fig. 3. Operationalizing commitments: an example of a finite-state machine for a coordinator that handles a delayed resource

To operationalize a commitment, we represent it as an FSM that processes commitments. The FSMs corresponding to different patterns can be combined with each other to yield the desired composite structure for the different agents. Figure 3 illustrates an example of a heuristic for handling a delayed resource. On the left is a part of an agent's FSM behavior where it deals with obtaining a resource from another party. An agent implemented according to this FSM would wait for the resource to arrive and then process it according to its current plan. However, such an agent would not be robust under certain kinds of enactment failures, specifically if the resource fails to materialize on time. The FSM on the right is an alternative for the same functional behavior. An agent implemented according to this FSM would be robust under the above failure, because it would time-out and generate reminders for the missing resource.

The above heuristic is promising, but has an obvious shortcoming in that, if the resource is dead rather than merely delayed, the agent will keep generating reminders, whereas it should drop the current plan altogether. As agents are designed for a rich variety of scenarios, more such heuristics will be needed. They might be invented at run-time via machine learning or during configuration when a team of agents is deployed.

We can validate if a set of agents will function together in a manner to produce the right behaviors. It is known that checking the correctness of a distributed system of complex components is not tractable. The FSM representation of the heuristics hides irrelevant detail and enables the correctness verification known as model checking. Examples of the kinds of errors that can be detected early via model checking are: (1) if all the agents in a system are implemented according to the simple FSM on the left in the figure above, then such a system will hang when a resource dies, and (2) when resource sharing, if the receiver of a resource is implemented according to the FSM on the right, then we can confirm that reminders will be generated in case of a delay, but there might still be unnecessary delays because the resource provider cannot notify the resource consumer and the resource consumer will be unable to terminate its current plan if the resource is in fact dead. Similarly, we can create additional sets of FSMs and verify their correctness. Previous work on this problem used a Computational Tree Logic (CTL) model checker to create FSMs that would guarantee specified combinations of commitment patterns [28, 27].

In simple terms, the methodology combines the power of heuristics and the learning of agent behaviors, while providing a sound underpinning in terms of commitments and their formal semantics. Heuristic classification is essential for practical knowledge acquisition and implementation; formalization gives us the essential guarantees of robustness and reliability that are necessary for mission-critical situations.

8 Conclusions

Commitments are a powerful representation for modeling intelligent interactions among agents distributed within an organizational structure. Previous approaches have considered the semantics of commitments and how to check compliance with them. However, for large-scale applications such as supply chains or military operations, these approaches do not capture implicit temporal task dependencies or the organizational authority and responsibilities among the participating entities. Our use of negotiated commitments for coordination lets us capture realistic task dependencies and avoid ambiguities. Consequently, it enables us to reason about whether, and at what point, a commitment is satisfied or breached, and whether it is or ever becomes unenforceable when replanning must be done.

Our use of deadlines for agent plans is similar to that for commitment lifecycles [7], which explains how operations can create, modify, delete, and satisfy commitments. This work operationalizes commitments, and we extend it to yield agent-internalized BDI semantics for temporal commitments.

The use of policy and organizational reasoning for coordination requires advances in the representation of policies in terms of commitments and obligations and an associated deontic reasoning mechanism. A temporal deontic logic for specifying obligations so that interaction protocols can take deadlines into account has been developed [4]. Other work on obligations [11] used them to represent and reason about policies, but did not incorporate commitments, as we do.

The choice of commitments as a basic data type for coordination enables the monitoring of performance by recording the satisfaction of prior commitments. This can be used to predict an agent's computational resource needs, and can be used to determine when an agent is not meeting expectations.

This chapter also investigates the coalition deal as a strategy for QoS-aware negotiation over commitments. Using equilibrium strategies, we prove that it makes better tradeoffs between utility optimization and computational efficiency than either the package deal or issue-by-issue negotiation.

Many real world systems are becoming service-oriented. In a service-oriented multiagent system, commitments represent agent associations and interactions. In such an environment, a participant agent's beliefs, desires, and intentions about the commitments in which it is involved are critical to modeling its behavior. By formalizing commitments in terms of BDI, we have provided the basic framework on which a more comprehensive commitment-driven coordination theory could be developed. The advantage of this framework is that it blends two established formalisms—BDICTL [3] and commitments—that together can model a service-oriented multiagent system. Our future research involves exploration of how agents decide what to commit (integrating earlier works on "capability" [15] with commitments), when to revoke a commitment, how a commitment ages, and how historical information of an agent's commitment adherence can be utilized to predict agent behavior.

References

1. William J. Clancey. Heuristic classification. *Artificial Intelligence*, 27(3):289–350, 1985.
2. Jiangbo Dang and Michael N. Huhns. Optimal multiple-issue negotiation over qos metrics of web service. *USC CIT Technical Report TR-CIT05-01*, 2005.
3. M. Dastani and L. van der Torre. An extension of bdictl with functional dependencies and components. In *Proceedings of LPAR'02*, volume LNCS 2514, pages 115–129. Springer, 2002.
4. Frank Dignum, H. Weigand, and E. Verharen. Meeting the deadline: On the formal specification of temporal deontic constraints. In *Foundations of Intelligent Systems, 9th International Symposium*, 1996.
5. E. A. Emerson. Temporal and modal logic. In J. van Leeuwen, editor, *Handbook of Theoretical Computer Science: Formal Models and Semantics*, volume B, pages 995–1072, 1990.
6. S. S. Fatima, M. Wooldridge, and N. Jennings. Optimal negotiation of multiple issues in incomplete information settings. In *Proc. Third International Joint Conference on Autonomous Agents and MultiAgent Systems (AAMAS'04)*, pages 1080–1089, New York, USA, 2004. ACM.
7. Nicoletta Fornara and Marco Colombetti. Operational specification of a commitment-based agent communication language. In *AAMAS '02: Proceedings of the First International Joint Conference on Autonomous Agents and Multiagent Systems*, pages 536–542. ACM Press, 2002.

8. D. Gouscos, M. Kalikakis, and P. Georgiadis. An approach to modeling web service qos and provision price. In *Proc. Fourth International Conference on Web Information Systems Engineering Workshops (WISEW'03)*, pages 121–130, Roma, Italy, 2003.

9. Bryan Horling, Victor Lesser, Regis Vincent, Tom Wagner, Anita Raja, Shelley Zhang, Keith Decker, and Alan Garvey. The TAEMS white paper. 2004. http://mas.cs.umass.edu/research/taems/white.

10. C. M. Jonker and V. Robu. Automated multi-attribute negotiation with efficient use of incomplete preference information. In *Proc. Third International Joint Conference on Autonomous Agents and MultiAgent Systems (AAMAS'04)*, pages 1056–1063, New York,USA, 2004. ACM.

11. Lalana Kagal, Tim Finin, and Anupam Joshi. A policy based approach to security on the semantic web. In *Proc. Second International Semantic Web Conference*, 2003.

12. Ashok U. Mallya and Michael N. Huhns. Commitments among agents. *IEEE Internet Computing*, 7(4):90–93, July-Aug 2003.

13. E. M. Maximilien and M. P. Singh. A framework and ontology for dynamic web services selection. *IEEE Internet Computing*, 8(5):84–93, Sept-Oct 2004.

14. T. D. Nguyen and N. Jennings. Coordinating multiple concurrent negotiations. In *Proc. Third International Joint Conference on Autonomous Agents and MultiAgent Systems (AAMAS'04)*, pages 1064–1071, New York,USA, 2004. ACM.

15. Lin Padgham and Patrick Lambrix. Agent capabilities: Extending BDI theory. In *AAAI/IAAI*, pages 68–73, 2000.

16. G. Petrone. Managing flexible interaction with web services. In *Proc. Workshop on Web Services and Agent-based Engineering (WSABE 2003)*, pages 41–47, Melbourne, Australia, 2003.

17. C. Preist. A conceptual architecture for semantic web services. In *Proceedings of the Third International Semantic Web Conference 2004 (ISWC2004)*, Hiroshima,Japan, 2004.

18. S. Ran. A model for web services discovery with qos. *ACM SIGecom Exchanges*, 4(1):1–10, 2003.

19. A. S. Rao and M. P. Georgeff. BDI-agents: from theory to practice. In *Proceedings of the First Intl. Conference on Multiagent Systems*, San Francisco, 1995.

20. Tuomas Sandholm and N. Vulkan. Bargaining with deadlines. In *Proc. National Conference on Artificial Intelligence (AAAI)*, pages 44–51, Orlando, FL, 1999.

21. Sandip Sen. Reciprocity; a foundational principle for promoting cooperative behavior among self-interested agents. In *Proc. International Conference on Multi-Agent Systems*, pages 322–329, Menlo Park, CA, 1996.

22. Devendra Shrotri and Michael N. Huhns. Formalization of multiagent commitments in a BDI_CTL framework. *USC CIT Technical Report TR-CIT05-02*, 2005.

23. Munindar P. Singh. Synthesizing coordination requirements for heterogeneous autonomous agents. *Autonomous Agents and Multi-Agent Systems*, 3(2):107–132, 2000.

24. Munindar P. Singh and Michael N. Huhns. Social abstractions for information agents. In Matthias Klusch, editor, *Intelligent Information Agents*, Boston, MA, 1999. Kluwer Academic Publishers.

25. Munindar P. Singh and Michael N. Huhns. *Service-Oriented Computing: Semantics, Processes, Agents*. Wiley, London, UK, 2005.

26. SWSA. Semantic web services architecture requirements. Semantic Web Services Initiative Architecture committee (SWSA). http://www.daml.org/services/swsa/swsa-requirements.html.

27. Mahadevan Venkatraman and Munindar P. Singh. Verifying compliance with commitment protocols. *Autonomous Agents and Multi-Agent Systems*, 2(3):217–236, 1999.

28. Jie Xing and Munindar P. Singh. Engineering commitment-based multiagent systems: A temporal logic approach. In *Proceedings of the Second International Joint Conference on Autonomous Agents and Multiagent Systems*, pages 891–898. ACM Press, 2003.

A Family of Graphical-Game-Based Algorithms for Distributed Constraint Optimization Problems

Rajiv T. Maheswaran[1], Jonathan P. Pearce[2], Milind Tambe[3]

[1] University of Southern California maheswar@usc.edu
[2] University of Southern California jppearce@usc.edu
[3] University of Southern California tambe@usc.edu

Summary. This paper addresses the application of distributed constraint optimization problems (DCOPs) to large-scale dynamic environments. We introduce a decomposition of DCOP into a graphical game and investigate the evolution of various stochastic and deterministic algorithms. We also develop techniques that allow for coordinated negotiation while maintaining distributed control of variables. We prove monotonicity properties of certain approaches and detail arguments about equilibrium sets that offer insight into the tradeoffs involved in leveraging efficiency and solution quality. The algorithms and ideas were tested and illustrated on several graph coloring domains.

1 Introduction

A distributed constraint optimization problem (DCOP) [8, 12] is a useful formalism in settings where distributed agents, each with control of some variables, attempt to optimize a global objective function characterized as the aggregation of distributed constraint utility functions. DCOP can be applied to many multiagent domains, including sensor nets, distributed spacecraft, disaster rescue simulations, and software personal assistant agents. For example, sensor agents may need to choose appropriate scanning regions to optimize targets tracked over the entire network or personal assistant agents may need to schedule multiple meetings in order to maximize the value of their users' time. As the scale of these domains become large, current complete algorithms incur immense computation costs. A large-scale network of personal assistant agents for instance, would require DCOP global optimization over hundreds of agents and thousands of variables, which is currently very expensive. On the other hand, if we let each agent or variable react on the basis of its local knowledge of neighbors and constraints utilities, we create a system that removes the necessity for tree-based communication structures and scales up very easily and is far more robust to dynamic environments.

Recognizing the importance of local search algorithms, researchers initially introduced DBA[13] and DSA[1] for Distributed CSPs, which were later extended to DCOPs with weighted constraints [14]. We refer to these as algorithms without coordination or *1-coordinated* algorithms. While detailed experimental analyses of these 1-coordination algorithms on DCOPs is available[14], we still lack theoretical tools that allow us to understand the evolution and performance of such algorithms on arbitrary DCOP problems. Our fundamental contribution in this paper is the decomposition of a DCOP into an equivalent graphical game. Current literature on graphical games considers general reward functions [3, 11] not necessarily tied to an underlying DCOP setting. This decomposition provides a framework for analysis of 1-coordinated algorithms and furthermore suggests an evolution to *k-coordinated* algorithms, where a collection of k agents coordinate their actions in a single negotiation round.

The paper is organized as follows. In Section 2, we present a formal model of the DCOP framework. In Section 3, we introduce a decomposition of the DCOP into a game, where the players are the variables whose utilities are aggregates of their outgoing constraint utilities. We prove that the optimal solution of the DCOP is a Nash equilibrium in an appropriate game. In Section 4, two algorithms that consider only unilateral modifications of values are presented. We prove monotonicity properties of one approach and discuss its significance. In Section 5, we devise two extensions to the unilateral algorithms that support coordinated actions and prove the monotonicity of one of the extensions, which indicates justification for improved solution quality. In Section 6, we discuss experiments and results and we conclude in Section 8.

2 DCOP: Distributed Constraint Optimization

We begin with a formal representation of a distributed constraint optimization problem and an exposition to our notational structure. Let $V \equiv \{v_i\}_{i=1}^{N}$ denote a set of variables, each of which can take a value $v_i = x_i \in X_i$, $i \in \mathcal{N} \equiv \{1, \ldots N\}$. Here, X_i will be a domain of finite cardinality $\forall i \in \mathcal{N}$. Interpreting each variable as a node in a graph, let the symmetric matrix E characterize a set of edges between variables/nodes such that $E_{ij} = E_{ji} = 1$ if an edge exists between v_i and v_j and $E_{ij} = E_{ji} = 0$, otherwise ($E_{ii} = 0 \ \forall i$). For each pair (i, j) such that $E_{ij} = 1$, let $U_{ij}(x_i, x_j) = U_{ji}(x_j, x_i)$ represent a reward obtained when $v_i = x_i$ and $v_j = x_j$. We can interpret this as a utility generated on the edge between v_i and v_j, contingent simultaneously on the values of both variables and hence referred to as a *constraint*. The global or team utility $\overline{U}(x)$ is the sum of the rewards on all the edges when the variables choose values according to the assignment $x \in X \equiv X_1 \times \cdots \times X_N$. Thus, the goal is to choose an assignment, $x^* \in X$, of values to variables such that

$$x^* \in \arg\max_{x \in X} \overline{U}(x) = \arg\max_{x \in X} \sum_{i,j:E_{ij}=1} U_{ij}(x_i, x_j)$$

where x_i is the i-th variable's value under an assignment vector $x \in X$. This constraint *optimization* problem completely characterized by (X, E, U), where U is the collection of constraint utility functions, becomes *distributed* in nature when control of the variables is partitioned among a set of autonomous agents. For the rest of this paper, we make the simplifying assumption that there are N agents, each in control of a single variable.

3 DCOP Games

Various complete algorithms [8] have been developed to solve a given DCOP. Though heuristics that significantly speed up convergence have been developed [6], the complexity is still prohibitive in large-scale domains. The tree-based communication structures are not robust to dynamics in problem structure. Finding a solution to a slightly modified problem requires a complete rerun which is expensive and may never terminate if the time-scale of the dynamics are faster than the time-scale of the complete algorithm.

Thus, we focus on non-hierarchical variable update strategies based on local information consisting of neighbors' values and constraint utility functions on outgoing edges. We remove the need to establish a parent-child relationship between nodes. Essentially, we are creating a game where the players are the variables, the actions are the choices of values and the information state is the context consisting of neighbor's values. The key design factor is how the local utility functions are constructed from the constraint utility functions. We present a particular decomposition of the DCOP (or equivalently a construction of local utility functions) below.

Let v_j be called a *neighbor* of v_i if $E_{ij} = 1$ and let $\mathcal{N}_i \equiv \{j : j \in \mathcal{N}, E_{ij} = 1\}$ be the indexes of all neighbors of the i-th variable. Let us define $x_{-i} \equiv [x_{j_1} \cdots x_{j_{K_i}}]$, hereby referred to as a *context*, be a tuple which captures the values assigned to the $K_i \equiv |\mathcal{N}_i|$ neighboring variables of the i-th variable, i.e. $v_{j_k} = x_{j_k}$ where $\cup_{k=1}^{K_i} j_k = \mathcal{N}_i$. We now define a local utility for the i-th agent (or equivalently the i-th variable) as follows:

$$u_i(x_i; x_{-i}) \equiv \alpha_i \sum_{j \in \mathcal{N}_i} U_{ij}(x_i, x_j)$$

where $\alpha_i > 0$. We now have a DCOP game defined by (X,E,u) where u is a collection of local utility functions. For simplicity, we will assume $\alpha_i = 1 \ \forall i \in \mathcal{N}$ in the rest of this paper, but all the results hold for arbitrary positive choice if α_i. This is the case because scaling the utility functions uniformly across all outgoing links does not change the global payoffs of any strategy, where a strategy is defined as a mapping from information state to action that maximizes local utility.

A *Nash equilibrium* assignment is a tuple of values $\hat{x} \in X$ where no agent can improve its local utility by unilaterally changing its value given its current context:

$$\hat{x}_i \in \arg\max_{x_i \in X_i} u_i(x_i; \hat{x}_{-i}), \ \forall i \in \mathcal{N}.$$

Given a DCOP game (X,E,u), let $X_{NE} \subseteq X$ be the subset of the assignment space which captures all Nash equilibrium assignments:

$$X_{NE} \equiv \{\hat{x} \in X : \hat{x}_i \in \arg\max_{x_i \in X_i} u_i(x_i; \hat{x}_{-i}), \ \forall i \in \mathcal{N}\}.$$

Proposition 1. *The assignment* x^* *which optimizes the DCOP characterized by* (X, E, U) *is also a Nash equilibrium with respect to the graphical game* (X, E, u).

Proof. Let us assume that x^* optimizes the DCOP (X, E, U) yet is not a Nash equilibrium assignment. Then, some agent can improve its local utility by altering the value of its variable. For some $n \in \mathcal{N}$ and $\hat{x}_n \neq x_n^*$, we have

$$u_n(\hat{x}_n; x_{-n}^*) > u_n(x_n^*; x_{-n}^*).$$

Let $\hat{x} = [x_1^* \cdots x_{n-1}^* \; \hat{x}_n \; x_{n+1}^* \cdots x_N^*]$. Then,

$$
\begin{aligned}
&\sum_{i,j:E_{ij}=1} U_{ij}(\hat{x}_i, \hat{x}_j) \\
&= \sum_{i,j:i \neq n, j \neq n, E_{ij}=1} U_{ij}(\hat{x}_i, \hat{x}_j) + \sum_{j:E_{nj}=1} U_{nj}(\hat{x}_n, \hat{x}_j) + \sum_{i:E_{in}=1} U_{in}(\hat{x}_i, \hat{x}_n) \\
&= \sum_{i,j:i \neq n, j \neq n, E_{ij}=1} U_{ij}(\hat{x}_i, \hat{x}_j) + 2u_i(\hat{x}_n; \hat{x}_{-n}) \\
&> \sum_{i,j:i \neq n, j \neq n, E_{ij}=1} U_{ij}(\hat{x}_i, \hat{x}_j) + 2u_i(x_n^*; x_{-n}^*) \\
&= \sum_{i,j:i \neq n, j \neq n, E_{ij}=1} U_{ij}(x_i^*, x_j^*) + 2u_i(x_n^*; x_{-n}^*) \\
&= \sum_{i,j:E_{ij}=1} U_{ij}(x_i^*, x_j^*)
\end{aligned}
$$

which implies that

$$x^* \notin \arg\max_{x \in X} \sum_{i,j:E_{ij}=1} U_{ij}(x_i, x_j)$$

which is a contradiction. ∎

Because we are optimizing over a finite set, we are guaranteed to have an assignment that yields a maximum. By the previous proposition, an assignment that yields a maximum is also a Nash equilibrium, thus, we are guaranteed the existence of a pure-strategy Nash equilibrium. This claim cannot be made for any arbitrary graphical game [3, 11]. Though it has been shown to exist in congestion games without unconditional independencies [10, 9], we have shown that the games derived from DCOPs have this property in a setting with unconditional independencies. The mapping to and from the underlying distributed constraint optimization problem yields additional structure. If there were only two variables, the agents controlling each variable would be coupled by the fact that they would receive identical payoffs from their constraint. In a general graph, DCOP-derived local utility functions reflect the amalgamation of multiple such couplings which reflects an inherent benefit to cooperation.

4 Algorithms without Coordination

Given this game-theoretic framework, how will agents' choices for values of their variables evolve over time? In a purely selfish environment, agents might be tempted to always react to the current context with the action that optimizes their local utility, but this behavior can lead to an unstable system [5]. Imposing structure on the dynamics of updating values can lead to stability and to improved rates of convergence [4]. We begin with algorithms that only consider unilateral actions by agents in a given context. The first is the MGM (Maximum Gain Message) Algorithm which is a modification of DBA (Distributed Breakout Algorithm) [13] focused solely on gain message passing. DBA cannot be directly applied because there is no global knowledge of solution quality which is necessary to detect local minima. The second is DSA (Distributed Stochastic Algorithm) [1], which is a homogeneous stationary randomized algorithm. Our analysis will focus on synchronous applications of these algorithms.

Let us define a *round* as the duration to execute one run of a particular algorithm. This run could involve multiple broadcasts of *messages*. Every time a messaging phase occurs in a round, we will count that as one *cycle* and cycles will be our performance metric for speed, as is common in DCOP literature. Let $x^{(n)} \in X$ denote the assignments at the beginning of the n-th round. We assume that every algorithm will broadcast its current value to all its neighbors at the beginning of the round taking up one cycle. Once agents are aware of their current contexts, they will go through a process as determined by the specific algorithm to decide which of them will be able to modify their value. Let $M^{(n)} \subseteq \mathcal{N}$ denote the set of agents allowed to modify the values in the n-th round. For MGM, each agent broadcasts a gain message to all its neighbors that represents the maximum change in its local utility if it is allowed to act under the current context. An agent is then allowed to act if its gain message is larger than all the gain messages it receives from all its neighbors (ties can be broken through variable ordering or another method). For DSA, each agent generates a random number from a uniform distribution on $[0, 1]$ and acts if that number is less than some threshold p. We note that MGM has a cost of two cycles per round while DSA only has a cost of one cycle per round. Through our game-theoretic framework, we are able to prove the following monotonicity property of MGM.

Proposition 2. *When applying MGM, the global utility $\overline{U}(x^{(n)})$ is strictly increasing with respect to the round (n) until $x^{(n)} \in X_{NE}$.*

Proof. We assume $M^{(n)} \neq \emptyset$, otherwise we would be at a Nash equilibrium. When utilizing MGM, if $i \in M^{(n)}$ and $E_{ij} = 1$, then $j \notin M^{(n)}$. If the i-th variable is allowed to modify its value in a particular round, then its gain is higher than all its neighbors gains. Consequently, all its neighbors would have received a gain message higher than their own and thus, would not modify their values in that round. Because there exists at least one neighbor for every variable, the set of agents who cannot modify their values is not empty: $M^{(n)^C} \neq \emptyset$. We have $x_i^{(n+1)} \neq x_i^{(n)} \ \forall i \in M^{(n)}$ and $x_i^{(n+1)} = x_i^{(n)} \ \forall i \notin M^{(n)}$. Also, $u_i(x_i^{(n+1)}; x_{-i}^{(n)}) > u_i(x_i^{(n)}; x_{-i}^{(n)}) \ \forall i \in M^{(n)}$, otherwise the i-th player's gain message would have been zero. Looking at the global utility, we have

$$\overline{U}\left(x^{(n+1)}\right)$$

$$= \sum_{i,j:E_{ij}=1} U_{ij}\left(x_i^{(n+1)},x_j^{(n+1)}\right)$$

$$= \sum_{\substack{i,j:i\in M^{(n)},\\ j\in M^{(n)},E_{ij}=1}} U_{ij}\left(x_i^{(n+1)},x_j^{(n+1)}\right) + \sum_{\substack{i,j:i\in M^{(n)},\\ j\notin M^{(n)},E_{ij}=1}} U_{ij}\left(x_i^{(n+1)},x_j^{(n+1)}\right)$$

$$+ \sum_{\substack{i,j:i\notin M^{(n)},\\ j\in M^{(n)},E_{ij}=1}} U_{ij}\left(x_i^{(n+1)},x_j^{(n+1)}\right) + \sum_{\substack{i,j:i\notin M^{(n)},\\ j\notin M^{(n)},E_{ij}=1}} U_{ij}\left(x_i^{(n+1)},x_j^{(n+1)}\right)$$

$$= \sum_{\substack{i,j:i\in M^{(n)},\\ j\notin M^{(n)},E_{ij}=1}} U_{ij}\left(x_i^{(n+1)},x_j^{(n)}\right) + \sum_{\substack{i,j:i\notin M^{(n)},\\ j\in M^{(n)},E_{ij}=1}} U_{ij}\left(x_i^{(n)},x_j^{(n+1)}\right) + \sum_{\substack{i,j:i\notin M^{(n)},\\ j\notin M^{(n)},E_{ij}=1}} U_{ij}\left(x_i^{(n)},x_j^{(n)}\right)$$

$$= \sum_{i\in M^{(n)}} u_i\left(x_i^{(n+1)};x_{-i}^{(n)}\right) + \sum_{j\in M^{(n)}} u_j\left(x_j^{(n+1)};x_{-j}^{(n)}\right) + \sum_{\substack{i,j:i\notin M^{(n)},\\ j\notin M^{(n)},E_{ij}=1}} U_{ij}\left(x_i^{(n)},x_j^{(n)}\right)$$

$$> \sum_{i\in M^{(n)}} u_i\left(x_i^{(n)};x_{-i}^{(n)}\right) + \sum_{j\in M^{(n)}} u_j\left(x_j^{(n)};x_{-j}^{(n)}\right) + \sum_{\substack{i,j:i\notin M^{(n)},\\ j\notin M^{(n)},E_{ij}=1}} U_{ij}\left(x_i^{(n)},x_j^{(n)}\right)$$

$$= \sum_{\substack{i,j:i\in M^{(n)},\\ j\notin M^{(n)},E_{ij}=1}} U_{ij}\left(x_i^{(n)},x_j^{(n)}\right) + \sum_{\substack{i,j:i\notin M^{(n)},\\ j\in M^{(n)},E_{ij}=1}} U_{ij}\left(x_i^{(n)},x_j^{(n)}\right) + \sum_{\substack{i,j:i\notin M^{(n)},\\ j\notin M^{(n)},E_{ij}=1}} U_{ij}\left(x_i^{(n)},x_j^{(n)}\right)$$

$$= \overline{U}\left(x^{(n)}\right).$$

The second equality is due to a partition of the summation indexes. The third equality utilizes the properties that there are no neighbors in $M^{(n)}$ and that the values for variables corresponding to indexes not in $M^{(n)}$ in the $(n+1)$-th round are identical to the values in the n-th round. The strict inequality occurs because agents in $M^{(n)}$ must be making local utility gains. The remaining equalities are true by definition. Thus, MGM yields monotonically increasing global utility until equilibrium. ∎

Why is monotonicity important? In anytime domains where communication may be halted arbitrarily and existing strategies must be executed, randomized algorithms risk being terminated at highly undesirable assignments. Given a starting condition with a minimum acceptable global utility, monotonic algorithms guarantee lower bounds on performance in anytime environments. Consider the following example.

Example 1. **The Traffic Light Game.** Consider two variables, both of which can take on the values *red* or *green*, with a constraint that takes on utilities as follows: $U(red,red)=0, U(red,green)=U(green,red)=1, U(green,green)=-1000$. Turning this DCOP into a game would require the agent for each variable to take the utility of the single constraint as its local utility. If (red,red) is the initial condition, each agent would choose to alter its value to *green* if· given the opportunity to move. If both agents are allowed to alter their value in the same round, we would end up in the adverse state *(green, green)*. When using DSA, there is always a positive probability for any time horizon that *(green, green)* will be the resulting assignment.

In domains such as independent path planning of trajectories for UAVs or rovers, in environments where communication channels are unstable, bad assignments could lead to crashes whose costs preclude the use of methods without guarantees. This is illustrated in Figure 1 which displays sample trajectories for MGM and DSA with identical starting conditions for a high-stakes scenario described in Section 6. The performance of both MGM and DSA with respect to a various graph coloring problems are investigated and discussed in Section 6.

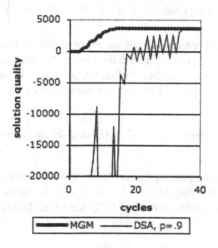

Fig. 1. Sample Trajectories of MGM and DSA for a High-Stakes Scenario

5 Algorithms with Coordination

When applying algorithms without coordination, the evolution of the assignments will terminate at a Nash equilibrium point within the set X_{NE} described earlier. One method to improve the solution quality is for agents to coordinate actions with their neighbors. This allows the evolution to follow a richer space of trajectories and alters the set of terminal assignments. In this section we introduce two *2-coordinated* algorithms, where agents can coordinate actions with one other agent. Let us refer to the set of terminal states of the class of *2-coordinated* algorithms as X_{2E}, i.e. neither a unilateral nor a bilateral modification of values will increase sum of all constraint utilities connected to the acting agent(s) if $x \in X_{2E}$. We will call X_{2E} the set of *2-equilibria* and X_{NE} the set of *1-equilibria*. Clearly the terminal states of a coordinated algorithm will depend on what metric the coordinating agents will use to determine if a particular joint action is acceptable or not. In a team setting (and in our analysis), a joint action that increases the sum of the utilities of the acting agents is considered acceptable, even if a single agent may see a loss in utility. This would be true in a purely selfish environment as well, if agents could compensate each other for possible losses in utility. An alternative choice would be to make a joint action acceptable only if both agents see utility gains. We consider the former notion of an acceptable joint action and define the terminal states as follows:

$$X_{2E} = \left\{ \hat{x} : (\hat{x}_i, \hat{x}_j) = \arg\max_{(x_i, x_j)} \left\{ u_i(x_i; \mu_{-i}(x_j, \hat{x}_{-ij})) \right. \right.$$

$$\left. \left. + u_j(x_j; \mu_{-j}(x_i, \hat{x}_{-ji})) \right\}, \ \forall i, j \in \mathcal{N}, i \neq j \right\}$$

where x_{-ij} is a tuple consisting of all values of variables except the i-th and j-th variable, and $\mu_{-i}(x_j, x_{-ji})$ is a function that converts its arguments into an appropriate vector of the form of x_{-i} described earlier, i.e. μ_{-i} takes values from the variables indexed by $\{j\} \cup \{\mathcal{N} \setminus \{i \cup j\}\}$ to a vector composed of the variables indexed by $\mathcal{N}_{-i}$.

Proposition 3. *For a given DCOP (X, E, U) and its equivalent game (X, E, u), we have $X_{2E} \subseteq X_{NE}$.*

Proof. We show this by proving the contrapositive. Suppose $x \notin X_{NE}$. Then, there exists a variable i such that $u_i(\hat{x}_i; x_{-i}) > u_i(x_i; x_{-i})$ for some $\hat{x}_i \neq x_i$. This further implies that there exists some variable $j \in \mathcal{N}_i$, for which $U_{ij}(\hat{x}_i, x_j) > U_{ij}(x_i, x_j)$. We then have

$$u_i(\hat{x}_i; \mu_{-i}(x_j, x_{-ij})) > u_i(x_i; \mu_{-i}(x_j, x_{-ij})) \quad \text{and} \quad u_j(x_j; \mu_{-j}(\hat{x}_i, x_{-ji})) > u_j(x_j; \mu_{-j}(x_i, x_{-ij}))$$

which implies that $x \notin X_{2E}$. ∎

Essentially, we are saying that a unilateral move which improves the utility of a single agent must improve the constraint utility of at least one link which further implies that the local utility of another agent must also increase given that the rest of its context remains the same. The interesting phenomenon is that our definition of X_{2E} above is sufficient to capture both unilateral and bilateral deviations within the context of bilateral deviations. This is due to the underlying DCOP structure and would not be true in a general game. If we wanted the terminal set of 2-coordinated assignments to be a strict subset of the Nash equilibrium set in a general game, we would have to augment the definition of X_{2E} to specifically include the $\hat{x}_i \in \arg\max_{x_i \in X_i} u_i(x_i; \hat{x}_{-i})$, $\forall i \in \mathcal{N}$ condition, as it is possible that there exists a local utility improvements due to a unilateral action that does not lead to a combined utility improvement for the acting agent and any neighbor.

It has been proposed that coordinated actions be achieved by forming coalitions among variables. In [2], each coalition was represented by a *manager* who made the assignment decisions for all variables within the coalition. These methods inherently undermine the distributed nature of the decision-making by essentially replacing multiple variables with a single variable in the graph. It is not possible in all situations for this to occur because utility function information and the ability to communicate with the necessary neighbors may not be transferable (due to infeasibility or preference). We introduce two algorithms that allow for coordination while maintaining the underlying distributed decision making process and the same constraint graph: MGM-2 (Maximum Gain Message-2) and SCA-2 (Stochastic Coordination Algorithm-2).

Both MGM-2 and SCA-2 begin a round with agents broadcasting their current values. The first step in both algorithms is to decide which subset of agents are allowed to make *offers*. We resolve this by randomization, as each agent generates a random number uniformly from $[0, 1]$ and considers themselves to be an *offerer* if the random number is below a threshold q. If an agent is an offerer, it cannot accept offers from other agents. All agents who are not offerers are considered to be *receivers*. Each offerer will choose a neighbor at random (uniformly) and send it an offer message which consists of all coordinated moves between the offerer and receiver that will yield a gain in local utility to the offerer under the current context. The offer message will contain both the suggested values for each player and the offerer's local utility gain for each value pair. Each receiver will then calculate the global utility gain for each value pair in the offer message by adding the offerer's local utility gain to it's own utility change under the new context and (very importantly) subtracting the difference in the link between the two so it is not counted twice. If the maximum global gain over all offered value pairs is positive, the receiver will send an *accept* message to the offerer with the appropriate value pair and both the offerer and receiver are considered to be committed. Otherwise, it sends a *reject* message to the offerer, and neither agent is committed.

At this point, the algorithms diverge. For SCA-2, any agent who is not committed and can make a local utility gain with a unilateral move generates a random number uniformly from $[0, 1]$ and considers themselves to be *active* if the number is under a threshold p. At the end of the round, all committed agents change their values to the committed offer and all active agents change their values according to their unilateral best response. Thus, SCA-2 requires three cycles (value, offer, accept/reject) per round. In MGM-2 (after the offers and replies are settled), each agent sends a gain message to all its neighbors. Uncommitted agents send their best local utility gain for a unilateral move. Committed agents send the global gain for their coordinated move. Uncommitted agents follow the same procedure as in MGM, where they modify their value if their gain message was larger than all the gain messages they received. Committed agents send their partners a *go* message if all the gain messages they received were less than the calculated global gain for the coordinated move and send a *no-go* message, otherwise. A committed agent will only modify its value if it receives a go message from its partner. We note that MGM-2 requires five cycles (value, offer, accept/reject, gain, go/no-go) per round. Given the excess cost of MGM-2, why would one choose to apply it? We can show that MGM-2 is monotonic in global utility.

Proposition 4. *When applying MGM-2, the global utility* $\overline{U}(x^{(n)})$ *is strictly increasing with respect to the round (n) until* $x^{(n)} \in X_{2E}$.

Proof. We begin by introducing some notation. At the end of the n-th round, let $C^{(n)} \subset \mathcal{N}$ denote the set of agents who are committed, $M^{(n)} \subset \mathcal{N}$ denote the set of uncommitted agents who are active, and $S^{(n)} \equiv \{C^{(n)} \cup M^{(n)}\}^C \subset \mathcal{N}$ denote the uncommitted agents who are inactive. Let $p(i) \in C^{(n)}$ denote the partner of a committed agent $i \in C^{(n)}$. The global utility can then be expressed as:

$$\overline{U}\left(x^{(n+1)}\right)$$

$$= \sum_{i,j:E_{ij}=1} U_{ij}\left(x_i^{(n+1)},x_j^{(n+1)}\right)$$

$$= \sum_{\substack{i,j:i\in C^{(n)},\\ j\in C^{(n)},E_{ij}=1}} U_{ij}\left(x_i^{(n+1)},x_j^{(n+1)}\right) + \sum_{\substack{i,j:i\in C^{(n)},\\ j\in S^{(n)},E_{ij}=1}} U_{ij}\left(x_i^{(n+1)},x_j^{(n+1)}\right)$$

$$+ \sum_{\substack{i,j:i\in S^{(n)},\\ j\in C^{(n)},E_{ij}=1}} U_{ij}\left(x_i^{(n+1)},x_j^{(n+1)}\right) + \sum_{\substack{i,j:i\in S^{(n)},\\ j\in S^{(n)},E_{ij}=1}} U_{ij}\left(x_i^{(n+1)},x_j^{(n+1)}\right)$$

$$+ \sum_{\substack{i,j:i\in M^{(n)},\\ j\in S^{(n)},E_{ij}=1}} U_{ij}\left(x_i^{(n+1)},x_j^{(n+1)}\right) + \sum_{\substack{i,j:i\in S^{(n)},\\ j\in M^{(n)},E_{ij}=1}} U_{ij}\left(x_i^{(n+1)},x_j^{(n+1)}\right)$$

$$= \sum_{i\in C^{(n)}} U_{ip(i)}\left(x_i^{(n+1)},x_{p(i)}^{(n+1)}\right) + \sum_{i\in C^{(n)}}\sum_{j\in \mathcal{N}_i\setminus\{p(i)\}} U_{ij}\left(x_i^{(n+1)},x_j^{(n+1)}\right)$$

$$+ \sum_{j\in C^{(n)}}\sum_{i\in \mathcal{N}_j\setminus\{p(j)\}} U_{ij}\left(x_i^{(n+1)},x_j^{(n+1)}\right) + \sum_{j\in C^{(n)}} U_{jp(j)}\left(x_{p(j)}^{(n+1)},x_j^{(n+1)}\right)$$

$$- \sum_{j\in C^{(n)}} U_{jp(j)}\left(x_{p(j)}^{(n+1)},x_j^{(n+1)}\right) + \sum_{\substack{i,j:i\in S^{(n)},\\ j\in S^{(n)},E_{ij}=1}} U_{ij}\left(x_i^{(n+1)},x_j^{(n+1)}\right)$$

$$+ \sum_{i\in M^{(n)}} u_i\left(x_i^{(n+1)},x_j^{(n+1)}\right) + \sum_{j\in M^{(n)}} u_j\left(x_i^{(n+1)},x_j^{(n+1)}\right)$$

$$= \sum_{i\in C^{(n)}} U_{ip(i)}\left(x_i^{(n+1)},x_{p(i)}^{(n+1)}\right) + \sum_{i\in C^{(n)}}\sum_{j\in \mathcal{N}_i\setminus\{p(i)\}} U_{ij}\left(x_i^{(n+1)},x_j^{(n)}\right)$$

$$+ \sum_{j\in C^{(n)}}\sum_{i\in \mathcal{N}_j\setminus\{p(j)\}} U_{ij}\left(x_i^{(n+1)},x_j^{(n)}\right) + \sum_{j\in C^{(n)}} U_{jp(j)}\left(x_{p(j)}^{(n+1)},x_j^{(n+1)}\right)$$

$$- \sum_{j\in C^{(n)}} U_{jp(j)}\left(x_{p(j)}^{(n+1)},x_j^{(n+1)}\right) + \sum_{\substack{i,j:i\in S^{(n)},\\ j\in S^{(n)},E_{ij}=1}} U_{ij}\left(x_i^{(n)},x_j^{(n)}\right) +$$

$$+ \sum_{i\in M^{(n)}} u_i\left(x_i^{(n+1)},x_j^{(n)}\right) + \sum_{j\in M^{(n)}} u_j\left(x_i^{(n)},x_j^{(n+1)}\right)$$

$$= \sum_{i \in C^{(n)}} u_i(x_i^{(n+1)}; \mu_{-i}(x_{p(i)}^{(n+1)}, x_{-ip(i)}^{(n)})) + \sum_{j \in C^{(n)}} u_j(x_j^{(n+1)}; \mu_{-j}(x_{p(j)}^{(n+1)}, x_{-jp(j)}^{(n)}))$$

$$- \sum_{j \in C^{(n)}} U_{jp(j)}\left(x_{p(j)}^{(n+1)}, x_j^{(n+1)}\right) + \sum_{\substack{i,j:i \in S^{(n)}, \\ j \in S^{(n)}, E_{ij}=1}} U_{ij}\left(x_i^{(n)}, x_j^{(n)}\right)$$

$$+ \sum_{i \in M^{(n)}} u_i\left(x_i^{(n+1)}, x_j^{(n)}\right) + \sum_{j \in M^{(n)}} u_j\left(x_i^{(n)}, x_j^{(n+1)}\right)$$

$$> \sum_{i \in C^{(n)}} u_i(x_i^{(n)}; \mu_{-i}(x_{p(i)}^{(n)}, x_{-ip(i)}^{(n)})) + \sum_{j \in C^{(n)}} u_j(x_j^{(n)}; \mu_{-j}(x_{p(j)}^{(n)}, x_{-jp(j)}^{(n)}))$$

$$- \sum_{j \in C^{(n)}} U_{jp(j)}\left(x_{p(j)}^{(n)}, x_j^{(n)}\right) + \sum_{\substack{i,j:i \in S^{(n)}, \\ j \in S^{(n)}, E_{ij}=1}} U_{ij}\left(x_i^{(n)}, x_j^{(n)}\right)$$

$$+ \sum_{i \in M^{(n)}} u_i\left(x_i^{(n)}, x_j^{(n)}\right) + \sum_{j \in M^{(n)}} u_j\left(x_i^{(n)}, x_j^{(n)}\right) = \overline{U}\left(x^{(n)}\right).$$

The first equality is by definition. The second equality partitions the indexes into update class, eliminating cross indexes of $M^{(n)}$ with anything other than $S^{(n)}$. In the third equality, we simplify the summations involving committed agents using expressions for partners and neighbors, we insert a zero value term in parenthesis, and transform the summations involving active agents into local utilities. In the fourth equality, we modify the round index for those agents who are inactive. In the fifth equality, we transform the summations involving committed agents into local utilities. The inequality is due to the fact that the global utility on the links of the committed partners and the local utility of the active agents must increase due to the positive gain messages. The key is that by setting $j = p(i)$ in the second and third summations, we recover the gain message of the committed teams. Note the subtraction of the utility gain on the link between partners to avoid double counting. The final equality can be achieved by reversing the transformation to yield the global utility at the previous round. Thus, MGM-2 yields monotonically increasing global utility until equilibrium is reached. ∎

Example 2. **Meeting Scheduling.** Consider two agents trying to schedule a meeting at either 7:00 AM or 1:00 PM with the constraint utility as follows: $U(7,7) = 1, U(7,1) = U(1,7) = -100, U(1,1) = 10$. If the agents started at $(7,7)$, any 1-coordinated algorithm would not be able to reach the global optimum, while 2-coordinated algorithms would.

It is not obvious that 2-coordinated algorithm will yield a solution with higher quality than a 1-coordinated algorithm in all situations. In fact, there are DCOPs and initial conditions for which a 1-coordinated algorithm will yield a better solution than a 2-coordinated algorithm. The complexity lies in that we cannot predict exactly what trajectory the evolution will follow. However, due the proposition above we can have some confidence that 2-coordinated algorithms will perform better on average as outlined in the following corollary.

Corollary 1. *For every initial condition $x_0 \in X_{NE} \setminus X_{2E}$, MGM-2 will yield a better solution than either MGM or DSA.*

Proof. Since $x_0 \in X_{NE}$, neither MGM nor DSA will move and the solution quality will be that obtained at the assignment x_0. However, since $x_0 \notin X_{2E}$, MGM-2 will continue to evolve from x_0 until it reaches an assignment in X_{2E}. Because $MGM - 2$ is monotonic in global utility, whatever solution in reaches in X_{2E} will have a higher global utility than x_0. ∎

Thus, MGM-2 dominates DSA and MGM for initial conditions in $X_{NE} \setminus X_{2E}$ and is identical to DSA and MGM on X_{2E} (as neither algorithm will evolve from there). The unknown is the behavior on $X \setminus X_{NE}$. It is difficult to analyze this space because one cannot pinpoint the trajectories due to the probabilistic nature of their evolution. If we assume that iterations beginning in $X \setminus X_{NE}$ are taken to points in X_{NE} in a relatively uniform manner on average with all algorithms, then we might surmise that the dominance of MGM-2 should yield a better solution quality. The performance of both MGM-2 and SCA-2 with respect to a various graph coloring problems are investigated and discussed in Section 6.

6 Experiments

We considered three different domains for our experiments. The first was a standard graph-coloring scenario, in which a cost of one is incurred if two neighboring agents choose the same color, and no cost is incurred otherwise. Real-world problems involving sensor networks, in which it may be undesirable for neighboring sensors to be observing the same location, are commonly mapped to this type of graph-coloring scenario. The second was a fully randomized DCOP, in which every combination of values on a constraint between two neighboring agents was assigned a random reward chosen uniformly from the set $\{1, \ldots, 10\}$. In both of these domains, we considered ten randomly generated graphs with forty variables, three values per variable, and 120 constraints. For each graph, we ran 100 runs of each algorithm, with a randomized start state. The third domain was chosen to simulate a high-stakes scenario, in which miscoordination is very costly. In this enviroment, agents are negotiating over the use of resources. If two agents decide to use the same resource, the result could be catastrophic. An example of such a scenario might be a set of unmanned aerial vehicles (UAVs) negotiating over sections of airspace, or rovers negotiating over sections of terrain. In this domain, if two neighboring agents take the same value, there is a large penalty incurred (-1000). If two neighboring agents take different values, they obtain a reward chosen uniformly from $\{10, \ldots, 100\}$. Because miscoordination is costly, we introduced a *safe* (zero) value for all agents. An agent with this value is not using any resource. If two neighboring agents choose zero as their values, neither a reward nor a penalty is obtained. In such a high-stakes scenario, a randomized start state would be a poor choice, especially for an anytime algorithm, as it would likely contain many of the large penalties. So, rather than using randomized start states, all agents started with the zero value. However, if all agents start

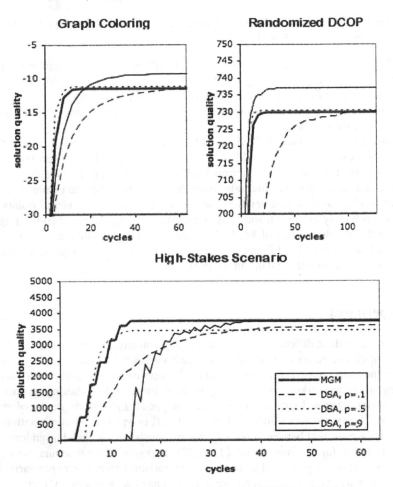

Fig. 2. Comparison of the performance of MGM and DSA

at zero, then DSA and MGM would be useless, since no agent would ever want to move alone. So, a reward of one was introduced for the case where one agent has the zero value, and its neighbor has a nonzero value. In the high-stakes domain, we also performed 100 runs on each of 10 randomly generated graphs with forty variables and 120 constraints, but due to the addition of the safe value, the agents in these experiments had four possible values.

For each of the three domains, we ran: MGM, DSA with $p \in \{0.1, 0.3, 0.5, 0.7, 0.9\}$, MGM-2 with $q \in \{0.1, 0.3, 0.5, 0.7, 0.9\}$ and SCA-2 with all combinations of the above values of p and q (where q is the probability of being an offerer and p is the probability of an uncommited agent acting). Each table shows an average of 100 runs on ten randomly generated examples with some selected values of p and q. Although

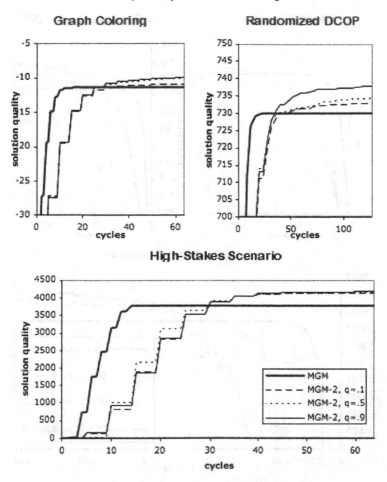

Fig. 3. Comparison of the performance of MGM and MGM-2

each run was for 256 cycles, most of the graphs display a cropped view, to show the important phenomena.

Figure 2 shows a comparison between MGM and DSA for several values of p. For graph coloring, MGM is dominated, first by DSA with $p = 0.5$, and then by DSA with $p = 0.9$. For the randomized DCOP, MGM is completely dominated by DSA with $p = 0.9$. MGM does better in the high-stakes scenario as all DSA algorithms have a negative solution quality (not shown in the graph) for the first few cycles. This happens because at the beginning of a run, almost every agent will want to move. As the value of p increases, more agents act simultaneously, and thus, many pairs of neighbors are choosing the same value, causing large penalties. Thus, these results show that the nature of the constraint utility function makes a fundamental difference in which algorithm dominates. Results from the high-stakes scenario contrast with

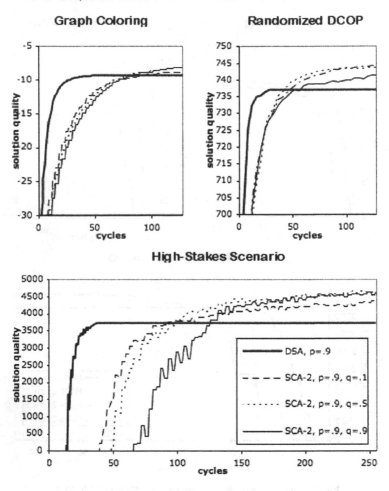

Fig. 4. Comparison of the performance of DSA and SCA-2

[14] and show that DSA is not necessarily the algorithm of choice when compared with DBA across all domains.

Figure 3 shows a comparison between MGM and MGM-2, for several values of q. In all domains, MGM-2 eventually reaches a higher solution quality after about thirty cycles, despite the algorithms' initial slowness. The stair-like shape of the MGM-2 curves is due to the fact that agents are changing values only once out of every five cycles, due to the cycles used in communication. Of the three values of q shown in the graphs, MGM-2 rises fastest when $q = 0.5$, but eventually reaches its highest average solution quality when $q = 0.9$, for each of the three domains. We note that, in the high-stakes domain, the solution quality is positive at every cycle, due to the monotonic property of both MGM and MGM-2. Thus, these experiments clearly verify the monotonicity of MGM and MGM-2, and also show that MGM-2 reaches a higher solution quality as expected.

Figure 4 shows a comparison between DSA and SCA-2, for $p = 0.9$ and several values of q. DSA starts out faster, but SCA-2 eventually overtakes it. The result of the effect of q on SCA-2 appears inconclusive. Although SCA-2 with $q = 0.9$ does not achieve a solution quality above zero for the first 65 cycles, it eventually achieves a solution quality comparable to SCA with lower values of q.

Figure 5 contains a graph and a pie-chart for each of the three domains, providing a deeper justification for the improved solution quality of MGM-2 and SCA-2. The graph shows a probability mass function (PMF) of solution quality for three sets of assignments: the set of all assignments in the DCOP (X), the set of 1-equilibria (X_{NE}), and the set of 2-equilibria (X_{2E}). Here we considered scenarios with twelve variables, 36 constraints, and three values per variable (four for the high-stakes scenario to include the zero value) in order to investigate tractably explorable domains. In all three domains, the solution quality of the set of 2-equilibria (the set of equilibria to which MGM-2 and SCA-2 must converge) is, on average, higher than the set of 1-equilibria. In the high-stakes DCOP, 99.5% of assignments have a value less than zero (not shown on the graph.)

The pie chart shows the proportion of the number of 2-equilibria to the number of 1-equilibria that are not also 2-equilibria. Notice that in the case of the randomized DCOP, most 1-equilibria are also 2-equilibria. Therefore, there is very little difference between the PMFs of the two sets of equilibria on the corresponding graph. We also note that the phase transition mentioned in [14] (where DSA's performance degrades for $p > 0.8$) is not replicated in our results. In fact, our solution quality gets better as $p > 0.8$, though with slower convergence.

7 Related Work

Algorithms for solving DCOPs are generally divided into two categories. Complete algorithms, such as Adopt[8] and OptAPO[7], are guaranteed to converge to an optimal solution. However, their comparatively long runtime, as well as other properties, such as Adopt's requirement that agents be organized in a depth-first-search tree or OptAPO's requirement that all agents reveal all their constraints to their neighbors, ensures that incomplete DCOP algorithms, including those presented here, will be preferred in many domains.

For incomplete DCOP algorithms, this paper provides a complement to recent experimental analysis of DSA and DBA[14] on graph coloring problems. The cited work provides insight into the effects of the choice between randomized and deterministic 1-coordinated algorithms on solution quality and convergence time, showing randomized algorithms to be the preferred choice in general. In contrast, this paper provides theoretical justifications for both monotonicity and 2-coordination, as well as providing new 2-coordinated algorithms, based on DSA and DBA, and experimental analysis of the new algorithms' performance. In addition, we show that

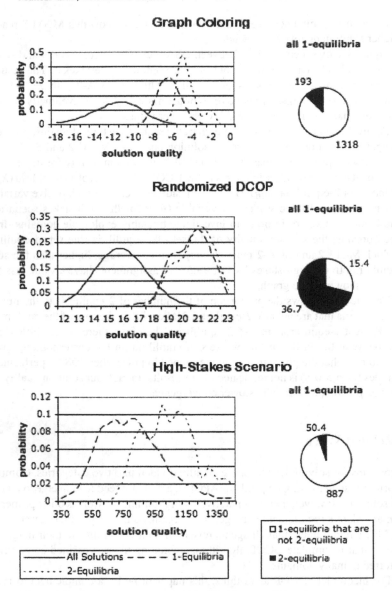

Fig. 5. The graphs show a comparison of the distribution of solution quality among the complete set of solutions, the set of 1-equilibria, and the set of 2-equilbria. The pie charts show the proportion of 1-equilibria that are also 2-equilibria.

randomized algorithms, while efficient, are not ideal for all domains, particularly in high-stakes, anytime scenarios.

In [7] and [2], coordination was achieved by forming coalitions represented by a *manager* or *mediator* who made the assignment decisions for all variables within the coalition. These methods require high-volume communication to transfer utility function information and the abdication of authority from one agent to another, which can be infeasible or undesirable in many distributed decision-making environments. Furthermore, in [2], the cost of forming a coalition may discourage rapid commitment and detachment from teams. MGM-2 and SCA-2, however, allow for coordination while maintaining the underlying distributed decision-making process and allowing dynamic teaming in each round.

Finally, also related is research in general graphical games, which has focused on centralized algorithms for finding mixed-strategy Nash equilibria [3, 11]. In contrast, distributed algorithms based on DCOP games are guaranteed to result at least in pure-strategy Nash equilibria (1-equilibria), but may also introduce 2-coordination and hence 2-equilibria.

8 Conclusions

The key contributions of this paper include: (i) a decomposition of a DCOP into an equivalent graphical game, (ii) the proof of monotonicity for MGM, a 1-coordinated algorithm, (ii) the development of 2-coordinated algorithms that maintain distributed control of variables, (iii) the proof of monotonicity of MGM-2, (iv) a theoretical analysis and comparison of the equilibria sets of algorithms of differing degrees of coordination, and (v) experimental verification and discovery when applying these algorithms to a variety of graph coloring problems. The key theoretical idea is that breaking a DCOP down to a game can lead to algorithms where we can guarantee strict improvement in global solution quality over time which is critical in anytime application in high-stakes environments. Also important is the idea of k-coordinated algorithms leading to progressively nested sets of equilibria, which yield both a higher average solution quality and a higher likelihood of obtaining the globally optimal solution. Through our experiments, we are able to show that randomized algorithms though very efficient are not ideal for all environments. Initial results imply that the nature of the constraint utility function makes a fundamental difference in the solution structure rather than the graph structure. Future work will entail development of distributed k-coordinated algorithms and deeper analysis of stochastic schemes to obtain analytic reasoning for choosing particular update rates. Also, it would be interesting to see if convergence rates can be reduced with the use of heterogeneous dynamic randomized algorithms.

References

1. S. Fitzpatrick and L. Meertens. Distributed coordination through anarchic optimization. In V. Lesser, C. L. Ortiz Jr., and M. Tambe, editors, *Distributed Sensor Networks: A*

Multiagent Perspective, pages 257–295. Kluwer, 2003.

2. K. Hirayama and J. Toyoda. Forming coalitions for breaking deadlocks. In *Proc. ICMAS*, pages 155–162, 1995.

3. M. Kearns, M. Littman, and S. Singh. Graphical models for game theory. In *Proc. UAI*, pages 253–260, 2001.

4. R. T. Maheswaran and T. Başar. Multi-user flow control as a Nash game: Performance of various algorithms. In *Proc. CDC*, Tampa, FL, December 1998.

5. R. T. Maheswaran and T. Başar. Decentralized network resource allocation as a repeated noncooperative market game. In *Proc. CDC*, Orlando, FL, December 2001.

6. R. T. Maheswaran, M. Tambe, E. Bowring, J. P. Pearce, and P. Varakantham. Taking DCOP to the real world: efficient complete solutions for distributed multi-event scheduling. In *AAMAS*, 2004.

7. R. Mailler and V. Lesser. Solving distributed constraint optimization problems using cooperative mediation. In *AAMAS*, 2004.

8. P. J. Modi, W. Shen, M. Tambe, and M. Yokoo. An asynchronous complete method for distributed constraint optimization. In *AAMAS*, 2003.

9. D. Monderer and L. S. Shapley. Potential games. *Games and Economic Behavior*, 14:124–143, 1996.

10. R. W. Rosenthal. A class of games possessing pure-stratgy Nash equilibria. *International Journal of Game Theory*, 2:65–67, 1973.

11. D. Vickrey and D. Koller. Multi-agent algorithms for solving graphical games. In *Proc. AAAI*, pages 345–351, 2002.

12. M. Yokoo, E. H. Durfee, T. Ishida, and K. Kuwabara. The distributed constraint satisfaction problem: formalization and algorithms. *IEEE Transactions on Knowledge and Data Engineering*, 10(5):673–685, 1998.

13. M. Yokoo and K. Hirayama. Distributed breakout algorithm for solving distributed constraint satisfaction and optimization problems. In *ICMAS*, 1996.

14. W. Zhang, Z. Xing, G. Wang, and L. Wittenburg. An analysis and application of distributed constraint satisfaction and optimization algorithms in sensor networks. In *AAMAS*, 2003.

Key-Based Coordination Strategies: Scalability Issues

Tom Wagner[1], John Phelps[2], Valerie Guralnik[2] and Ryan VanRiper[2]

DARPA-IPTO
Honeywell Labs

Summary. We describe a key-based approach to multi-agent coordination, where certain coordination decisions are done only when the agent holds a coordination key. This approach is primarily decentralized, but has some centralized aspects, including synchronization of coordination decisions and schedule information sharing. The approach is described within the context of the application requirements that motivated its development. Finally, its scalability properties are discussed.

1 Introduction

In this paper we examine an approach to multi-agent coordination in the context of two different multi-agent applications and discuss their response to scaling in the three coordination dimensions identified by Durfee [4]: agent population, task environment, and solution.

In the first application, agents with heterogeneous and interacting capabilities are coordinated. In the other, agents with homogenous capabilities are coordinated. The coordination solution to both problems is distributed. However, the use of a coordination "key" passed between agents introduces elements of centralization, including partial global sharing of schedule information and synchronization of coordination decisions.

Before we delve into the applications and specifics of their coordination protocols, it is worthwhile to ask the basic question of "what is coordination and when do we need it?" Typically a multi-agent systems (MAS) model of development is pursued when distributed processing and distributed control are required. As with other distributed processing models, one important problem of MAS research is how to obtain globally coherent behavior from the system when the agents operate autonomously and asynchronously. In general, when the agents share resources or the tasks being performed by the agents interact, the agents must explicitly work to coordinate their activities. Consider a simple physical example. Let two maintenance robots, R1 and R2, be assigned the joint task of moving a long table from one room to another. Let both robots also have an assortment of other independent activities that must be performed, e.g., sweeping the floor. Assume that neither robot can lift the table by him/herself. In order for the robots to move the table together they must coordinate their activities by 1) communicating to determine when each of the robots will be able to schedule the table moving activity, 2) possibly negotiating over the time at which they should move the table together, 3) agreeing on a time, 4) showing up at the table at the specified time, 5) lifting the table together, and so forth. This is an example of communication-based coordination that produces a temporal sequencing of activities enabling the robots to interact and carry out the joint task (over a shared resource – the table). Without the coordination process, it is unlikely that the table would ever be moved as desired unless the robots randomly decided to move the table at the same moment in time. Note that if the robots are designed to "watch" each other and "guess" when the other is going to move the table that this is an instance of coordination by plan inference and still counts as a coordination episode. In general, achieving global coherence in a MAS where tasks interact requires coordination.

In the robot/table example, the coordination episode is peer-to-peer. Imagine now a room full of maintenance robots, each having multiple joint tasks with other agents and all sharing physical resources such as tools and floorspace or X/Y coordinates. Without coordination said room full of robots would have much in common with a preschool "free play session" with robots moving about, unable to perform tasks due to obstacle avoidance systems always diverting them from their desired directions or due to the lack of a required tool. There are two primary ways to coordinate this room full of robots – either in a distributed peer-to-peer (or group to group) fashion or in a centralized fashion. When coordination is distributed each agent is responsible for determining when to interact with another agent and then having a dialog to determine how they should sequence their activities to achieve coherence. When coordination is centralized generally one agent plans for the others or manages a shared resource. Note that in the example above coordination focuses on *when* to perform a given task. Coordination can also be about *which* tasks to perform, *what resources* to use, *how* to perform a task, and so forth.

While the robot domain is good for illustrating conceptually the coordination problem, the need for coordination is not limited to robots. Software agents, humans, and systems composed of mixes of agents, humans, and robots [10] all have a need for some kind of coordination. When the tasks or activities of different parties interact, in a setting where control is distributed (parties are autonomous), coordination is needed.

We now examine two MAS applications, the coordination protocols that are used to achieve global coherence, and the scalability properties of each. One application, Dynamic Readiness and Repair Service, is a system for dynamic coordination of distributed aircraft service teams. The other application is a system for coordination of First Responder teams. Coordination requirements in these two systems are similar – achieve global coherence and do this in "real-time" (response time fast enough for the application). However, in these two systems the coordination solutions implemented are different and these differences are driven by the different characteristics of the underlying problem spaces.

DFOISR 05-S-1456

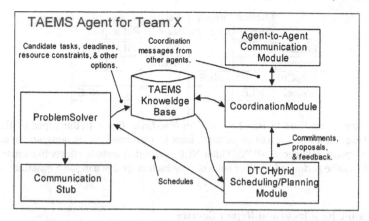

Fig. 1. A Single TÆMS-based Agent Ready to Coordinate Its Activities With Other Agents

2 Aircraft Service Team Coordination

2.1 The Application

We describe an agent-based solution to aircraft service team coordination called Dynamic Readiness and Repair Service[14]. For this application we employed GPGP-based [3, 2, 6] agent technologies to coordinate the aircraft service team activity. We compared the performance of the algorithm to a centralized scheduling oracle that generates optimal schedules for the teams.

2.2 TÆMS and TÆMS Agents

By establishing a domain independent language (TÆMS) for representing agent activity, we have been able to design and build a core set of agent construction components and reuse them on a variety of different applications (mentioned above). TÆMS agents are created by bundling our reusable technologies with a domain specific component, generally called a domain problem solver, that is responsible for knowing and encapsulating the details of a particular application domain.

It is sufficient to understand that TÆMS agents have components for scheduling and coordination that enable them to 1) reason about what they should be doing and when, 2) reason about the relative value of activities, 3) reason about temporal and resource constraints, and 4) reason about interactions between activities being carried out by different agents. A high-level view of a TÆMS agent is shown in Figure 1; everything except for the domain problem solver is reusable code. Note that each module is a research topic in its own right. The agent scheduler is the Design-to-Criteria [9, 13, 16] scheduler and the coordination module is derived from GPGP [2]. Other modules, e.g., learning, can be added to this architecture in a similar (conceptual) plug and play fashion.

DFOISR 05-S-1456

	Repair Engines	Repair Avionics	Repair WeapCtrl	Refuel	Rearm
Engines				NLE	NLE
Avionics			NLE		
WeapCtrl		NLE			
Refuel	NLE				NLE
Rearm	NLE			NLE	

Table 1. Tasks Interactions Indicated by *NLE* for *Non-Local Effect*. In this paper, NLEs are all mutual exclusion where tasks that interact cannot be performed on the same aircraft at the same time (spatial + temporal MUX). Other NLEs supported include effects like hindering where tasks can be performed together but will slow each other down in some quantified way.

2.3 Dynamic Readiness and Repair Service

For the Dynamic Readiness and Repair Service project we simulated aircraft returning from an engagement and needing repairs and readiness operations to be performed. Three types of aircraft are modeled in the prototype: F16s, A10s, and C9 surveillance craft. When an aircraft returns it is potentially in need of (to varying degrees): 1) fuel, 2) missiles, 3) repairs to engines, 4) repairs to cockpit avionics, or 5) repairs to cockpit weapons controls. Each incoming aircraft is assigned a deadline which is its take-off time for redeployment. Mission Control is responsible for assigning the deadline and for identifying the areas of the aircraft that need service.

There are five teams on the ground that repair, refuel and rearm the aircraft for their next mission. Each team is controlled by a coordination decision support agent that uses TÆMS agent technology to reason about what the team should be doing, when, and with which resources. In this scenario the following teams handle aircraft preparation: 1) refuel, 2) rearm (replaces depleted missiles), 3) avionics repair, 4) weapons controls repair, and 5) engines repair. As aircraft land the Mission Control agent notifies the service teams of the aircrafts' service needs and readiness deadlines. The agents then coordinate how best to select and sequence operations so that the most aircraft can be ready by their respective launch times. Not all problem instances given to the MAS contained fully satisfiable constraints.

The tasks required to repair an individual plane do not need to be performed in any specific sequence. However, there are sets of tasks that cannot be performed simultaneously because they involve the same spatial regions of the aircraft. For instance, the engines cannot be serviced while a plane is rearmed as both of these activities take place on or near the wings. In contrast, avionics can be serviced while an aircraft is rearmed because avionics reside in the cockpit region and the rearming takes place on or about the wings. A full specification of task interactions is shown in Table 1.

This problem instance requires three classes of simulation activities: 1) simulating the outcome of the last mission in terms of aircraft condition, 2) simulating the activities of Mission Control and the initial damage assessment team, 3) simulating the activities of the repair crews. While detailed description is beyond the scope of

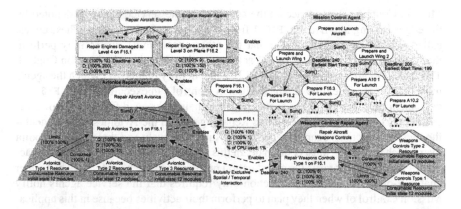

Fig. 2. Portions of the TÆMS Task Structures for Mission Control and Three of the Service Team Agents

the paper, from a high level, the aerial battle is simulated using either a problem space generator or a human generator who selects aircraft from a palette and "breaks" the aircraft. The activities of Mission Control and the initial damage assessment team are captured in TÆMS task structures that are produced by the generation tools. In essence, the Mission Control agent is first notified that there is an aircraft requiring service when it lands. At that same time a description of the aircraft's service needs is transmitted to Mission Control in TÆMS format. Mission Control then disseminates the information to the service teams. The activities of the service teams are simulated using the TÆMS agent simulation environment [12]. In this environment the agents, which are distributed on different machines and execute as different processes co-ordinated simulated tasks. These tasks like real tasks, take a specified amount of time to execute and consume resources, e.g., replacing an avionics module of type 1 consumes one type 1 avionics module.

We will now discuss an example problem for this domain. Figure 2 shows portions of TÆMS task structures for Mission Control and three of the service teams. The Mission Control task structure is a hierarchical decomposition of a top level goal which is simply to Prepare and Launch Aircraft. The top level goal, or task, has two subtasks which are to Prepare and Launch Wing1 and Prepare and Launch Wing2. Each of these tasks are decomposed into subtasks to service a particular aircraft in the given wing, e.g., Prepare F16.1 For Launch, and finally into primitive actions. Tasks are represented with oval boxes, primitive actions with rectangles. Note that most of the decompositions are omitted from the figure for clarity. The details are shown for the Prepare F16.1 For Launch task – it is decomposed into a single primitive action, Launch F16.1, which denotes the time required for Mission Control to launch the aircraft when the plane is ready. The operative word here is *ready*. In order for a given aircraft to be launched on its next mission, it must be serviced. The service activities are not carried out by Mission Control. In the figure,

Mission Control's dependence on the activities of the service agents is denoted by the edges leading into Launch F16.1 from the actions of other agents. These edges, called *enables* in TÆMS, denote that the other agents must successfully perform their tasks before the Launch F16.1 activity can be carried out by Mission Control. These *enables* are *non-local-effects* (NLEs) and identify points over which the agents must coordinate. The time at which Mission Control can execute Launch F16.1 is dependent on when the other agents perform their tasks. A different type of NLE exists between the Weapons Controls Repair agent and the Avionics Repair agent – the two F16.1 actions cannot be performed simultaneously and that is another point over which the agents must coordinate. In this problem, this spatial/temporal interaction of the service teams is the coordination problem on which we focus. The former enabling-of-the-launch-task interaction only requires that the service agents notify Mission Control of when they plan to perform their activities because in this application Mission Control sets and maintains deadlines and the other agents negotiate over the temporal/spatial MUX NLEs to satisfy the stated deadlines if possible. Note that within a task structure deadlines and earliest-start-times are inherited (unless those lower in the tree are tighter) so the temporal constraints on Prepare and Launch Wing1 also apply to Launch F16.1. The same deadlines are propagated through the *enables* coordination to the service team agents – note that F16.1's engines must be serviced by 240 also.

Note that all of the primitive actions (leaf nodes) also have Q (quality), C (cost), and D (duration) discrete probability distributions associated with them. For simplicity in this paper we do not use uncertainty and all values will have a density of 100%. Repairing the engines of F16.1 thus takes 200 time units while servicing the engines of F16.2, which are less damaged, requires 150 time units. The two activities produce qualities of 12 and 9 respectively. The sum() function under most of the parent tasks is called a *quality-accumulation-function* or *qaf*. It describes how quality (akin to utility) generated at the leaf nodes relates to the performance of the parent node. In this case we sum the resultant qualities of the subtasks – other TÆMS functions include min, max, sigmoid, etc. Quality is a deliberately abstract concept into which other attributes may be mapped. In this paper we will assume that quality is a function of the importance of the repair.

In the sample task structure there is also an element of choice – this is a strong part of the TÆMS construct and important for any dynamic environment in which resources or time may be constrained. The Repair Aircraft Engines task, for example, has two subtasks joined under the sum() qaf. In this case the Engine Repair agent may perform either subtask or it may perform both depending on what activities it has time for and their respective values. The explicit representation of choice – a choice that is quantified by those discrete probability distributions attached to the leaf nodes – is how TÆMS agents make contextually dependent decisions.

Space precludes a more detailed specification of tasks and attributes, however, it is important to note that different tasks require different resources, different amounts of resources, and require different time to perform. For instance, refueling an aircraft that is fully depleted requires more time and consumes more fuel (a resource). Other examples: repairing engines damaged to level 4 (heavily damaged) requires more time than engines that are damaged to level 1 (lightly damaged), rearming four missiles requires more time than rearming two missiles, etc. Similarly, different aircraft consume different resources and not all aircraft need a particular class of service. For instance, the C9 surveillance aircraft does not carry missiles and does not contain a weapons controls module. In contrast, both the A10 and the F16 carry missiles and both have weapons controls modules but the modules for the two aircraft are different and require different amounts of time to service. The teams themselves also maintain different resources, e.g., the refueling team is the only team that consumes the fuel resource. However, in the problem instance discussed in this paper the teams do not interact over consumable resources so the coordination problem is one of spatial and temporal task interaction.

The characteristics of the solution to this particular application problem can be found in other problem domains. The underlying technical problem is to coordinate distributed processes that affect one another when the environment is dynamic and the coordination problem cannot be predicted offline / *a priori* but instead must be solved as it evolves.

2.4 Coordination via Don't Commitments

The goals of coordination in the Dynamic Readiness and Repair Service application are: 1) to adapt to a dynamic situation, 2) to maximize the number of planes that are completely repaired by their respective deadlines, 3) to provide mutual access to shared physical resources, 4) achieve global optimization of individual service team (agent) schedules through local mechanisms and peer-to-peer coordination. When examining the coordination problem, it became clear that this application domain has a unique property not generally found in TÆMS agent applications – for agents whose tasks interact, *all* of their tasks will interact. By way of example, all of the engine repair tasks interact with all of the refueling tasks interact with all of the rearming tasks. Similarly for the tasks that pertain to the cockpit. All avionics tasks interact with all weapons controls tasks.

The implications of this property for coordination are that: 1) there is no reason for a service team that operates on the wing region to interact with a team that operates in the cockpit and vice versa[1], 2) agents that operate on the same spatial area (wing or cockpit) must always coordinate their activities. This translates into a discrete partitioning of the agents into *coordination sets*.

Within each coordination set the tasks of the member agents form a fully connected graph via TÆMS *non-local-effects*. This means that for any agent of a given set, e.g., the engine repair agent of $Agent_{wing}$, to schedule a repair task it must dialog

---

[1] An indirect interaction occurs when the problem instance contains deadlines that cannot be met. In such cases both wing and cockpit agents should forgo work on selected planes in order to avoid having an entire fleet of aircraft that are partially complete, none of which are ready for their next mission. This interaction is dealt with using value for commitment satisfaction and algorithms/experiments pertaining to that topic must be presented separately due to space limitations.

with the other agents to ensure that mutual exclusion over the shared resource, e.g., the wing on plane F16.1, is maintained.

This coordination problem could be solved in typical GPGP [3, 2, 6] fashion. However, GPGP operates in a *pairwise* peer-to-peer fashion. For agents in $Agents_{wing}$ this means that coordination could require a significant amount of time to propagate and resolve the interacting constraints and it is unclear given the dynamics of the environment and the speed with which coordination must occur whether convergence on a reasonable, if suboptimal, solution would ever occur. This would also apply to other agent sets if the problem scaled in the number and type of mutually exclusive methods. Because of the strong interconnectedness of the tasks and the partitioning of agents into coordination sets, we developed a new algorithm for problem classes of this type.

```
If (coordinationKey is not null) and
(needCoordinate or coordianationKey.othersNeedCoordinate) {
    primarySchedule = evaluate(taems,
                coordinationKey.getPrimaryDontCommitments());
    if (coordinationKey.getSecondaryDontCommitments() interractWith taems.getDeadlineCommitments()) {
        secondarySchedule = evaluate(taems, coordinationKey.getSecondaryDontCommitments());
        if (primarySchedule.quality > secondarySchedule.quality) {
            preferredSchedule = primarySchedule;
            coordinationKey.discardSecondaryDontCommitments();
        } else {
            preferredSchedule = secondarySchedule;
            coordinationKey.replacePrimaryDontCommitmentsWithSecondaryDontcommitments()
        }
    } else {
        preferredSchedule = primarySchedule;
    }
    taems.setSchedule(preferredSchedule);
    violatedDeadlines = taems.getViolatedDeadlines(preferredSchedule);
    newViolatedDeadlines = violatedDeadlines.getNewDeadlines();
    whatifDontCommitments = coordinationKey.getPrimaryDontCommitments();
    whatifDontCommitments.discardInteractions(newViolatedDeadlines);
    whatifSchedule = evaluate(taems, whatifDontCommitments);
    if (whatifSchedule != preferredSchedule)
        coordinationKey.addSecondaryDontCommitments(whatifSchedule);
    whatifViolatedDeadlines = taems.getViolatedDeadlines(whatifSchedule);
    taems.markAsOldDeadlines(whatifViolatedDeadlines)
}
oldViolatedDeadlines = violatedDeadlines.getOldDeadlines();
communicateDeadlineViolation(oldViolatedDeadlines);
```

Fig. 3. Pseudo-code for an Individual Agent's GPGP protocol for Dynamic Readiness and Repair.

The algorithm uses a *coordination key* data structure and concepts from token-passing [11, 5] algorithms to coordinate the agents. The general operation of the algorithm is that there is one coordination key per coordination set that is passed from agent to agent in a circular fashion. When an agent is holding the coordination key for its coordination set, it can 1) declare its intended course of action / schedules, 2) evaluate existing proposals from other other agents, 3) confirm or negate proposals of other agents, 4) make its own proposals, or 5) read confirmations or negations of its own proposals by other agents. The coordination key itself is the vehicle by which this information is communicated. Each key contains intended courses of action, proposals, and proposal responses, and this information is modified as the agents circulate the given key. The pseudo-code of the algorithm is shown in Figure 3.

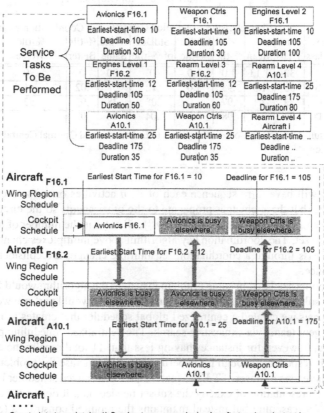

Constraints to maintain: 1) Service team on a single aircraft at a given instant in time. 2) One service team in each region at a given instant in time. 3) Earliest start times which denote when the aircraft lands. 4) Deadlines which denote when the aircraft is due for its next mission.

Fig. 4. The Centralized Exhaustive Scheduling Oracle Has An Omnipotent View – Figure Shows One Scheduling Instance

The coordination key algorithm is effective but approximate and heuristic. The crux of the matter is that in order for the agents to coordinate optimally over a single issue, e.g., when agent X should perform task T_1, the key must circulate through the coordination set multiple times. The number of times that each agent must hold the key is dependent on the changes made during each iteration. In the worst case

DFOISR 05-S-1456

		Mean # Solutions Possible						
Exp	Num	Missing X Aircraft Deadlines						
Class	Trials	X=0	X=1	X=2	X=3	X=4	X=5	X=6
A	32	.31	1.09	.75	.31	.13	0	0
B	32	.31	2	3.1	3.6	2.9	0	0
C	32	0	3.2	13	24.1	16.3	2.53	.4
D	28	0	3.1	16.8	33.0	49.6	36.3	2.7

		Characteristics of Solution Generated by Coordination Keys						
Exp	Num			Median	StdDev	%-tile	%-tile	%-tile
Class	Trials	Mean	%-tile	%-tile	of %-tile	Same	Better	Worse
A	32	1.13	1.0	1.0	0	.80	0	.20
B	32	1.5	.98	1.0	.12	.58	.02	.41
C	32	2.1	.97	1.0	.08	.38	.03	.62
D	28	2.4	.98	1.0	.04	.26	.02	.73

Table 2. Results Comparing Coordination Keys to Exhaustive and Optimal Centralized Schedule Generation

each agent will have to re-sequence each of its n activities once for every change that is made, but these changes propagate to the other agents so the circulation-to-convergence factor is $O(a^n)$ rather than $O(n^a)$, where a is the number of agents in a coordination set. The coordination key algorithm above multiplexes changes so that in a given pass through a coordination set multiple changes are considered by the agents at once.

We hypothesized that in some problem instances the algorithm would fail to find an optimal solution but that in most problem instances it would perform well. To test this hypothesis we created a centralized global scheduler that creates schedules for all of the agent teams via exhaustive search. The centralized scheduling problem is exponential, however, for instances having less than 11 total repairs the exhaustive scheduler is responsive enough for experimentation.[2] Because the problem instance presented here uses a subset of TÆMS features, the centralized scheduler is designed to solve a representation of exactly the subset needed, i.e., it does not perform detailed TÆMS reasoning but instead maintains the required constraints (e.g., deadlines, earliest start times, service teams can only service one aircraft at a time, and only one service team can work in a cockpit or the wing region at a given point in time). The centralized scheduler algorithm is outlined in Figure 4. The function of the centralized scheduler is twofold. First, it determines the minimum number of aircraft deadlines that will be missed by an optimal solution. In some cases all deadlines can be met and in others aircraft deadlines represent unsatisfiable constraints. The second role of the centralized scheduler is to determine the relative size of the different solution spaces. For instance, for a given problem there may be zero solutions that

---

[2] The centralized scheduler requires on the order of 10 minutes to schedule 11 repairs on a dual-processor Xenon 2Ghz linux workstation. A problem instance of that size will generate about 250,000 schedules, some subset of which are unique.

don't miss any deadlines, X (optimal) solutions that miss one aircraft deadline, Y solutions that miss two aircraft deadlines, Z solutions that miss three aircraft deadlines, etc. By tabulating this information we can determine a percentile ranking for the solutions produced by the distributed coordination key algorithm. The centralized scheduler does not compete with the distributed coordination key algorithm on a completely level playing field. The centralized scheduler sees all the repairs that will be needed for all planes on a given problem instance at time 0. The agents in the distributed system only see repairs as the aircraft land. Thus, for the instance shown in Figure 4, the service team agents will not see aircraft A10.1 until time 25 (when it lands). At this time they may be committed to a suboptimal course of action that the centralized omnipotent scheduler will avoid because it can see A10.1's repairs at time 0 along with all of the other repairs that will need to be scheduled. This difference is due to a need to keep the centralized scheduler development costs down and has its roots in design/implementation issues with the simulation environment. A related bias in favor of the centralized scheduler is that the distributed coordination mechanisms operate in the same simulated clock as the repairs themselves. This enables the simulation environment to control and measure coordination costs but causes a skew in terms of the apparent cost of coordination relative to domain tasks, e.g., in some cases the ten clicks (about 5 seconds in wall clock time) that the agents require to coordinate will take as much simulation time as it takes the service teams to rearm one missile on an aircraft. The skew is of primary relevance when comparing the distributed algorithm to the centralized scheduler and is less of an issue when comparing different distributed algorithms.

Table 2 presents the results of comparing the coordination key algorithm to the optimal and exhaustive centralized scheduler. Each row is the statistical aggregation of one set of trials where each set of trials is drawn from one difficulty class. The rows lower in the table represent increasingly more difficult problem instances – aircraft having more repairs and tighter deadlines relative to their landing times and the time required for their repairs [3]. All rows except for the last represent 32 random trials. Row D contains 28 because of the occasional exception thrown by the exhaustive scheduler caused by running out of RAM. As the difficulty increases, note that the density of the solution space increases and shifts right. This is represented by the columns $X=0$, $X=1$, ..., which contain the mean number of solutions produced by the oracle that miss 0 deadlines, 1 deadline, etc., respectively. As the problem instances get harder more aircraft are likely to miss deadlines. Note that the coordination key algorithm generally performs well for all of the tested conditions. The *Mean* value denotes the average number of aircraft deadlines missed during a batch of trials. The more descriptive statistics are those about the percentile ranking of the solutions generated by coordination keys. This is because how well the keys algorithm performs is determined not by the absolute number of missed deadlines (the average of which is presented in the *mean* column) but instead by the solutions possible for a given trial.

---

[3] The seven trial parameters are: (1) land time, (2) takeoff time deadlines, (3) level of avionics damage, (4) level of weapons control damage, (5) level of engines damage, (6) level of rearm damage, and (7) refuel level.

For instance, in some trials the best solution possible may miss two deadlines. As the difficulty increases the *mean* value for the keys algorithm increases because there are more instances where the optimal solution is to miss one deadline, or two deadlines, etc. Looking at the percentiles, in experiment class A the keys algorithm performed in the 100th percentile, in experiment class B the 98th percentile, in experiment class C the 97th percentile, and in class D (the most difficult class), the 98th percentile. The percentile rating is computed as follows:

- The centralized scheduler generates all of the unique schedules that exist for a given individual trial.
- These schedules are binned according to the number of deadlines missed, e.g., in X of the schedules 0 aircraft miss a deadline, in Y of the schedules 1 aircraft misses a deadline, in Z of the schedules 2 of the aircraft miss a deadline, etc. Think of the centralized scheduler as producing a histogram of possible solutions where solutions are binned by the number of deadlines missed.
- Let $CKDLM_i$ be the number of aircraft deadlines missed by the coordination key algorithm in trial i.
- Let Bin_CK_i denote the histogram bin in which $CKDLM_i$ falls (the bin that pertains to $CKDLM_i$ missed deadlines).
- Let $Density\_at\_or\_above_i$ be the $\sum$ of the densities of solutions that are in bins $>$ or $=$ to Bin_CK_i. Bins $> Bin\_CK_i$ represent solutions that are *worse* because they entail missing more deadlines.
- Let $Percentile\_Ranking_i = Density\_at\_or\_above_i / TN_i * 100$, where TN_i is the total number of solutions generated by the centralized scheduler for trail i. $Percentile\_Ranking_i$ is the percentile ranking for the coordination key algorithm for trial i of the set of 32.
- Let $Overall\_Percentile\_Ranking =$
  $(\sum_{i=1}^{32} Percentile\_Ranking_i)/32$ be the overall percentile ranking for one batch of 32 trials.

In all cases the median percentile is 100% and the standard deviation is low. Because there are generally multiple solutions that perform as well as the solutions actually generated by the coordination keys, its percentile is broken down in the last three columns of Table 2. The column marked %-*tile Same* indicates the mean % of possible solutions that miss exactly as many deadlines as the keys algorithm did. %-*tile Better* indicates the number that performed *strictly better* (missing fewer aircraft deadlines) and %-*tile Worse* indicate the number that performed strictly worse. Note that as the problem space gets harder the number of solutions possible that are worse than those found by the keys algorithm increases. At the same time the band of solutions as good as those generated by keys narrows, as does the band of solutions that are strictly better than those found by the keys algorithm.

While the data suggests that the algorithm performs well on average, there are circumstances where the algorithm performs less well. We examined several such instances in detail and while we have intuitions about when the algorithm will perform in a suboptimal fashion, the experiments in which performance is suboptimal pertain

DFOISR 05-S-1456

to a more basic issue. To illustrate let us assume a three-aircraft problem instance with the following characteristics:

- Aircraft F16 arrives at time 15 with a deadline or take-off time of 400 and requires repair of engines damaged to level 2 (the duration of this repair is 100).
- Aircraft A10 arrives at time 18 with a deadline of 450 and requires complete refueling (the duration of this task is 100).
- Aircraft C9 arrives at time 24 with a deadline of 240 and requires repair of engines damaged to level 2 (the duration of this repair is 100) and refueling of a quarter tank (duration of this tank 25).

The F16 lands at time 15 and the engine service team obtains the coordination key and schedules the engine repair of the F16 to run from time 17 to 117. The A10 lands at time 18 and at time 19 the refuel team gets the coordination key and schedules refueling of the A10 to last from 19 to 119. When the C9 lands at time 24 the engine service team is thus occupied with the F16 until time 117 and the refueling team is occupied with the A10 until time 119. To respond to the C9's landing and repair needs, the engine service team obtains the coordination key at time 25 and schedules C9's repair to run from time 117 to time 217. At a subsequent time-step, the refueling team attempts to schedule C9's refueling, however, because both refueling and engine repair are mutually exclusive tasks, the earliest time the refueling team can schedule the C9 is at time 217. This means it is impossible to service the C9 by its deadline (take-off time) of 240. In response to this pending failure, the refuel service team attempts to negotiate with the engine service team via the coordination key to obtain a wing access slot between 119 and 217. However, the engine service team needs that time slot to complete its portion of the C9's engine repairs on time. The end result is that the C9's deadline cannot be met. For this same problem instance, however, the centralized scheduler was able to produce a solution in which all of the deadlines are met.

The underlying issue is that service activities are not interruptible in this problem instance – otherwise repair teams could run from aircraft to aircraft and the optimization problem would be much simpler. If activities were interruptible, when the C9 first landed either the engine service team or the refuel service team could disengage from their respective current activities (servicing the F16 or the A10) and attend to the C9, which is the aircraft with the tightest deadline. The reason the centralized scheduler is able to produce a better solution in this problem instance – a solution which eludes the distributed coordination approach – is that the centralized oracle sees all of the repair tasks *a priori*. It thus considers the possibility of not servicing the F16 or A10 immediately upon arrival so that the C9 can be serviced by engines or refueling immediately upon its arrival and all deadlines can be met.

This particular performance issue derives from the somewhat imbalanced playing field (discussed earlier) between the distributed algorithm and the centralized oracle. Interestingly, we can hypothesize two instances where the distributed algorithm will fail to perform well, even on a level playing field, but such instances occur infrequently in randomly generated problem instances – even those with tight deadline constraints and numerous repairs per aircraft.[4]

One instance where the the coordination key algorithm will perform less well entails semi-independent coordination problems that occur simultaneously in the coordination set of more than two agents. Imagine a coordination set of the rearm, refuel, and engine repair agents. Let the key pass from agent to agent in the following order: rearm to refuel to engine (then the cycle repeats). Now, let us assume that at time t the rearm agent needs a time slot that is held by the engine agent, and that refuel needs a time slot that is held by the rearm agent. The implications are that multiple unrelated proposals must reside on one key for part of the coordination set traversal, i.e., the proposal from rearm to engine and the proposal from refuel to rearm both reside on the key during the refuel to engine to rearm circuit. The key algorithm is designed with the assumption that, in general, multiple proposals will pertain to a single (sometimes multi-step) coordination process. Therefore, when the engine agent receives the coordination key it either accepts or rejects the set of current proposals (from the rearm and refuel agents) *en masse* even though it may only be affected by the rearm agent's proposal. In this case, when the set of proposals arrives and the engine agent determines that it cannot satisfy the rearm agent's request, it rejects the proposals *en masse* and the proposal from refuel to rearm is never evaluated by the rearm agent. This may result in a missed opportunity for the refuel agent. The shortcoming described here can be fixed by making the agents more selective in proposal rejection.

Another instance where the coordination key algorithm may perform less well is when a long chain of multi-step inter-locking resource releases are required. The factor at work is the algorithm's approximate limited-cycle-to-action model. However, as noted, neither class of problems occur frequently with random instances. We are currently exploring creating a generator and experiments to test performance under these circumstances.

2.5 Scalability Issues

The Dynamic Readiness and Repair Service application could conceivably be deployed in a situation where dozens of agents needed to be coordinated. This is based on superficial studies of modern air support crew structures and responsibilities, which appear to typically be disparate in space and in time to utilize the airstrip to its maximum capacity. In such a scenario, an Air Traffic Control agent would hand off returning airplanes to the Mission Control agent, which would setup the coordination problems for the service team repair agents to solve. Thus, the problem's complexity as a function of scaling the number of agents could plausibly be controlled by information hiding – agents would only be required to solve relatively small spatially and temporally local problems.

Scaling in the task environment dimension for this application could mean increasing the number and kind of repairs required for each aircraft and increasing

---

[4] If the repairs are spread over a large number of aircraft there is little spatial resource contention and service teams can basically function in parallel.

the rate at which aircraft land. It could also mean increasing the number of pairs of service operations that are mutually exclusive. Scaling in this dimension would present a more significant problem for the protocol described above due to the afore-mentioned worst case performance of key-circulation to convergence ratio. For each change introduced, it is $O(a^n)$, where n is the number of tasks per agent and a is the number of agents in a coordination set. Obviously, in such degenerative cases, less optimal results could be tolerated, but ideally, we would like to at least bound the performance for a given problem type. This is an area of future research.

This brings us quite naturally to consideration of the solution properties dimension which concerns solution quality, robustness, and overhead limitations. In the evaluation that we conducted, the key-based coordination protocol performed well, although it utilized a heuristic search. This was due to the fact that the relatively hard problems vis-a-vis the protocol we developed were sparse in the set of problems generated to test it. Whether these problems would be sparse in real-world setting was beyond the scope of our research.

With respect to robustness in the face of uncertainty, to an extent we can rely on mechanisms built into the TÆMS task structure evaluation [9, 13, 16]. However, the precise manner by which uncertainty of task finish times and accrued quality are handled in commitment information between agents would need to be further developed. For instance, each agent would need to decided, based on its unique task environment, whether it could afford to choose a commitment with higher expected quality with uncertainty of finish time or one with lower expected quality and certainty of finish time.

Finally, communication overhead limitations were not a consideration in the development of the key-based coordination protocol. There are numerous obvious ways to compact the schedule information for each agent sent in the coordination key that we would need to implement in order to reduce the key size. Another aspect of this dimension is what would happen if one of the agents in a coordination set was disabled. Again, we assumed that none would be disabled. At the very minimum, the loss of an agent in a coordination set would need to be detectable by at least one other agent in the coordination set, who could notify the other agents in the set. Also, a key-caching mechanism would need to be implemented to warrant against the loss of the key if the agent who was disabled possessed the key.

3 First Response Coordination

3.1 The Application

COORDINATORs [18, 17] are coordination managers for fielded first responders. They provide decision support for first response teams and the incident commander by reasoning about mission structures, resource limitations, time considerations, and *interactions* between the missions of *different teams* to decide who should be doing what, and when, so as to get the best overall result. COORDINATORs provide global

Fig. 5. A Network of COORDINATORs Handling Task Coordination Between Responders

team activity optimization – helping the teams to respond to the dynamics of the environment and to act in concert, supporting one another, as appropriate for the current circumstances. When the situation changes, the COORDINATORs communicate, evaluate the implications of change, and potentially decide (or suggest, depending on their role) on a new course of action for the teams. Fiture 5 depicts the network of COORDINATOR-enabled teams performing activities. The two COORDINATOR-first responder pairings on the left of the figure are connected to each other and to the COORDINATOR-incident commander pairing on the right by communications as well as task interrelationships.

The underpinnings of COORDINATORs are TÆMS agents [3, 7, 14, 15] equipped with a new coordination module derived from the coordination keys [14] technology. This means that each distributed COORDINATOR is able to reason about complex mission task structures and communicate with other coordinators to determine who should be supporting whom, when, in order to save the most lives, make the best use of assets or resources, reduce risk to the response teams, and so forth.

COORDINATORs are implemented and functioning and have been experimented with using staged first response exercises. However, this project and the work described here is only the potential starting point for COORDINATORs and technology that supports human activity coordination.

There are several characteristics of this problem instance that make it a hard problem:

The situation is dynamic – it is not known with any detail at the time of the 911 call what sort of state the site or victims will be in when response teams arrive. Thus the agents must coordinate and decide which operations to perform in real-time. This is especially true when fire is involved; in an unmitigated average office fire, gas temperature inside the burning, enclosed space can easily reach 1200 degrees Fahrenheit in less four minutes[8].

Agents must make quantified / value decisions – different tasks have different values and require different amounts of time and labor resources. It may be critical to provide water supply support to suppress fire spread until victims are discovered during a search, at which point, priorities require adjustment.

Coordination is dynamic – the operations being performed by the first responder teams interact and the occurrence of the interactions are also not known *a priori*. For instance, until victims are found, it is not known whether ventilation in a hallway will be required.

Deadlines are present – a fire suppression team will need to put out a fire in one area within a deadline in order for a rescue operation to be able to effectively complete their evacuation operation. Deadlines require the agents to reason about end-to-end processes and to coordinate with other agents to optimize their activities.

Tasks are interdependent – tasks interact in two different ways: 1) over shared resources in a spatial/temporal fashion, 2) multiple tasks must be performed to accomplish a goal, e.g., a fire has not been met with a satisfactory response until all the people threatened by it have been evacuated, and it has been extinguished in the most effective manner possible (though in TÆMS this generally pertains to degrees of satisfaction rather than a boolean or binary value).

COORDINATORs have been constructed using off-the-shelf wireless PDAs and desktop PCs. COORDINATORs also leverage a Honeywell-proprietary asset location technology to track the physical location of first response teams, victims, and important resources such as a wall cutting saw or a multi-story portable ladder. A screen snapshot of a the incident commander display as well as the PDA-based coordinators running in simulation is shown in Figure 6. The left of the incident commander display is a scrollable map of the area of concern – in our scenario our lab building. The map can display first responders moving about as well as situation information, such as the location and intensity of fire, smoke, or building damage as well as the location of first responder resources, such as saws or hoses. Below the map is a dispatch command bar that the incident commander can use to send teams to specific locations in the building to do situation assessment. In the center of the display are cameras that track the first responders through the building. There is one camera per team. Whenever the team enters a region that is covered by a camera, the incident commander display switches the team's camera view to the feed from the covering camera. To the right of the camera displays are the team Gantt displays which show the task schedules for each team.

Note that herein we use the term "first responder" to mean personnel ranging from fire fighters to emergency medical teams. For the details of this project, however, we have focused primarily on the needs of the fire fighters and the incident commander because we were able to get domain expertise in that area.

In this section we discuss the first response domain and the motivation for COORDINATORs. We then provide architectural and technical details of the agent technologies that make COORDINATORs possible and illustrate their role using a first response episode. Human-based first response exercises using COORDINATORs are then discussed, followed by important research directions and next steps for COORDINATORs.

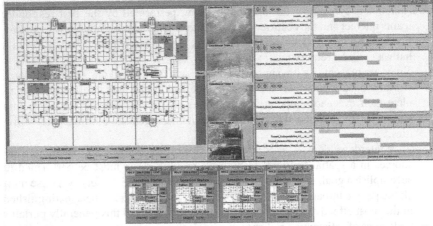

Fig. 6. The Incident Commander display and Simulated PDAs for the First Response Coordination application.

3.2 Coordination via Commitment Value

The goals of coordination in the COORDINATORs application are similar to those for the Dynamic Readiness and Repair Service application. However, since first responders are concerned with the safety of life and property, COORDINATORs attempts to maximize the number of civilians that are saved while minimizing facility damage and risk to first responders.[5]

This application augments the decision-making powers first responders capable of performing *any* task in the domain. The implication homogeneous first responder capabilities for coordination is that agents do not have a partition of coordination based on task types that they had in the Dynamic Readiness and Repair Service application. Each agent coordinates with every other agent. Each agent must maximize the quality of its local tasks performed, while cooperatively assisting other agents to maximize the quality of their local tasks performed. It does this by satisfying support needs. Figure 7 gives the high-level pseudocode for the key-based COORDINATOR protocol.

The algorithm's *coordination key* is derived from the Dynamic Readiness and Repair Service application data structure [14]. The general operation of the algorithm is that there is one coordination key for the entire application that is passed from agent to agent (fielded first responder agents only). As with the previous application of the key-based protocol, when an agent is holding the coordination key for its coordination set, it can evaluate, confirm, or negate existing or proposed commitments from other agents. However, the mechanism by which it does this is significantly changed. In this application, we used commitment value for the proposed support tasks instead of the avoidance of mutually exclusive activities to drive the coordination. When an

---

[5] Although risk-reward tradeoffs are supported by the DTC TÆMS scheduler, we did not leverage these capabilities in our GPGP implementation.

```
if(coordinationKey is not null) {
    if(needCoordinate or coordinationKey.othersNeedToCoordinate()){
        coordinationKey.addNewCommitmentRequests(requests);
        needChoice = coordinationKey.setCommitments(taems, PRIMARY);
        primarySchedule= evaluate(taems);
        coordinationKey.determineSatisfiedCommitments(taems, primarySchedule, PRIMARY);
        if(needChoice is false) {
            preferredSchedule = primarySchedule;
            coordinationKey.setCommitments(taems, PROPOSAL);
            whatifSched = evaluate(whatIfCond);
            coordinationKey.determineSatisfiedCommitments(taems, whatifSched, PROPOSAL);
        } else {
            coordinationKey.setCommitments(taems, SECONDARY);
            secondarySchedule = evaluate(taems);
            coordinationKey.determineSatisfiedCommitments(taems, secondarySchedule, SECONDARY);
            if(coordinationKey.pickChoiceCommitments()) {
                preferredSchedule = firstBestSched;
            } else {
                preferredScheudle = secondarySchedule;
                generateNegotiationEvents();
            }
        }
    }
}
```

Fig. 7. Pseudo-code for an Individual Agent's GPGP protocol for First Response Coordination.

agent proposes tasks for other agents to commit to doing in its service, the commitment value associated with task performance is associated with the value the overall task (requiring support). This leads to a global utility accounting irregularity, but this is a approximate, heuristic mechanism that, while not perfect, works well in practice.

3.3 Evaluation

Arguably, the most important overall evaluation question for COORDINATORs is whether they improve the performance of first responders. In a perfect world with unlimited resources, one might design a set of experiments in which first responders engage in a series of first response episodes both with and without COORDINATORs providing support. In each case, one would like to measure specific metrics like number of lives saved, number of assets saved, time required to perform the mission tasks, number of responders necessary to address the situation, amount of risk incurred by the responders and the civilians, etc. In this perfect world, one would have buildings to burn and the ability to recreate, verbatim, scenarios so that the measurement and comparison could be one-to-one.

We elected to use a somewhat more economic approach. To evaluate COORDINATORs from an application view, rather than simply evaluating the performance of the underlying technology (e.g., time required for coordination), we staged first response exercises and had human performers take the role of first responders. Note that the lessons learned from this process are anecdotal but are also more meaningful as an early viability test of the concept.

DFOISR 05-S-1456

In the exercises there are four teams and an incident commander (IC). The scenario is set in a petrochemical plant though the plant is mapped back onto the Honeywell Lab's building. During the exercise, responders must move around the building, perform situation assessment tasks, respond to the situations they discover, and coordinate to rescue civilians. The scenario is setup in such a way that teams must coordinate in order to rescue the civilians. Failure to do so results in (simulated) loss of life – a metric that can be tabulated.

To assess the benefits of having COORDINATORs, we first deploy the teams on the first response exercise using walkie-talkies for communication (they are also equipped with stop-watches and building maps to make the simulation more complete). After the walkie-talkie exercise, during which loss of (prop) life is recorded, the teams are rotated and the scenario run again, this time with COORDINATORs providing automated support.

In doing this exercise, we rapidly discovered the degree to which humans are overwhelmed when faced with lots of temporal and task related data that is in a state of constant change. The initial plan was to host VIPs and to have a VIP take the role of incident commander – the individual who generally handles coordination in the walkie-talkie exercise. Not only was the IC task too difficult for the VIPs, it was too difficult for most of the research team members. In practice, only someone who had memorized the flow of events in the exercise could help the teams to rescue all the civilians. We resorted to this model in order to get human performers through the walkie-talkie exercise at all.

Thus VIPs and visitors (with varying degrees of domain expertise) generally took the role of first response teams. At the start of the scenario, the teams are deployed by the IC and given situation assessment tasks. In enacting the scenario, at this point teams move throughout the building and go to assigned zones (generally conference rooms). To simulate the situation assessment task, we created a series of props representing the situation. For instance, a first response team might find fire props, debris props, and a civilian prop pinned by a girder prop. This would indicate that a civilian was trapped and that the fire needed to be put out and the debris cleared before the girder could be cut away. Cutting the girder also requires some other team (generally) to fetch a power saw from the simulated truck. In the exercise, props are reinforced by staging data sheets that describe the situation textually and explicitly cull out resource needs and potential temporal issues (e.g., "you must evacuate these civilians before the adjacent wall collapses at time T=40").

Because fielded first responders must coordinate while carrying out domain tasks, we also require our first response stand-ins to carry out simulated domain tasks. In general, this translates into putting props into one another and moving them physically throughout the building. For example, to extinguish the fire, it goes into a *fire extinguishment box* and the box must then be carried to a staging area on a specific floor of the building. Similarly, evacuation of an injured civilian requires that the civilian prop be put into the gurney prop box, a box that must be fetched from the staging area, and then the gurney box must be put into a stairwell box (if that is the exit route chosen) and the stairwell box carried to the staging area.

Dynamics are introduced into the environment using secondary envelopes on which is printed a time at which they are to be opened. Thus teams may coordinate, decide on a course of action, then open an envelope and discover that the situation has changed (e.g., a ceiling fell-in) and then they must recoordinate to adapt to the new situation.

As one might guess from the description, human performers generally fared poorly during this exercise. Only with an expert IC who knew the complete scenario *a priori* and had figured out exactly who should be supporting whom, and when, could get both the teams and the cardboard civilians out of the facility in time. What is more interesting is that the stress incurred by the human performers during the exercise was pronounced and observable even to the non-expert. Trying to battle one's props while processing all the cross chatter on the walkie-talkie and interact with the IC proved to be a difficult task even without the heat, smoke, sound, and inherent danger of a crisis situation. Few performers were able to coordinate properly. Few were able to evaluate their mission structures properly. Not once did a guest team make it through the scenario with the optimal course of action chosen. Notable among our VIPs was a Honeywell VP who processed the temporal data without hand drawn Gantt charts and who carried the props with great vigor while barking commands into his walkie-talkie. (Confidence in management rose a fraction during this episode.)

In contrast to the walkie-talkie scenario, the run with COORDINATORs handling the activity coordination is almost boring – despite the scenario being run at a faster clock rate. In the COORDINATOR scenario, the teams perform situation assessment and describe their situation to the COORDINATORs. The COORDINATORs then handle all of the exchange of local information, the analysis, and the formation of commitments. Teams are then informed of what they should be doing, when, who will be supporting them, and so forth.

After both exercises, the VIPs are then debriefed and shown a simplified Gantt chart of the major coordination points and support needs of the different teams. While the evidence gathered during these exercises is anecdotal, the reaction of our visitors, some with first response and military domain expertise, has served to reinforce our belief that this line of work is valuable. In practice, the "fog of war" caused by flames, screaming, smoke, etc., makes a set of tasks that humans have difficulty with under normal circumstances nearly impossible. Information exchange and coordination analysis should be off-loaded from the humans to automated assistants that are better equipped to reason precisely and respond in a (near) optimal and timely fashion.

3.4 Scalability Issues

Unlike the Dynamic Readiness and Repair Service application, the agent population for this application could quite reasonably number in the hundreds or thousands – incorporating first response teams from local, state and federal police, fire, hazardous materials, and other agencies. However, in the exercises that we ran, there were only five agents: one for the incident commander and four for each of the first responders. The solution, although providing a good basis for further development, is currently not well suited to deployment in large-scale crisis response situations. There are a number of important issues related to crisis response management that are not addressed in the current application, including coordination between incident commander agents, coordination of domain-relevant resources such as hazardous materials cleanup kits, and a generally richer, more extensible model for situation assessment and information sharing.

We can again hypothesize that information through hierarchical task abstraction and assignment can lessen the coordination burden on an individual COORDINA-TOR as the number of COORDINATORs increases. However, we must still address the rate and complexity of tasks generated by interactions with the environment could affect the coordination protocol. Specifically, we would like to know how it affects the distributed solution convergence time. The rate of protocol convergence is dependent on the rate and quantity of commitment requests from each agent for assistance with their local tasks. Each commitment request can mean the addition of one or more tasks to an agent's local task structure. So, as with the Dynamic Readiness and Repair Service application, in the worst case, for each change introduced, the key-circulation to convergence ratio is $O(a^n)$, where n is the number of tasks per agent and a is the number of agents in a coordination set.

The solution dimension for COORDINATORs, including quality, robustness, and overhead limitations is further complicated by its mixed-initiative qualities. The baseline solution is human performance unmediated by COORDINATOR technology, and humans are typically not very good at solving coordination problems without optimization assistance. This brings up the problem of how best to enable a human user of COORDINATORs to interact with the coordination optimization protocols as the number of agents and rate and quantity of task change increases. Abstraction and information hiding based on natural problem decompositions (based on physical or other inherent problem constraints) seem to be again the best approach to addressing these problems. That is, ensuring that if a person is looking at a state-wide coordination problem via COORDINATORs, he will not be burdened by low-level resource information, like how many oxygen packs are stationed in a given municipal fire station.

4 General Scalability Limitations and Future Work

We have examined two different applications that use a key-based approach to coordinate interactions of multiple agents and discussed its scalability properties in each along the three dimensions identified by Durfee [4]: agent population, task environment, and solution. We now discuss in general some of the limitations of the key-based coordination protocols and lay out directions for future work.

One limitation of the current key-based implementation is a notion of hierarchy in the coordination protocol. For instance, coordination sets (the agents where one key circulates) can overlap, but the notion of a decision in one coordination set preempting the decision in another coordination set is not supported. This could be useful especially in the COORDINATOR application, where the "upper management" of a crisis response could direct resources based on strategic priorities in a way that might contradict local resource needs or commitment requests.

Another limitation of the key-based protocols when scaling in the rate of task change or arrival is that the decisions of a coordination set can be made no faster than its slowest member – the complexity of one agent's local coordination problem could bring the group's decision making to a stand-still. One way around this would be to enforce time-bounded computation at each agent. Each agent would then be required to gauge the level of heuristic analysis it does s based on the amount of time it has to compute and the complexity of the problem it must solve.

Yet another direction we could take to make the solution more robust and quite possibly faster would be to switch to a centralized, black-board [1] mechanism. This would open up the possibility (and complexity) of asynchronous coordination decisions.

5 Acknowledgments

The applications described herein were based on agent TÆMS-agent infrastructure and coordination work that has a long history and we would like to acknowledge those many other researchers who have contributed to their growth and evolution – some of the individuals are Victor Lesser, Keith Decker, Alan Garvey, Bryan Horling, Regis Vincent, Ping Xuan, Shelley XQ. Zhang, Anita Raja, Roger Mailler, and Norman Carver.

The Dynamic Readiness and Repair Service project was sponsored by the Defense Advanced Research Projects Agency (DARPA) and the Office of Naval Research under agreement number N00014-02-C-0262 and by Honeywell International under project number I10105BB4.

The COORDINATORs project was sponsored by DARPA through AFRL under agreement number F30602-03-C-0010 and by Honeywell under project numbers I10133AC1000, I10155AD1000, and I10171AJ2000. We would also like to acknowledge the efforts of the other Honeywell Lab's project team who performed first hand interviews with fire marshals and first responders. These include Tom Plocher, Walt Heimerdinger, Tony Faltesek, and Michelle Raymond. This work was partially supported by DARPA's IPTO office, through AFRL, and by Honeywell International. We would like to thank Ron Brachman, Barbara Yoon, Zach Lemnios, John Beane, Mike Lynch, and Andrew Berezowski for their support.

The U.S. Government is authorized to reproduce and distribute reprints for Governmental purposes notwithstanding any copyright annotation thereon. Disclaimer: The views and conclusions contained herein are those of the authors and should not be interpreted as necessarily representing the official policies or endorsements, either expressed or implied, of the Defense Advanced Research Projects Agency (DARPA), Office of Naval Research, the National Institute of Standards and Technology, the U.S. Government or Honeywell International.

DFOISR 05-S-1456

References

1. Norman Carver and Victor Lesser. Blackboard Architectures for Knowledge-Based Signal Understanding. In *Symbolic and Knowledge-Based Signal Processing*, pages 205–250, Alan Oppenheim and S. Hamid Nawab, (eds.), January 1992. Prentice Hall.
2. K. Decker and J. Li. Coordinated hospital patient scheduling. In *ICMAS '98: Proceedings of the 3rd International Conference on Multi Agent Systems*, page 104. IEEE Computer Society, 1998.
3. Keith S. Decker. *Environment Centered Analysis and Design of Coordination Mechanisms*. PhD thesis, University of Massachusetts, 1995.
4. Edmund Durfee. Scaling up agent coordination strategies. In *IEEE Computer*, pages 39–46. IEEE, July 2001.
5. IEEE. *802.5: Token Ring Access Method*. IEEE, New York, NY, 1985.
6. V. Lesser, K. Decker, T. Wagner, N. Carver, A. Garvey, B. Horling, D. Neiman, R. Podorozhny, M. NagendraPrasad, A. Raja, R. Vincent, P. Xuan, and X.Q Zhang. Evolution of the GPGP/TAEMS Domain-Independent Coordination Framework. *Proceedings 1st International Conference on Autonomous Agents and Multi-Agent Systems (Plenary Lecture/Extended Abstract)*, pages 1–2, 2002.
7. Victor Lesser, Bryan Horling, and et al. The taems whitepaper / evolving specification. http://mas.cs.umass.edu/research/taems/white.
8. National Fire Protection Association. *Fire Protection Handbook*, 18th edition, 1997.
9. Anita Raja, Victor Lesser, and Thomas Wagner. Toward Robust Agent Control in Open Environments. In *Proceedings of 5th International Conference of Autonomous Agents(AA 2000). Also Umass CS Technical Report 1999-059*, pages 84–91, Barcelona, Spain, June 2000.
10. Paul Scerri, David Pynadath, Lewis Johnson, Paul Rosenbloom, Nathan Schurr, Mei Si, and Milind Tambe. "A Prototype Infrastructure for Distributed Robot-Agent-Person Teams. In *AAMAS*. ACM, 2003.
11. Andrew S. Tanenbaum. *Computer Networks*. Prentice Hall, New Jersey, 1996.
12. Regis Vincent, Bryan Horling, and Victor Lesser. An agent infrastructure to evaluate multi-agent systems: The java agent framework and multi-agent system simulator. In Thomas Wagner and Omer Rana, editors, *Infrastructure for Agents, Multi-Agent Systems, and Scalable Multi-Agent Systems, Lecture Notes in AI*, pages 102–127. Springer, 2001.
13. Thomas Wagner, Alan Garvey, and Victor Lesser. Criteria-Directed Heuristic Task Scheduling. *International Journal of Approximate Reasoning, Special Issue on Scheduling*, 19(1-2):91–118, 1998. A version also available as UMASS CS TR-97-59.
14. Thomas Wagner, Valerie Guralnik, and John Phelps. A key-based coordination algorithm for dynamic readiness and repair service coordination. In *Proceedings of the 2nd International Conference on Autonomous Agents and Multi-Agent Systems (AAMAS2003), 2003.*, 2003. Nominated for most novel application award.
15. Thomas Wagner, Valerie Guralnik, and John Phelps. Software Agents: Enabling Dynamic Supply Chain Management for a Build to Order Product Line. *International Journal of Electronic Commerce Research and Applications, Special issue on Software Agents for Business Automation*, 2(2):114–132, 2003.
16. Thomas Wagner and Victor Lesser. Design-to-Criteria Scheduling: Real-Time Agent Control. In Wagner/Rana, editor, *Infrastructure for Agents, Multi-Agent Systems, and Scalable Multi-Agent Systems*, LNCS. Springer-Verlag, 2001. A version is also available as UMASS CS Tech Report TR-99-58.

17. Thomas Wagner, John Phelps, Valerie Guralnik, and Ryan VanRiper. An application view of coordinators: Coordination managers for first responders. In *Sixteenth Innovative Applications of Artificial Intelligence Conference (IAAI04)*, 2004.
18. Thomas Wagner, John Phelps, Valerie Guralnik, and Ryan VanRiper. Coordinators - coordination managers for first responders. In *3rd International Joint Conference on Autonomous Agents and Multi-Agent Systems (AAMAS04)*, 2004.

Designing Agent Utilities for Coordinated, Scalable and Robust Multi-Agent Systems

Kagan Tumer

NASA Ames Research Center ktumer@mail.arc.nasa.gov

Summary. Coordinating the behavior of a large number of agents to achieve a system level goal poses unique design challenges. In particular, problems of scaling (number of agents in the thousands to tens of thousands), observability (agents have limited sensing capabilities), and robustness (the agents are unreliable) make it impossible to simply apply methods developed for small multi-agent systems composed of reliable agents. To address these problems, we present an approach based on deriving agent goals that are aligned with the overall system goal, and can be computed using information readily available to the agents. Then, each agent uses a simple reinforcement learning algorithm [26] to pursue its own goals. Because of the way in which those goals are derived, there is no need to use difficult to scale external mechanisms to force collaboration or coordination among the agents, or to ensure that agents actively attempt to appropriate the tasks of agents that suffered failures.

To present these results in a concrete setting, we focus on the problem of finding the subset of a set of imperfect devices that results in the best aggregate device [5]. This is a large distributed agent coordination problem where each agent (e.g., device) needs to determine whether to be part of the aggregate device. Our results show that the approach proposed in this work provides improvements of over an order of magnitude over both traditional search methods and traditional multi-agent methods. Furthermore, the results show that even in extreme cases of agent failures (i.e., half the agents failed midway through the simulation) the system's performance degrades gracefully and still outperforms a failure-free and centralized search algorithm. The results also show that the gains increase as the size of the system (e.g., number of agents) increases. This latter result is particularly encouraging and suggests that this method is ideally suited for domains where the number of agents is currently in the thousands and will reach tens or hundreds of thousands in the near future.

1 Introduction

Coordinating a large number of agents to achieve complex tasks collectively presents new challenges to the field of multi-agent systems. The research issues in this area present significant departures from those in traditional multi-agent systems coordination problems where a handful of agents interact with one another. When dealing with a handful of agents, it is reasonable to assume that in many cases agents react to one another, can model one another, and/or enter into contracts with one another [6, 8, 12, 21]. When dealing with thousands of agents on the other hand, such assumptions become more difficult to justify. At best each one can assume that the agents are aware of other agents as part of a background. In such cases, agents have to act within an environment that may be shaped by the actions of other agents, but cannot be interpreted as the the by-product of the actions of any single agent.

This distinction is crucial and makes the coordination problem fundamentally different than that traditionally encountered in many domains, and thus requires new approaches. In this work, we focus on an agent coordination method that aims to handle systems which have the following four characteristics:

1. The agents have limited sensing and decision making capabilities. Therefore, rather than rely on carefully designed agents, the interactions among the agents will be leveraged to achieve the complex task;
2. The agents will not be able to model the other agents in the system. Therefore, they will "react" to the signals they receive from their environment;
3. The agents will not necessarily perform reliably, and a non-negligible percentage of the agents will to fail during the life-cycle of the system. Therefore, the agents will not rely on other agents performing specific tasks at specific performance levels.
4. The number of agents will be in the thousands. Therefore, the agents will need to act with local information and without direct regard for the full system performance.

To study such multi-agent systems within a concrete domain, we focus on the problem of imperfect device subset selection. This problem consists of a set of imperfect devices, and the task is to find the subset of those devices that results in the best aggregate device [5]. It can be viewed as an abstraction of what will likely loom as a major challenge in achieving coordination in large scale multi-agent systems (e.g., systems of nano or micro-scale components) meeting the four criteria listed above. This is a hard optimization problem, and brute force approaches cannot be used for any but its smallest toy instances [5, 10].

We propose addressing this problem by associating each device with an adaptive Reinforcement-Learning (RL) agent [15, 17, 26, 33]) that decides whether or not its device will be a member of the subset. In this problem, there is a well-defined, system-level objective function that needs to be achieved. As such we focus on how the agents' actions further that system-level goal (i.e., global utility). Furthermore, because we intend to scale this system to a large number of agents, the agents need to take their actions without actively soliciting information from other agents in the system. The design problem we face then, is to determine how best to set the private utility functions of the agents in a way that will lead to good values of the global utility, without involving difficult to scale external mechanism that ensure cooperation among the agents. Note that though the agents have simple decisions to make, this is still fundamentally a multi-agent problem: Each agent autonomously makes a decision at each time step based on its estimate of the reward it will receive; and the system is fully distributed as each agent has full autonomy over its actions.

For the joint action of agents working in such a system to provide good values of the global utility, we must both ensure that the agents do not work at cross-purposes, and that each one has a learning problem that is relatively easy to solve. Typically these two requirements are in conflict with one another. For example, providing each agent with the system-level goal will ensure that they will not work at cross purposes. However, such a choice will leave the agents with a difficult problem: each of the agents' utilities will depend on the actions of all the other agents, making it all but impossible for the agents to determine the best actions to follow in most systems of interest. At the other extreme, providing each agent with a simple, local utility function will provide a clear signal, but may not necessarily lead the system to high values of global utility.

The challenge is is to find the best trade-off between these two requirements. This design problem is related to work in many other fields, including multi-agent systems (MAS's), computational economics, mechanism design, computational ecologies and game theory [4, 20, 13, 18, 25]. However, because of issues related to the scale of the system, the reliability of the agents and the limited availability of information, they do not provide a full solution to this problem. (See [30] for a detailed discussion of the relationship between these fields, involving hundreds of references.)

This chapter presents an agent utility based multi-agent coordination algorithm that is well-suited for large and noisy multi-agent systems where coordination among simple and coomperative agents is required. In Section 2 we summarize the background material for agent utility derivation and define the desirable properties an agent utility needs to possess for coordination in large multi-agent systems. In Section 3 we present the imperfect device combination problem and derive the specific agent utilities for this domain. In Section 4 we describe the simulations and present results showing the performance of the various utilities, their scaling properties and their robustness to agent failures. Finally, in Section 5 we provide a summary and discuss the implications and general applicability of this work.

2 Background

In this work, we focus on multi-agent systems that aim to maximize a global utility function, $G(z)$, which is a function of the joint move of all agents in the system, z. Instead of maximizing $G(z)$ directly, each agent, i, tries to maximize its private utility function $g_i(z)$. Our goal is to devise private utility functions that will cause the multi-agent system to produce high values of $G(z)$ [2, 28, 34]. Because this method is based on assigning a utility function to each agent, it is better suited for inherently cooperative distributed domains such as multi-rover coordination [1], or the imperfect device combination problem presented here. On the other hand, with some modifications, it is also applicable to more general domains such as data routing [32], job scheduling over heterogeneous servers [29] or multivariate search [35].

In this work, the notation z_i refers to the parts of z that are dependent on the actions of i, and z_{-i} to refer to the components of z that do not depend on the actions of agent i. Instead of concatenating these partial states to obtain the full state vector, we use zero-padding for the missing elements in the partial state vector. This allows us to use addition and subtraction operators when merging components of different states (e.g., $z = z_i + z_{-i}$).

2.1 Properties of Utility Functions

Now, let us formalize the two requirements discussed above that a private utility should satisfy. First, the private utilities have to be aligned with respect to G, quantifying the concept that an action taken by an agent that improves its private utility also improves the global utility. Formally, for systems with discrete states, the degree of factoredness for a given utility function g_i is defined as:

$$\mathcal{F}_{g_i} = \frac{\sum_z \sum_{z'} u[(g_i(z) - g_i(z')) (G(z) - G(z'))]}{\sum_z \sum_{z'} 1} \tag{1}$$

for all z' such that $z_{-i} = z'_{-i}$ and where $u[x]$ is the unit step function, equal to 1 if $x > 0$, and zero otherwise. Intuitively, the higher the degree of factoredness between two utilities, the more likely it is that a change of state will have the impact on the two utilities (e.g., make both of them go up). A system is fully factored when $\mathcal{F}_{g_i} = 1$. As a trivial example, a system in which all the private utility functions equal G [7] is fully factored.

Second, the private utilities have to have high **learnability**, intuitively meaning that an agent's utility should be sensitive to its own actions and insensitive to actions of others. Formally we can quantify the learnability of utility g_i, for agent i at z:

$$\lambda_{i,g_i}(z) = \frac{E_{z'_i}[|g_i(z) - g_i(z_{-i} + z'_i)|]}{E_{z'_{-i}}[|g_i(z) - g_i(z'_{-i} + z_i)|]} \tag{2}$$

where $E[\cdot]$ is the expectation operator, z'_i's are alternative actions of agent i at z, and z'_{-i}'s are alternative joint actions of all agents other than i. Intuitively, learnability provides the ratio of the expected value of g_i over variations in agent i's actions to the expected value of g_i over variations in the actions of agents other than i. So at a given state z, the higher the learnability, the more $g_i(z)$ depends on the move of agent i, i.e., the better the associated signal-to-noise ratio for i. Higher learnability means it is easier for i to achieve a large values of its utility. Note that, though a system where all agents' private utilities are set to G is fully factored, such a system will have low learnability since each agent's utility will depend on the actions of all the other agents in the system.

2.2 Private Utility Functions

Now, let us present two utilities that are fully factored and have high learnability. The **Estimated Difference Utility** is given by:

$$EDU_i \equiv G(z) - E_{z_i}[G(z)|z_{-i}] \tag{3}$$

where $E_{z_i}[G(z)|z_{-i}]$ gives the expected value of G over the possible actions of agent i. Such a private utility for the agents is fully factored with G because the second term does not depend on agent i's state [34] (these utilities are referred to as AU in [34]). Furthermore, because it removes noise from an agent's private utility, EDU yields far better learnability than does G [34]. This noise reduction is due to the subtraction which (to a first approximation) eliminates the impact of states that are not affected by the actions of agent i.

The second utility we consider is the **Wonderful Life Utility** [34], given by:

$$WLU_i \equiv G(z) - G(z_{-i}). \tag{4}$$

The major difference between EDU and WLU is in how they handle z_{-i}. EDU provides an estimate of agent i's impact by sampling all possible actions of agent i whereas WLU simply removes agent i from the system WLU is also factored with G, because the second term does not depend on the actions of agent i [34]. In general, WLU also has better learnability than G, and in the next section we discuss this in more detail for this problem domain.

3 Combination of Imperfect Devices

We now explore the use of these private utility functions for the problem of combining imperfect devices [5]. A typical example of this problem arises when many simple and noisy observational devices (e.g., nano or micro devices, low power sensing devices) attempt to accurately determine some value pertinent to the phenomenon they're observing. Each device will provide a single number that is slightly off, similar to sampling a Gaussian centered on the value of the real number. The problem is to choose the subset of a fixed collection of such devices so that the average (over the members of the subset) distortion is as close to zero as possible.

3.1 Problem Definition

Formally, the problem is to minimize

$$\varepsilon \equiv \frac{|\sum_{j=1}^{N} n_j a_j|}{\sum_{k=1}^{N} n_k}, \tag{5}$$

where $n_j \in \{0, 1\}$ is whether device j is or is not selected, and there are N devices in the collection, having associated distortions $\{a_j\}$. This is a hard optimization problem that is similar to known NP-complete problems such as subset sum or partitioning [5, 10], but has two twists: the presence of the denominator and that $a_j \in R \ \forall j$. In this work we set the system-level utility function to $G = -\varepsilon$ (we do this so that the goal is to "maximize" G, which is more consistent with the concept of "utility" design).

The system is composed of N agents, each responsible for setting one of the n_j. Each of those agent has its own private utility function, though the overall objective is to maximize system level performance. The aim is to give those agents private utilities so that, as they learn to maximize their private utilities, they also maximize G.

3.2 Expected Difference Utility

For this application, the EDU discussed in the previous section becomes:

$$EDU_i(z) = -\frac{|\sum_{j=1}^{N} n_j a_j|}{\sum_{k=1}^{N} n_k}$$
$$+ \left(p(n_i = 1) \frac{|\sum_{j \neq i}^{N} n_j a_j + a_i|}{\sum_{k \neq i}^{N} n_k + 1} + p(n_i = 0) \frac{|\sum_{j \neq i}^{N} n_j a_j|}{\sum_{k \neq i}^{N} n_k} \right) \qquad (6)$$

where $p(n_i = 1)$ and $p(n_i = 0)$ give the probabilities that agent i set its n_i to 1 or 0 respectively. In what follows, we will assume that those two actions are equally likely (i.e., for all agents i, $p(n_i = 1) = p(n_i = 0) = 0.5$).

Depending on which action agent i chose (0 or 1), EDU can be reduced to:

$$EDU_i(z) = 0.5 \frac{|\sum_{j=1}^{N} n_j a_j - a_i|}{\sum_{k=1}^{N} n_k - 1} - 0.5 \frac{|\sum_{j=1}^{N} n_j a_j|}{\sum_{k=1}^{N} n_k} \qquad \text{if } n_i = 1, \qquad (7)$$

or:

$$EDU_i(z) = 0.5 \frac{|\sum_{j=1}^{N} n_j a_j + a_i|}{\sum_{k=1}^{N} n_k + 1} - 0.5 \frac{|\sum_{j=1}^{N} n_j a_j|}{\sum_{k=1}^{N} n_k} \qquad \text{if } n_i = 0. \qquad (8)$$

Note that in this formulation, EDU provides a very clear signal. If EDU is positive, the action taken by agent i was beneficial to G, and if EDU is negative, the action was detrimental to G. Thus an agent trying to maximize EDU will efficiently maximize G, without explicitly trying to do so. Furthermore, note that the computation of EDU requires very little information. Any system capable of broadcasting G can be minimally modified to accommodate EDU. For each agent to compute its EDU, the system needs to broadcast the two numbers needed to compute G: the number of devices that were turned on (i.e., the denominator in Equation 5) and the associated subset distortion as a real number (i.e., the numerator in Equation 5 before the absolute value operation is performed. Based on those two numbers, the agent can compute its EDU.

3.3 Wonderful Life Utility

For this application, the WLU discussed in the previous section becomes:

$$WLU_i(z) = -\frac{|\sum_{j=1}^{N} n_j a_j|}{\sum_{k=1}^{N} n_k} + \frac{|\sum_{j \neq i}^{N} n_j a_j|}{\sum_{k \neq i}^{N} n_k} \qquad (9)$$

Note however, that unlike with EDU, the action chosen by agent i has a large impact on the WLU. If agent i chooses action 0, the two terms in Equation 9 are identical, resulting in a WLU of zero. Depending on which action agent i chose (0 or 1), WLU can be reduced to:

$$WLU_i(z) = \frac{|\sum_{j=1}^{N} n_j a_j - a_i|}{\sum_{k=1}^{N} n_k - 1} - \frac{|\sum_{j=1}^{N} n_j a_j|}{\sum_{k=1}^{N} n_k} \qquad \text{if } n_i = 1 , \qquad (10)$$

or:

$$WLU_i(z) = 0 \qquad\qquad\qquad\qquad \text{if } n_i = 0 . \qquad (11)$$

In this formulation, unlike EDU, WLU provides a clear signal only if agent i had chosen action 1. In that case, a positive WLU means that the action was beneficial to G, and a negative WLU means that the action was detrimental for G. However, if agent i had chosen action 0, it receives a reward of 0 regardless of whether that action was good or bad for G. This means that on average half the actions an agent takes will be random as far as G is concerned. Considering learnability implications, this means that on average WLU will have half the learnability of EDU for this problem.

4 Experimental Results

In this work we purposefully used computationally unsophisticated and easy to build agents for the following reasons:

1. To ensure that we remained consistent with our purpose of showing that a large scale system of potentially failure-prone agents can be coordinated to achieve a system level goal. Indeed, building thousands of sophisticated agents may be prohibitively difficult; therefore though systems that will scale up to thousands may use sophisticated agents, they cannot rely on such sophistication.
2. To focus on the design of the utility functions. Having sophisticated agents can obscure the differences in performance due to the agent utility functions and the algorithms they ran. By having each agent run a very simple algorithm we kept the emphasis on the effectiveness of the utility functions.

Each agent had a data set and a simple reinforcement learning algorithm. Each agents' data set contained time, action, utility value triplets that the agent stored throughout the simulation. At each time step each agent chose what action to take, which provided a joint action which in turn set the system state. Based on that state the system level utility, and the private utility of all the agents are computed. The new time, action take and utility value for agent i then gets added to the data set maintained by agent i. This is done for all agents and then the process repeats.

To choose its actions, an agent uses its data set to estimate the values of the utility it would receive for taking each of its two possible move. Each agent i picks its action at a time step based on the utility estimates at that time. Instead of simply picking the largest estimate, to promote exploration it probabilistically selects an action, with a higher likelihood of selecting the actions with higher utility estimates (e.g., it uses a Boltzmann distribution across the utility values). Because the experiments were run for short periods of time, the temperature in the Boltzmann distribution did not decay in time. However to reflect the fact that the environment in which an agent is operating changes with time (as the other agents change their moves), and therefore the optimal action changes in time, the two utility estimates are formed using exponentially aged data: for any time step t, the utility estimate i uses for setting either of the two actions n_i is a weighted average of all the utility values it has received at previous times t' that it chose that action, with the weights in the average given by an exponential of the values $t - t'$. Finally, to form the agents' initial data sets, there is an initialization period in which all actions by all agents are chosen uniformly randomly, with no learning used. It is after this initialization period ends that the agents choose their actions according to the associated Boltzmann distributions.

For all learning algorithms, the first 20 time steps constitute the data set initialization period (note that all learning algorithms must "perform" the same during that period, since none are actually in use then). Starting at $t = 20$, with each consecutive time step a fixed fraction of the agents switch to using their learner algorithms instead, while others continue to take random actions. Because the behavior of the agents starting to use their learning algorithm changes, having all agents start learning simultaneously provides a sudden "spike" into the system which significantly slows down the learning process. This gradual introduction of the learning algorithms is intended to soften the "discontinuity" in each agent's environment. In these experiments, for $N = 50$ and $N = 100$, three agents turned on their learning algorithms at each time step, and for $N = 1000$, sixty agents turned on their learning algorithms at each time step.

4.1 Agent Utility Performance

Figures 1-3 show the convergence properties of different agent utilities and a search algorithm in systems with 50, 100 and 1000 agents respectively. The results reported are based on 20 different $\{a_i\}$ configurations, where each $\{a_i\}$ is selected from a Gaussian distribution with zero mean and unit variance. For each configuration, the experiments were run 50 times (i.e., each point on the Figures is the average of $20 \times 50 = 1000$ runs). The graphs labeled G, EDU and WLU show the performance of agents using reinforcement learners with those reinforcement signals provided by G (team game), EDU and WLU respectively. S shows the performance of local search where new n_i's are generated at each step by perturbing the current state and selected if the solution is better than the current best solution (in the experiments reported here, 25% of the actions were randomly changed at each time step, though somewhat surprisingly, the results are not particularly sensitive to this parameter). Because the runs are only 200 time steps long, algorithms such as simulated annealing do not outperform local search: there is simply no time for an annealing schedule. This local search algorithm provides the performance of an algorithm with centralized control.

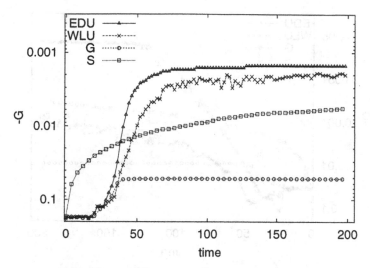

Fig. 1. Combination of Imperfect Devices Problem, N=50.

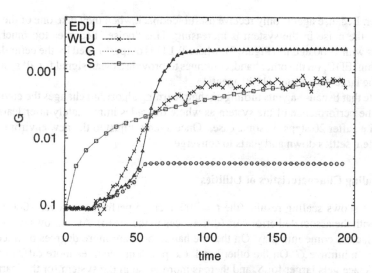

Fig. 2. Combination of Imperfect Devices Problem, N=100.

In all cases in which agents use the G utility, they have a difficult time learning. Even for 50 agents, the noise in the system is too large for such agents to learn how to select their actions. For 50 agents (Figure 1) both WLU and EDU outperform the centralized search algorithm. In this case, both utility functions sufficiently "clean-up" the signal for the agents to perform well. For 100 agents (Figure 2), WLU starts

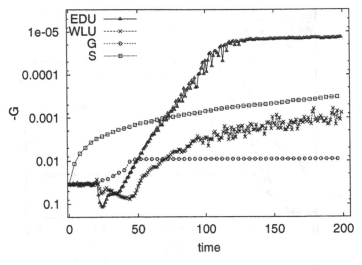

Fig. 3. Combination of Imperfect Devices Problem, N=1000.

to suffer. Because agents only receive useful feedback when they take one of the two actions, the noise in the system is increasing. This "noise" becomes too much for systems with 1000 agents (Figure 3), where WLU is outperformed by the centralized algorithm. EDU, on the other hand, continues to provide a clean signal for all systems up to the largest we tested (1000 agents).

Note that because agents turning on their learning algorithm changes the environment, the performance of the system as whole degrades immediately after learning starts (i.e., after 20 steps) in some cases. Once agents adjust to the new environment, the system settles down and starts to converge.

4.2 Scaling Characteristics of Utilities

Figure 4 shows scaling results (the $t = 200$ average performance over 1000 runs) along with the associated error bars (differences in the mean). As N grows two competing factors come into play. On the one hand, there are more degrees of freedom to use to minimize G. On the other hand, the problem becomes more difficult: the search space gets larger for S, and there is more noise in the system for the learning algorithms. To account for these effects and calibrate the performance values as N varies, we also provide the baseline performance of the "algorithm" that randomly selects its action ("Ran"). Note that the difference between the performances of all algorithms and EDU increases when the system size increases, reaching a factor of twenty for S and over 600 for G for $N = 1000$.

Also note that all algorithms but EDU have slopes similar to that of "Ran", showing that they cannot use the additional degrees of freedom provided by the larger N. Only EDU effectively uses the new degrees of freedom, providing gains that are

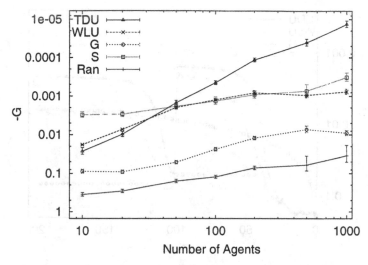

Fig. 4. Scaling in the Combination of Imperfect Devices Problem.

proportionally higher than the other algorithms (i.e., the rate at which *EDU*'s performance improves outpaces what is "expected" based on the random algorithm's performance).

4.3 Robustness

In order to evaluate the robustness of the proposed utility functions for multiagent coordination, we tested the performance of the system when a subset of the agents failed during the simulation. At a given time ($t = 100$ in these experiments), a certain percentage of agents failed (e.g., were turned off) simulating hazardous condition in which the functioning of the agents cannot be ascertained. The relevance of this experiment is in determining whether the proposed utility functions require all or a large portion of the agents to perform well to be effective, or whether they can handle sudden changes to their environment.

Figure 5 shows the performance of EDU, WLU, and G for 50 agents when 10% of the agents fail at time step $t = 100$. Similarly Figure 6 shows the performance of 100 agents where 20% of them fail. The results of the centralized search algorithm with no failures ("S" from Section 4.1), is also included for comparison.

In these experiments, none of the agent learning algorithms were adjusted to account for the change in the environment. In agents that continued to function, the learning proceeded as though nothing had happened. As a consequence, not only did the agents need to overcome the sudden change in their task but they had to do so with parameters tuned to the previous environment. Despite these limitations, EDU and WLU recover rapidly for the 50 agent case, whereas G does not. For the case with 100 agents and 20% agent failure, only EDU outperforms the centralized

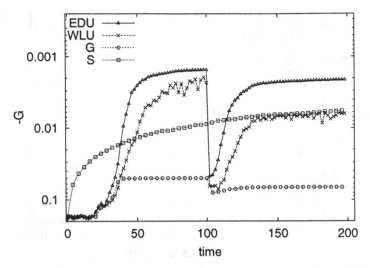

Fig. 5. System performance for 50 agents, 10% of which fail at time t=100.

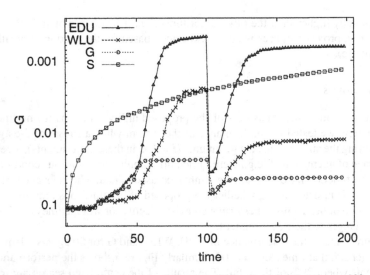

Fig. 6. System performance for 100 agents, 20% of which fail at time t=100.

search algorithm. Note this is a powerful results: a distributed algorithm with only 80% functioning agents, each tuned to a different environment outperforms a 100% functioning centralized algorithm.

Figures 7 and 8 show the performance of EDU when the percentage of agent failures increases from 10 to 50% for 50 and 100 agents respectively. For comparison

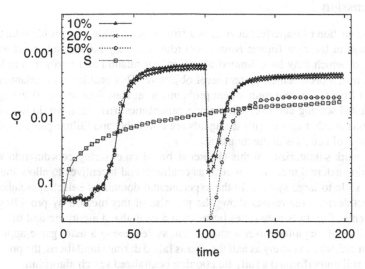

Fig. 7. Effect of agent failures on EDU for 50 agents (S has no agent failures).

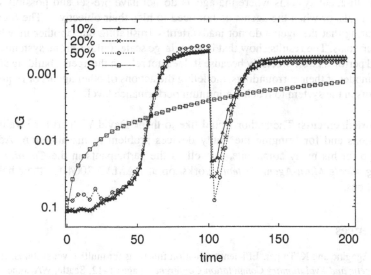

Fig. 8. Effect of agent failures on EDU for 100 agents (S has no agent failures).

purposes, the search results (From Section 4.1) are also included. After the initial drop in performance when the agents stop responding, EDU trained algorithms recover rapidly and even with half the agents outperform the fully functioning and centralized search algorithm. These results demonstrate both the adaptability of the EDU and its robustness to failures of individual agents, even in extreme cases.

5 Discussion

The combination of imperfect devices is a simple abstraction of a problem that will loom large in the near future: How to coordinate a very large numbers of agents – many of which may have limited access to information and perform unreliably – to achieve a prespecified system-level objective. This problem is fundamentally different from traditional multi-agent problems in at least four ways: (i) the agents have limited sensing and decision making capabilities; (ii) the agent do not model the actions of other agents; (iii) the agents are unreliable and failure-prone; and (iv) the number of agents is in the thousands.

The work summarized in this chapter is based on ensuring coordination while eliminating external mechanisms such as contracts and incentives to allow the systems to scale to large system. In the experimental domain of selecting a subset of imperfect devices, the results shows the promise of this method by providing improvements of up to twenty times better than a centralized algorithm and of nearly three orders of magnitude over a multi-agent system using a team game approach. Furthermore, when as many as half the agents failed during simulations, the proposed method still outperformed a fully functioning centralized search algorithm.

This approach is well-suited for addressing coordination in large scale cooperative multi-agent systems where the agents do not have pre-set and possibly conflicting goals, or when the agents do not need to hide their objectives. The focus is on ensuring that the agents do not inadvertently frustrating one another in achieving their goals. The results show that in such large scale, failure-prone systems, this method performs well precisely because it does not rely on the agents building an accurate model of their surroundings, modeling the actions of other agents or requiring all agents in the system to reach a minimum performance level.

Acknowledgements: The author would like to thank David Wolpert for invaluable discussions and for bringing the faulty devices problem to his attention, Adrian Agogino for his many comments, as well as the participants in the *Coordination of Large Scale Multi-Agent Systems* workshop at AAMAS 2004 for their helpful suggestions.

References

1. A. Agogino and K. Tumer. Efficient evaluation functions for multi-rover systems. In *The Genetic and Evolutionary Computation Conference*, pages 1–12, Seatle, WA, June 2004.
2. A. Agogino and K. Tumer. Unifying temporal and structural credit assignment problems. In *Proceedings of the Third International Joint Conference on Autonomous Agents and Multi-Agent Systems*, New York, NY, July 2004.
3. S. Arai, K. Sycara, and T. Payne. Multi-agent reinforcement learning for planning and scheduling multiple goals. In *Proceedings of the Fourth International Conference on MultiAgent Systems*, pages 359–360, July 2000.
4. C. Boutilier. Planning, learning and coordination in multiagent decision processes. In *Proceedings of the Sixth Conference on Theoretical Aspects of Rationality and Knowledge*, Holland, 1996.

5. D. Challet and N. F. Johnson. Optimal combinations of imperfect objects. *Physical Review Letters*, 89:028701, 2002.
6. B. Clement and E. Durfee. Theory for coordinating concurrent hierarchical planning agents. In *Proceedings of the National Conference on Artificial Intelligence*, pages 495–502, 1999.
7. R. H. Crites and A. G. Barto. Improving elevator performance using reinforcement learning. In D. S. Touretzky, M. C. Mozer, and M. E. Hasselmo, editors, *Advances in Neural Information Processing Systems - 8*, pages 1017–1023. MIT Press, 1996.
8. K. Decker and V. Lesser. Designing a family of coordination mechanisms. In *Proceedings of the International Conference on Multi-Agent Systems*, pages 73–80, June 1995.
9. J. Fredslund and M. J. Mataric. Robots in formation using local information. In *Proceedings, 7th International Conference on Intelligent Autonomous Systems (IAS-7)*, pages 100–107, Marina del Rey, CA, March 2002.
10. M. R. Garey and D. S. Johnson. *Computers and Intractability: A Guide to the Theory of NP-Completeness*. W.H. Freeman and Company, San Fransisco, 1979.
11. T. Hogg and B. A. Huberman. Controlling smart matter. *Smart Materials and Structures*, 7:R1–R14, 1998.
12. J. Hu and M. P. Wellman. Multiagent reinforcement learning: Theoretical framework and an algorithm. In *Proceedings of the Fifteenth International Conference on Machine Learning*, pages 242–250, June 1998.
13. B. A. Huberman and T. Hogg. The behavior of computational ecologies. In *The Ecology of Computation*, pages 77–115. North-Holland, 1988.
14. N. F. Johnson, S. Jarvis, R. Jonson, P. Cheung, Y. R. Kwong, and P. M. Hui. Volatility and agent adaptability in a self-organizing market. preprint cond-mat/9802177, February 1998.
15. M. Kearns and D. Koller. Efficient reinforcement learning in factored MDPs. In *Proceedings of the Sixteenth International Joint Conference on Artificial Intelligence*, pages 740–747, 1999.
16. S. Kraus. Negotiation and cooperation in multi-agent environments. *Artificial Intelligence*, pages 79–97, 1997.
17. M. L. Littman. Markov games as a framework for multi-agent reinforcement learning. In *Proceedings of the 11th International Conference on Machine Learning*, pages 157–163, 1994.
18. D. C. Parkes. *Iterative Combinatorial Auctions: Theory and Practice*. PhD thesis, University of Pennsylvania, 2001.
19. D. Pynadath and M. Tambe. The communicative multiagent team decision problem: Analyzing teamwork theories and models. *Journal of Artificial Intelligence Research*, 16:389–423, 2002.
20. T. Sandholm and R. Crites. Multiagent reinforcement learning in the iterated prisoner's dilemma. *Biosystems*, 37:147–166, 1995.
21. T. Sandholm and V. R. Lesser. Coalitions among computationally bounded agents. *Artificial Intelligence*, 94:99–137, 1997.
22. P. Scerri, Y. Xu, E. Liao, J. Lai, and K. Sycara. Scaling teamwork to very large teams. In *Proceedings of the Third International Joint Conference on Autonomous Agents and Multi-Agent Systems*, New York, NY, July 2004.
23. Sandip Sen, Mahendra Sekaran, and John Hale. Learning to coordinate without sharing information. In *Proceedings of the Twelfth National Conference on Artificial Intelligence*, pages 426–431, Seattle, WA, 1994.
24. P. Stone. *Layered Learning in Multi-Agent Systems: A Winning Approach to Robotic Soccer*. MIT Press, Cambridge, MA, 2000.

25. P. Stone and M. Veloso. Multiagent systems: A survey from a machine learning perspective. *Autonomous Robots*, 8(3), 2000.
26. R. S. Sutton and A. G. Barto. *Reinforcement Learning: An Introduction*. MIT Press, Cambridge, MA, 1998.
27. M. Tambe. Towards flexible teamwork. *Journal of Artificial Intelligence Research*, 7:83–124, 1997.
28. K. Tumer, A. Agogino, and D. Wolpert. Learning sequences of actions in collectives of autonomous agents. In *Proceedings of the First International Joint Conference on Autonomous Agents and Multi-Agent Systems*, pages 378–385, Bologna, Italy, July 2002.
29. K. Tumer and J. Lawson. Collectives for multiple resource job scheduling across heterogeneous servers. In *Proceedings of the Second International Joint Conference on Autonomous Agents and Multi-Agent Systems*, Melbourne, Australia, July 2003.
30. K. Tumer and D. Wolpert, editors. *Collectives and the Design of Complex Systems*. Springer, New York, 2004.
31. K. Tumer and D. Wolpert. A survey of collectives. In *Collectives and the Design of Complex Systems*, pages 1,42. Springer, 2004.
32. K. Tumer and D. H. Wolpert. Collective intelligence and Braess' paradox. In *Proceedings of the Seventeenth National Conference on Artificial Intelligence*, pages 104–109, Austin, TX, 2000.
33. C. Watkins and P. Dayan. Q-learning. *Machine Learning*, 8(3/4):279–292, 1992.
34. D. H. Wolpert and K. Tumer. Optimal payoff functions for members of collectives. *Advances in Complex Systems*, 4(2/3):265–279, 2001.
35. D. H. Wolpert, K. Tumer, and E. Bandari. Improving search algorithms by using intelligent coordinates. *Physical Review E*, 69:017701, 2004.
36. P. Xuan, V. Lesser, and S. Zilberstein. Communication decisions in multi-agent cooperation: Model and experiments. In *Proceedings of the Fifth International Conference on Autonomous Agents*, pages 616–623, Montreal, January 2001. ACM Press.
37. Y. C. Zhang. Modeling market mechanism with evolutionary games. *Europhysics Letters*, March/April 1998.

Part III

New Approaches for Large Scale Coordination

Learning Scalable Coalition Formation in an Organizational Context[*]

Sherief Abdallah and Victor Lesser

University of Massachusetts Amherst
shario,lesser@cs.umass.edu

1 Introduction

Agents can benefit by cooperating to solve a common problem [2, 11]. For example, several robots may cooperate to move a heavy object, sweep a specific area in short time, etc. However, as the number of agents increases, having all agents involved in a detailed coordination/negotiation process will limit the scalability of the system. It is better to first *form a coalition* of agents that has enough resources to undertake the common problem. Then only the agents in this coalition coordinate and negotiate among themselves.

This situation is common in domains where a task requires more than one agent and there are more than one task competing for resources. Computational grids and distributed sensor networks are examples of such domains. In computational grids a large number of computing systems are connected via a high-speed network. The goal of the grid is to meet the demands of new applications (tasks) that require large amounts of resources and reasonable responsiveness. Such requirements cannot be met by an individual computing system. Only subset of the available computing systems (aka a coalition) has enough resources to accomplish an incoming task.

The work in [8] defined the coalition formation problem as follows (a formal definition is given in Section 2). The input is a set of agents, each controlling some amount of resources, and a set of tasks, each requiring some amount of resources and each worth some utility. The solution assigns a coalition of agents to each task, such that each task's requirements are satisfied and total utility is maximized. It should

---

[*] This material is based upon work supported in part by the National Science Foundation under Grant No. IIS-9988784 and the Defense Advanced Research Projects Agency (DARPA) and Air Force Research Laboratory Air Force Materiel Command, USAF, under agreement F30602-99-2-0525. The U.S. Government is authorized to reproduce and distribute reprints for Governmental purposes notwithstanding any copyright annotation thereon. Any opinions, findings, and conclusions or recommendations expressed in this material are those of the author(s) and do not necessarily reflect the views of the National Science Foundation, the Defense Advanced Research Projects Agency (DARPA), Air Force Research Laboratory or the U.S. Government.

be noted that the coalition formation problem is not concerned with how agents in a coalition cooperate to actually executes its assigned task. Such cooperation can be achieved by other complementing frameworks such as teamwork [11].

In this chapter we propose a novel approach for solving the coalition formation problem approximately using an *underlying organization* to guide the formation process. The intuition here is to exploit whatever knowledge is known *a priori* in order to make the coalition formation process more efficient. For instance, in many domains, agents' capabilities remain the same throughout the lifetime of the system. Additionally, incoming tasks may follow some statistical pattern. Can we *organize* agents to exploit this knowledge (of their capabilities and task arrival patterns) to make the search for *future* coalitions more efficient? If so, will all organizations yield the same performance, or do some organizations perform better than others? In the remainder of this chapter we try to provide answers to these questions. The main contributions of this work are:

- an organization-based distributed algorithm for approximately solving the coalition formation problem
- the use of reinforcement learning to optimize the local allocation decisions made by agents in the underlying organization

The chapter is organized as follows. In Section 2 we define the problem formally, laying out the framework we will use throughout the chapter. In Section 4 we present our approach. Section 5 describes our experimental results. We compare our approach to similar work in Section 6. Conclusions and future work are discussed in Section 7.

2 Problem definition

To focus on the coalition formation problem, some simplifying assumptions are made to avoid adding the scheduling problem to it.[2] We assume time is divided into episodes. At the beginning of each episode each agent receives a sequence of tasks.[3] Once a task is allocated a coalition, agents in that coalition can not be assigned to another task until the end of the episode. At the end of every episode all agents are freed and ready to be allocated to the next sequence of tasks. More formally:

Let $T = \langle T_1, T_2, ..., T_q \rangle$ be the sequence of tasks arriving in an episode. Each task T_i is defined by the tuple $\langle u_i, rr_{i,1}, rr_{i,2}, ..., rr_{i,m} \rangle$, where u_i is the utility gained if task T_i is accomplished; and $rr_{i,k}$ is the amount of resource k required by task T_i. Let $I = \{I_1, I_2, ..., I_n\}$ be the set of individual agents in the system. Each agent I_i is defined by the tuple $\langle cr_{i,1}, cr_{i,2}, ..., cr_{i,m} \rangle$, where $cr_{i,k}$ is the amount of resource k controlled by agent I_i.

The coalition formation problem is finding a subset of tasks $S \subseteq T$ that maximizes utility while satisfying the coalition constraints, i.e.:

---

[2] In future we plan to integrate scheduling in our framework.

[3] Note that the overall system may receive more than one task at the same time but at different agents.

- $\sum_{i|T_i \in S} u_i$ is maximized
- and there exists a set of coalitions $\bar{C} = \{C_1, ..., C_{|S|}\}$, where $C_i \subseteq I$ is the coalition assigned to task T_i, such that $\forall T_i \in S, \forall k : \sum_{I_j \in C_i} cr_{j,k} \geq rr_{i,k}$, and $\forall i \neq j : C_i \cap C_j = \emptyset$

In other words, each task is assigned a coalition capable of accomplishing it and any agent can join at most one coalition. This means if the resources controlled (collectively) by a coalition exceed the amount of resources required by the assigned task, the excess resources are wasted. Having more than one type of resource means that there will be trade-offs, where decreasing the excess of one resource type may increase the excess of another resource type. Next section shows that the coalition formation problem (as defined above) is NP-hard.

2.1 Complexity

In this section we prove that the Coalition Formation Problem (CFP), as we formulated it, is NP-hard. We do so by reducing the multidimensional knapsack problem, which is known to be NP-hard, to CFP.

The Multi-dimensional Knapsack Problem, MDKP

The input of this problem consists of a set of constraints $C = \{c_1, c_2, ..., c_m\}$ and a set of objects $O = \{o_1, o_2, ..., o_q\}$, where each object is defined by the tuple $o_i = <u_i, w_{i,1}, w_{i,2}, ..., w_{i,m}>$, where u_i is its value and $w_{i,j}$ is its weight for dimension j. The goal is to find a subset of objects $S \subset O$, s.t. $\sum_{o_i \in S} u_i$ is maximized, while $\forall c_j \in C, \sum_{o_i \in S} w_{i,j} \leq c_j$

Theorem 1. *Coalition Formation Problem, CFP, is NP-hard*

Proof. This is proved by reducing an MDKP instance to a CFP instance. This is done as follows. The decision version of the MDKP problem is:

Q1: given a set of objects O and a set of constraints C, is there a valid subset of objects S_k that satisfy the constraints and has total utility of k or more?

The mapping from MDKP to CFP is as follows. For each object $o_i = <u_i, w_{i,1}, ..., w_{i,m}>$ in MDKP, we define an agent $a_i = <w_{i,1}, ..., w_{i,m}>$ and a task $T_i = <u_i, w_{i,1}, ..., w_{i,m}>$. We also add task $T' = <U, W_1, ..., W_m>$, where $U = \sum_{o_i \in O} u_i$ and $W_j = (\sum_{o_i \in O} w_{i,j}) - c_j$ (this amount can be viewed as the gap between the demand of a resource and its supply). As will be described shortly, T' encodes the constraints of the MDKP instance such that the coalition assigned to this task corresponds to the set of objects left **outside** the knapsack. The CFP decision problem then becomes:

Q2: given the set of tasks T and the set of agents A, is there a a valid set of Coalitions $\bar{C}$ that results in $U + k$ utility or more?

To prove the theorem, we need to show that the answer to Q1 is yes iff the answer to Q2 is yes. Let $\bar{C}_k = \{\{a_i\} : o_i \in S_k\}$ be the set of coalitions corresponding to S_k (i.e. $\bar{C}_k$ is a set of singular coalitions). Let $C_{-k} = \{a_i : o_i \notin S_k\}$, i.e. the coalition corresponding to all objects not in S_k. By definition, every coalition $\{a_i\} \in \bar{C}_k$ can be assigned to T_i, resulting in k utility. The hard part is to prove that the constraints of the MDKP problem is not violated by this assignment. This is where T' comes into play. If S_k satisfies the MDKP constraints, then

$$\forall j, \sum_{i:o_i \in S_k} w_{i,j} \leq c_j$$

$$\therefore \forall j \sum_{i:o_i \in O} w_{i,j} - \sum_{o_i \in S_k} w_{i,j} \geq \sum_{i:o_i \in O} w_{i,j} - c_j$$

$$\therefore \forall j \sum_{i:o_i \notin S_k} w_{i,j} \geq W_j$$

$$\therefore \forall j \sum_{i:a_i \in C_{-k}} w_{i,j} \geq W_j$$

i.e., C_{-k} is a valid coalition to undertake T'. This means there exists a set of coalitions $\bar{C} = \bar{C}_k \cup \{C_{-k}\}$ that yield $k + U$ utility.

3 Control

In a real multiagent system, which implements the coalition formation approach, a task may arrive at any agent. How can this agent *know* which agents have the right capabilities? We refer to the problem of *locating and assigning* an agent to a coalition as the control problem. While the control problem is crucial to the coalition formation process, it has received little attention in previous work that deals with coalition formation. This section tries to pin down the different approaches to solve this problem.

Figure 1 illustrates three possible approaches to the control problem. The first approach is having a fully distributed control paradigm where every agent is a manager. Each manager knows about and controls every other agent. The other extreme is the fully centralized approach, where there is only one manager in the system. The third approach is having a hierarchy. In this case there is a *tree* of managers. Each manager controls a *fixed* number of neighbors. The remainder of this section discusses the trade-offs between these three approaches in light of the following issues: state consistency, scalability, and reliability.

Communication is needed when a new task arrives for two reasons. First to inform agents that are chosen in the coalition which task they are assigned to. Second, to inform other managers of the change of state in the system, i.e. maintaining *state consistency*. State consistency is the property that every manager in a system sees the same system's state. This is important to avoid conflicts among managers as early as possible. For example, assume manager m_1 asks agent a_1 to undertake task T_1. a_1 accepts and hence is no longer available to be assigned to another task. On the other hand, manager m_2 does not know of the change in a_1's state. m_2 receives another task, decomposes it, and starts contracting subtasks, relying on its incorrect system state. After contracting and committing some subtasks, m_2 asks a_1 to do subtask T_2.

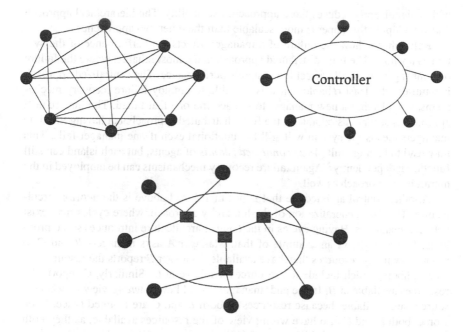

Fig. 1. Different control structures: fully distributed (top left), fully centralized (top right), and hierarchy (bottom).

a_1 rejects the request as it is still working on T_1. m_2 fails to find a substitute for a_1 and starts decommitting the subtasks already committed.

Naturally, maintaining state consistency becomes a problem as the number of managers in a system increases. For example, in the fully distributed approach where every agent is itself a manager, the number of managers is maximum and maintaining state consistency needs a lot of communication overhead.[4] This makes the fully distributed approach the least efficient. On the other hand, in the fully centralized approach there is only one manager in the system that handles all allocations, therefore maintaining state consistency is free. The hierarchical approach strikes a balance between the other two approaches (the overhead for maintaining state consistency depends on the number of managers in the system).

Scalability is also an issue. A manager that needs to know the state of 1000 agents and control them is much more overloaded than a manager that needs to know the state of only 10 agents and control just these 10 agents. In both the centralized and the fully distributed approaches a manager is connected to all agents in the system,

---

[4] It is also possible to leave other managers have an *old* state of the system, hoping that no conflict will occur (e.g. they will never ask for the same agent, or even if they ask, the other agent will be already done from the old task.) This may lead to communication savings in some domains. We do not cover this approach in this chapter.

which significantly reduces these approaches scalability. The hierarchical approach that we adopt in this paper is more scalable than the other two approaches.

Reliability is how the failure of a manager affects the performance of the system as a whole. The fully distributed approach is the most reliable, where the failure of a manager minimally affect the system's performance. The centralized approach is naturally the least reliable, but it is possible to employ failure recovery mechanisms, e.g. electing a new manager to replace the one that failed. The hierarchical approach is still not as reliable as the fully distributed approach, but having multiple managers means the system will still be functional even if one manager fails. This may lead to having multiple *disconnected islands* of agents, but each island can still function independently.[5] Again failure recovery mechanisms can be employed in the hierarchical approach as well.

Another control architecture that is not mentioned above is the *network* architecture. This is a generalization of the hierarchy approach, where cycles may exist between managers. Having cycles in the control architecture introduces some problems. Figure 2 shows an example of that. Manager A asks managers B and C to report how many resources they have available. Manager B reports the resources of its neighbors, which include the resources available at C. Similarly, C reports the resources available at B. In the end, manager A will have a *wrong* view of what resources are available, because resources of both B and C are counted twice. Even worse, both B and C also have wrong view of the resources available, as they both may ask A for its state (which wrongfully indicates that A has a lot of resources). Having cycles also requires care with contracting tasks. Without careful protocol design, a task may circulate indefinitely being continuously contracted. For these reasons we did not consider control structures that include cycles.

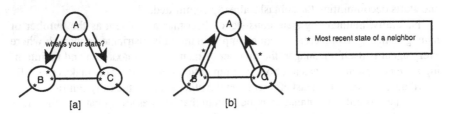

Fig. 2. Problems with cycles in control architectures.

4 Proposed Solution

Because the coalition formation problem is NP-hard, an optimal algorithm will need exponential time in the worst case (unless NP = P). An approximation algorithm,

---

[5] Because islands are now disconnected, it is possible that some tasks that were achievable by the connected hierarchy are no longer achievable.

which can exploit information about the problem, is needed. If the environment (in terms of incoming task classes and patterns) does not follow any statistical model, and agents continually and rapidly enter and exit the system, there is little information to be exploited. Luckily, in many real applications the environment does follow a model, and the system can be assumed closed.

In such cases, it is intuitive to take advantage of this stability and *organize* the agents in order to guide the search for future coalitions. We chose to organize agents in a hierarchy, which is both distributed and scalable as discussed in Section 3. Figure 3 shows a sample hierarchical organization. An *individual* (the leaves in Figure 3) represents the resources controlled by a single agent. A *manager* (shown as a circle in Figure 3) is a computational role, which can be executed on any individual agent, or on dedicated computing systems. A manager *represents* agents beneath it when it comes to interaction with other parts of the organization.

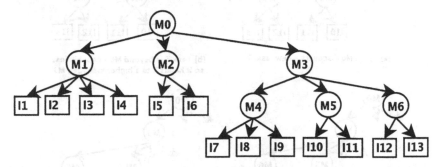

Fig. 3. An Organization Hierarchy

Each manager M has a set of children, $children(M)$, which is the set of nodes directly linked below it. So for instance, in the organization shown in Figure 3, $children(M6) = \{I12, I13\}$, while $children(M3) = \{M4, M5, M6\}$. Conversely, each child C has a set of managers $managers(C)$. For example, $managers(M4) = \{M3\}$. For completeness, children of an individual are the empty set, and so are the managers of a root node.

Each agent A (either a manager or an individual) controls, either directly or indirectly, a set of individuals, $cluster(A)$ (i.e., the leaves reachable from agent A). In the example above, $cluster(M6) = \{I12, I13\}$, $cluster(M3) = \{I7, I8, I9, I10, I11, I12, I13\}$, and $cluster(I6) = \{I6\}$. Also for each agent A, we define $members(A)$ to be the set of all agents reachable from A. In the above example, $members(M3) = \{M3, M4, M5, M6, I7, I8, I9, I10, I11, I12, I13\}$. Sections 4.3 and 4.6 show how agents in such organizations learn to work with each other.

4.1 Example

Figure 4 shows how a group of agents, organized in a hierarchy, can cooperate to form a coalition. A task $T = \langle u = 100, rr_1 = 50, rr_2 = 150 \rangle$ is discovered by agent

*M*6. Knowing that *members*(*M*6) does not have enough resources to accomplish *T*, *M*6 sends task *T* to its manager *M*3. Since *members*(*M*3) has enough resources to achieve *T*, *M*3 uses its local policy to chose the best child to contribute in achieving *T*, which is *M*5. *M*3 partially decomposes *T* into subtask $T_5 = \langle u_5 = 50, rr_{5,1} = 0, rr_{5,2} = 100 \rangle$, and asks *M*5 to allocate a coalition for it. *M*5 returns a committed coalition $C_{T_5} = \{I10, I11\}$. The process continues until the whole task *T* is allocated. Finally, *M*3 integrates all sub-coalitions into C_T and sends it back to *M*6.

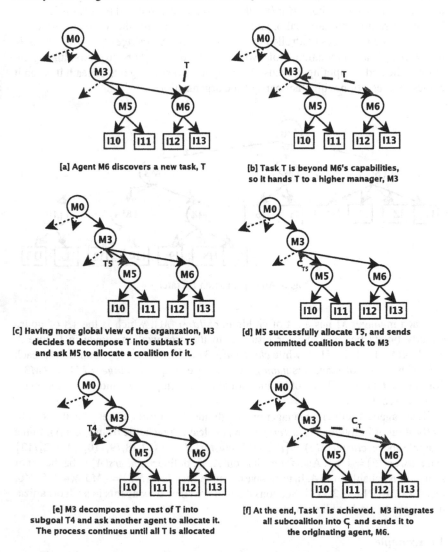

[a] Agent M6 discovers a new task, T

[b] Task T is beyond M6's capabilities, so it hands T to a higher manager, M3

[c] Having more global view of the organzation, M3 decides to decompose T into subtask T5 and ask M5 to allocate a coalition for it.

[d] M5 successfully allocate T5, and sends committed coalition back to M3

[e] M3 decomposes the rest of T into subgoal T4 and ask another agent to allocate it. The process continues until all T is allocated

[f] At the end, Task T is achieved. M3 integrates all subcoalition into C_T and sends it to the originating agent, M6.

Fig. 4. An example of organization-based coalition formation.

4.2 Architecture

In the system we developed, managers are concurrently and distributively learning their local policies. A local policy determines the order by which a manager decomposes a high-level task into subtasks and allocate these subtasks to its children. The combination of local policies constitutes a global hierarchical policy of the whole system. Figure 5 illustrates a block diagram of a manager's architecture in the system. There is a handler for every child. Each handler includes a neural net, which approximates the value of choosing the corresponding child to form a sub-coalition (for the task at hand). The weights of a neural net are optimized using reinforcement learning, as Algorithm 3 shows (described in Section 4.3). To speedup learning using neural nets, the state encoder encodes the current state differently for the neural net of different children, depending on the amount of resources available at each child. More on learning in Section 4.6.

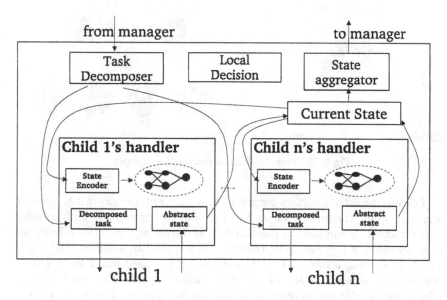

Fig. 5. A manager architecture.

The state aggregator aggregates the state of a manager m before it is sent to higher managers $managers(m)$. When a higher manager m_h receives the aggregated state from its child m, m_h will store the aggregated state in the *abstract state* field of child m's handler. The current state of a manager is a combination of the abstract states of its children and the current status of the task at hand (i.e. the resources the task requires and not yet allocated and the utility to be gained if the remainder of the task is completed). The task decomposer stores arriving tasks. When the local policy chooses a child to form a sub-coalition, the task decomposer decomposes the task for this child (storing it in the child's handler). More details of the operation of a manager in Section 4.3.

4.3 Local Decision

Algorithm 3 describes the decision process used by manager A in the organization once it receives a task T_A. Figure 6 illustrates the algorithm. Though in this figure T_A comes from another agent, T_A can also arrive directly from the environment as well. The algorithm works as follows.

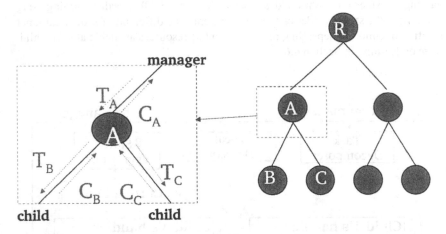

Fig. 6. The recursive decision process of a manager.

LOC_M is the list of coalitions committed by manager M for tasks that M received previously in the current episode. LOC_M is reset at the beginning of each episode. M evaluates its current state s_M (Section 4.4). M then selects an action a based on its policy (Section 4.6). Each action corresponds to a child $M_i \in children(M)$. Once a child is selected, a subtask T_i of T is dynamically created based on M_i's state (Section 4.5). M then asks M_i to form a sub-coalition capable of accomplishing T_i. (The notion $M_i.allocateCoalition(T_i)$ means that the function $allocateCoalition$ is called remotely on agent M_i). M_i forms a sub-coalition C_{T_i} and sends a commitment back to M. M updates C_T and learns about this action. M updates its state, including the amount of resources to be allocated (UR_M) and the corresponding utility to be gained (uu_M).

M selects the next best child and the process continues as long as the following conditions hold (step 3): T requires more resources than currently allocated AND M still controls some unallocated resources that are required by T. At the end, if enough resources are allocated to T, M adds the formed coalition C_T to its list of commitments LOC_M and returns C_T. Otherwise T is passed up the hierarchy. Also to simplify handling of multiple tasks, we do not allow coalition formation of a task to be interrupted. This means that if a new task T_{new} arrives at manager M while M is still forming a coalition for an older task T_{old}, then M will finish forming the coalition for T_{old} before considering T_{new}.

Algorithm 3: allocateCoalition(T)

INPUT: task $T = \langle u, rr_1, ..., rr_m \rangle$

OUTPUT: coalition $C_T = \{I_1, ..., I_{|C_T|}\}$

1: let $C_T = \{\}$, $uu \leftarrow u$, $UR \leftarrow \langle rr_1, ..., rr_m \rangle$, $stop \leftarrow$ false, $AR \leftarrow$ the amount of available
    resources controlled by $M = availableResources()$
    $= totalResources(M) - \sum_{C \in LOC} totalResources(C)$

2: $s \leftarrow$ encodeState(uu, UR)

3: **while** $UR > \bar{0}$ AND $UR.AR > 0$ AND $stop =$ false **do**

4:      $a \leftarrow$ selectAction(s)

5:      let M_i be the child corresponding to a.

6:      $T_i \leftarrow$ decomposeTask($\langle UR, uu \rangle$, M_i)

7:      $C_{T_i} \leftarrow M_i$.allocateCoalition(T_i)

8:      $C_T \leftarrow C_T \cup C_{T_i}$

9:      $UR \leftarrow UR - totalResources(C_{T_i})$, $uu \leftarrow uu - uT_i$, and $AR \leftarrow AR - totalResources(C_{T_i})$

10:     $r \leftarrow$ time and communication costs of forming C_{T_i}

11:     **if** $UR = \bar{0}$ /* T does not need more resources */ **then**

12:         $r \leftarrow r + u$

13:     **end if**

14:     $s' \leftarrow$ encodeState(uu, UR) /* the next state */

15:     learn(s, a, r, s')

16:     $s \leftarrow s'$

17: **end while**

18: **if** $UR > \bar{0}$ /* task T successfully allocated */ **then**

19:     $LOC \leftarrow LOC \cup C_T$ /* to exclude agents in C_T from next allocations */

20:     return C_T

21: **else**

22:     **if** $\exists M' \in managers(M)$ /* if not root */ **then**

23:         M'.allocateCoalition(T) /* pass T up */

24:     **else**

25:         fail.

26:     **end if**

27: **end if**

4.4 State Abstraction

For a manager M, the function *encodeState* encodes the current state at manager M to produce the current state of $members(M)$. This encoding is then fed to neural nets to get action values, as discussed in Section 4.6. Since the higher the manager in the hierarchy the exponentially more individuals it controls, state abstraction is necessary to achieve scalability. Otherwise, one is effectively centralizing the problem. In this work, each manager M abstracts the state of its organization, through the state aggregator (Section 4.2). This abstraction involves aggregating the states of underlying children recursively as described below.

Due to the large state space and to facilitate recursive abstraction, we defined the state by a set of features. Each state feature of manager M is defined recursively in terms of the features of M's children. For example, let the feature vector $totalResources(M) = \langle tr_1, ..., tr_m \rangle$ be the total amount of resources controlled by manager M (where m is the number of different resource types). It can be defined recursively as follows: $totalResources(M) = \sum_{c \in children(M)} totalResources(c)$. That is, the total resources controlled by a manager is the sum of the total resources controlled by its children. For an individual I_i, $totalResources(I_i) = I_i$.

Some features cannot be defined recursively in a straightforward way. Instead, they are defined in terms of other recursive features. For example, let $averageResources(M)$ be a feature vector of the average amount of resources controlled by any individual in $members(M)$. This feature can be defined as $averageReources(M) = totalResources(M)/size(M)$. $totalResources(M)$ is described above, while $size(M)$ is the total number of individuals in an organization and is recursively defined as $size(M) = \sum_{c \in children(M)} size(c)$.

The recursive features defined above are assumed constant throughout the system lifetime. For example, $size(M)$ will return the number of individuals controlled by manager M, even if at a specific time none of these individuals is free. Clearly, for allocation purposes, one needs more *dynamic* features that reflect the *current* state of the system. For each static feature, a corresponding dynamic feature is defined preceded by the keyword *avail*. For example, the number of individuals not allocated to tasks $= availSize(M) = size(M) - \sum_{C \in LOC(M)} size(C)$, and their aggregated resources $=$

$$availTotalResources(M) = totalResources(M) - \sum_{C \in LOC(M)} totalResources(C)$$

In our implementation, tasks allocation always starts from the root manager (even if a task is received/discovered at a lower manager it is propagated up the hierarchy to the root manager). This restriction and the strict tree control architecture simplify communication and maintaining state consistency. The reason is that an agent can receive a request to do a task only from its manager. Since there is only one manager for each agent, each manager knows the state of its children through the request/response messages exchange. For example, manager M initially knows its child M_1 has 100 of CPU resource. M asks M_1 to form a coalition with at least 50 CPU resource. M_1 replies that it formed a coalition of 60 CPU resource (because, for example, M_1 controls 5 agents of 20 CPU resource each). M now knows that M_1 has only 40 CPU resource available.

As a result, when a manager asks a child to form a coalition, the manager knows *a priori* that a capable coalition will be formed. What is not known is how much resources will be wasted. In the last example, manager M knows that its child M_1 has 100 units of CPU resource. When M asks M_1 to form a sub-coalition with at least 50 CPU units, M knows that M_1 will commit a coalition with 50 or more CPU units, but M does not know exactly how much CPU units. For example, if M_1 controls only one agent with 100 CPU units then this agent will be the formed coalition and 50 extra CPU units might be wasted.

As usual, nothing comes for free. While abstraction significantly enhances the scalability of the system, the price of abstraction is loss of information. A manager higher in the hierarchy "sees" fewer details about its organization. This leads to uncertainty in the manager state, and hence makes the local decision process more difficult to optimize. Section 4.7 discusses how the hierarchy affect the quality of abstraction.

4.5 Task Decomposition

When a manager M selects a child M_i to be asked for resources (for an incoming task T), M partially decomposes T to T_i (using heuristics that will be described shortly). As described in Section 4.4, a manager M only sees abstract features of its child M_i. Using this information, M needs to find T_i such that the expected excess of resources is minimized. What makes this difficult is that when a manager M decomposes T into T_i it does not know the exact state of M_i, but only an abstraction of it.

The partial decomposition heuristic we use, which is outlined in Algorithm 4, is to request from each child a multiple, α, of the average available resources it controls; i.e., $\alpha \times \frac{availTotalResources(M_i)}{availSize(M_i)}$. The intuition behind the heuristic is as follows. If all individuals controlled by M_i are identical, the heuristic is optimal. As individuals become more diverse in the resources they control, the heuristic still gives a good approximate decomposition that may succeed without wasting many resources.

Let us elaborate at Algorithm 4 in more detail. Because agents can not participate in more than one coalition, the minimum of the ratio l_j (in the algorithm) over all resource types is selected and used for all other resource types. Also to ensure progress, α is at least 1. Finally, the utility of the decomposed task is proportional to the total of the decomposed resources.

Algorithm 4: decomposeTask(T, M_i)

    INPUT: task $T = \langle u, rr_1, ..., rr_m \rangle$ AND manager M_i
    OUTPUT: task $T_i = \langle u_i, rr_{i,1}, ..., rr_{i,m} \rangle$
  1: $AR_i \leftarrow availTotalResources(M_i) = \langle ar_{i,1}, ..., ar_{i,m} \rangle$
  2: $z_i \leftarrow availSize(M_i)$
  3: $\forall j : l_j \leftarrow \lfloor z_i \times \frac{rr_j}{ar_j} \rfloor$
  4: $\alpha \leftarrow min_j(l_j)$
  5: $\alpha \leftarrow max(\alpha, 1)$
  6: $rr_{i,j} \leftarrow min(\alpha \times \frac{ar_{i,j}}{z_i}, rr_j)$
  7: $u_i \leftarrow u \times \frac{\sum_j rr_{i,j}}{\sum_j rr_j}$
  8: return T_i

For example, let $T = \langle u = 100, rr_1 = 50, rr_2 = 150 \rangle$, $availTotalResources(M_4) = \langle ar_{4,1} = 100, ar_{4,2} = 100 \rangle$, and $availSize(M_4) = 10$. Using the algorithm below we get $\alpha = 5$ and hence $T_4 = \langle u_4 = 50, rr_{4,1} = 50, rr_{4,2} = 50 \rangle$. Note that asking M_4 for as much as possible will result in wasted resources. For example, the decomposed task $T_4' = \langle u_4' = 50, rr_{4,1}' = 50, rr_{4,2}' = 100 \rangle$ can only be satisfied if all individuals controlled by M_4 are allocated, resulting in 50 units of resource type 1 being wasted.

Note that the above heuristic algorithm is not optimal. In the previous example, if the whole organization only has 150 units of resource type 2 available, then the decomposed task T_4' may be better than T_4. Because of that, we allow each manager to select the same child more than once to fine tune the decomposition at the expense of more communication and time cost.

4.6 Learning

A key factor in the performance of our system is how a manager selects its actions (function *selectAction* in Algorithm 3). In particular, in what order a manager should ask each child for its contribution. We modeled this as a Markov Decision Process, MDP, then used reinforcement learning (RL) techniques to learn a good local policy for each manager. This section briefly describes the MDP model and the RL algorithm this work uses to learn the manager's policy. The section also describes how this work uses neural nets in conjunction with RL to cope with large state space. Before getting into the details of the model, some terms need to be defined:

System/Environment. These terms are used interchangeably to refer to anything outside the agent. A state of manager M (when it receives task T) consists of the abstract states of each child $M_i \in children(M)$, the resources required by T and its utility.

Action. Whatever an agent can do is an action. In a manager, there is an action corresponding to each child.

Reward. A real number indicating the quality of the last executed action. In other words, the agent executes an action and then receives its immediate reward (utility) from the system. From Algorithm 3, intermediate rewards are small negative rewards to reflect the communication and the processing costs of each additional step spent forming the coalition. Once a manager M successfully allocates a coalition to task T, it gains a reward equal to T's utility. Note that we can implicitly indicate our preferences by modifying the reward function. For example, in [8] the author prefers coalitions of smaller size. This can be achieved by adjusting the reward function accordingly (e.g., dividing the utility gained by the size of the coalition formed). Note that even if T is a subtask of another task T', the rewards received by M are independent of whether the coalition formation for T' will succeed or not. This *recursive optimality* speeds up learning, while not affecting the quality of the formed coalitions.

State. Ideally, the state of the system at a certain time should include every bit of detail about this system. However, for all practical purposes, only part of the system that would affect decision is important. If the state of an agent does not capture enough details of the real world, the agent may fail to learn an optimal policy and the best it can do is to learn a near optimal policy.

Policy. The policy $\pi(s)$ is a table that specifies for every state the action that should be taken. The goal of a learning algorithm is to learn an *optimal* policy $\pi^*(s)$, i.e., a policy that specifies for every state the *best* action such that the total reward gained (by the agent) is maximized.

Decision Cycle. When an agent starts in a given state s, executes an action a, receives a reward r, and moves to the next state s', then this completes a decision cycle. This decision cycle is defined by the tuple $\langle s, a, r, s' \rangle$.

The model used in this work is Markov Decision Process, or MDP. In this model, the agent starts in a certain state s. The agent decides which *action* to execute. Upon executing an action a, the agent receives a *reward* r and the system moves to another state s'. The process continues until the system reaches a terminal state (if none exists, the process continues). An MDP model is completely defined by four components: $\langle S, A, P, R \rangle$, where

- S is the set of system states.
- A is the set of actions available for the agent to choose from.
- $P(s, a, s')$ is a transition probability function, i.e., the probability that the system will transit from state s to state s' if the agent executes action a. The uncertainty in coalition formation is due to the abstraction and the fact that a child might have allocated a task that its parent does not know about. Because it is difficult to analytically compute such transition probability, we used a model free learning algorithm as we discuss shortly.
- $R(s, a, s')$ is the expected reward function, if the system is in state s, the agent applies action a, and the system's next state is s'

In the field of operations research, it is assumed that all four components of the MDP are known and the optimal policy can be found using dynamic programming techniques [10]. However, in real domains, the P and R components are usually unknown. These two components together characterize the dynamics of the system in which the agent operates. They are called the *environment model*.

Reinforcement learning algorithms can be used in these cases as they make no assumptions regarding the environment model, and hence they are *model free*. These algorithms use *decision cycle tuples* to approximate the P and R functions. Decision cycle tuples can be obtained by executing actions in the system and receiving rewards. i.e., an agent observes its current state s and executes the best action a according to its policy, then observes the resulting reward r and next state s'. These four values constitute a decision cycle tuple.

This work uses a well-known algorithm, *Q-learn*[10] to automatically find the optimal policy. The main idea of the original algorithm is as follows. For every state and action pair $\langle s, a \rangle$, a real value $Q(s, a)$ is stored. These values are initialized randomly (or in any arbitrary way). They are then updated using the following equation (also known as Bellman's Equation):

$$Q(s,a) \leftarrow Q(s,a) + \alpha[r + \gamma \max_{a'} Q(s',a') - Q(s,a)]$$

Where $\langle s, a, r, s' \rangle$ is a decision cycle tuple; α and γ are learning parameters and are called *learning rate* and *discounting factor* respectively. As the agent moves from state to state, executing actions and receiving rewards, the values stored in Q converges and can be used to determine the optimal policy. Q-learning learns in an incremental and interactive manner; as an agent gains more experience, its performance improves. This is important in domains containing huge number of states, many of which will not be visited. The best action to perform in a given state s is $a^* = \pi^*(s) = argmax_a Q(s, a)$. The details explaining the intuition behind the algorithm and a proof of its correctness is beyond the scope of this chapter and can be found in [10]. We used the Q-learning algorithm with neural nets to approximate action values.

It should be noted that for this algorithm (and any other Reinforcement Learning algorithm) to work correctly, the agent needs to try all actions at every state "a large enough" number of times. One way to achieve this is to select an action randomly $\varepsilon\%$ of the time, and in the remaining $1 - \varepsilon\%$ pick the best action. This simple algorithm is called ε-*greedy exploration* algorithm [10] and ε is called the *exploration rate*. Typically, ε is initially large (to allow the agent to try more actions) and then decreases over time. We use a decaying exploration rate so that agents explore less as they gain more experience. We also tried using eligibility tracing, but the learning algorithm often diverged so this approach was dropped.

Neural Nets

Since the state of a manager includes the amount of available resources of each of its children and the amount of recourses required by the incoming task, the state space is very large. This prohibits the use of traditional Q-learning algorithm which uses a table to store the value of every state and action pair. Alternatively, functional approximators can be used. The idea here is to use a parametrized function instead of a table to approximate the values of actions (i.e. approximates $Q(s, a)$). In this case, Q-learning algorithm is used to update the parameters of the function, which implicitly updates the value of the action.

Here we use neural nets as the functional approximator. Q-learning is used to update the weights of the neural net. The details are beyond the scope of this document but can be found in [10]. A separate neural net is used to approximate the value of each action/child as shown in Figure 5. This uses more memory space (because of storing more neural nets), but provides better approximation as the weights of each neural net can be better fitted to the corresponding action/child.

We explored several techniques to speed up the learning further. One technique involved minimizing the input fed to each neural net. The key observation is that the value of choosing a child M_i depends mainly on M_i's state, and to a lesser extent on the other children's states.

4.7 Organization Structure

In this work, the underlying organization can be viewed as a search tree. Our distributed algorithm searches the same search tree several times for each task and for each episode. Each time, the search has a different start state (where and when the task is discovered) and different goal state (the set of individuals — leaves — that form the coalition.)

To optimize performance, not only does one need to learn a good *search mechanism*, as we do here, but also to find an *organization* that for a specific environment model and agent population yields the best performance. The interesting question is whether by modifying the search tree can the search mechanism perform better. The closest analogue in classical AI is the use of macro operators, which adds edges to the search tree to speedup the search. In our case there is more flexibility, as the search tree can be modified in whatever way.

While in this work we do not tackle the hard problem of optimizing the organization, we verify the effect of the underlying organization on the performance of the overall system. Our experiments verify this by testing different organization structures of the same agent population and same tasks distribution, as described in Section 5.

5 Experiments and Results

5.1 Setup

In our experiments we compare three possible policies: random, greedy, and learning. The random policy just picks a child at random. The greedy policy selects the child M_i with the highest preference value $p_i = \sum_{k=1}^{m} min(cr_{i,k}, rr_k)$, which measures how much resources M_i can contribute to the incoming task. For example, let the incoming task $T = \langle u = 100, rr_1 = 50, rr_2 = 150 \rangle$ and let manager M has two possible children M_1 and M_2 where $availTotalResources(M_1) = \langle cr_{1,1} = 200, cr_{1,2} = 0 \rangle$, $availTotalResources(M_2) = \langle cr_{2,1} = 0, cr_{2,2} = 200 \rangle$, $p_1 = 50$ and $p_2 = 150$. Thus M will select M_2.

The experiments try to evaluate the effect of both the underlying organization and learning the local policy on the system's performance. To do so, we compared the performance of the same agent population under five organizations and the three local policies described above. In the tested agent population, agents control two types of resources, and the fall into 6 types of agents:

Type A controls $\langle cr_{A,1} = 2, cr_{A,2} = 2 \rangle$ resources
Type B controls $\langle cr_{B,1} = 10, cr_{B,2} = 10 \rangle$ resources
Type C controls $\langle cr_{C,1} = 0, cr_{C,2} = 30 \rangle$ resources
Type D controls $\langle cr_{D,1} = 1, cr_{D,2} = 10 \rangle$ resources
Type E controls $\langle cr_{E,1} = 20, cr_{E,2} = 2 \rangle$ resources
Type F controls $\langle cr_{F,1} = 8, cr_{F,2} = 0 \rangle$ resources

These classes represent different specializations among agents. Four of the studied organizations are shown in Figure 7. Organization *HOMOGEN* is homogeneous. Agents of each type are clustered together, then similar types (e.g., A and B) are clustered together. Organization *SEMI − HOMOG* is semi-homogeneous. Each couple of agents of similar types are clustered together, then similar clusters are clustered together. Organization *SHORT* is similar to *HOMOGEN*, but one level of the hierarchy is omitted. Finally, organization *RANDOM* has the same "structure" of *SHORT*, but individual agents are assigned randomly to each cluster.

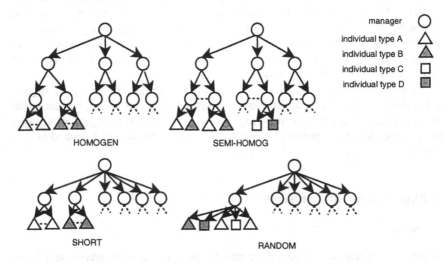

Fig. 7. Different Organization Structures.

Because the above four organizations (unlike the fifth organization described below) involve distributed decision making, we refer to the three local policies as: distributed learned policy (Distrib-Learn), distributed random policy (Distrib-Random), and distributed greedy policy (Distrib-Greedy), whenever we compare performance against the fifth organization.

The fifth organization is the centralized organization, *CENTRALIZED*, where there is only one manager connected to every other agent. This organization is tested using the random policy (Center-Random) and the greedy policy (Center-Greedy). The learned policy is not tested for this organization because the state of the centralized manager is exponential in the number of individuals, which is 40 in our experiments. We use this organization as a base line for comparison.

Results for every organization/technique combination were computed over 10 simulation runs. Each simulation run consisted of 30,000 episodes. Seven tasks arrive at every episode and are randomly picked from a bag of tasks. Tasks in the bag are generated randomly such that each task requires between 4 and 10 agents to be accomplished. Each task has an associated payoff, which is 1750 on average (it depends on the amount of resources each task requests). At any episode, the resources required by arriving tasks exceed the resources available to the system. The cost of every message (requesting a coalition or responding with a formed coalition) costs -1. Each Decision cycle (i.e. a time-step in forming a coalition) costs -1.

Our experiments focused only on 40 individuals and 10 managers so we can easily hand code different organization structures and study their effect. However, to verify the scalability of our approach, we tested it in a population of 90 agents and 13 managers. Agents were organized in a way similar to organization H and were randomly generated (using 9 distributions to represent 9 different classes of agents). Tasks were also randomly generated (from two different distributions). We plan further experiments on even larger populations and on the use of clustering techniques to automatically generate different organizations.

5.2 Results

Figure 8 shows the average utility for different organizations and policies when things have stabilized (i.e. learned policy converged). As expected, Center-Random performed worst. Distrib-Random performed better than Center-Random.[6] Center-Greedy is better than both. Our approach, Distrib-Learn, outperformed all other policies for all organization structures, except when using a random organization structure.

Figure 9 illustrates how the performance of our system improves as agents gain more experience (i.e., witness more episodes). Interestingly, Distrib-Greedy, performed worse than Distrib-Random and Distrib-Learn in all organizations except RANDOM, where it performed better than both. We think this is due to the fact that the greedy policy is based on a heuristic, which might perform best in some contexts and worst in others. That is also why the greedy policy has the highest deviation. In our experiments with larger agent population (90 agents), Distrib-Learn was better than other policies, achieving 35% more utility than Center-Random and at least 20% better than Distrib-Random and Distrib-Greedy.

More importantly, Distrib-Learn is more stable than other approaches as Figure 10 shows. The standard deviation (of achieved utility) using Center-Greedy is 70% worse than Distrib-Learn with SE organization. Center-Random is 30% worse than Distrib-Learn. Also Distrib-Greedy was the worst for all organizations except *RANDOM*. We had similar results with the larger agent population. Distrib-Learn had the least standard deviation, which was around one third that of Distrib-Greedy.

While it is expected that our approach performs better than distributed random and greedy policies, one might expect centralized policies to perform better than our approach, due to the inaccuracies (incurred by abstraction) and the limitations on managers' choices (imposed by the organization). We believe the reason our system performed better is the underlying organization, which implicitly encodes domain knowledge. In other words, limiting the actions of a manager is actually a good thing if these actions are the best actions this manager can take. This is also why a bad organization may lower performance. The underlying organization also affects the abstraction quality. A random organization contains more information, hence it will be abstracted poorly (the entropy principle).

---

[6] We believe this is due to the goal decomposition component of the organization, which encodes part of the domain knowledge.

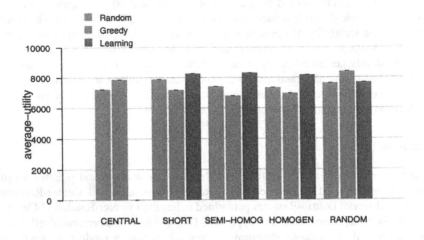

Fig. 8. Average utility for random, greedy and learned policies and for different organizations.

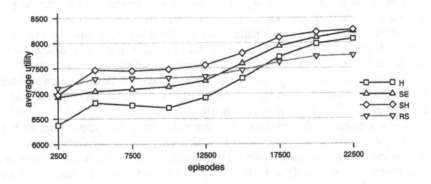

Fig. 9. Learning curve.

Figure 11 compares the average number of exchanged messages per task. As expected this measure increases as the organization hierarchy gets taller. Centralized approaches exchange fewer messages. Still, learning the local decision reduces the number of exchanged messages. Finally, Figure 12 shows the average resources wasted. Center-Greedy wasted 20% more resources than Distrib-Learn, while Center-Random wasted 40% more. We got similar results for the larger agent population.

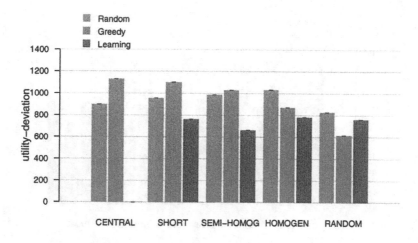

Fig. 10. Utility standard deviation for random, greedy and learned policies and for different organizations.

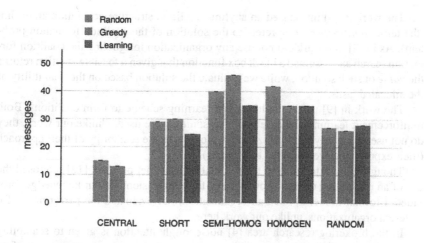

Fig. 11. Messages average for random, greedy and learned policies and for different organizations.

6 Related work

In [8], the authors presented a distributed algorithm for solving the coalition formation problem. The algorithm requires exponential time but is optimal. It neither used learning nor an underlying organization. Our algorithm is an approximation algorithm that returns a solution in polynomial time.

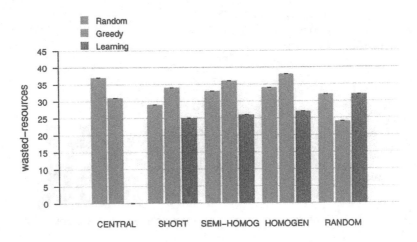

Fig. 12. Average percentage of wasted resources for random, greedy and learned policies and for different organizations.

The work in [6] introduced an anytime coalition structure generation algorithm (the term *coalition structure* refers to the solution of the coalition formation problem). As in [8], the work did not use any organization for guiding the coalition formation search and assumed a black box function that given a feasible solution returns the *value* of such solution, while we evaluate the solution based on the total utility of the allocated tasks.

The work in [9] used a multi-leveled learning scheme to form coalitions. Both reinforcement learning and case based reasoning were used. Unlike our work, they do not use an underlying organization, which limits the scalability of their approach (their experiments were limited to 4 agents).

Though some extensions to the original contract net protocol [12] proposed the use of an underlying organization, none of these extensions (to our knowledge) provided a formal model of such an organization, nor evaluated the performance for different organizations, unlike our work here.

In the brokering research area [4] not enough attention is given to scalability or coalition formation, the main focus of our work. In some sense, our use of an underlying organization can be viewed as a hierarchy of brokering agents. Integrating brokering techniques into our framework is an interesting future work direction.

The coalition formation problem can be mapped to a multi-unit combinatorial auction. However, none of the algorithms developed for combinatorial auctions [7] make use of *stable knowledge*, which remains relatively unchanged throughout the system lifetime. This includes agents' capabilities (e.g., same bids repeat for consecutive auctions) and task patterns (e.g., consecutive auctions follow some statistical model). We on the other hand try to exploit this knowledge implicitly using an underlying organization and learning the local decision of each agent in the organization.

The work in [3] tried to provide a unified framework for coordination in MAS. In this framework each agent follows a set of behaviors that differ in their level of abstraction. As behaviors become more and more abstract, an (implicit) underlying organization becomes more and more apparent. The goal of such an organization is to optimize the immediate individual goals. In our work, the goal of the organization is to optimize the coalition formation process, which *indirectly* optimizes the performance of the MAS as a whole.

In [5], the authors proposed and analyzed a simplified and restricted model of an organization, which takes only processing and communication costs into account. While they tried also to analyze the performance of different organizations, unlike our work there was no notion of resources, individual capabilities, coalition capabilities, task requirements, coalition formation, and learning.

In our approach a group of agents co-learn to work together in an organization. This can be viewed as distributed learning of a hierarchical policy that targets recursive optimality [1]. However, none of the work in hierarchical learning area (HRL) introduced the concepts of quantitative/dynamic state *abstraction* and task *decomposition*. We defined these concepts to decouple agents' local decision problems while minimizing communication, and hence achieve scalability. Our work also quantitatively evaluates how different action hierarchies affect the learning performance. Figure 13 illustrates the relationship between our work and HRL. HRL learns a policy for the whole action hierarchy in a single agent. In our approach each agent concurrently learn a *sub-policy*. Collectively, these sub-policies constitute a global hierarchical policy, but learning of sub-policies is distributed.

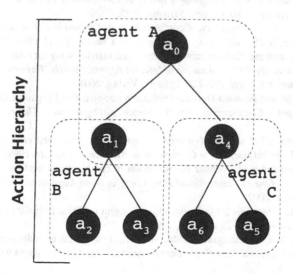

Fig. 13. Relationship between Hierarchical Reinforcement Learning and our approach.

7 Conclusions and Future work

In this work we defined a generic problem solving framework using an underlying organization, and applied it to the coalition formation problem. We provided an algorithm for the local decision to be made by each agent, given state abstractions from other agents and its decomposed task. We used Q-learning with neural nets as functional approximators to improve the local decision. Our initial results show that our approach outperformed both random and greedy policies for most of the organizations we studied. It achieved higher utility and more stability with a smaller percentage of wasted resources and fewer exchanged messages. The results also verify the scalability of our approach as it still outperforms the other approaches we studied for larger systems.

In future, we aim to study a wider variety of organizations for different types of environments. We will also investigate further our abstraction and decomposition schemes, as we believe better schemes can considerably improve the learned policy performance. We also plan to study the optimization of the underlying organization and how this interacts with optimizing the hierarchical policy.

References

1. A Barto and S Mahadevan. Recent advances in hierarchical reinforcement learning. In *Discrete Event Systems journal*, volume 13, pages 41–77, 2003.
2. K Decker and V Lesser. Designing a family of coordination algorithms. In *1st International Conference on Multi-Agent Systems*, 1995.
3. E. Durfee and T. Montgomery. Coordination as distributed search in a hierarchical behavior space. *IEEE Trans. on Systems, Man, and Cybernetics*, 21:1363–1378, 1991.
4. Matthias Klusch and Katia Sycara. Brokering and matchmaking for coordination of agent societies: A survey. In *Coordination of Internet Agents: Models, Technologies and Applications*, chapter 8, pages 197–224. Springer Verlag, 2001.
5. Young pa So and Edmund Durfee. Designing tree-structured organizations for computational agents. *Computational and Mathematical Organization Theory*, 2(3):219–246, 1996.
6. T. Sandholm and et al. Coalition structure generation with worst case guarantee. *Proceedings of the 3rd Internation Conference on Autonomous Agents*, 1999.
7. T. Sandholm and et al. Winner determination in combinatorial auction generalizations. *Proceedings of the 1st International Joint Conference on Autonomous Agents and Multiagent Systems*, 2002.
8. Onn Shehory. Methods for task allocation via agent coalition formation. *Artificial Intelligence Journal*, 101(1–2):165–200, 1998.
9. K. Soh and X. Li. An integrated multilevel learning approach to multiagent coalition formation. *International Joint Conference on Artificial Intelligence*, pages 619–624, August 2003.
10. R Sutton and A Barto. *Reinforcment Learning: An Introduction*. MIT Press, 1999.
11. M. Tambe. Towards flexible teamwork. *Journal of Artificial Intelligence Research*, 7:83–124, 1997.

12. D. Norrie W. Shen. An agent-based approach for dynamic manufacturing scheduling. *Proceedings of the 3rd International Conference on the Practical Applications of Agents and Multi-Agent Systems*, 1998.

Multi-Agent Coordination in Open Environments

Myriam Abramson[1], Ranjeev Mittu[2]

[1] U.S. Naval Research Laboratory Myriam.Abramson@nrl.navy.mil
[2] U.S. Naval Research Laboratory ranjeev.mittu@nrl.navy.mil

Summary. This paper proposes a new approach to multi-agent systems leveraging from recent advances in networking and reinforcement learning to scale up teamwork based on *joint
intentions*. In this approach, teamwork is subsumed by the coordination of learning agents.
The intuition behind this approach is that successful coordination at the global level generates opportunities for teamwork interactions at the local level and vice versa. This unique
approach scales up model-based teamwork theory with an adaptive approach to coordination.
Some preliminary results are reported using a novel coordination evaluation.

1 Introduction

Open environments such as Peer-to-Peer (P2P) and wireless or Mobile AdHoc
Networks (MANET) provide new challenges to communication-based coordination algorithms such as *joint intentions*[13] as well as the opportunity to scale-up.
Our framework is based on the proxy architecture of Machinetta[17] where *proxy*
agents perform the domain-independent coordination task on behalf of *real*, domain-
dependent agents. This framework is extended with a coordination mechanism of
individual actions based on reinforcement learning. This adaptive proxy agent architecture is illustrated in Figure 1. In this approach, local teamwork outcomes provide the feedback for learning the coordination task on a larger scale. The teamwork
theory of joint intentions and its associated problems in open environments are presented first and then our general approach, OpenMAS, is introduced with illustration
from the prey/predator example[3]. An implementation addressing some of the issues
is presented followed by conclusions for future work.

2 Joint intentions and Open Environments

Joint intentions[5, 13] form the cornerstone of teamwork theory of BDI (Belief, De-
sire, Intention) agents. It differentiates joint actions from individual actions by the
presence of a common internal state (beliefs) and the joint commitment of achieving

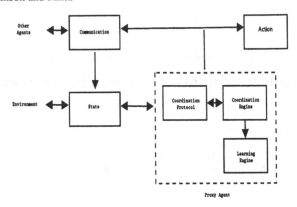

Fig. 1. Adaptive proxy agent architecture

a goal. It is based on the communication of critical information among team members. However, the mutual responsiveness expected of team members at a local level is difficult to achieve on a larger scale. Open environments are characterized by their dynamic nature and the heterogeneity of the agents as well as asynchronous and unreliable communication on a large scale. The problems addressed can be categorized as follows: team formation, role allocation, synchronization of beliefs, communication trade-offs, and information sharing.

1. **Team Formation.** An open environment gives the opportunity to find teammates appropriate for a task instead of relying on a fixed group of agents. What is the best way to find teammates? When is the best time to find teammates? How to decide whether to join a team? In open environments, peers form "groups" by similarity of individual interests. Likewise, similarity of individual intentions is a necessary stepping stone for team formation in open environments. An intention is defined here[5] as the decision to do something in order to achieve a goal and can be construed as a partial plan.

2. **Role Allocation.** While direct point-to-point communication with any node can be expensive and uncertain, access to neighbors is readily available in open environments. P2P middleware, such as JXTA (Juxtapose)[1], provides the functionality needed to communicate reliably and cheaply with *neighbors*. In MANET, the possibility of disconnecting the network is another constraint in accepting a role requiring a change in location. Figure 2 describe the connection role that peers play in communication in MANET. In open environments, multiple teams are involved. How to adjust the connectivity role of the agents so that each team can accomplish its goals most effectively?

3. **Synchronization of Beliefs.** The theory of joint commitments is based on the ability to synchronize beliefs regarding "who is doing what". Teamwork breaks down when roles do not match expected beliefs leading to *coordinated attack* dilemmas[14]. How to adjust gracefully to uncertainties in communication?

4. **Communication Selectivity**. The tradeoffs involve the robustness that redundancy of messages can provide in open environments versus the costs of communication to the network. When reliable communication cannot be assumed, selective communication of critical information might be detrimental to the coordination task.
5. **Information Sharing.** Sharing information is critical to the formation of a common internal state. The redundancy of messages from different sources provides corroborative evidence to support the information transmitted while conflicts undermine certainty. However, a problem in open systems is the unnecessary replication of messages from the same source through the network leading to false corroborative evidence.

Synchronization of beliefs, communication selectivity and information sharing are areas that are complicated by open environments, while team formation as well as role allocation are the problems we are interested in addressing given these complicating factors.

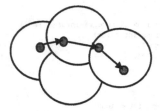

Fig. 2. Multi-hop routing in a MANET

3 OpenMAS Approach

Our proactive approach consists of leveraging from the belief framework of cognitive agents at the local level but endowing the agents with the adaptative capabilities of reinforcement learners as an additional coordination mechanism at the global level where communication is unsure and unreliable. The objective is to find a continuum between large-scale coordination and local teamwork. The overarching issues addressed in support of this objective are (1) how to integrate general models of cooperation with reinforcement learning in distributed, open environments (2) what are good evaluation measures for the propagation of beliefs to heterogeneous agents and (3) how to integrate multiple teams.

Methodology

Through the propagation of beliefs, the agents have some knowledge of the global situation, albeit imperfect and decaying with time. This capability relaxes the invalidation of the Markov property for multi-agent reinforcement learning systems. Instead of committing to a non-local role, the agents just commit to the next individual step. This is a least-commitment approach that addresses the problems outlined above of teamwork in open environments. Local environmental beliefs on the other hand trigger a role allocation mechanism among neighbors sharing the same beliefs. Role allocation of mutually exclusive tasks among agents can be modeled with distributed resource allocation algorithms based on constraint satisfaction[24]. The joint actions generated are preferred over the individual actions generated by the coordination learning mechanism. Similarities between joint actions and individual actions produce the terminal rewards needed for the learning algorithm. In this approach, there is a tight integration between the local level of teamwork and the global level of coordination. The overall approach is described in Algorithm 5. Figure 3 illustrates the approach in the prey/predator example.

Algorithm 5: Intention/Action loop

```
INPUT: intentions
OPENMAS-interpreter:
do
    <information, intention> ← receive-information()
    if similar-intentions(intention)
      accept-information()
      update-current-state()
    endif
    state-estimation()
    take-next-step()
    reinforce-learn()
    propagate <next-step, intentions>
forever
```

The information received includes information communicated from peers and/or perceived local information from the environment

---

The environment of agents acting under uncertainty can be conveniently modeled as a POMDP (Partially-observable Markov Decision Process). POMDP can be reformulated as continuous-space Markov decision processes (MDPs) representing belief states[10] and solved using an approximation technique. When propagating local environmental beliefs, the redundancy of messages reinforces current state beliefs through corroborative evidence while discrediting others. The most likely state of the global situation is then modeled as an MDP and the action to take determined by a stochastic policy approximated by a policy gradient method [19]. Through communication, the agents are able to construct a global, albeit imperfect, view of the world validating their assumption of the Markov property for independent autonomous decision-making based on trial and error. However, even assuming the same global knowledge of the world and optimization algorithm, coordination imposes the additional constraint that the agents choose the action leading to pareto optimality. For a deterministic policy, this constraint can be met through conventions or through the

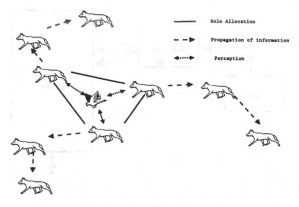

Role Allocation

Propagation of information

Perception

Fig. 3. Prey/predator example

The agents propagate changes of position and changes in the prey's status to their neighbors recursively according to a time-to-live (TTL) parameter. The TTL parameter ensures that a message does not bounce around needlessly when the destination cannot be found and can also be used to disseminate information within a certain range. Role allocation strategies resolve local conflicts.

transmission of knowledge. Another way to meet this coordination constraint is to learn a stochastic policy that approximates a mixed strategy.

Role allocation endows the agents with a goal-driven behavior. In addition to accomplishing their roles and searching for possible role instantiations, agents in open environments have the additional implicit task of maintaining the connectivity of the network. It is necessary to balance those sometimes conflicting goals. The capability to assume multiple roles is a characteristic of intelligent and flexible behavior. Instead of modeling each goal separately in an MDP given the state of the environment, the goals themselves, as formulated by a role allocation strategy for each target, are part of the environment. This soft-subsumption architecture for multiple roles is illustrated in Figure 4.

4 Problem Modeling

The world is modeled as the problem space:

$$W = \{S, S', A, T, R\}$$

where

- S is the believed perceived local state of the world.
- S' is the believed global state of the world through propagation of information.
- A is the set of actions.

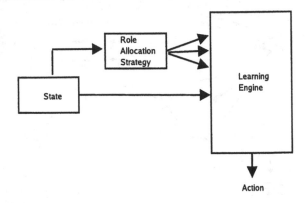

Fig. 4. Soft-subsumption architecture for multiple roles

- T is the set of transition probabilities

$$S \times A \times S \rightarrow [0,1]$$

- R is the set of roles.

and

$$S \times R \rightarrow A_i$$

$$S' \times A_j \rightarrow \Re$$

where

- A_i is the action determined to achieve a role.
- A_j is the action determined by coordination in the believed state space S'.

A reward r is obtained if $A_i = A_j$.

The goal of each agent is to find a policy π maximizing the sum of expected rewards such that:

$$\forall s \in S', V^\pi(s) = r + \sum_{s' \in S'} T(s, \pi(s), s') \gamma V^\pi(s')$$

where s' is the next state following the action prescribed by $\pi(s)$, r is the reward in state s, and γ is the discount factor weighting the importance of future rewards.

5 An Example

An prototype evaluation of the OpenMAS general methodology has been conducted with some simplifying assumptions with the RePast simulation tool[6]. Further experiments are planned for a large-scale MANET simulation in ns-2[2] using P2PS[22], a P2P agent discovery infrastructure designed to work in ns-2 simulations.

5.1 Prey/Predator Example

The prey/predator pursuit game is a canonical example in the teamwork literature[3, 11] because one individual predator alone cannot accomplish the task of capturing a prey. Practical applications of the prey/predator pursuit game include, for example, unmanned ground/air vehicles target acquisition, distributed sensor networks for situation awareness, and rescue operations. The original problem can be extended to multiple teams by including more than one prey. Prey/predators can sense each other if they are in proximity but do not otherwise communicate. Predators communicate with other predators individually or can broadcast messages through their neighbors. Four predators are needed to capture a prey by filling out four different roles: surround the prey to the north, south, east and west. Those roles are independent of each other and can be started at any time obviating the need for scheduling. The only requirement is that they have to terminate at the same time either successfully when a capture occurs or unsuccessfully if no team can be formed. The predator agents are homogeneous and can assume any role but heterogeneity can be introduced by restricting the role(s) an agent can assume. The prey and predators move concurrently and possibly asynchronously at different time steps. In addition to the four orthogonal navigational steps, the agents can opt to stay in place. In case of collision, the agents are held back to their previous position. Several escape strategies are possible for the prey. A linear strategy, i.e. move away in the same random direction, has been shown to be an effective strategy while a greedy strategy, i.e. move furthest away from the closest predator, can lead to capture situations[9].

The preference or utility u_{ij} of predator agent i for a role j is inversely proportional to the Manhattan distance d required to achieve the role. Other factors such as fatigue, speed, resources, etc. can affect the preference for a role and are grouped under a capability assessment C[16].

$$u_{ij} = \frac{1}{d} \times C_{ij} \qquad (1)$$

The predators move in the direction of their target when assigned a role or explore the space according to a pre-defined strategy. The decision space for the role allocation of P predators and p preys is $O(p^T)$ where T is the number of teams of size t that can be formed with P predators[3]. This problem belongs to the most difficult class of problems for constraint satisfaction in multi-agent systems[15] due to the dynamic nature of the environment and the mutually-exclusive property of role allocation.

5.2 Role Allocation Strategy

An optimization algorithm can be used in parallel fashion by each agent based on sensed and communicated information from the other agents in the group to autonomously determine which role to assume. It is assumed that the other agents

---

3 $\frac{P!}{(P-t)!}$

reach the same conclusions because they use the same optimization algorithm[8]. The Hungarian algorithm[12] (see below) is used as the optimization method by each agent. Information necessary to determine the payoff of each role needs to be communicated. Therefore, it is the current local state within the perception range, or augmented with second hand information, that is communicated to the neighbors instead of the intended role in a trade-off between performance and privacy.

This algorithm, also known as the bipartite weighted matching algorithm, solves constraint optimization problems such as the job assignment problem in polynomial time. The implementation of this algorithm follows Munkres' assignment algorithm[4]. The algorithm is run over a utility matrix of *roles* × *agents*. The maximization of utilities is transformed to a cost minimization problem:

$$cost = \arg\max \sum_{i,j} u_{ij}$$

$$Minimize \sum_{i,j} (cost - u_{ij})$$

The algorithm consists of transforming the matrix into equivalent matrices until the solution can be read off as independent elements of an auxiliary matrix. While additional rows and columns with maximum value can be added to square the matrix, the optimality is no longer guaranteed if the problem is over-constrained, i.e. there are more roles to be filled than agents. A simple example is illustrated in Table 1.

Table 1. A 4×4 assignment problem

The optimal assignment is $(r_1, x_3), (r_2, x_2), (r_3, x_4), (r_4, x_1)$

	x_1	x_2	x_3	x_4
r_1	0.79	0.28	1.00	0.89
r_2	0.29	0.51	0.83	0.38
r_3	0.33	0.03	0.47	0.91
r_4	0.92	0.14	0.82	0.80

When multiple teams are involved, an agent chooses the role in the team that has the maximum sum of utilities rather than maximizing the sum of utilities across teams, thereby ensuring team formation.

5.3 Policy Search

In reinforcement learning, there are two ways to search the state space of a problem. We can search the policy space which is a mapping from current state to actions or we can search the value space which is a mapping from possible states to their evaluation. Because there are only a limited number of actions that can be taken from a state, it is usually faster to search the policy space. Both methods however, should converge to the optimal greedy strategy whether by taking the best state-action value or the action that leads to the best valued state as the expected sum of rewards.

A function approximator generalizes to large state space. For gradient methods, it was shown that a small change in the parameter space can lead to large changes in the output space when searching for the value function while policy search where the output are action probabilities is assured locally optimal convergence[19]. Learning a stochastic policy has some advantages in dynamic and uncertain environments especially in pursuit games where the opponent might learn to escape a deterministic adversary.

5.4 Coordination Evaluation

Because coordination is an emergent property of interactive systems, it can only be measured indirectly through the performance of the agents in accomplishing a task where a task is decomposed in a number of goals to achieve. The more complex the task, the higher the number of goals needed to be achieved. While performance is ultimately defined in domain-dependent terms, there are some common characteristics. Performance can be measured either as the number of steps taken to reach the goal, i.e. the time complexity of the task, or as the amount of resources required. An alternative evaluation for coordination is the absence of failures or negative interactions such as collisions, lost messages, or fragmentation of the network when no messages are received. Figure 5 illustrates a taxonomy of coordination solution metrics. To show the scalability of a solution, the evaluation must vary linearly with the complexity of the task[7].

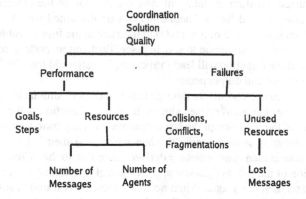

Fig. 5. Taxonomy of coordination solution quality for communicating agents

A combined coordination quality measure is defined as the harmonic mean of goals achieved g, net resources expanded r and collisions c as follows:

$$g = \frac{\#Preys\,Captured}{\#Preys} \tag{2}$$

$$r = \frac{\#Predators}{log_2(\#Messages\,Received) + \#Predators} \tag{3}$$

$$c = \frac{\#Predators}{\#Collisions + \#Predators} \tag{4}$$

$$coordination = \frac{3grc}{gr + rc + cg} \tag{5}$$

Although the message size required by the different predator strategies was roughly equivalent, further work should measure the number of information bits per message [20].

5.5 Experimental Evaluation

In the prey/predator example, actions leading to collisions with other predators are negatively reinforced while actions leading to the capture of the prey are rewarded. Experiments were conducted on a 20x20 grid with 2 preys and a variable number of predators moving concurrently but synchronously at each time steps. The preys move to a random adjacent free cell 70% of the time except edge cells to avoid toroidal world ambiguities. The predators communicate their location and sensory information about the preys to their neighbors according to pre-defined communication and perception range. The probability of receiving a message vary according to a normal distribution based on (Euclidean) distance and the communication range of each agent. The current state is represented by the one-dimensional locations of the preys, the current location of the agent, and the location of the closest other three predators known. A feed-forward neural net was implemented with 54 binary input nodes, 7 hidden nodes and 5 output nodes to translate to the four possible orthogonal directions to move and an option to stay in place. Each output node o_i represents the probability that the direction will lead to success. The sigmoid transfer function was used for all internal and output nodes.

The agents learn to coordinate through trial and error in simulation using temporal difference learning between the value of the current direction in the output vector and the value of the direction in the last output vector. They train following the optimized role allocation strategy (see 5.2) when available as their behavior policy. The direction to take is then *conventionally* derived according to the differences between the destination of the role assignment and the current location of the agent along the x-axis first and then the y-axis. When no role allocation is found, a softmax policy is followed where the direction i is selected stochastically according to the probability $P(i) = \frac{e^{o_i}}{\sum_i e^{o_i}}$. A reward of 1.0 is received when a goal is reached or when a role allocation was found and a penalty of 1E-6 is received when colliding.

In the performance phase, the neural net from the most successful agent is selected. Table 2 summarizes the different parameters used. Figure 6 shows coordination quality results averaged over 1000 runs comparing different policies followed when restricting the optimized role allocation strategy above a certain utility threshold comprising about 5% of the interactions. There is a significant difference between the results obtained following the greedy policy learned through reinforcement learning and a random policy (t-test p-values were 2E-5, 0.0001, 0.004 for 7, 8 and 9 predators respectively). The memory-based approach consists of moving to an adjacent cell that was not visited in the last 7 steps. Interestingly, although memory-based exploration performs better than random walk for a single reinforcement learner agent[21], they rate worse for multi-agent coordination. Those experiments have shown that learning from past experiences can produce a viable behavioral policy on a larger scale that is conducive to teamwork on a local scale and that can produce domain-dependent coordination rules. Further application of state estimation techniques should enhance this approach.

Table 2. Parameters

Input nodes	54
Hidden nodes	7
Output nodes	5
Learning rate α*	0.3
Penalty	1E-6
Reward	1.0
Role utility threshold	3.0
Communication range	7
Perception range	2
Cycles	1000
Tmax	3000

*decreasing with time t at the rate $\frac{\alpha}{1+\frac{t}{Tmax}}$

6 Related Work

The dissemination of information enables agents to obtain some global, though imperfect, knowledge of the world. This capability is taken into account in scaling up teamwork approaches based on communication and our approach also takes this capability into account to enhance multi-agent learning. Our approach is different from the large-scale coordination of Machinetta proxies[18] because (1) individual actions lead to joint actions through on-line adaptation and (2) the uncertainty and ambiguity of information is taken into account through state estimation. Our least-commitment approach is however similar to a token-based approach to teamwork[16].

The importance of communication in solving decentralized Markov decision processes was noted in [23] where the goal was to develop a communication policy in addition to the navigation policy. For agents in open environments, those policies overlaps since the location of the agent determines its communication range.

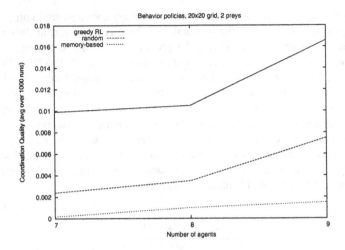

Fig. 6. Behavior policies

7 Conclusions and Future Work

Open environments such as P2P and MANET forces a reexamination of teamwork in large scale systems relying more on adaptive coordination than explicit cooperation requiring synchronization points. The capability to acquire global, albeit imperfect, knowledge through the propagation of information makes it possible to use independent reinforcement learners for coordination tasks in multi-agent systems. Similarity of intentions can help relieve the burden placed on the network by selectively propagating information while state estimation based on evidence reasoning calibrates incoming information. A local teamwork model drives the rewards of the overall coordination task. This proactive approach scales well to any dimensions and its precision can be modulated by the TTL parameter. Future experiments are planned for large MANET network simulations and P2P agent discovery of heterogeneous agents.

Acknowledgement

The authors want to acknowledge useful discussions with Joe Macker, William Chao, and Joe Collins.

References

1. Project jxta. http://www.jxta.org.
2. The network simulator. Retrieved from http://www.isi.edu/nsnam/ns/, 2003.

3. M. Benda, V. Jagannathan, and R. Dodhiawalla. On optimal cooperation of knowledge sources. Technical Report BCS-G2010-28, Boeing AI Center, Boeing Computer Services, 1985.

4. F. Burgeios and J. C. Lassalle. An extension of the munkres algorithm for the assignment problem to rectangular matrices. *Communication of the ACM*, 14:802–806, 1971.

5. Philip R. Cohen and Hector J. Levesque. Teamwork. *Nous*, 25(4):487–512, 1991.

6. Nick Collier. Repast: the recursive porous agent simulation toolkit. Retrieved from http://repast.sourceforge.net, 2001.

7. E. H. Durfee. Scaling up agent coordination strategies. *IEEE Computer*, 2001.

8. Brian P. Gerkey and Maja J. Mataric. *RobotCup 2003*, volume 3020, chapter On Role Allocation in RobotCup. Springer-Verlag Heidelberg, 2004.

9. Thomas Haynes and Sandip Sen. Evolving behavioral strategies in predator and prey. In *IJCAI-95 Workshop on Adaptation and Learning in Multiagent Systems*, 1995.

10. L. Kaelbling, M. Littman, and A. Cassandra. Planning and acting in partially observable stochastic domains. *Artificial Intelligence*, (101):99–134, 1998.

11. Richard E. Korf. A simple solution to pursuit games. In *Working Papers of the 11th International Workshop on Distributed Artificial Intelligence*, pages 183–194, 1992.

12. H. W. Kuhn. The hungarian method for the assignment problem. *Naval Research Logistics Quarterly*, 2(83), 1955.

13. H. J. Levesque, P. R. Cohen, and J. Nunes. On acting together. In *Proceedings of the National Conference on Artificial Intelligence*, 1990.

14. Nancy Lynch. *Distributed Algorithms*. Morgan Kaufmann, 1996.

15. P. J. Modi, H. Jung, M. Tambe, W. Shen, and S. Kulkarni. Dynamic distributed resource allocation: A distributed constraint satisfaction approach. In *Proceedings of the 7th International Conference on Principles and Practice of Constraint Programming*, 2001.

16. P. Scerri, A. Farinelli, S. Okamoto, and M. Tambe. Token approach for role allocation in extreme teams: Analysis and experimental evaluation. In *Proceedings of 2nd IEEE International Workshop on Theory and Practice of Open Computational Systems*, 2004.

17. P. Scerri, D. Pynadath, N. Schurr, A. Farinelli, S. Gandhe, and M. Tambe. Team oriented programming and proxy agents: The next generation. Workshop on Programming MultiAgent Systems, Autonomous Agents and Multi-Agent Systems Conference, 2003.

18. Paul Scerri, Elizabeth Liao, Justin Lai, and Katia Sycara. *Cooperative Control*, chapter Coordinating Very Large Groups of Wide Area Search Munitions. Kluwer Publishing, 2004.

19. R. Sutton, D. McAllester, S. Singh, and Y. Mansour. Policy gradient methods for reinforcement learning with function approximation. In *Advances in Neural Information Processing Systems*, volume 12, pages 1057–1063. MIT Press, 2000.

20. Ming Tan. Multi-agent reinforcement learning: Independent vs. cooperative learning. In Michael N. Huhns and Munindar P. Singh, editors, *Readings in Agents*, pages 487–494. Morgan Kaufmann, San Francisco, CA, USA, 1997.

21. S. B. Thrun. Efficient exploration in reinforcement learning. Technical Report CMU-CS-92-102, Pittsburgh, Pennsylvania, 1992.

22. Ian Wang and Ian Taylor. P2ps, peer-to-peer simplified. Retrieved from http://srss.pf.itd.nrl.navy.mil/, 2003.

23. Ping Xuan and Victor Lesser. Multi-agent policies: From centralized ones to decentralized ones. In *Autonomous Agents and Multi-Agent Systems*, 2002.

24. M. Yokoo. *Distributed Constraint Satisfaction*. Springer-Verlag, 1998.

Mobile Agents

Ichiro Satoh

National Institute of Informatics ichiro@nii.ac.jp

Summary. Mobile agent technology has been promoted as an emerging technology that makes it much easier to design, implement, and maintain distributed systems. It also provides an infrastructure for multi-agent computing. This chapter discusses the potential uses of mobile agents in distributed systems, lists their potential advantages and disadvantages. The body of the chapter has descriptions of technologies for executing, migrating, and implementing mobile agents. It also presents several actual and potential applications of mobile agents. A brief review of other research in the area and prospects for the future conclude the chapter.

1 Introduction

Mobile agents are autonomous programs that can travel from computer to computer in a network, at times and to places of their own choosing. The state of the running program is saved, by being transmitted to the destination. The program is resumed at the destination continuing its processing with the saved state. They can provide a convenient, efficient, and robust framework for implementing distributed applications including mobile applications for several reasons, including improvements to the latency and bandwidth of client-server applications and reducing vulnerability to network disconnection. Although not all applications for distributed systems will need mobile agents, many other applications will find mobile agents the most effective technique for implementing all or part of their tasks. In fact, many mobile agent systems have been released over the last few years ([10, 9, 2, 23]).

This chapter discusses the potential uses of mobile agents in distributed systems and presents a number of their potential advantages and disadvantages. It also describes technologies for executing, migrating, and implementing mobile agents and presents several actual and potential applications for them. A brief review of other research in the area and prospects for the future conclude the chapter.

1.1 Advantages of Mobile Agents

Mobile agents have several advantages in the development of various distributed applications.

- **Reduced communication costs:** Distributed computing needs interactions between different computers through a network. The latency and network traffic of interactions often seriously affect the quality and coordination of two programs running on different computers. As we can see from Figure 1, if one of the programs is a mobile agent, it can migrate to the computer the other is running on communicate with it locally. That is, mobile agent technology enables remote communications to operate as local communications.

- **Asynchronous execution** After migrating to the destination-side computer, a mobile agent does not have to interact with its source-side computer. Therefore, even when the source can be shut down or the network between the destination and source can be disconnected, the agent can continue processing at the destination. This is useful within unstable communications.

- **Direct manipulation** A mobile agent is locally executed on the computer it is visiting. It can directly access and control the equipments for the computer as long as the computer allows it to do so. This is helpful in network management, in particular in detecting and removing device failures. Installing a mobile agent close to a real-time system may prevent delays caused by network congestion.

- **Easy-development of distributed applications** Most distributed applications consist of at least two programs, i.e., a client-side program and a server side program and often spare codes for communications, including exceptional handling. However, since a mobile agent itself can carry information to another computer, we can only write a single program to define distributed computing. A mobile agent program does not have to define communications with other computers. Therefore, we can easily modify standalone programs as mobile agent programs.

As we can see from Figure 2, mobile agents can save themselves through persistent storage, duplicate themselves, and migrate themselves to other computers under their own control so that they can support various types of processing in distributed systems.

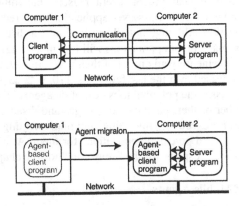

Fig. 1. Reduced communication

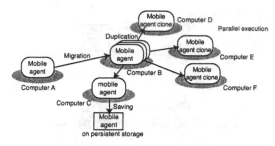

Fig. 2. Functions of mobile agents in distributed system

Remarks

Mobile agent technology may be treated as a type of software agent technology, but it is not always required to offer intelligent capabilities, e.g., reactive, pro-active, and social behaviors that are features of existing software agent technologies. This is because these capabilities tend to be large in terms of scale and processing, and no mobile agent should consume excessive computational resources, such as processors, memory, files, and networks, at its destinations. Also, all mobile agents must be as small as possible because their size seriously affects the cost of migrating over a network.

1.2 Mobility and Distribution

Fuggetta, et al [5] provided a description of mobile software paradigms for distributed applications. These are classified as client/server (CS), remote evaluation (REV), code on demand (COD), and mobile agent (MA) approaches. By decompiling distributed applications into code, data, and execution, most distributed executions can be modeled as primitives of these approaches as we can see from Figure 3.

- The client-server approach is widely used in traditional and modern distributed systems (Figure 3 a)). The code, data, and execution remain fixed at computer A. Computer B requests a service from the server with some data arguments of the request. The code and remaining data to provide the service are resident within computer B. As a response, computer B provide the service requested by accessing computational resources provided in it. Computer B returns the results of the execution to computer A.
- The remote evaluation approach assumes that the code to perform the execution is stored at computer A (Figure 3 b)). Both the code and data are sent to computer B. As a response, computer B executes the code and data by accessing computational resources, including data, provided in them. An additional interaction returns the results from computer B to computer A.

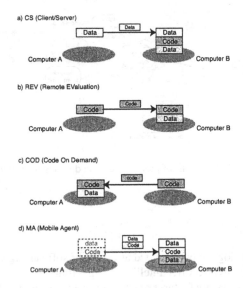

Fig. 3. Client/server, remote evaluation, code on demand, and mobile agent

- The code-on-demand approach is an inversion of the remote evaluation approach. (3 c)). The code and data are stored at computer A and execution is done at computer B. Computer A fetches code and data from computer B and then executes the code with its local data as well as the imported data. An example of this is Java applets, which are Java codes that web-browsers download from remote HTTP servers to execute locally.
- The mobile agent approach assume that the code and data are initially hosted by computer A (Figure 3 d)). Computer A migrates the data and code it need to computer B. After it has moved to computer B, the code is executed with the data and the resources available on computer B.

2 Mobile Agent System

Mobile agent systems consist of two parts: mobile agents and runtime systems. The former defines the behavior of software agents. The latter are called agent platforms, agent systems, and agent servers, and support their execution and migration. The same architecture exists on all computers at which agents are reachable. That is, each mobile agent runs within a runtime systems on its current computer. When an agent requests the current runtime system to migrate itself, the runtime system can migrate the agent to a runtime system on the destination computer, carrying its state and code with it. Each runtime system itself runs on top of the operating system as a middleware. It provides interpreters or virtual machines for executing agent programs, or the system themselves are provided on top of virtual machines, e.g., the Java virtual machine (JVM).

2.1 Remote Procedure Call

Agent migration is similar to RPC (Remote Procedure Calling) or RMI (Remote Method Invocation). RPC enables a client program to call a procedure for server programs running in separate processes, generally in different computers from the client [3]. RMI is an extension of local method invocation that allows an object to invoke the methods of the object on a remote computer. RPC or RMI can pass arguments to a procedure or method of a program on the server and receives a return value from the server. The mechanism for passing arguments and results between two computers through RPC or RMI correspond to that for agent migration between two computers. Figure 4 shows flow for the basic mechanism of RPC between two computers.

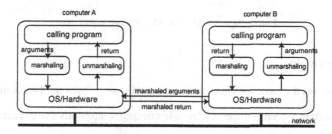

Fig. 4. Remote procedure call between two computers

Agent Marshaling

Data items, e.g., objects and values, in a running program cannot be directly transmitted over a network. They must be transformed into external data representation, e.g., a binary form or text form, before migrating them (Figure 5). Marshaling is the process of collecting data items and assembling them into a form suitable for transmission in a message. Unmarshaling is the process of disassembling them on arrival to produce an equivalent collection of data items at the destination.[1] The marshaling and unmarshaling processes are carried out by runtime systems in mobile agent systems. The runtime system at the left (at sender-side computer) of Figure 6 marshals an agent to transmit it to a destination through a communication channel or message and then the runtime system at the right (at receiver-side computer) of Figure 6 receives the data and unmarshals the agent.

---

[1] Note that marshaling and serialization are often used without any distinction between them. The latter is a process of flattening and converting an object, including its referring objects, into a sequence of bytes to be sent across network or saved on a disk.

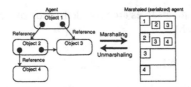

Fig. 5. Marshaling agent

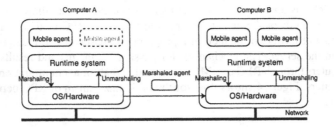

Fig. 6. Agent migration between two computers

Agent Migration

Figure 6 shows the basic mechanism for agent migration between two computers.

1) The runtime system on the sender-side computer suspends the execution of the agent.
2) It marshals the agent into a bit-chunk that can be transmitted over a network.
3) It transmits the chunk to the destination computer through the underlying network protocol.
4) The runtime system on the receiver-side computer receives the chunk.
5) It unmarshals the chunk into the agent and resumes the agent.

Most existing mobile agent systems use TCP channels, SMTP, or HTTP as their underlying communication protocols. Mobile agents themselves are separated from the underlying communication protocols.

Strong Migration vs. Weak Migration

The state of execution is migrated with the code so that computation can be resumed at the destination. According to the amount of detail captured in the state, we can classify agent migration into two types: strong and weak.

- **Strong Migration:** is the ability of an agent to migrate over a network, carrying the code and execution state, where the state includes the program counter, saved processor registers, and local variables, which correspond to variables allocated in the stack frame of the agent's memory space, global variables. These correspond to variables allocated in the heap frame. The agent is suspended, marshaled, transmitted, unmarshaled and then restarted at the exact position where it was previously suspended on the destination node without loss of data or execution state.

- **Weak Migration:** is the ability of an agent to migrate over a network, carrying the code and partial execution state, where the state is variables in the heap frame, e.g., instance variables in object oriented programs, instead of its program counter and local variables declared in methods or functions. The agent is moved to and restarted on the destination with its global variables. The runtime system may explicitly invoke specified agent methods.

Strong migration can cover weak migration, but it is a minority. This is because the execution state of an agent tends to be large and the marshaling and transmitting of the state over a network need heavy processing. Moreover, like the latter, the former cannot migrate agents that access the computational resources only available in current computers, e.g., input-and-output equipments and networks. The former unfortunately has no significant advantages in the development and operation of real distributed applications as discussed by Srasser et al. [2].

The program code for an agent needs to be available at the destination where the agent is running. The code must to be deployed at the source at the time of creation and at the destination to which it moves. Therefore, existing runtime systems offer a facility for statically deploying program code that is needed to execute the agent, for loading the program code on demand, or for transferring the program code along with the agent.

2.2 Mobile Agent Languages

Since mobile agents are programming entities, programming languages for defining mobile agents are needed. There has been a huge number of programming languages, but all of these are not available for mobile agents. Programming languages for mobile agents must support the following functions. They should enable programs to be marshaled into data and vice versa. They should also download code from remote computers and link it at run-time. A few researchers have provided newly designed languages for defining mobile agents, e.g., Telescript [23], and most current mobile agent systems use existing general-purpose programming languages that can satisfy the above requirements, e.g., Java [1]. Telescript provides primitives for defining mobile agents, e.g, go operation, and enables a thread running on an interpreter to migrate to another computer. The Java language itself offers no support for the migration of executing code, but offers dynamic class loading, a programmable class loader, and a language-level marshaling mechanism, where these can be directly exploited to enable code mobility. Creating distributed systems based on mobile agents is a relatively easy paradigm because most existing mobile agents are object oriented programs, e.g., Java, and can be developed by using rapid application development (RAD) environments.

Distributed systems are characterized by heterogeneity in hardware architectures and operating systems. To achieve heterogeneity, the state and code of an agent need to be saved in a platform-independent representation. Hidden differences between platforms is provided at the language level, by using intermediate byte code representation in Java or by relying on scripting languages such as Tcl/Tk. Therefore, Java-based mobile agents are executed on Java virtual machines and Tcl/Tk-based mobile agents on Tcl/Tk interpreters. The costs of running agents in a Java virtual machine on a device are decreasing by using just-in-compiler technologies.

2.3 Agent Execution Management

The runtime system manages execution and monitoring of all agents on a computer. It allows several hundred agents to be present at any one time on a computer. It also provide these agents with an execution environment and executes them independently of one another. It manages the life-cycle of its agents, e.g., creation, termination, and migration.

Each agent program can access basic functions provided by its runtime system by invoking APIs (Table 1). The agent uses the go command to migrate from one computer to another with the destination system address (and its target agent's identifier) and does not need to concern itself with any other details of migration. Instead, the runtime system supports the migration of the agent. It stops the agent's execution and then marshals the agent's data items to the destination via the underlying communication protocol, e.g., tcp channel, HTTP (hyper text transfer protocol), and SMTP (simple mail transfer protocol). The agent is unpacked and reconstituted on the destination.

Table 1. Functions available in agents

command	parameters	function
go	destination address, agent-identifier	agent migration
terminate	agent-identifier	agent termination
duplicate	agent-identifier	agent duplication
identify	agent-type	identification
lookup	agent-type, runtime system address	discovery of available agents
communicate	agent-identifier	inter-agent communication

2.4 Inter-agent communication

Mobile agents can interact with other agents residing within the same computer or with agents on remote computers as other multi-agents. Existing mobile agent systems provide various inter-agent communication mechanisms, e.g., method invocation, publish/subscribe-based event passing, and stream-based communications.

2.5 Locating Mobile Agents

Since mobile agents can autonomously travel from computer to computer, a mechanism for tracking the location of agents is needed by the users to control their agents and for agents to communicate with other agents. Several mobile agent systems provide such mechanisms, which can be classified into three schemes:

- A name server multicasts query messages about the location of an agent the to computers and receives a reply message from a computer hosting the agent (Figure 7 (a)).
- An agent registers its current location at a predefined name server whenever it arrives at another computer (Figure 7 (b)).
- An agent leaves a footprint specifying its destination at its current computer whenever it migrates to another computer to track the trails of the agent (Figure 7 (c)).

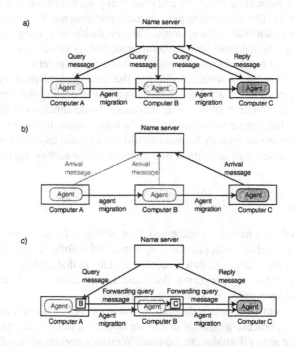

Fig. 7. Discovery for migrating agents

In many cases, locating agents is application specific. For example, the first scheme is suitable for an agent moving within a local region. It is not suitable for agents visiting distant nodes. The second scheme is suitable for an agent migrating within a far away region; in the case of a large number of nodes, registering nodes are organized hierarchically. However, it is not suitable for a large number of migrations. The third scheme is suitable for a small number of migrations; it is not appropriate for long chains.

2.6 Security

Security is one of the most important issues with mobile agent systems. Most security issues in mobile agents are common to existing computer security problems in communication and the downloading of software. In addition, many researchers have explored mechanisms to enhance security with mobile agent systems. There are two problems in mobile agent security: the protection of hosts from malicious mobile agents and the protection of mobile agents from malicious hosts. It is difficult to verify with complete certainty whether an incoming agent is malicious or not. However, there are two solutions to protecting hosts from malicious mobile agents. The first is to provide access-control mechanisms, e.g., Java's security manager. They explicitly specify the permission of agents and restrict any agent behaviors that are beyond their permissions. The second is to provide authentication mechanisms by using digital signatures or authentication systems. They explicitly permit runtime systems to only receive agents that have been authenticated, have been sent from authenticated computers, or that have originated from authenticated computers.

There have been no general solutions to the second problem, because it is impossible to keep agent private from runtime systems executing the agent. However, (non-malicious) runtime systems can authenticate the destinations of their agents, to check whether these are non-malicious, before they migrate the agents to these destinations. While strong security features would not immediately make mobile agents appealing, the absence of security would certainly make mobile agents unattractive and unpractical.

2.7 Remarks

Several technologies have been presented for enabling software to migrate between computers, e.g., mobile code, process-migration, and mobile objects. Mobile agents differ from mobile codes, e.g., downloadable applets, in that mobile codes can maintain the states of running programs. As a result, they must start their initial states after they have been deployed at remote computers.

One of the most important differences between mobile agents and traditional techniques, e.g., process-migration or mobile objects is in their acceptable levels of mobility-transparency. Introducing too much transparency can adversely affect other characteristics, such as complexity, or the scope of modifications made to the underlying environment. For example, a solution allowing the migration of processes or objects at any time in response to a request from any other object would require significant changes to the underlying environment, e.g., balancing the processor load and escaping from a shutdown computer, whereas mobile agents can move where and when they choose, typically through a go statement. Similarly, solutions that insist on continuous communication and name resolution could be achieved for naming and open channel handling, but they would incur significant complexity in communication support and the naming model. Process-migration and mobile object technologies require fully transparent solutions at the operating system level to minimize complexity. For example, processes and objects still continue to access the computational resources, e.g., file systems, database systems, and channels, that they accessed at their source-side computers, even after they have moved. With a reasonable choice of transparency-requirements, mobile agents can access computational resources provided in current computers after mobile agents have moved to their destinations. Although mobile agents are similar to mobile objects at the programming-level, they contain threads and they are therefore active and can act autonomously, whereas most mobile objects are implemented as passive entities.

3 Mobile Agent Agent Systems

There have been a huge number of mobile agent systems. This section presents several traditional mobile agent systems, which offer common functions to other existing mobile agent systems, and modern mobile agent systems for large-scale and dynamic distributed systems.

3.1 Telescript

Telescript is the first commercial mobile agent implementation developed by General Magic [23]. It provides an object-oriented language designed for mobile agents, which employs an intermediate, portable language across servers, and introduces three essential concepts for mobile agents: agents, places, and the go command. Places are essentially stationary agents that can contain other agents or places. Agents migrate to places, which reside at local or remote computers. Telescript supports strong migration so that the execution of a moving agent can be resumed after it arrives at the destination. Each agent and place has an associated authority. A place can query an incoming agent's authority and potentially deny entry to the agent or restrict its access rights. The agent receives a permit, which encodes its access rights and resource-consumption quotas. The system terminates agents that exceed their quota and raises exceptions when they attempt unauthorized operations. Agents interact with the place or other agents at a meeting place by issuing a meet primitive.

```
Shopper: class (Agent, EventProcess) = (
  public
    see initialize
    see meeting
  private
    see goHome
  property
    ....
);
```

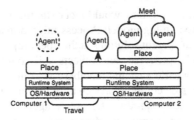

Fig. 8. Telescript Agent

List: Telescript class definition

```
initialize: op (
  desiredProduct: owned String;
  desiredPrice: Integer) = {
  ^();
  clientName = sponsor.name.copy()
};

goHome: op (homeName: Telename;
  homeAddress: Teleaddress) = {
  ....
  *.go(Ticket(homeName,homeAddress));
  *.enableEvents(PartEvent(clientName));
  here@MeetingPlace.meet(Petition(clientName));
  *.getEvent(nil, PartEvent(clientName))
};
```

List: Telescript method definition

Although Telescript was commercially unsuccessful, it has influenced other mobile agent systems. General Magic provided a Java-based system named Odyssey that used the same design framework. It did not feature strong migration.

3.2 Agent TCL

Agent Tcl is a mobile-agent system developed at Dartmouth College [6]. It primarily supported the Tcl scripting language (a later version, named DAgents, supported Java and Scheme as well as Tcl). It provided an extended interpreter for Tcl-based agent programs and a server that received agents from other servers (Figure 9).

Agent Tcl supports the notion of strong migration, because, when an agent migrate to another computer, the system captures the stack frame and program counters as well as the heap frame of the agent and sends these data items to the destination. It also extends the Tcl scripting language with several primitives. For example, The agent_jump command captures the internal state of the agent and sends the

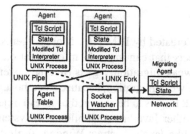

Fig. 9. System Structure Agent Tcl

state information to the destination machine through SMTP. The server on the destination machine restores the migrated agent's state information in this execution environment, and resumes the agent's execution at the statement immediately after the command is executed.

```
proc who machines {
    global agent
    set list ""
    foreach m $machines {
        if ([catch {agent_jump $m} result]) {
            append list
                "$m:nunable to JUMP here ($result)nn"
        } else {
            set users [exec who]
            append list
                "$agent(local-server):n$usernn"
        }
    }
    agent_send $agent(root) 0 $list
    exit
}
```

List: Agent Tcl Program

The above is an Agent Tcl program to migrate to another computer and then execute UNIX's who command. The agent continues this through its list of machines until it has visited them all. No agent has a reference is bound to other agents or components.

3.3 Aglets

The Aglets system was created by IBM [10]. Mobile agents, called Aglets, are implemented as Java objects that can move from one host on the Internet to another based on the notion of weak migration. Aglets runtime system itself is built on Java. It supports the notion of weak migration, because since Java, the underlying technology, does not allow stack frames to be captured or thread objects to be marshaled. To solve this, Aglets (and other Java-based mobile agent systems) provides a callback mechanism for agents, like Java's Abstract Window Toolkit (AWT). That is, when the life-cycle state of an agent is changed, e.g., creation, destruction, and migration, specified methods for the agent's program are invoked by the runtime system so that a moving agent may close windows and file handles. The global variables are marshaled and sent to the destination node. On arriving an event can be generated to instruct the agent to do something, e.g., set up resources. The following program is an agent in Aglets.

```
public class SimpleAglet extends Aglet implements MobileListener {
  public String name;
  // onCreation() invoked after the agent is created.
  public void onCreation(Object init) {
    addMobilityListener(this);
    name = new String("Agent");
    try {
      // dispatch() is a migration command
      dispatch("atp://some.where.com");
    } catch (Exception e) {/* migration fail */}
  }
  // onDispatching() is invoked before migrating.
  public void onDispatching(MobiltyEvent e) {
    System.out.println(name+" is going to "
      +e.getLocation());
  }
  // onArrival() is invoked after arriving.
  public void onArrival(MobileEvent e) {
    System.out.println(name+" came from "
      +e.getLocation());
  }
  // main program.
  public void run() {
    ....
  }
}
```

Figure 10 shows the execution of the agent defined in the above program. The onCreation() method is invoked before the agent is created and then the run() method is invoked to perform the agent's behavior with the Aglets runtime system. The MobileListener interface defines callback methods invoked when an agent migrates to another computer. The onDispatching() method is invoked before the migration of the agent. After arriving at the destination, the onArrival() method is invoked and then run() is invoked again. The Aglets system provides several primitives for invoking methods of other agents, e.g., a one-way asynchronous message, a synchronous method call, and an asynchronous method call (future-based mechanism).

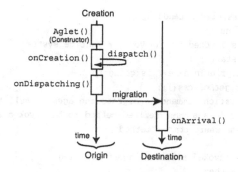

Fig. 10. Execution of Agent in Aglets system

Table 2. Lifecycle events of Aglets

lifecycle state	method invoked before	method invoked after
creation		onCreation()
migration	onDispatching(URL)	onArrval()
termination	onDisposing()	
duplication	onCloning()	onClone()

3.4 Voyager

Voyager [9] is a Java-based Object Request Broker (ORB) system, which is not compatible with CORBA, developed by ObjectSpace Inc. It not only supports mobile agents but also distributed objects. It supports a universal naming service, universal directory, activation framework, publish-subscribe, and mobile agent technology. Runtime system can be used as an agent server to host objects as mobile agents. It provides a mechanism for the creation of distributed applications through the use of its core ORB so that a programmer wishing to deploy remote objects needs to first define the object's interface. It provides typical inter-agent communication primitives, such as Future (asynchronous), OneWay (no return value is required), OneWayMulticast (sending a one way message to a group of objects or to objects who satisfy a certainly criteria) and finally the default Sync (synchronous). Voyager uses Java's standard object serialization and sockets for communication so that it can migrate agents to other computers based on the notion of weak migration. It can dynamically generate proxies which removes the need for stub generators to support the notion of mobility-transparency. That it, it enables an object to communicate other agents even after they have moved to remote computers. A mobile agent with Voyager is defined as follows:

```
public class Traveler extends Agent {
   Sting name = null;
   // start() is invoked by the Voyager runtime system
   public void start() {
      System.out.println(name+" is going to "
         +Voyager.getAddress());
      // the migration command to migrate the agent itself to the destination
      // and specifies a user defined method to be invoked at the destination.
      moveTo("some.where.com", "method");
   }
   // method is invoked after the agent arriving.
   public void method() {
      System.out.println(name+" am in "
         +Voyager.getAddress());
   }
}
```

There is a migration primitive, called moveTo(), which the programmer uses to specify a destination host or destination object; a call-back method is used to restart the object.

3.5 FarGo

FarGo is an infrastructure for Java-based distributed objects developed by the Israel Institute of Technology [8]. It supports Java-based mobile agents and migrate them between computers based on the notion of weak migration. Its goal is to separate the application logic of an object program from the dynamic deployment of the program since a developer is unlikely to know a priori how to an application can be structured in a way that best leverages the available infrastructure. Therefore, FarGo introduces the notion of complet references, which are proxies of objects that forward messages to their target objects. The references can explicitly specify the deployment policies of objects as relationships between the locations of two objects. If an object has a reference to another object, when the former object migrates to another computer, the latter migrates to the same destination or specified locations, according to the policy specified in the reference. This mechanism provides a dynamic application layout and elevates system scalability and adaptability

3.6 MobileSpaces

MobileSpaces [14] is a Java-based mobile agent system like Aglets, Voyager, and FarGo, but is unique among other existing similar systems because it can dynamically organize multiple mobile agents. The system introduces two concepts, *agent hierarchy* and *group migration*. The former means that each mobile agent can be a container of other mobile agents inside itself, and the latter allows mobile agents to move inside other mobile agents as well as inside other computers. These concepts enable us to organize more than one mobile agent into a single mobile agent and they introduce agent migration as a meta mechanism of dynamically changing and extending mobile agent-based applications. Although existing software development methodologies, including object orientation, construct large and complex mobile applications, such applications are essentially static and monolithic in the sense that they cannot be adapted adaptable. Moreover, a large-scale application software program is often constructed as a collection of subcomponents. Consequently, a mobile application needs to be migrated as a whole with all its subcomponents. MobileSpaces can naturally use mobile agents as mobile software components and can easily construct a large-scale and adaptable mobile application as a compound mobile agent.

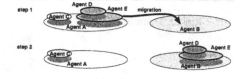

Fig. 11. Agent Hierarchy and Inter-agent Migration

The MobileSpaces runtime system is characterized by allowing a group of mobile agents to be composed hierarchically and its architecture is structured based on agent hierarchy and group migration. For example, agent migration between different computers is offered by subcomponents, called *transmitter* mobile agents, instead of a runtime system. Transmitter agents are allocated on hosts. Each transmitter agent can exchange its inner agents with one another through its favorite communication protocol as we can see in Figure 12. When a mobile agent is preparing for a trip, the agent migrates itself into an appropriate transmitter agent. The transmitter suspends the moving agent (including its nesting agents) and then serializes its state, classes, and destination address into a proper form for its communication protocol. It next transfers the serialized agent to a transmitter agent on the destination side. The transmitter agent receives the data and then reconstructs the agent (including its nesting agents) according to the data. Each runtime system can be equipped with more than one transmitter agent to exchange agents through various communication protocols and networks, e.g., TCP, UDP, HTTP, and SMTP, studied by Satoh [14, 19].

The MobileSpaces system can dynamically change and evolve its facilities by migrating agents implementing these facilities. For example, while the system is running, it can add a new function to itself by migrating a new mobile agent which implements the function to the system. The system can be open to evolve and adapt itself to its execution environment and the requirements of visiting agents.

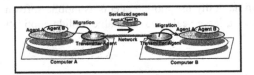

Fig. 12. Transmitter Mobile Agents

4 Mobile Agent Applications

Many researchers have stated that there are no killer applications for mobile agent technology [11], because almost everything you can do with MAs can be done with more traditional technologies. However, mobile agents make it easier, faster, and more effective to develop, manage, and execute distributed applications than other technologies. We describe typical applications of mobile agents as follows:

4.1 Remote Information Retrieval

This is one of the most traditional applications of mobile agents. If all information were stored in relational databases, a client could send a message containing SQL commands to database servers. However, given that most of the world's data is in fact maintained in free text files on different computers, remote searching and filtering require the ability to open, read, and filter files. Since mobile agents can perform most of their tasks locally at the destination, Client can send its agents to database servers so that they locally perform a sequence of query or update tasks on the servers. Communications between the client and server can be minimized, i.e., the migration of a search agent to the server and the migration of an agent to the client. Since agents contain program codes for filtering information that is of interest to their users from databases, they only need to carry wanted information back to the client to reduce communication traffic. Furthermore, agents can migrate among multiple database servers to retrieve and gather the interesting data from the servers. They can also determine the destinations based on information they have acquired from the database servers that they have thus far visited.

4.2 Network Management

Mobile agent technology provides a solution to the flexible management of network systems. Mobile agents can locally observe and control equipment at each node by migrating among nodes. Mobile agent-based network management has several advantages in comparison with traditional approaches, such as the client/server one.

- As code is very often smaller than the data it processes, the transmission of mobile agents to sources of data creates less traffic than transferring the data itself. Deploying a mobile agent close to the network nodes that we want to monitor and control prevents delays caused by network congestion.
- Since a mobile agent is locally executed on the node it is visiting, it can easily access the functions of devices on this node.
- The dynamic deployment and configuration of new or existing functionalities into a network system are extremely important tasks, especially as they potentially allow outdated systems to be updated in an efficient manner.
- Network management systems must often handle networks that may have various malfunctions and disconnections and whose exact topology may not be known. Since mobile agents are autonomous entities, they may be able to detect proper destinations or routings on such networks.

Adopting mobile agent technology eliminates the need for administrators to constantly monitor many network management activities, e.g., the installation and upgrading of software and periodic network auditing. There have been several attempts to apply this technology to network management tasks. Karmouch presented typical mobile agent approaches to network management [12]. Satoh proposed a framework for building and operating agent itineraries for network management systems [16, 20].

4.3 Load Balancing

This is a legacy application of process migration and mobile agent technologies. In a distributed system, e.g., a grid computing system, computers tend to be heterogeneous so that their computational loads are different. Computers may also be dynamically added to or removed from the system. Tasks should be dynamically deployed at computers which loads light rather than those lose with heavy loads. Since mobile agents can migrate to other computers, tasks that are implemented as mobile agents can be relocated at suitable computers whose processors can execute the tasks. This is practical in implementing massively multi agent systems that must operate a huge number of agents, which tend to be dynamically created or which terminate, on a distributed system that consists of heterogeneous computers.

4.4 Active Documents

Mobile code technology is widely used in plug-in modules for rich internet applications (RIA) in web-browsers, e.g., Java Applet and Macromedia Flash. Such modules provide us with interactive user experiences because their virtual machines, e.g., Java virtual machines and Flash players, can locally execute and render them across multiple platforms and browsers without having to communicate with remote servers. However, it is not easy to save their results on local computers or remote servers, and to resume them with the previous results later, since their code can be transported but not their state. Mobile agents solve this problem and provide a next-generation RIA. Mobile agent-based modules for RIA can naturally carry both their code and state at client computers. For example, MobiDoc [15] is a mobile agent-based framework for building mobile compound documents where a compound document can be dynamically composed of mobile agent-based components, which view or edit their contents, e.g., text, images, and movies. It can migrate itself over a network as a whole, with all its embedded components. Each component is self-contained in the sense that it maintains its content and program code for viewing and modifying the content inside it, and multiple components can be combined into an active and mobile document.

4.5 Mobile Computing

Mobile agents use the capabilities and resources of remote servers to process their tasks. When a user wants to do tasks beyond the capabilities of his or her computers, the agents that perform the tasks can migrate to and be executed at a remote server. Mobile agents can also mask temporal disconnections in networks. Mobile computers are not always connected to networks, because their wired networks are disconnected before they are moved to other locations or wireless networks become unstable or non-available due to deteriorating radio conditions or are not uncovered by the area at all. A stable connection is only requested at the beginning to send the agent, and to take the agent back at the end of the task, but this is not requested during the execution of the whole application execution. Several researchers have explored mechanisms for migrating agents through unstable networks [4, 7, 19]. When a mobile agent requests a runtime system to migrate itself, the system tries to transmit the moving agent to the destination. If the destination cannot be reached, the system automatically stores the moving agent in a queue and then periodically tries to transmit the waiting agent to either the destination or another runtime system on a reachable intermediate node as close to the destination as possible. These relay runtime systems repeat the process until the agent arrives at its destination.

4.6 Active Networking

There are two approaches to implementing active networks (for example, see [22]). The active packet approach replaces destination addresses in the packets of existing architectures with miniature programs that are interpreted at nodes on arrival. The active node approach enables new protocols to be dynamically deployed at intermediate and end nodes using mobile code techniques. Mobile agents are very similar to active networks, because a mobile agent can be regarded as a specific type of active packet, and an agent platform in traditional networks can be regarded as a specific type of active node. There have been a few attempts to incorporate mobile agent technology with active network technology (for example, see [12]). Of these, the MobileSpaces system [19] provides a mobile agent-based framework for integrating the both approaches. The framework enables us to implement network processing of mobile agents with mobile agent-based components, where the components are still mobile agents so that they can be dynamically deployed at computers to customize network processing.

4.7 Ubiquitous Computing

Ubiquitous computers often have limited resources, such as restricted levels of CPU power and amounts of memory. Mobile agents can help to conserve these limited resources, since each agent only needs to be present at the computer when the computer needs the services provided by that agent. The SpatialAgent framework [13, 17] provides a bridge between the movement of physical entities, e.g., people and things, and the movement of mobile agents to support and annotate the entities using location-tracking systems, e.g., RFID technology. It binds physical entities with mobile agents and navigate agents to stationary or mobile computers near the locations of the entities and places to which the agents are attached, even after their locations have changed. Figure 13 (a) shows that a moving entity carrying an RF-tagged agent host and a space containing a place-bound RF-tag and RF reader. When the reader detects the presence of the RFID tag that is bound to the agent host, the framework instructs the agents attached to the tagged place to migrate to the visiting agent host to offer location-dependent services of for that place. Figure 13 (b) shows that an RF-tagged agent host and an RF reader have been allocated. When an RF-tagged moving entity enters the coverage area of the reader, the framework instructs the agents attached to the entity to migrate to the agent host within the same coverage area to offer entity-dependent services to the entity.

4.8 Software Testing

Mobile agents are useful in the development of software as well as the operation of software in distributed and mobile computing settings. An example of these applications is testing methodology for software running on mobile computers, called *Flying Emulator* [18, 21]. Wireless LANs or 4G-networks incorporate wireless LAN technologies, and mobile terminals can access the services provided by LANs, as well as

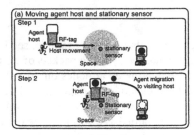 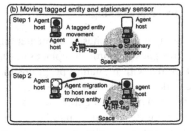

Fig. 13. Linkages between physical and logical worlds

global network services. Therefore, software running on mobile terminals may depend on not only its application-logic but also on services within the LANs that the terminals are connected to. Effective software constructed to run on mobile terminals for 4G wireless networks and wireless LANs must be tested in all networks to which the terminal could be moved and then connected to. Like existing approaches, this provides software-based emulators for mobile terminals for software designed to run on the terminals. It also constructs the emulators as mobile agents that can travel between computers. As we can see from Figure 14, these emulators can carry target software to networks that the terminals are connected to and allow it to access services. These services are provided by the networks in the same way as if the software had been carried by and executed on terminals connected to the networks.

5 Conclusion

Mobile agents are just an implementation technique used in the development and operation of distributed systems, as other software agents, including multi-agents, are themselves not goals but tools for modeling and managing our societies and systems. Therefore, the future of mobile agents is not specifically as mobile agents. They will be used as essential technologies in real distributed systems, even though they will not be called mobile agents. In fact, although monolithic mobile agent systems were developed in the past decade to illustrate the concepts of mobile agents, recent several mobile agent systems have been developed based on several slightly different semantics for mobile agents.

References

1. Ken Arnold, James Gosling, and David Holmes. *The Java Programming Language (3rd ed.)*. Addison-Wesley, 2000.
2. J. Baumann, F. Hohl, K. Rothermel, and M. Straßer. Mole: Concepts of a mobile agent system. *World Wide Web*, 3(3):123–137, 1998.
3. Andrew D. Birrell and Bruce Jay Nelson. Implementing remote procedure calls. *ACM Transactions on Computer Systems*, 2(1):39–59, 1984.

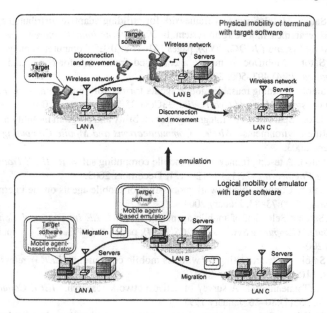

Fig. 14. Corelation between the movement of target mobile computer and migration of mobile agent-based emulator

4. Jiannong Cao, Xinyu Feng, Jian Lu, and Sajal K. Das. Mailbox-based scheme for design-ing mobile agent communication protocols. *IEEE Computer*, 35(9):54–60, 2002.
5. Alfonso Fuggetta, Gian Pietro Picco, and Giovanni Vigna. Understanding code mobility. *IEEE Transactions on Software Engineering*, 24(5):342–361, 1998.
6. Robert S. Gray. In *CIKM Workshop on Intelligent Information Agents*, 1995.
7. Robert S. Gray, David Kotz, Saurab Nog, Daniela Rus, and George Cybenko. Mobile agents for mobile computing. Technical report, Dartmouth College Technical Report: PCS-TR96-285, 1999.
8. Ophir Holder, Israel Ben-Shaul, and Hovav Gazit. System support for dynamic layout of distributed applications. In *19th IEEE International Conference on Distributed Comput-ing Systems*, pages 403–411, 1999.
9. ObjectSpace Inc. ObjectSpace voyager technical overview. Technical report, Ob-jectSpace, 1999.
10. Danny B. Lange and Oshima Mitsuru. *Programming and Deploying Java Mobile Agents Aglets*. Addison-Wesley, 1998.
11. Dejan Milojicic. Mobile agent applications. *IEEE Concurrency*, 7(4):80–90, July-September 1999.
12. Vu Anh Pham and Ahmed Karmouch. Mobile software agents: An overview. *IEEE Communications Magazine*, 36(7):26–37, July 1998.
13. Ichiro Satoh. Physical mobility and logical mobility in ubiquitous computing environ-ments. In *6th International Conference on Mobile Agents (MA'2002)*, Lecture Notes in Computer Science 2535, pages 186–202. Springer, October.

14. Ichiro Satoh. MobileSpaces: A framework for building adaptive distributed applications using a hierarchical mobile agent system. In *20th International Conference on Distributed Computing Systems (ICDCS 2000)*, pages 161–168. IEEE Computer Society, April 2000.
15. Ichiro Satoh. MobiDoc: A mobile agent-based framework for compound documents. *Informatica*, 25(4):493–500, 2001.
16. Ichiro Satoh. Building reusable mobile agents for network management. *IEEE Transactions on Systems, Man and Cybernetics*, 33C(3):350–357, August 2003.
17. Ichiro Satoh. SpatialAgents: Integrating user mobility and program mobility in ubiquitous computing environments. *Wireless Communications and Mobile Computing*, 3(4):411–423, June 2003.
18. Ichiro Satoh. A testing framework for mobile computing software. *IEEE Transactions on Software Engineering*, 29(12):1112–1121, December 2003.
19. Ichiro Satoh. Configurable network processing for mobile agents on the internet. *Cluster Computing*, 7(1):73–83, January 2004.
20. Ichiro Satoh. Selection of mobile agents. In *24th IEEE International Conference on Distributed Computing Systems (ICDCS'2004)*, pages 484–493. IEEE Computer Society, March 2004.
21. Ichiro Satoh. Software testing for wireless mobile computing. *IEEE Wireless Communications*, 11(5):58–64, October 2004.
22. David L. Tennenhouse. A survey of active network research. *IEEE Communications Magazine*, 35(1):80–86, January 1997.
23. James E. White. *Software Agents*, chapter Telescript Technology: Mobile Agents, pages 437–472. 1997.

WIZER: Automated Model Improvement in Multi-Agent Social-Network Systems

Alex Yahja[1] and Dr. Kathleen M. Carley[2]

[1] Computation, Organizations, and Society Program, Institute for Software Research International, Center for the Analysis of Social and Organizational Systems, Carnegie Mellon University, 5000 Forbes Avenue, Pittsburgh, PA 15213 ay@cmu.edu
[2] Institute for Software Research International, Center for the Analysis of Social and Organizational Systems, Carnegie Mellon University, 5000 Forbes Avenue, Pittsburgh, PA 15213 kathleen.carley@cmu.edu

Summary. There has been a significant increase in the use of multi-agent social-network models due to their ability to flexibly model emergent behaviors in complex socio-technical systems while linking to real data. These models are growing in size and complexity which requires significant time and effort to calibrate, validate, improve the model, and gain insight into model behavior. In this paper, we present our knowledge-based simulation-aided approach for automating model-improvement and our tool implementing this approach (WIZER). WIZER is capable of calibrating and validating multi-agent social-network models, and facilitates model-improvement and understanding. By employing knowledge-based search, causal analysis, and simulation control and inference techniques, WIZER can reduce the number of simulation runs needed to calibrate, validate, and improve a model and improve the focus of these runs. WIZER automates reasoning and analysis of simulations, instead of being a multi-agent programming language or environment. We ran a preliminary version of WIZER on BioWar a city-scale social agent network simulation of the effects of weaponized biological attacks on a demographically-realistic population within a background of naturally-occurring diseases. The results demonstrate the efficacy of WIZER.

1 Introduction

Currently, a paradigm shift is occurring in how we model and think about knowledge, individuals, teams, groups, networks, organizations, markets, institutions, and other societal systems due to developments in the field of computational modeling and analysis [1][8][16][32][39][19][40]. Computational modeling and analysis has emerged as a useful scientific tool for addressing socio-technical problems with complex dynamic inter-related parts, such as natural disaster response and biological attacks. These problems do not occur in vacuum but within a context constrained by social, organizational, geographical, technological, regulatory, cultural, and financial factors. As opportunities and challenges emerge dynamically in, say tsunami relief, existing rescue and aid plans often need major adaptations. For members of a rescue and aid team to cohesively follow a joint course action, it helps if the development in the environment, the consequent change of plans, and the effects of the intervention carried out according to the plans can be thought over and analyzed both in advance and in real/ongoing time.

There has been a rapid increase in the use of multi-agent models [12][26][28] – as well as social network analysis [41] – to address complex socio-technical problems. Model assessment determining how valid, how explainable, and how robust a model is is becoming a major concern [11]. Indeed, identifying reliable validation methods for complex systems such as electronic medical surveillance systems is a critical research area [34]. Calibration and validation serve as a foundation for model improvement through simulation and inference.

Models contain both explicit and implicit assumptions about some portion of the real world. These assumptions form abstractions of reality and these abstractions may or may not be sound. Moreover, the real world changes continuously and in unexpected ways. A cohesive joint course action by a group(s) responding to ongoing socio-technical problems is crucial to the efficiency and success of the action. How to adapt existing plans in ongoing socio-technical environments and how to coordinate members of a group(s) depend on how valid the underlying models and assumptions are. It is also desirable to automate improvement of models and assumptions based on live empirical data. Validation and model-improvement serve as a foundation for the coordination of large number of agents and their distributed tasks, goals, and organizations to deal with live socio-technical problems. The required fidelity of the model varies as a function of the research, policy, and/or mission questions being asked. Calibration, validation, and model-improvement are hard due to the changes in the real world, altered goals, inherent assumptions and abstractions, and human cognitive limitations such as bounded rationality [38].

Information exploitation is a technique that has yet to be fully employed to deal with the problem of calibration, validation, and model improvement. (The term "validation" will be used from now on to denote calibration, validation, and model-improvement.) Few multi-agent simulations have exploited the depth and breadth of available knowledge and information for validation that resides in journals, books, websites, human experts, and other sources. Typically, simulation results are designed solely for human analysis and validation is provided by subject matter experts announcing that the model "feels right" face validity. While this may be sufficient for small-scale simulations, it is woefully inadequate for large-scale simulations designed to inform decision-makers. In particular, automated help for validation and analysis is crucial. However, little work to date probes the important aspect of automating validation and analysis (this is conventionally left to humans to perform: there is an invisible wall of separation between simulation and analysis/knowledge inference). To successfully automate validation and analysis, domain knowledge must be exploited, for example by an expert systems inference engine. A simulation and inference engine that can do virtual experiments and knowledge inference in concert would facilitate focused search by using both the simulation engines search space and the inference engines knowledge space to arrive at better parameter and meta-model values for validation. This paper describes our approach for doing knowledge-based simulation-aided validation in multi-agent social-network systems, embodied in a tool called WIZER (What-If AnalyZER). WIZER applies knowledge control of the simulation, inference and intelligent search in multi-agent social-network simulations.

The results presented in this paper are based on WIZER runs using BioWar. BioWar is a city-scale multi-agent social-network simulator capable of modeling the effects of weaponized biological attacks on a demographically-realistic population within a background of naturally-occurring diseases [7][6]. BioWar currently runs a few thousand to several million agents. Unlike traditional models that look at hypothetical cities (such as the Brookings smallpox model [17] and the SARS model [22]), BioWar is configured to represent real cities by loading census data, school district boundaries, etc. It models both healthy and infected agents as they go about their lives, enabling observation of absenteeism, drug purchases, hospital visits, and other data streams of interest.

2 Validation Experience

The complexity of ensuring valid results of agent-based simulations is shown during the validation of BioWar outputs. BioWar has many input and model parameters and these parameters can be stochastic. Brute-force search in the space of input and model parameters to fit the non-computational data is all but impossible. BioWar also has a complex response surface(s) and is knowledge intensive. Putting BioWar in specification can be viewed as a multi-dimensional numeric and symbolic optimization problem, with the knowledge component (e.g., school district announcements). The validation experience shows that there is a need for:

- Sophisticated analysis and response techniques to optimize the space over which parameters must be varied for correctness, and thus increase the number of parameters which can be studied.
- Tools to semi-automatically create and execute parametric studies to minimize the manual intervention currently required for these studies.
- New approaches to simulation scaling so as to reduce the size of the simulations which produce validated output streams.

WIZER addresses the first two points above.

3 Related Work

Multi-agent systems are usually "validated" by strictly applying requirements engineering. In software engineering terms [31], validation means the determination of the correctness of the final program or software produced with respect to the user needs and requirements not necessarily the empirical data or the real world. The usual emphasis in multi-agent system development is on language, programming, and design principles such as agent autonomy, team work, roles/types, and interaction protocols [12][28]. Formal methods [13] used in software engineering for control and understanding of complex multi-agent systems lack an effective means of determining if a program fulfills a given formal specification [15]. Complex societal problems contain "messy" interactions, dynamic processes, and emergent behaviors, so it is often problematic to apply requirements engineering and/or formal methods.

Another validation method is evolutionary verification and validation or EVV [37][36], which utilizes evolutionary algorithms, including genetic algorithms and scatter search, for verification and validation. While EVV allows testing and exploitation of unusual combinations of parameter values via evolutionary processes, it employs knowledge-poor genetic and evolutionary operators, not the scientific method, for doing experiments, forming and testing hypotheses, refining models, and inference, precluding non-evolutionary solutions.

Docking is another approach to validating multi-agent systems [2]. Docking is based on the notion of repeating a scientific experiment to confirm findings or to ensure accuracy. It considers whether two or more different simulation models align (produce similar results), which is used in turn as a basis to determine if one model can subsume another. The higher the degree of alignment among models, the more they can be assumed to be valid, especially if one (or both) of them has been previously validated. The challenges in applying docking are the limited number of previously validated models, the implicit and diverse assumptions incorporated into models and the differences in data and domains among models.

One application of docking is to align complex multi-agent simulations against mathematical or system dynamics models. BioWar's anthrax simulation has been successfully docked against the IPF (Incubation-Prodromal-Fulminant) mathematical model, a variant for anthrax of the well-known SIR (Susceptible-Infected-Recovered) epidemiological model [9] and BioWar's smallpox model has been docked against a SIR model of smallpox [10]. While aligning a multi-agent model with a widely used mathematical model can show the differences and similarities between these two models, the validity is limited by the type of data the mathematical model uses. For example, the IPF model mentioned above operates on population-level data, so the result of the alignment will be only valid at the granularity of population-level data. Mathematical models also have difficulties representing non-numerical (symbolic) knowledge, including the knowledge base underlying complex context-sensitive agent interactions.

Validating complex multi-agent simulations by statistical methods alone [23] is problematic due to the coarse granularity required for statistical methods to operate properly and the insufficient representation of symbolic knowledge. Statistical methods are good at describing data and inferring distributional parameters from samples, but statistic methods alone are insufficient to handle the highly dynamic, symbolic, causal, heterogeneous, and emergent nature of societal systems.

Complex multi-agent simulations are not normally validated using expert systems (such as OrgCon [5]) as it is thought that it is sufficient to let human experts alone perform the analyses, experiment design, and quantitative and symbolic reasoning. This view is especially prevalent as most simulations are in the realm of purely numeric models.

Human experts can do validation by focusing on the most relevant part of the system and thinking about the problem intuitively and creatively. These subject matter experts (SMEs) have the knowledge needed to judge model performance in their specialized fields. Applying learned expertise and intuition, SMEs can exploit hunches and insights, form rules, judge patterns, and analyze policies. Managed and administered properly, SMEs can be effective. Pitfalls include bounded rationality, implicit biases, implicit reasoning steps, judgment errors, and others.

Another approach to validation is direct comparison with real world data and knowledge. Validation can be viewed as experimenting with data and knowledge, using models as the lab equipment for performing computational experiments [20][3]. Simulation models to be validated should reflect the real world and results from experiments in simulation should emulate changes in the real world. If results from virtual or computational experiments are compared to real world data and match sufficiently, the simulation is sufficiently valid. Simulation [24][33] has an advantage over statistics and formal systems as it can model the world closely, free of the artifacts of statistics and formal systems.

There is related work in engineering design methods using Response Surface Methodology or RSM [27] and Monte Carlo simulations [35] to do direct validation, but only with numerical data and limited to a small number of dimensions. RSM is collection of mathematical and statistical techniques for the modeling and analysis of problems in which a response of interest is influenced by several variables. It can include virtual experiments using Monte Carlo simulation. It usually tests only a few variables and operates to find the best fit equation so that the correlation of equations predictions with real data is statistically significant.

4 Our Approach: Knowledge-Based Simulation-Aided Model-Improvement

WIZER (What-If AnalyZER) is a coupled inference and simulation engine that improves upon Response Surface Methodology to deal with the high dimensional, symbolic, stochastic, emergent, and dynamic nature of multi-agent social-network systems. Viewing simulation systems as knowledge systems, WIZER is designed for controlling and validating them directly with empirical data and knowledge using pattern analyses and knowledge inferences (mimicking those of SMEs) and virtual experiments (mimicking those of RSM).

WIZER integrates an inference engine and simulation virtual experiments to do calibration and validation for model-improvement and to provide explanations. It improves on RSM features by performing knowledge-intensive data-driven search steps via an inference engine constrained by simulation outputs, instead of just doing statistical and mathematical calculations. WIZER facilitates knowledge-based simulation control and simulation-assisted inference, enabling reasoning about simulations and simulation-assisted reasoning. It enables the management of model assumptions, contradictory or incomplete data, and increases the speed and accuracy of model validation and analysis. It is capable of explaining the reasoning behind inferences using both the simulation and inference engine. Search in WIZER is performed using both simulation and knowledge inference. The amount of search is reduced as the knowledge inferences, empirical data and knowledge, and virtual experiments constrain the search space.

WIZER seeks to emulate scientists doing experiments and analyses via the scientific method, instead of simply emulating an experimental setup. While other toolkits such as Swarm (http://wiki.swarm.org), TAEMS [25], and Repast (http://repast.sourceforge.net) are designed with the goal of assisting the design and implementation of agent-based systems, WIZER is designed to help with scientific experimentation, validation, analysis, and model improvement. WIZER is conceptually able to run on top of any simulation system, including those constructed using Swarm and Repast toolkits. WIZER is basically a logical reasoning, experimentation, and simulation control engine with statistical and pattern recognition capabilities. This is similar to techniques scientists employ when designing, executing, and analyzing experiments. WIZER differs from Evolutionary Programming [18] as it does not need a population of mutation candidates and the mutation operator. Instead, WIZER applies knowledge inference to simulations to design the next simulation run, based on scientific experimental method. If the result of inferences mandates a radical change, a revolution would occur. WIZER also differs from Evolutionary Strategies and Genetic Algorithms [14] as it does not use recombination/crossover operators. In short, WIZER employs a unique logical reasoning, simulation control and scientific method for doing virtual experiments. Explaining what a simulation system does and what happens in simulation to SMEs is important from validation perspective. Utilizing its inference engine, WIZER can provide automated explanation of the happenings and emergent behaviors within a multi-agent simulation system.

As shown in Figure 1, Alert WIZER takes in the simulation output data and determines which data streams of the simulation outputs do not fall within the empirical data value ranges and how. The WIZER Inference Engine takes the simulators causal diagram of what parameter influences which output data and the empirical constraints and confidence intervals on parameters to make a judgment on which parameters to change and how (including causal links and the model or agent submodel itself, if necessary). This results in new parameters for the next simulation. This simulation in turn yields new outputs which are fed back into WIZER.

This cycle repeats until a user-defined validity level is achieved. Thus, WIZER consists of:

- A system for determining which outcome variables match or fall within the acceptable range of the real data Alert WIZER. This system will create an "alert" when there is not a match. Inputs to Alert WIZER include real and virtual data. Real data include various types of data such as subject matter experts (SMEs) estimation of behavior, 1st, 2nd, and 3rd order statistics for data streams at the

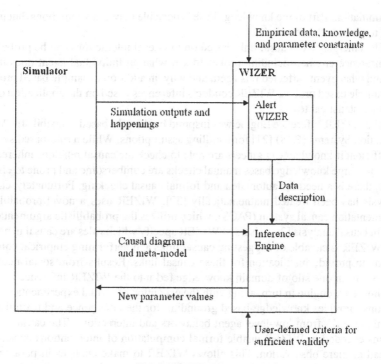

Fig. 1. WIZER Diagram

yearly, seasonal, monthly, and day of week level, and actual streams of data. Alert WIZER includes statistical tools.

- An intelligent system for identifying which of the "changeable" parameters should be changed and how to improve the fit of the virtual to the real data the WIZER Inference Engine. This component uses a database relating parameters to the variables and modules they impact. This includes assumptions about the expected range for parameter values (according to SMEs) or best guesses, thus placing confidence measures on parameters.
- A local response surface analysis feature that can run simple virtual experiments for parametric studies.

The knowledge bases in the inference engine are populated with the knowledge about the simulator, simulation outcomes, domain facts and knowledge, assumptions, ontology, problem solving strategies, information about statistical tools it employs and other data. The knowledge bases contain both knowledge (hard or certain rules and facts) and assumptions (soft or uncertain rules and facts). Simulation outcomes provide measurements of the degree-of-support an assumption has. These different types of knowledge are included to enable the inference engine to reason about its reasoning. For example, knowledge about the simulation allows the inference engine to back up its symbolic reasoning with simulation outcomes and also to reason about the simulation. Part of the knowledge base is portable between simulations, but users need to provide the remainder.

The emergence of causal links based on low-level interactions can be probed by the inference engine, including probes to see what an individual agent does in its life and what events affected this agent and why, in addition to sample based probes. For sample based probes, WIZER conducts inferences based on the application of its included statistical tests.

The WIZER Inference Engine was inspired by the rule-based Probabilistic Argumentation Systems (PAS) [21] for handling assumptions. While a rule-based system is sufficient if knowledge engineers are able to check the causal relations inherent in rules, for large knowledge bases manual checks are cumbersome and prone to errors. Thus, there is a need for automated and formal causal checking. Fortunately, causal analysis has been treated mathematically [30]. WIZER uses a novel probabilistic argumentation causal system (PACS), which utilizes the probabilistic argumentation [21] in causal analysis [29]. Users of WIZER specify which rules are causal in nature and WIZER is capable of suggesting causal links and performing empirical computations to provide justification for these causal links. Results from social network analysis form one silo of domain knowledge fed into the WIZER inference engine. The inference engine in turn, along with the execution of virtual experiments in simulations, provides knowledge-based grounding for the emergence and evolution of social networks from low-level agent behaviors and interactions. The causal mechanisms encoded in WIZER enable formal computation of interventions or actions, instead of mere observation. This allows WIZER to make changes in parameters, causal links, and meta-models, and to analyze the consequences. In other words, WIZER can emulate what scientists do by changing and analyzing experiments.

Causal analysis involves mechanisms (stable functional relationships), interventions (surgeries on mechanisms), and causation (encoding of behavior under interventions). Associations common in statistics can characterize static conditions, while causal analysis deals with the dynamics of events under changing conditions. Simply turning off some potential causal links and re-simulating is insufficient and while counterfactual testing – checking would happen if (true) facts were false – can uncover causal effects, the method can fail in the presence of other causes or when other causes are preempted and it ignores the sufficiency aspect. These weaknesses of this (global) counterfactual test can be addressed by sustenance, providing a method to compute actual causation [29]. Sustenance means minimally supporting an effect. Actual cause is computed by constructing causal beams and doing local counterfactual test within the beams. Causal beams are causal links that have been pruned to retain a subset of causal links that sustains the occurrence of an effect. Dynamic beams are simply causal beams with a time dimension [29].

To account for the probability of causation, the causal model [30][29] specifies the use of Bayesian priors to encode the probability of an event given another event. It does not distinguish between different kinds of uncertainty. It is unable to model ignorance, ignores contradictions and is incapable of expressing evidential knowledge without the use of the probability distribution format. Since the intended use of WIZER is to do validation in environments with incomplete, contradictory, and uncertain knowledge and because WIZER needs to clearly delineate between assumptions and facts, we need an improved causal model, built by borrowing concepts from the Probabilistic Argumentation Systems (PAS). Table 1 shows the encoding of facts, assumptions, and rules for rule-based systems using probabilistic argumentation, while Table 2 shows the encoding of facts, assumptions, and causations for causal analysis enhanced with PAS-like assumption management. In both tables, let P_i be proposition i, a_i be assumption i, *causes* be the causation operator, and $\Rightarrow$ be the implication operator.

Table 1. Rule-Based Encoding

Type of Knowledge	Logical Representation	Meaning
A fact	P1	P1 is true
A rule	P1 $\Rightarrow$ P2	P1 implies P2
An uncertain fact	a1 $\Rightarrow$ P1	If a1 is true then P1 is true
An uncertain rule	a2 $\Rightarrow$ (P1 $\Rightarrow$ P2)	If a2 is true then P1 implies P2

Table 2. Causation Encoding

Type of Knowledge	Logical Representation	Meaning
A fact	P1	P1 is true
A rule	P1 causes P2	P1 causes P2
An uncertain fact	a1 $\Rightarrow$ P1	If a1 is true then P1 is true
An uncertain rule	a2 $\Rightarrow$ (P1 causes P2)	If a2 is true then P1 causes P2

We call Table 2's formalism the probabilistic argumentation causal systems (PACS). WIZER includes both rule-based and causal formalisms. PACS algorithmic details are derived from both PAS [21] and causal analysis [30]. Simulation virtual experiments can be seen as a proxy for real world experiments when doing real world interventions would be unrealistic or unethical. Causal analysis uses computations based on real-world experimental and non-experimental data. WIZER adds another dimension to causal analysis: allowing quasi-experimental that is, simulated data.

The internal workings of the WIZER Inference Engine are complex, but its basic operations are simple. Let $P = p_1, \ldots, p_n$ be propositions, $A = a_1, \ldots, a_n$ be assumptions, h be the hypothesis and $K = c_1 \cap \ldots \cap c_n$ be the knowledge base of clauses, where c_i is an element of the set of all possible A and P clauses. Let a be the (conjunctive) arguments supporting h. We have

$a \cap K \Rightarrow h$

or equivalently

$a \Rightarrow \neg K \cup h$

or equivalently

$$\neg(\neg K \cup h) \Rightarrow \neg a$$

$$K \cap \neg h \Rightarrow \neg a$$

In other words, if we know K and h, we can compute the supports, that is, the arguments supporting h. The hypothesis h is a clause produced by Alert WIZER after comparing simulation data streams with empirical data. After finding the arguments supporting h, the degree of support can be found, defined as

$$dsp(h, K) = prob(a \text{ support } a \text{ of } h \text{ is valid} \mid no \text{ contradiction}, K)$$

Similarly, the degree of plausibility can be found, defined as

$$dpl(h, K) = prob(no \text{ support of } \neg h \text{ is valid} \mid no \text{ contradiction}, K)$$

These two measures are used to determine which arguments are the most relevant to the hypothesis at hand, pinpointing which parameter values, causal links, and/or submodels should be changed. In other words, hypothesis h is the input to WIZER Inference Engine and the arguments supporting h are the output, leading to changes in parameter and meta-model values.

The operations described above are performed for both rule-based and causal clauses. Then, for clauses denoted as causal, additional operations are performed to see whether and to what degree the causal relations are empirically correct, partially based on the degree of support and the degree of plausibility. Sustenance, causal beams and actual cause are also computed. WIZER also performs virtual experiments as needed.

The intertwining causal computation and virtual experimentation capability of WIZER enhances PACS and is useful in simulations to:

- Provide a formal computational means to convert simulation results or happenings to user-friendly causal sentences and also a mechanism to arrive at probability distributions or profiles for assumption variables.
- Allow probing of existing and potential causal assumptions and links and examination of the robustness of causal links using empirical data and quasi-experimental data obtained by simulations based on other known mechanisms and empirical data. For example, a simulation may have modeled Washington DC and policy analysts would like to know the effects of quarantining certain city blocks or closure of some major roads to mitigate the spread of smallpox. The mechanisms, data values, and stochastic processes in the city model themselves do not contain direct answers to the above causal question. Utilizing causal computation would allow this question to be answered.
- Allow the formal modeling of interventions in simulations.
- Allow symbolic values/events to be considered in determining causal relations. For example, the recent shortage of flu vaccine caused the CDC to recommend restrictions on who received the vaccine, resulting in a stockpile of unused flu vaccine, partly because some eligible people believed that none were available due to the news. WIZER would be able to probe similar kinds of cause and effect relationships.
- Allow experimentation and simulation control. As WIZER modifies, runs, re-modifies, and re-runs simulations, it uses causal mechanisms to keep track of

and help inform what causes a certain series of modifications to work or fail and to suggest possible next steps.

- Allow better inference by letting the inference engine run simulations in the midst of causal inferences as needed. This allows the examination of the empirical claims of causal inferences.
- Provide a way to automatically tweak agent meta-models and individual agents so that they are both realistic and able to coordinate in a realistic environment.

5 Run Setup and Empirical Data

WIZER was used to validate BioWar. As mentioned earlier, BioWar [7] is a city-scale spatial multi-agent social-network model capable of bioattack simulations. BioWar has a large number of variables and interactions. Application of the Spiral Development model [4] to BioWar code development means that any previous validation of model predictions may no longer apply to a new version.

We have implemented Alert WIZER, which takes the empirical data on school absences, workplace absenteeism, doctor visits, emergency room visits, with additional emergency room visitation data from SDI (Surveillance Data Inc.), and over-the-counter drug purchase data. It also uses the outputs of the BioWar simulator and conducts minimum bound checking, maximum bound checking and mean comparison.

The following empirical data was used to compute the empirical bounds and means for the Alert WIZER:

- NCES Indicator 17, 2002 (Year 2000 data), for calculating school absenteeism http://nces.ed.gov/programs/coe/2002/section3/indicator17.asp
- CDC Advance Data, from Vital and Health Statistics, no. 326, 2002, for calculating ER visits http://www.cdc.gov/nchs/data/ad/ad326.pdf
- CDC Advance Data, from Vital and Health Statistics, no. 328, 2002, for calculating doctor visits http://www.cdc.gov/nchs/data/ad/ad328.pdf
- 1997 US Employee Absences by Industry Ranked for determining work absenteeism http://publicpurpose.com/lm-97absr.htm
- Over-the-counter (OTC) Drug Sales extracted from Pittsburgh Supercomputing Centers "FRED" data containing pharmacy sales data.

BioWar simulation outputs include the data streams matching the above empirical data such as daily absences for each school.

6 Preliminary Results

WIZER was run on "Challenge 3" and "Challenge 4" data from BioWar [6] using an implementation of Alert WIZER. Challenge 3 data consists of 4 data streams with 10 simulation runs for each attack case (no attack, anthrax attack, and smallpox attack) for each of 4 cities. The city population and locations (buildings and facilities) were scaled at 20%. The parameters were adjusted following an execution of preliminary inference engine steps based on a partial causal diagram of BioWar. We present the means from the four Challenge 3 simulation output data streams in Tables 3-6.

Table 3 shows that the simulated means of school absenteeism rates for normal simulation cases (no bioattack) fall between lower and upper empirical bounds for the simulations of Norfolk, Pittsburgh, San Diego, and "Veridian Norfolk" (a part of Norfolk specified by Veridian, Inc.). For anthrax attack cases, the simulated means are higher than normal means but still lower than the empirical higher bounds. This is plausible as the empirical higher bound contains (contagious) influenza outbreaks and other disease cases. For smallpox attacks, however, the simulation mean for one city – San Diego – is higher than the empirical higher bound. Smallpox is highly contagious so this is also plausible. For other cities, the simulated means of school absenteeism remain within expected bounds.

Table 3. School Absenteeism

City, scale	Lower bound	Higher bound	No attack	Anthrax	Smallpox
Norfolk, 20%	3.04%	5.18%	3.45%	3.75%	3.55%
Pittsburgh, 20%	3.04%	5.18%	3.52%	4.67%	4.46%
San Diego, 20%	3.04%	5.18%	3.78%	3.81%	5.57%
Veridian Norfolk, 20%	3.04%	5.18%	3.73%	4.05%	4.31%

For the workplace absenteeism (Table 4), the simulated means are within the empirical bounds for normal (no attack) cases for all the cities. In case of anthrax attack, the workplace absenteeism means are higher than those for normal cases; and in three of four cities, higher than the empirical higher bound. For smallpox attack, the simulated means are higher than those for normal cases, and higher than the empirical higher bound for one of the four cities.

Table 4. Workplace Absenteeism

City, scale	Lower bound	Higher bound	No attack	Anthrax	Smallpox
Norfolk, 20%	2.30%	4.79%	2.72%	4.65%	2.82%
Pittsburgh, 20%	2.30%	4.79%	2.77%	5.79%	3.99%
San Diego, 20%	2.30%	4.79%	3.26%	4.99%	5.78%
Veridian Norfolk, 20%	2.30%	4.79%	3.16%	5.50%	3.81%

Table 5 shows that for doctor visits the simulated means for the four cities fall within the empirical bounds for normal (no attack) cases. For anthrax attack cases, the simulated means are higher than those for normal cases for two cities, and slightly lower for two other cities. For smallpox attacks, the means are higher than those for normal cases for three cities and the same for one city. The results for attack cases are imperfect but indicate correct trends. All means for anthrax and smallpox attacks are within the empirical bounds.

Table 5. Doctor Visit per Person per Year

City, scale	Lower bound	Higher bound	No attack	Anthrax	Smallpox
Norfolk, 20%	0.415	1.611	0.499	0.476	0.499
Pittsburgh, 20%	0.415	1.611	0.493	0.485	0.573
San Diego, 20%	0.415	1.611	0.726	0.753	0.796
Veridian Norfolk, 20%	0.415	1.611	0.707	0.821	0.738

For emergency room visits (Table 6), the simulated means for four cities fall within the empirical bounds for normal (no attack) cases. For anthrax attacks, the simulated means are higher than those of normal cases for two cities and slightly lower for two others. For smallpox attacks, the simulated means are higher than those for normal cases for three cities and the same for one city. The results for attack cases are imperfect but indicate correct trends.

Table 6. Emergency Room Visit per Person per Year

City, scale	Lower bound	Higher bound	No attack	Anthrax	Smallpox
Norfolk, 20%	0.056	0.232	0.112	0.108	0.112
Pittsburgh, 20%	0.056	0.232	0.109	0.106	0.129
San Diego, 20%	0.056	0.232	0.149	0.159	0.188
Veridian Norfolk, 20%	0.056	0.232	0.161	0.187	0.168

Challenge 4 data has 12 data streams: school absenteeism, work absenteeism, doctor visits, emergency room visits, emergency room visits using the Surveillance Data Inc. data, and seven drug type purchase data streams. Table 7 shows the percentage of validated data streams for six cities for the no attack case.

Table 7. Percentage of "Challenge 4" Simulation Output Data Streams Validated

City	Data Streams Validated
San Francisco	5 out of 12, or 41.67%
San Diego	7 out of 12, or 58.33%
Pittsburgh	7 out of 12, or 58.33%
Norfolk	6 out of 12, or 50.00%
Hampton	4 out of 12, or 33.33%
Washington DC	4 out of 12, or 33.33%

7 Discussion

Automation of simulation experiment control and analysis is rarely viewed as a critical feature of simulation systems; instead, experimental control, analysis, intervention, validation, and model-improvement are left for humans to perform. Most simulation platforms aim to provide tools to ease the coding of simulation systems, rather than automating the analysis, control, validation, intervention, and model-improvement. WIZER indicates that such automation can be very useful, especially when dealing with socio-technical and public health problems which have a high degree of uncertainty and interactions. Based on empirical data and knowledge, simulations can bound the inferences and allow the empirical claims of the inferences to be investigated. At the same time, knowledge-based inference and control of simulation can reduce the number of simulation searches and virtual experiments that need to be conducted. Simulations and inferences on them here act like a dynamic version space on both search and knowledge spaces.

The results presented in this paper are preliminary. More WIZER and simulation runs are needed to get better statistics – such as the median and variance –, and to evaluate error margins, the effects of sample choices, search space traversal, and the performance of combined simulation and knowledge search, including the metrics for measuring the amount of search reduction in both search space and knowledge space. The performance of WIZER will be compared with that of human subject matter experts.

8 Acknowledgements

This research was supported, in part, by DARPA for work on Scalable Biosurveillance Systems, the NSF IGERT9972762 in CASOS, the MacArthur Foundation, and by the Carnegie Mellon Center on Computational Analysis of Social and Organizational Systems. The computations were performed on the National Science Foundation Terascale Computing System at the Pittsburgh Supercomputing Center. Any opinions, findings, conclusions or recommendations expressed in this material are those of the authors and do not necessarily reflect the views of DARPA, the National Science Foundation, the Pittsburgh Supercomputing Center, the MacArthur Foundation, or the US Government.

References

1. R Axelrod. Advancing the art of simulation. In *Simulating Social Phenomena*, pages 21–40. Springer-Verlag, Berlin, Germany, 1997.
2. R Axtell, R Axelrod, J.M Epstein, and M.D Cohen. Aligning simulation models: A case study and results. *Computational and Mathematical Organization Theory*, 1(2):123–141, 1996.

3. S Bankes. Models as lab equipment: Science from computational experiments. In *Proceedings of the North American Association for Computational Social and Organizational Science Conference*. Center for Computational Analysis of Social and Organizational Systems, Pittsburgh, PA, 2004.

4. B Boehm. Spiral development: Experience, principles, and refinements. In *Spiral Development Workshop, Special Report CMU/SEI-2000-SR-008*. Carnegie Mellon University, Pittsburgh, PA, 2000.

5. R Burton and B Obel. *Strategic Organizational Diagnosis and Design: Developing Theory for Application*. Kluwer Academic Publishers, Dordrecht, the Netherlands, second edition, 1998.

6. K Carley, N Altman, B Kaminsky, D Nave, and A Yahja. Biowar: A city-scale multi-agent model of weaponized biological attacks. Technical report, Carnegie Mellon University, Pittsburgh, PA, 2004.

7. K Carley, D Fridsma, E Casman, N Altman, J Chang, B Kaminsky, D Nave, and A Yahja. Biowar: Scalable multi-agent social and epidemiological simulation of bioterrorism events. In *Proceedings of North American Association for Computational Social and Organizational Science Conference*. Center for Computational Analysis of Social and Organizational Systems, Pittsburgh, PA, 2004.

8. K Carley and M Prietula, editors. *Computational Organizational Theory*. Lawrence Erlbaum Associates, Mahwah, NJ, 1999.

9. L-C Chen, K Carley, D Fridsma, B Kaminsky, and A Yahja. Model alignment of anthrax attack simulations. *Decision Support Systems in the special issue on Intelligence and Security Informatics*, 2003.

10. L-C Chen, B Kaminsky, T Tummino, K Carley, E Casman, D Fridsma, and A Yahja. Aligning simulation models of smallpox outbreaks. In *Intelligence and Security Informatics*, volume 3073 of *Lecture Notes on Computer Science*, pages 1–16. Springer-Verlag, Berlin, Germany, 2004.

11. C Cioffi-Revilla. Invariance and universality in social agent-based simulations. In *Proceedings of the National Academy of Sciences of the U.S.A*, volume 99 (Supp. 3), pages 7314–7316. National Academy Press, Washington, DC, 2002.

12. M Dastani, J Dix, and A.E.F Seghrouchni, editors. *Programming Multi-Agent Systems*, volume 3067 of *Lecture Notes in Artificial Intelligence*. Springer-Verlag, Berlin, Germany, 2004.

13. N Dershowitz, editor. *Verification: Theory and Practice*. Springer-Verlag, New York, NY, 2004.

14. M Dianati, I Song, and M Treiber. An introduction to genetic algorithms and evolution strategies. Technical report, University of Waterloo, 2003.

15. B Edmonds and JJ Bryson. The insufficiency of formal design methods: the necessity of an experimental approach for the understanding and control of complex mas. In *Proceedings of Autonomous Agents and Multi Agent Systems Conference*. Association for Computing Machinery, 2004.

16. J Epstein and R Axtell. *Growing Artificial Societies*. MIT Press, Cambridge, MA, 1996.

17. J Epstein, D.A.T Cummings, S Chakravarty, R.M Singa, and D.S Burke. Toward a containment strategy for smallpox bioterror: An individual-based computational approach. Technical report, Brookings Institution Press, Washington, DC, 2004.

18. LJ Fogel. *Intelligence Through Simulated Evolution: Forty Years of Evolutionary Programming*. Wiley Series on Intelligent Systems, New York, NY, 1999.

19. N Gilbert and KG Troitzsch. *Simulation for the Social Scientist*. Open University Press, Berkshire, United Kingdom, 1999.

20. HS Guetzkow, P Kotler, and RL Schultz, editors. *Simulation in Social and Administrative Science: Overviews and Case-Examples.* Prentice Hall, Englewood Cliffs, NJ, 1973.
21. R Haenni, J Kohlas, and N Lehmann. Probabilistic argumentation systems. Technical report, University of Fribourg, Fribourg, Switzerland, 1999.
22. C-Y Huang, C-T Sun, J-L Hsieh, and H Liu. Simulating sars: Small-world epidemiological modeling and public health policy assessments. *Journal of Artificial Societies and Social Simulation,* 7(4), 2004.
23. NP Jewell. *Statistics for Epidemiology.* Chapman and Hall/CRC, Boca Raton, FL, 2003.
24. AM Law and WD Kelton. *Simulation Modeling and Analysis.* McGraw-Hill, New York, NY, third edition, 2000.
25. V Lesser, K Decker, T Wagner, N Carver, A Garvey, B Horling, D Neiman, R Podorozhny, M NagendraPrasad, A Raja, R Vincent, P Xuan, and XQ Zhang. Evolution of the gpgp/taems domain-independent coordination framework. *Autonomous Agents and Multi-Agent Systems,* 9(1):87–143, 2004.
26. C Lucena, A Carcia, A Romanovsky, J Castro, and P Alencar, editors. *Software Engineering for Multi-Agent Systems II,* volume 2940 of *Lecture Notes in Computer Science.* Springer-Verlag, New York, NY, 2004.
27. RH Myers and DC Montgomery. *Response Surface Methodology: Process and Product Optimization using Designed Experiments.* John Wiley and Sons, New York, NY, second edition, 2002.
28. M Nickles, M Rovatsos, and G Weiss, editors. *Agents and Computational Autonomy: Potential, Risks, and Solutions,* volume 2969 of *Lecture Notes on Artificial Intelligence.* Springer-Verlag, Berlin, Germany, 2004.
29. J Pearl. *Causality: Models, Reasoning, and Inference.* Cambridge University Press, Cambridge, United Kingdom, 2000.
30. J Pearl. Statistics and causal inference: A review. *Test Journal,* 12(2):281–345, 2003.
31. RS Pressman. *Software Engineering.* McGraw-Hill, New York, NY, 2001.
32. M Prietula, K Carley, and L Gasser. *Simulating Organizations.* AAAI Press/The MIT Press, Menlo Park, CA, 1998.
33. S Rasmussen and CL Barrett. Elements of a theory of simulation. In *Proc. of the Third European Conference on Artificial Life (ECAL'95),* volume 929 of *Lecture Notes in Computer Science,* pages 515–529. Springer, Berlin, Germany, 1995.
34. J Reifman, G Gilbert, M Parker, and D Lam. Challenges of electronic medical surveillance systems. In *RTO HFM Symposium on NATO Medical Surveillance and Response: Research and Technology Opportunities and Options.* NATO, Budapest, Hungary, 2004.
35. CP Robert and G Casella. *Monte Carlo Statistical Methods.* Springer-Verlag, New York, NY, 1999.
36. S Shervais and W Wakeland. Evolutionary strategies as a verification and validation tool. Technical report, Portland State University, Portland, OR, 2003.
37. S Shervais, W Wakeland, and D Raffo. Evolutionary verification and validation of software process simulation models. In *5th International Workshop on Software Process Simulation and Modeling.* IEEE Computer Society, Washington, DC, 2004.
38. H Simon. A behavioural model of rational choice. *Quarterly Journal of Economics,* 69:99–118, 1957.
39. CS Taber and RJ Timpone. *Computational Modeling.* Sage, Newbury Park, CA, 1996.
40. MD Ward. *Theories, Models, and Simulations in International Relations.* Westview Press, Boulder, CO, 1985.
41. S Wasserman and K Faust. *Social Network Analysis: Methods and Applications.* Cambridge University Press, Cambridge, United Kingdom, 1994.

Part IV

Robustness and Flexibility for Large Scale
Coordination

Handling Coordination Failures in Large-Scale Multi-Agent Systems

Gal A. Kaminka

Bar Ilan University

Summary. Agents monitor other agents to coordinate and collaborate robustly. The goals of such monitoring include detection of coordination failures. However, as the number of monitored agents is scaled up, two key challenges arise: (i) Agents become physically and logically unconnected (unobservable) to their peers; and (ii) the number of possible coordination failures grows exponentially, with all potential interactions. This paper examines these challenges in teams of cooperating agents. We provide a brief survey of the evolution of two key approaches to handling coordination failures in large-scale teams: Restricting the number of agents that must be monitored, and using model-based rather than fault-based detection methods. We focus on a monitoring task that is of particular importance to robust teamwork: detecting disagreements among team-members.

1 Introduction

Agents in realistic, complex, domains must monitor other agents to accomplish their tasks, detect failures, coordinate, and collaborate. Indeed, the importance of agent monitoring in deployed multi-agent systems has long been recognized in theory (e.g., [2, 7, 9]), and in practice. Monitoring has been discussed in the context of industrial systems (e.g., [16]), to virtual environments for training and research (e.g., [36, 37, 30, 31]), to human-computer interaction (e.g., [27]), and multi-robot teams (e.g., [28, 5, 21]). Agent monitoring infrastructure is of particular importance in teams of cooperating agents, since the correct execution of teamwork mandates that team-members come to agree on the task that is jointly executed by the team, and manage interdependencies among team-members [2, 9].

One specific goal of monitoring in teams is detection and resolution of teamwork and coordination failures [24, 29, 38]. These may occur because of unanticipated environment states—likely in complex, dynamic environments—or from communication, sensor, or actuator uncertainties. For instance, intermittent failures in communications may cause a failure where one agent has sent a message, while its peers have not received it.

Thus deployed multi-agent systems must include facilities for detecting, diagnosing, and resolving failures. Indeed, a number of investigations have begun to explore mechanisms for detecting failures in coordination and teamwork [23, 25, 24, 3, 29, 38] and for diagnosing such failures [22, 32, 33, 12, 17]).

However, large-scale multi-agent systems—where the number of agents is the principal scale factor—pose a number of challenges to the ability of agents to monitor each other, and thus to handle failures. Two of these challenges are: (i) *Limited connectivity*, where agents become physically and logically separated, and thus less able to monitor each other; and (ii) a *combinatorial complexity* of possible failures, as the number of possible failures grows with the number of all possible interactions between failures.

This paper discusses these challenges in depth, and explores their significance in large-scale multi-agent systems. We also discuss the implications of these challenges with respect to existing approaches to failure detection. We find in the literature two approaches to failure detection. Some investigations take an approach based on fault-models, where possible faults are enumerated at design time and recognized at run-time. Other investigations take a model-based approach where agents detect failures at run-time as deviations from a model of the normative coordination in the system.

To illustrate, we focus on the example of detecting disagreements—a principal failure in multi-agent teamwork—to show the evolution of existing methods in recent years to address large-scale systems. We show how an analysis of the monitoring requirements of disagreement detection can lead to improved, reduced, bounds on the connectivity of team-members. We also discuss relevant model-based detection work, which can represent the state of multiple agents together, and can therefore be utilized for highly-scalable disagreement detection.

This chapter is organized as follows. Section 2 provides motivation for this work by showing concrete examples of limited connectivity and combinatorial failure complexity in monitoring for disagreements. Section 3 focuses on limited connectivity, and discusses a general approach in which only specific key agents must be monitored, while detection is guaranteed. Section 4 focuses on the exponential complexity of the number of possible coordination failures. Finally, Section 5 concludes.

2 Motivation and Background

Teamwork literature, addressing human and synthetic teams, has often emphasized the importance of team-members being in agreement on various features of their state, such as goals, plans, and beliefs[1]. Teamwork theory often defines agreement as a state of mutual belief, where agents reason to infinite recursion about their beliefs and their beliefs in others' beliefs in a proposition. For instance, *SharedPlans* theory requires team-members to mutually believe in a shared recipe [9] during the planning and execution phases of the task; the *Joint Intentions* framework emphasizes mutual belief in the team goals' selection, as well as in team-members' beliefs about the goals' achievability and relevance [2, 26]. Other investigations of agent teams have

---

[1] Of course, the literature also addresses other critical features of teamwork aside from agreement. But agreement is a repeating theme in recent work.

emphasized agreement on team plans to be jointly executed by team-members [16], on hierarchical team operators [35], on tasks to be executed collectively [28, 6, 21], etc. Investigations of human teamwork have not only emphasized agreement on the joint task, but also agreement on features of the environment that are important to the task being carried out by the team [1].

However, the literature also recognizes that achieving and maintaining agreement can be difficult. Teamwork theory recognizes that attainment of agreement by mutual belief is undecidable [10] and must therefore be approximated in practice. Such approximations frequently involve assumptions of trustworthiness of team-members, of foolproof communications [16], of team-members being able to observe each other [14], and/or of a mutually-visible environment [8]. As is often the case with approximations, they sometimes fail in practice (e.g., due to communications failures, sensing differences due to different physical locations of agents, etc.), and therefore team-members may find themselves in disagreement with each other. Such disagreements are often catastrophic, due to the unique importance of agreement in collaboration.

It is therefore critical that teams are monitored to detect such disagreements. A monitoring agent that identifies the state of team-members can compare the state of different team-members and detect differences on state features that, by design or by selection, should have been agreed upon [24]. However, as the number of monitored agents is scaled up, two challenges arise: (i) difficulty to observe or communicate with all agents, due to latency, range, occlusion and other separation factors (Section 2.1); and (ii) an exponential number of possible coordination failures (Section 2.2).

2.1 Limited Connectivity

As the number of agents grows, agents become logically and physically distributed, and cannot maintain continuous contact with each other. This may occur due to physical separation factors, such as occlusion and limited sensor range; or it may occur due to logical separation, such as limited communication reliability, interference, latency, or bandwidth. We use the term *limited connectivity* in a general sense to describe this phenomenon. Limited connectivity thus denotes both limited ability to observe a particular agent's actions as well as limited ability to communicate with the agent.

The challenge of limited connectivity is of course only of limited concern in small-scale systems. Given a few cycles, the agents can typically integrate multiple attempts at communications and sensing of the world, over time, to form a fairly coherent mental picture of what their peers are up to. However, as the number of agents grows, the ability to integrate such information over time diminishes rapidly. For instance, existing peer-to-peer (P2P) include millions of simultaneously-active nodes. Yet not one node is able to communicate directly with all of its peers at once, due to both bandwidth and processing power issues. Even spreading the efforts over time will not be sufficient, as the duration of time required is too long for any practical interest.

2.2 Combinatorial Failure Complexity

A different concern with large scale system is the number of potential coordination failures it may get into. Suppose each of N agents may be in one of k internal states. Then the number of possible joint states is k^N. In loosely-coupled systems, each agent is essentially independent of its peers, and may select between its k possible states freely. In such systems, the vast majority of joint states—if not all—are considered valid states.

However, in a coordinated multi-agent system, the selection of an internal state by an agent is conditional by the selection of its peers' internal state. In other words, agents move between joint states together. Typically, only a limited portion of these states would be valid coordinated states, from the designer's perspective. Thus most joint states may in fact be invalid from a coordination point of view.

Disagreements are a good example of this. Suppose a team of N agents agrees that their selection of internal state would be synchronous, i.e., for every selected state of one agent, all others must be in some agreed-upon internal state. For simplicity in notation, we describe this case as mutual selection of states $1 \ldots k$, i.e., all all agents select the same state. There would be $O(k)$ valid agreement joint states, and the rest of the k^n joint states would be considered invalid—coordination failure—states.

Note that the number of possible coordination failure states grows exponentially in the number of agents. Thus large-scale systems where agents coordinate may have to face an exponential number of possible faults.

3 Monitoring Graphs for Limited Connectivity

As the number of monitored team-members increases, it becomes increasingly difficult to monitor all of them (Section 2). Thus a key question is how to guarantee failure-handling results while limiting the number of agents that must be monitored.

The approach we take to this involves the construction and analysis of monitoring graphs, which represent information about which agent can monitor whom. We show that for disagreement detection, one can set conditions on the structure of the graph which, when satisfied, guarantee that detection is *complete* and *sound*. Complete detection guarantees all failures will be detected (i.e., no false negatives). Sound detection guarantees only failures will be detected (i.e., no false positives). Using the conditions we explore in this section, one can guarantee sound and complete detection of disagreements while setting conditions on the connectivity of agents.

Definition 1. *A monitoring graph of a team T is a directed (possibly cyclic) graph in which nodes correspond to team-members of T, and edges correspond to monitoring conditions: If an agent A is able to monitor an agent B (either visually or by communicating with it), then an edge (A, B) exists in the graph. We say that monitoring graph is connected, if its underlying undirected graph is connected.*

If the monitoring graph of a team is not connected, then there is an agent which is not monitored by any agent, and is not monitoring any agent. Obviously, a disagreement can go undetected in such a team: If the isolated agent chooses an internal state different from what has been agreed upon with its peers, it would go undetected.

It is easy to see that if the graph is connected, and each agent knows exactly the selection of its monitored peer, than sound and complete detection is possible, in a distributed fashion. Each agent A monitors at least one other agent B (or is monitored by another agent B). If A selects an internal state different from B, than at least one of them would detect the disagreement immediately. For instance, if A monitors B— and knows with certainty B's state—than simple comparison with A's selected state is all that is needed.

In the general case, however, connectivity is insufficient. Suppose an agent A has selected state P_1, and is monitoring another agent B that has selected state P_2. A disagreement exists here since agent B should have selected P_1. However, since the internal state of B may not be known to A with certainty, A may have several interpretations of B's chosen state. The set of these interpretations may contain P_1, in which case A may come to incorrectly believe that B is *not* in a state of disagreement with A.

To treat this formally, let us use the following notation when discussing agent A's hypotheses as to the state of an agent B: Suppose B's state is P (for instance, P is a plan selected by B). We denote by $M(A, B/P)$ the set of agent-monitoring hypotheses that A constructs based on communications from B, or inference from B's observable behavior (i.e., via plan recognition). In other words, $M(A, B/P)$ is the set of all A's hypotheses as to B's state, when B's state (e.g., selected plan) is P. Note that when A monitors itself, it has direct access to its own state and so $M(A, A/P) = \{P\}$.

We make the following definitions which ground our assumptions about the underlying monitoring process that implements M:

Definition 2. *Given a monitoring agent A, and a monitored agent B, we say that A's monitoring of B is* complete *if for any state P that may be selected by B, $P \in M(A, B/P)$. If A is monitoring a team of agents $B_1, \ldots, B_n$, we say that A's team-monitoring of the team is* complete *if A's monitoring of each of $B_1, \ldots, B_n$ is complete.*

Monitoring completeness is commonly assumed (in its individual form) in plan-recognition work, (e.g., [34, 4, 15]), and generally holds in many applications. It means that the set $M(A, B/P)$ includes the correct hypothesis P, but will typically include other matching hypotheses besides P. Using this notation, we can now formally explore disagreement detection under uncertainty in monitoring.

Centralized Disagreement Detection

In general, as discussed above, the condition of monitoring graph connectivity is necessary, but insufficient, to guarantee complete and sound detection. Indeed, in [23], Kaminka and Tambe show that if a single centralized monitoring agent monitors all others, it can guarantee either sound or complete detection of disagreements, but not both (Figure 1-a).

However, Kaminka and Tambe found that if certain *key agents* exist, then it may be possible to reduce the monitoring requirements in the system. Key agents have the property that their behavior, when selecting one of two given states, is sufficiently unambiguous, such that any agent that monitors them and has selected either one of the two states can identify with certainty whether a disagreement exists between it and the key agents. We repeat here the formal definition of key agents from [24]:

Definition 3. *Let P_1, P_2 be two agent states. Suppose an agent A is monitoring an agent B. If $M(A, B/P_1) \cap M(A, B/P_2) = \emptyset$ for any agent A, we say that B has observably-different roles in P_1 and P_2, and call B a* key agent *in $\{P_1, P_2\}$. We assume symmetry so that if two states are not observably different, then $M(A, B/P_1) \cap M(A, B/P_2) \supseteq \{P_1, P_2\}$.*

The key-agent is the basis for the conditions under which a team-member A_1 will detect a disagreement with a team-member A_2. This is done by preferring *maximally-coherent* hypotheses as to the state of the monitored agent. Maximally-coherent hypotheses are optimistic—they are hypotheses that minimize the number of disagreements between the two agents. The use of such hypotheses leads to sound disagreement detection [23, 24].

An agent A_1 (selecting state P_1) will detect a disagreement with a team-member A_2 (selecting a different state P_2) if A_2 is a key agent for the plans P_1, P_2 [24, Lemma 1]. A_1 knows that it has selected P_1. If A_2 has selected P_2, and is a key-agent in P_1 and P_2, then A_1 is guaranteed to notice that a disagreement exists between itself and A_2, since A_2 is acting observably different than it would if it had selected P_1. A_1 can now alert its teammate, diagnose the failure, etc.

When key agents exist in a team, it is sufficient for a single agent to monitor them to guarantee sound detection in the centralized case [20]. More accurately, if the team is observably-partitioned, i.e., a key agent exists for any pair of internal states potentially selected by team-members, then it is sufficient for a single agent to monitor only the key agents, to guarantee sound detection of disagreements. However, all key agents must be monitored (Figure 1-b).

Distributed Disagreement Detection

We now consider the case of distributed monitoring settings, where team-members monitor each other. First, in [23] Kaminka and Tambe have shown that if at least a single key agent exists for every pair of plans (i.e., the team employs an *observably-partitioned set of team plans*), and if all team-members monitor *all* agents, then detection is not only sound, but also complete (see Figure 2-a for illustration). Later on [24, Theorem 4], the result was clarified: All agents must monitor the key agents only—all of them—and the key agents must monitor each other (Figure 2-b). Guaranteed sound and complete detection here means that at least one team-members will detect a disagreement if one occurs, and no false detections will take place.

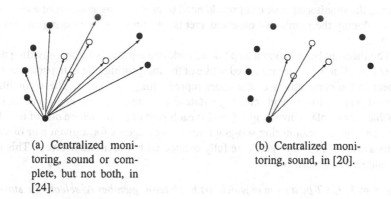

(a) Centralized moni-
toring, sound or com-
plete, but not both, in
[24].

(b) Centralized moni-
toring, sound, in [20].

Fig. 1. Illustration of centralized monitoring graphs. Non-filled dots indicate key agents.

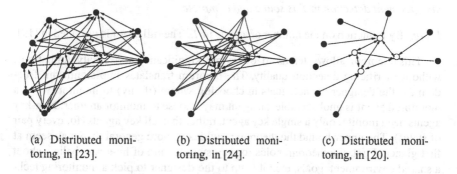

(a) Distributed moni-
toring, in [23].

(b) Distributed moni-
toring, in [24].

(c) Distributed moni-
toring, in [20].

Fig. 2. Illustration of distributed monitoring graphs. Non-filled dots indicate key agents. All
cases allow for sound and complete disagreement detection.

This result is of particular interest to building practical robust teams, and fortunately the conditions for it are often easy to satisfy: Teams are very often composed
such that not all agents have the same role in the same plan, and in general, roles
do have observable differences between them. Often, the set $M(A, B/P)$ can be computed offline, in advance; this allows the designer to identify the key agents in a
team prior to deployment. Furthermore, any agent can become a key-agent simply
by communicating its state to the monitoring agent and therefore eliminating ambiguity; thus a team can use highly-focused communications to guarantee detection.

However, the requirement that *all* key-agents be monitored prohibits deployment
of scaled-up applications: First, as the size of the team grows, limited connectivity
becomes more common, since agents become more physically and logically distributed. Thus not all agents, and in particular key agents, are going to be visible.

Second, the monitoring task itself would need to process observations of each agent. Thus reducing the number of observed agents can improve monitoring run-time in practice.

The theorem below takes a step towards addressing this issue by providing more relaxed conditions on the connected nature of the monitoring graph, in particular with respect to the connectivity of the nodes representing key agents. These conditions are: (i) every non-key agent selecting a state P monitors *a single* key agent for each possible pair of plans involving P (i.e., for each pair of plans, where one of the plans is P); and (ii) the monitoring sub-graph for all key agents for a given pair of states forms a clique (i.e., key agents are fully connected between themselves). This case is illustrated in Figure 2-c.

Theorem 1. *Let T be a team in which: (i) Each team-member A, selecting a state P_1, who is not a key agent for P_1, P_2 monitors one key agent for P_1, P_2; (ii) all key agents for a pair of states X, Z monitor all other key agents for X, Z (forming a bidirectional clique in the underlying monitoring graph); (iii) the team is observably-partitioned; and (iv) all monitoring carried out is complete, and uses maximal-coherence. Then disagreement detection in T is sound and complete.*

Proof. By induction on the number of agents in T. The full proof is provided in [19].

This theorem allows teams to overcome significant connectivity limitations, without sacrificing detection quality. The theorem translates into significant freedom for the designer or the agents in choosing whom (if any) to monitor; when a monitored agent is unobservable, an agent may choose to monitor another: Non-key agents need monitor only a single key agent, rather than all key agents (for every pair of states). The upper-bound the theorem provides is more general than may seem at first glance. First, the theorem holds for any state feature of interest—beliefs about a shared environment, goals, etc.; it is up to the designer to pick a monitoring technique that acquires the needed information for constructing the monitoring hypotheses. Second, the theorem does not depend at all on the method by which monitoring occurs, whether by communications or by observations. Thus the connectivity of a monitoring graph does not have to be maintained visually. Some or all of the edges in the monitoring graph may actually correspond to communication links between agents.

Though this theorem represents a significant advance in lowering the bound on the number of agents that must be monitored, all key agents must still monitor each other. This is a critical constraint in practice. For instance, we have reconstructed the visual monitoring graph in *thousands* of RoboCup game situations, to find that even with this new bound, sound and complete disagreement detection would have been possible without communications only in small percentage (approximately 5%) of a game. Typically, each RoboCup player can only see 2–3 key agents, this means that key agents cannot typically monitor all others. To illustrate, Figure 3 shows the monitoring graph of two teams overlayed on a screen-shot of an actual game situation. For both teams, the monitoring graph does not guarantee sound and complete disagreement detection under the known bound, despite the fact that it is connected.

This empiric constraint raises the bar on the challenge to find a lower bound on the number of agents that must be monitored to guarantee detection.

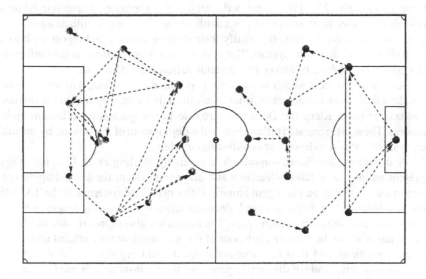

Fig. 3. Monitoring graphs in a RoboCup simulation-league game situation.

4 Model-Based Disagreement Detection

There are, in general, two approaches for detecting (and later, diagnosing) failures [11]. The first is called a consistency-based approach (and sometimes, model-based). A model of the correct behavior of the system is utilized to make predictions as to the observed output of the system in question. When these predictions fail, a fault is detected. Provided that the model is sufficiently detailed, it may be used to identify the exact nature of the failure by a process of model-based diagnosis. The second approach is fault-model-based (fault-based, for short). Here, models of possible faults are matched against the observed behavior of the system. When the observed behavior matches the models, an alarm is triggered. Often, fault-models are used together with prescribed resolution procedures, which are called into action to resolve the faults that were detected.

The same two approaches can be found in literature addressing coordination failure detection and diagnosis. On one hand, investigations such as [22, 23, 24, 20, 29] focus on using models of the correct behavior of agents to detect failures as deviations from the model, while others take a fault-based approach [25, 13, 3, 12, 38].

4.1 Detection Based on Fault-Models

We begin by examining the use of fault models to detect coordination failures. Dellarocas and Klein [25, 3] have proposed a centralized approach to detecting failures (which they refer to as *exceptions*) in coordination. Their work utilizes agent sentinels, which monitor agents to identify their state or actions, and report on it to a centralized fault detection system. The system then matches the reported information against a database of known coordination failures, for detection.

An important facet to this work is the population of the fault database. Unlike standard fault-model approaches, where fault models are closely tied to the domain and task at hand, Klein and Dellarocas propose to use general coordination fault-models. These are generated offline, before the deployment of the system, by manual analysis of domain-independent coordination models.

A different—distributed—approach is taken by Horling et al. [13, 12]. They present an integrated failure-detection and diagnosis system for a multi-agent system in the context of an intelligent home environment. The system uses the TAEMS domain-independent multi-agent task-decomposition and modeling language to describe the ideal behavior of each agent. The agents are also supplied with additional information about the expected behavior of the environment they inhabit under different conditions, and their role within the multi-agent organization. A distributed diagnosis system, made of diagnosis agents that use fault-models, is used to identify failures in components (such as erroneous repeated requests for resources) and inefficiencies (such as over- or under-coordination). The fault-models are used in planning monitoring actions, in identifying failures responsible for multiple symptoms, and in guiding recovery actions. Multiple diagnosis agents may use communications to inform each other of their actions and diagnoses.

A key issue with fault-model approaches is their scalability, given that the number of possible faults in large-scale multi-agent systems is likely to be exponential. Models that attempt to be specific to agents (e.g., "If A does X and B does Y then that is a failure", "If A does X and C does Z then that is a failure") are not likely to scale well. On the other hand, fault models that can utilize some abstraction or capture general failure conditions may do better.

As an example, Wilkins, Lee, and Berry [38] offer an execution monitoring approach which encompasses both coordination and task-execution failures. Their work introduces a taxonomy of generic failure types, which must be adapted and specialized to the domain and task. Agents responsible for monitoring rely on communicated state reports from the monitored agents to identify failures. While experiments with the system were carried out only on relatively small multi-agent systems, the modeling of the failures shows example of how fault-models can be sufficiently non-specific so that they may be reused in larger-scale systems. For instance, the fault models included distance failures (units getting too close), which are triggered when an adversary gets closer to a friendly unit). It does not matter who the adversary or friendly units are, nor their specific location, etc.

A common theme running through all of the above works is that they mostly ignore the issue of uncertainty in monitoring, and utilize communications or direct observations to acquire knowledge as to the state of monitored agents. This is a potentially limiting factor in their use in large-scale networks, where limited connectivity will necessarily lead to uncertainty in monitoring.

4.2 Model-Based Detection

Our own work—and those of others—took a different approach to detecting failures. This consistency-based approach utilizes a model of ideal behavior (in terms of the relationships), not a model of how failure symptoms relate to possible failure diagnoses. The model-based approach has the advantages of generality and model re-use [11]. In particular, fault models, as described above, are anticipatory; they are only able to capture failures which the designer has been able to anticipate in advance. A consistency-based approach to diagnosing failures is not limited in this respect.

We focus here on disagreement detection. In order to detect disagreements, the monitoring agent must first know which internal states are ideally to be agreed upon. Executable teamwork models such as STEAM [35] or GRATE* [16] allow the designer to specify hierarchical team plans whose execution must be synchronized across agents. To detect a disagreement, we compare the team plans selected by different agents. If they do not match, then a disagreement has occurred [24].

The seeming simplicity of the task is misleading. In the general monitoring case, there can be multiple hypotheses as to the plan selected by each individual. As a result, there can be an exponential number of hypotheses for the team as a whole. To address this, the techniques described in the previous section can guarantee detection results, as long as we select maximally-coherent hypotheses. However, this would seem to require going over the exponential number of hypotheses.

Fortunately, this is not the case. Initial work used the RESL plan-recognition algorithm to represent—implicitly—all possible hypotheses [24]. The savings here were significant, as each agent was modeled individually, and so memory use was $O(NL)$ where N is the number of agents, and L the size of all possible plans for a single agent. However, run-time was still essentially $O(L^N)$, as the algorithm still had to go through multiple hypotheses.

Recently, this result was improved, with the YOYO algorithm [20]. YOYO represents all agents in a single structure, which can only represent fully-coherent hypotheses, i.e., no disagreements. The key observation here is that if something is not representable in YOYO, than it must indicate a disagreement. Thus YOYO detects failures essentially by trying to interpret their actions as if they are not in disagreement. If there is no way to do it, then a disagreement must have occurred. YOYO is thus maximally coherent, and perfectly suited to the monitoring techniques discussed in the previous section. Its space requirements are $O(N+L)$ and runtime is $O(N+L)$. We refer the interested reader to [20] for additional details.

5 Discussion and Future Work

Multi-agent literature has often emphasized that an agent must monitor other agents in order to carry out its tasks. However, as the numbers of agents in deployed teams is scaled up, the challenges of limited connectivity and an exponential number of potential failures are raised. This paper has discussed recent approaches addressing these challenges, in the context of a critical monitoring task—detection of critical disagreements between teammates.

However, many open challenges exist in monitoring large-scale multi-agent systems. One important challenge is in reducing the load on the monitoring agent. Durfee [7] discussed decision-theoretic and heuristic methods for reducing the amount of knowledge that agents consider in coordinating. The methods include pruning nested (recursive) models, using communications to alleviate uncertainty, using hierarchies and abstractions, etc. This work is complementary to the methods discussed above. We focus on monitoring in teams of cooperating (rather than self-interested) agents, allowing exploitation of the fact that agents are coordinating, both to limit connectivity, as well as to use model-based techniques in detection. Thus, while Durfee's work focuses on reducing computational loads in monitoring each single agent, our work focuses on reducing the number of monitored agents, and on savings possible only when monitoring teams together.

Recent work on model-based diagnosis has also begun to address limited connectivity, though indirectly, and only to a limited extent. Work by Roos et al. [32, 33] has examined the use of model-based diagnosis by agents diagnosing a distributed system. While the methods describe do not address coordination failures, they are certainly relevant in terms of discussing the type of connectivity assumptions required for the diagnosis to work. Our recent preliminary work [18] on the use of model-based diagnosis of disagreements also limits connectivity: A key focus is on using only a handful of agents to represent all others in the diagnosis process, thus limiting runtime and communication load.

Acknowledgment

This work was partially supported by BSF grant #2002401. We thank Michael Bowling, Michael Lindner, and Meir Kalech for useful discussions. As always, thanks to K. Ushi.

References

1. John J. Burns, Eduardo Salas, and Janis A. Cannon-Bowers. Team training, mental models, and the team model trainer. In *Advancements in Integrated Delivery Technologies*, Denver, CO, 1993.
2. Philip R. Cohen and Hector J. Levesque. Teamwork. *Nous*, 35, 1991.
3. Chrysanthos Dellarocas and Mark Klein. An experimental evaluation of domain-independent fault-handling services in open multi-agent systems. pages 95–102, Boston, MA, 2000. IEEE Computer Society.
4. Mark Devaney and Ashwin Ram. Needles in a haystack: Plan recognition in large spatial domains involving multiple agents. pages 942–947, Madison, WI, 1998.

5. M. Bernadine Dias, R. Zlot, M. Zinck, J. P. Gonzalez, and Anthony Stentz. A versatile implementation of the traderbots approach for multirobot coordination. 2004.

6. M Bernardine Dias and Anthony (Tony) Stentz. A free market architecture for distributed control of a multirobot system. In *6th International Conference on Intelligent Autonomous Systems (IAS-6)*, pages 115–122, July 2000.

7. Edmund H. Durfee. Blissful ignorance: Knowing just enough to coordinate well. pages 406–413, 1995.

8. Maier Fenster, Sarit Kraus, and Jeffrey S. Rosenschein. Coordination without communication: Experimental validation of focal point techniques. pages 102–108, California, USA, June 1995.

9. Barbara J. Grosz and Sarit Kraus. Collaborative plans for complex group actions. 86:269–358, 1996.

10. J. Y. Halpern and Y. Moses. Knowledge and common knowledge in a distributed environment. *distributed computing*, 37(3):549–587, 1990.

11. Walter Hamscher, Luca Console, and Johan de Kleer, editors. *Readings in Model-Based Diagnosis*. Morgan Kaufmann Publishers, San Mateo, CA, 1992.

12. Bryan Horling, Brett Benyo, and Victor Lesser. Using self-diagnosis to adapt organizational structures. pages 529–536, May 2001.

13. Bryan Horling, Victor R. Lesser, Regis Vincent, Ana Bazzan, and Ping Xuan. Diagnosis as an integral part of multi-agent adaptability. Technical Report CMPSCI Technical Report 1999-03, University of Massachusetts/Amherst, January 1999.

14. Marcus J. Huber and Edmund H. Durfee. Deciding when to commit to action during observation-based coordination. pages 163–170, 1995.

15. Stephen S. Intille and Aaron F. Bobick. A framework for recognizing multi-agent action from visual evidence. pages 518–525. AAAI Press, July 1999.

16. Nicholas R. Jennings. Controlling cooperative problem solving in industrial multi-agent systems using joint intentions. 75(2):195–240, 1995.

17. Meir Kalech and Gal A. Kaminka. On the design of social diagnosis algorithms for multi-agent teams. 2003. socially-attentive monitoring, diagnosis, plan-recognition, belief ascription.

18. Meir Kalech and Gal A. Kaminka. Diagnosing a team of agents: Scaling-up. In *Proceedings of the International Workshop on Principles of Diagnosis (DX 2004)*, 2004.

19. Gal A. Kaminka and Michael Bowling. Towards robust teams with many agents. Technical Report CMU-CS-01-159, Carnegie Mellon University, 2001.

20. Gal A. Kaminka and Michael Bowling. Robust teams with many agents. 2002.

21. Gal A. Kaminka, Yehuda Elmaliach, Inna Frenkel, Ruti Glick, Meir Kalech, and Tom Shpigelman. Towards a comprehensive framework for teamwork in behavior-based robots. 2004.

22. Gal A. Kaminka and Milind Tambe. What's wrong with us? Improving robustness through social diagnosis. pages 97–104, Madison, WI, 1998. AAAI Press.

23. Gal A. Kaminka and Milind Tambe. I'm OK, You're OK, We're OK: Experiments in distributed and centralized social monitoring and diagnosis. pages 213–220, Seattle, WA, 1999. ACM Press.

24. Gal A. Kaminka and Milind Tambe. Robust multi-agent teams via socially-attentive monitoring. 12:105–147, 2000.

25. Mark Klein and Chris Dellarocas. Exception handling in agent systems. ACM Press, May 1999.

26. Sanjeev Kumar, Philip R. Cohen, and Hector J. Levesque. The adaptive agent architecture: Achieving fault-tolerance using persistent broker teams. pages 159–166, Boston, MA, 2000. IEEE Computer Society.

27. Neal Lesh, Charles Rich, and Candace L. Sidner. Using plan recognition in human-computer collaboration. Banff, Canada, 1999.
28. Lynne E. Parker. ALLIANCE: An architecture for fault tolerant multirobot cooperation. *IEEE Transactions on Robotics and Automation*, 14(2):220–240, April 1998.
29. David Poutakidis, Lin Padgham, and Michael Winikoff. Debugging multi-agent systems using design artifacts: The case of interaction protocols. 2002.
30. Jeff Rickel and W. Lewis Johnson. Animated agents for procedural training in virtual reality: Perception, cognition, and motor control. *Applied Artificial Intelligence*, 13:343–382, 1999.
31. Jeff Rickel and W. Lewis Johnson. Virtual humans for team training in virtual reality. In *Proceedings of the Ninth International Conference on Artificial Intelligence in Education*, pages 578–585. IOS Press, 1999.
32. Nico Roos, Annette ten Teije, Andre Bos, and Cees Witteveen. An analysis of multi-agent diagnosis. *in Proceedings of Autonomous Agents and Multi Agent Systems (AAMAS-02)*, July 2002.
33. Nico Roos, Annette ten Teije, and Cees Witteveen. A protocol for multi-agent diagnosis with spatially distributed knowledge. *in Proceedings of Autonomous Agents and Multi Agent Systems (AAMAS-03)*, pages 655–661, July 2003.
34. Milind Tambe. Tracking dynamic team activity. August 1996.
35. Milind Tambe. Towards flexible teamwork. 7:83–124, 1997.
36. Milind Tambe, W. Lewis Johnson, Randy Jones, Frank Koss, John E. Laird, Paul S. Rosenbloom, and Karl Schwamb. Intelligent agents for interactive simulation environments. *AI Magazine*, 16(1), Spring 1995.
37. Milind Tambe, Gal A. Kaminka, Stacy C. Marsella, Ion Muslea, and Taylor Raines. Two fielded teams and two experts: A robocup challenge response from the trenches. volume 1, pages 276–281, August 1999.
38. D. E. Wilkins, T. Lee, and P. Berry. Interactive execution monitoring of agent teams. 18:217–261, March 2003.

Towards Flexible Coordination of Large Scale Multi-Agent Teams

Yang Xu[1], Elizabeth Liao[2], Paul Scerri[2], Bin Yu[2], Mike Lewis[1], Katia Sycara[2]

[1] School of Information Sciences, University of Pittsburgh
{yxu, ml}@sis.pitt.edu
[2] School of Computer Science, Carnegie Mellon University
{eliao, pscerri, byu, katia}@cs.cmu.edu

Summary. As a paradigm for coordinating cooperative agents in dynamic environments, *teamwork* has been shown to be capable of leading to flexible and robust behavior. However, when teamwork is applied to the problem of building teams with hundreds of members, its previously existing, fundamental limitations become apparent. In this paper, we address the limitations of existing models as they apply to very large agent teams. We develop algorithms aimed at flexible and efficient coordination, applying a decentralized social network topology for team organization and the abstract coordination behaviors of Team Oriented Plans (TOPs). From this basis, we present a model to organize a team into dynamically evolving subteams, in order to flexibly coordinate the team. Additionally, we put forward a novel approach to sharing information within large teams, which provides for targeted, efficient information delivery with a localized reasoning process model built on previously incoming information. We have developed domain- independent software proxies, with which we demonstrate teams of an order of magnitude larger than those previously discussed in known published work. We implement the results of our approach, demonstrating its ability to handle the challenges of coordinating large agent teams.

1 Introduction

When a group of agents coordinates via *teamwork*, they can flexibly and robustly achieve joint goals in a distributed, dynamic and potentially hostile environment[7, 12]. Using basic teamwork ideas, many systems have been successfully implemented, including teams supporting human collaboration[4, 26], teams for disaster response[19], for manufacturing[12], for training[28] and for games[14]. While such teams have been very successful, their sizes have been severely limited. To address larger and more complex problems, we need teams that are substantially larger, yet retain the desirable properties of teamwork.

The key to the success of previous teamwork approaches is the explicit, detailed model each agent has of the other agents and the joint activity of the team. Team members use these models to reason about actions that will aid the achievement of joint goals[11, 28]. However, when the size of a team is scaled up, it becomes unfeasible to maintain up-to-date, detailed models of all other teammates, or even of all team activities. Specifically, the communication required to keep the models up to date does not scale well with the number of agents. Without these models, key elements of both the theory and operationalization of teamwork break down. For example, without accurate models of team activities, STEAM's communication reasoning[28] cannot be applied, nor can Joint Intention's reasoning about committments[11].

In this paper, we present a model of teamwork that does not rely on the accurate models of the team that previous approaches to teamwork use. By not requiring accurate models, we limit the required communication and thus make the approach applicable to very large teams. However, giving up the accurate models means that the cohesion guarantees provided by approaches such as Joint Intentions can no longer be provided. Instead, our algorithms are designed to lead to cohesive, flexible and robust teamwork *with high probability*.

The basic idea is to organize the team into dynamically evolving, overlapping subteams that work on sub-goals of the overall team goal. Members of a subteam maintain accurate models of each other and the specific subgoal on which they are working. To ensure cohesion and minimize inefficiency across the whole team, we connect all agents of the whole team into a network. By requiring agents to keep their neighbors in the network informed of the subgoals of subteams they are members of, there is high probability that inefficiencies can be detected and subsequently addressed. Using this model we have been able to develop teams that were effective, responsive and cohesive despite having 200 members. We identify three ideas in the model as being the keys to its success.

The first idea is to break the team into subteams, working on subgoals of the overall team goal. The members of a subteam will change dynamically as the overall team rearranges its resources to best meet the current challenges, respond to failures or sieze opportunities. Within these subteams, the agents will have accurate models of each other and the joint activity, in the same way a team based on the STEAM model would. Thus, using techniques developed for small teams, the subteam can be flexible and robust. Moreover, we identify two distinct groups within the subteams: the team members actually performing roles within the plan; and team members who are not, e.g., agents involved via role allocation. The fidelity of the model maintained by the role performing agents is higher than that of the non-role performing agents, which is in turn higher than other agents in the wider team. Because models are limited to subteams, communication overhead is limited.

To avoid potential inefficiencies due to subteams working at cross purposes, our second idea is to introduce an *acquaintance network*. This network connects *all agents in the team and is independent of any relationships due to subteams*. Specifically, the network is a *small world network* [30](see figure 1), so that any two team members are separated by a small number of neighbors. Agents share information about their current activities with their direct neighbors in the network. Although the communication required to keep neighbors in the acquaintance network informed is low, due to the small world properties of the network, there is high probability for every possible pair of plans. Some agents will know both, and thus, can identify inefficiencies due to conflicts among the plans. For example, it may be detected that two subteams are attempting to achieve the same goal or one subteam is using plans that interfere with the plans of another subteam. Once detected by any agent the subteams involved can be notified and the inefficiency rectified. Moreover, in this paper we investigate the influences of other social network properties to the efficiency of coordinating large scale teams.

When limiting models of joint activities to the members of a subteam, the overall team loses the ability to leverage the sensing abilities of all its members. Specifically, an agent may locally detect a piece of information unknown to the rest of the team but does not know which members would find the information relevant[8, 33]. For example, in a disaster response team, a fire fighter may detect that a road is impassable but not know which other fire fighters or paramedics intend to use that road. While communication in teams is an extensively studied problem, [5, 13, 21, 32], current algorithms for sharing information in teams either require infeasibly accurate models of team activities, e.g., STEAM's decision theoretic communication[28], or require that centralized information *brokers* are kept up to date[27, 3], leading to potential communication bottlenecks. Our solution for information sharing among large teams is to perform distributed information sharing without the cost of maintaining accurate models of all the teammates. An agent can easily know what information it needs, but it will not know who has the information, while another agent has the information but does not know who needs it. By allowing the agents to simply forward the information to an acquaintance in a better position to make the decision, we spread the reasoning across the team, leveraging the knowledge of many agents. We also leverage the idea that information is always interrelated and a received piece of information can be useful in deciding where to send another piece of information, if there is a relationship between two pieces of information. For example, when coordinating an agent group in urban search and rescue, if agent *a* tells agent *b* about a fire at 50 Smith St, when agent *b* has the information about the traffic condition of Smith St, sending that information to agent *a* is a reasonable thing to do, since *a* likely either needs the information or knows who does. By utilizing the interrelationship between pieces of information, agents can more quickly route new information through the acquaintance network. Moreover, agents do not model information, rather they model the acquaintances to which they send information. It may take several hops for a message to get to an agent that needs the information. Since each piece of information informs the delivery of other pieces and models are updated as the message moves, as the volume of information to be shared among the team increases, the amount of effort required per piece of information actually decreases. Moreover, since agents need to only know about their acquaintances, the approach scales as the number of agents in the team increases.

To evaluate our method for building large teams, we have implemented the above approach in software proxies[22] called Machinetta. A proxy encapsulating coordination algorithm works closely with a "domain level" agent and coordinates with other proxies. Although Machinetta proxies build on the successful TEAMCORE proxies[28] and have been used to build small teams[24], they were not able to scale to large teams without the fundamentally new algorithms and concepts described above. In this paper, we report results of coordinating teams of 200 proxies that exhibit effective, cohesive team behavior. Such teams are of an order of magnitude larger than previously discussed in known published work proxy-based teams[24], hence they represent a significant step forward in building large teams. To ensure that the approach is not leveraging peculiarities of a specific domain for its improved performance, we tested the approach in two distinct domains using identical proxies.[3]

2 Toward Flexible Team Coordination

In this section, we provide a detailed model of the organization and coordination of the team. At a high level, the team behavior can be understood as follows: A team is organized as a social network and team members detect events in the environment that result in plans to achieve the team's top-level goal. The team finds subteams to work on those plans and within the subteams the agents communicate to maintain accurate models to ensure cohesive behavior. Across subteams, agents communicate the goals of the subteams so that interactions between subteams can be detected and conflicts resolved. Finally, agents share locally sensed information on the associates' network to allow the whole team to leverage the local sensing abilities of each team member.

2.1 Building Large Scale Teams

A typical large scale team meets the following basic characteristics: there are large number of widely distributed team members with limited communication bandwidth. As a part of a large team, agents coordinate closely only with a subset of the total agents of the team. Based on these characteristics, we can define a logical model of the team organized as an *acquaintance network*. The *acquaintance network* is a directed graph $G = (A, N)$, where A is the team of agents and N is the set of links between any two agents. Specifically, for $< \alpha_i, \alpha_j > \in N$ for any two agents $\alpha_i, \alpha_j \in A$ denotes that α_i and α_j are acquaintances able to exchange tokens. Specifically, $n(\alpha)$ is defined as all the acquaintances of agent α. Note that the number of each agent's acquaintances is much less than the size of the agent team $|A|$. We additionally require that the acquaintance network be a *small world network*. Such networks exist among people and are popularized by the notion of "six degrees of separation" [18]. When agents are arranged in a network, having a small number of neighbours relative to the number of members in the team, the number of agents through which a message must pass to get from any agent to any other, going only from neighbour to neighbour, is typically very small. A subset of a typical acquaintance network for a large team is shown as Figure 1. In the Figure, each node represents an agent member in the team. When pairs of agents are connected, they can directly communicate with each other as acquaintances.

---

[3] A small amount of code was changed to interface to different domain agents.

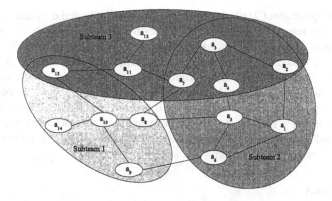

Fig. 1. Relationship between subteams and the acquaintance network

2.2 Team Oriented Plans

Team Oriented Plans (TOPs) are the abstraction that define team behavior. The TOPs provide the mapping from team level goals to individual *roles* that are performed by individual team members. Suppose the team A has a top level goal, G. The team *commits*, with the semantics of STEAM to G [28]. Achieving G requires achieving sub-goals, g_i, that are not known in advance but are functions of the environment. For example, sub-goals of a high-level goal to respond to a disaster could be to extinguish a fire and provide medical attention to particular injured civilians. To achieve sub-goals, the team follows plan templates represented in a library. These templates are parameterized while instantiated plans contain the specific details [23]. For example, when a particular fire in a building is detected by a team member, the plan will be instantiated because it matches a template for disaster response.

Each sub-goal is addressed with a plan, $plan_i = < g_i, recipe_i, roles_i, d_i, m_i >$, that matches a plan template in the library. The overall team thus has plans $Plans(t) = \{plan_1, \ldots, plan_n\}$. Individual team members will not necessarily know all plans. To maximize the responsiveness of the team to changes in the environment, we allow any team member to commit the team to the execution of a plan, when it detects that subgoal g_i is relevant. Team members can determine which sub-goals are relevant by the plan templates specified in the library. *Recipe_i* is a description of the way the sub-goal will be achieved[11] including the execution order of the components in the plan. $Roles_i = \{r_1, r_2, r_3, \ldots r_r\}$ are the individual activities that must be performed to execute *recipe_i*. d_i is the domain specific information pertinent to the plan. For convenience, we write $perform(r,a)$ to signify that agent, a, is working on role, r. *Subteam_i* includes any agents working on *plan_i* *and* their neighbors in the acquaintance network. The identities of those agents involved in role allocation is captured with $allocate(plan_i)$. In the cases where either a conflict or synergy is detected, all but one of the plans must be terminated. The domain specific knowledge of a termination of a plan can be defined as $^{term}recipe_i$.

We can think about TOPs as active objects in a distributed database. Each TOP "object" captures the state of a particular team plan. Team members involved in the execution of that plan need to have up-to-date versions of the TOP "object", e.g., knowing which team members are performing which roles and when TOPs are complete. Information needs to be shared to ensure there is synchronization across the same object held by different team members. Viewed in this manner, coordination can be thought of as a set of algorithms to fill in fields on the TOP objects and ensure synchronized objects across the team. For example, some coordination algorithms are triggered when there are open roles in the TOP objects and other algorithms are triggered when the post-conditions on the plan are satisfied.

2.3 Subteams

Although individual agents commit the team to a sub-goal, it is a subteam that will realize the sub-goal. The subteams formation process commences when an individual agent detects all the appropriate preconditions that matches a plan template in the library and subsequently instantiates a plan, $plan_i$. For each of the $roles_i$ in $plan_i$, a role token is created to be allocated to the team. We are using LA-DCOP for role allocation[6], which results in a dynamically changing subset of the overall team involved in role allocation. This works as follows: the token is passed from one team member to the next until an agent finally accepts the role. Once accepted, the agent becomes a member of the subteam and makes a temporary commitment to perform the role represented by the token. Note that agents can accept multiple tokens and therefor can perform more than one role and thus, belong to multiple subteams. Since allocation of team members to roles may change due to failures or changing circumstances, the members of a subteam also change. One example of this is when a member decides to drop a role for a more suitable task. This will lead to the best use of team resources because team members will execute roles that they are most capable of doing.

All subteam members, agents performing roles and their informed acquaintances, must be kept informed of the state of the plan, e.g., they must be informed if the plan becomes irrelevant. This maximizes cohesion and minimizes wasted effort. Typically $|subteam_i| < 20$, although it may vary with plan complexity and notice that typically, $subteam_i \cap subteam_j \neq \emptyset$ where $i \neq j$. In the experiments that follow, a simple plan contains 1-2 roles and 1-2 preconditions compared to a complex plans that have 4-5 roles and 9-10 preconditions. This occurs because agents can accept more than one role and usually belong to more than one subteam due the acquaintance network. These subteams are the basis for our coordination framework and leads to scalability in teams.

2.4 Plan Deconfliction

In this section, we describe how to resolve plan conflicts. When using distributed plan creation, two problems may occur. Upon detecting the appropriate preconditions, different team members may create identical plans or plans with the same p_g but different p_{recipe}. To reduce the need for plan deconfliction, we need to choose a rule for plan instantiation to reduce the number of plans created with the same p_g. These instantiation rules include *always instantiate, probabilistic* and *local information*. The choice of the plan instantiation rule will vary with the domain setting.

If two plans, $plan_i$ and $plan_j$ have some conflict or potential synergy, then we require $subteam_i \cap subteam_j \neq \emptyset$ to detect it. There must be a common team member on both subteams to maintain mutuals beliefs of the plans and hence detect the conflict. A simple probability calculation reveals that the probability of a non-empty intersection between subteams, i.e., the probability of an overlap between the teams, is:

$$Pr(overlap) = 1 - \frac{_{(n-k)}C_m}{_nC_m}$$

where $_aC_b$ denotes a combination, n = number of agents, k = size of $subteam_i$ and m = size of $subteam_j$.

Hence, the size of the subteams is critical to the probability of overlap. For example, if $|subteam_i| = |subteam_j| = 20$ and $|A| = 200$, then $P(overlap) = 0.88$, despite each subteam involving only 10% of the overall team. Since the constituents of a subteam change over time, this is actually a lower bound on the probability that a conflict is detected.

After a conflict is detected, the plan needs to be terminated; the same follows with completion of goals or recipes and irrelevant or unachievable plans. We capture the domain specific knowledge that defines these conditions with $^{term}p_{recipe}$. In exactly the same way as STEAM, when any $a \in subteam_i$ detects any conditions in $^{term}p_{recipe}$, it is obliged to ensure that all other members of $subteam_i$ also know that the plan should be terminated. In this way, the team can ensure that $plan_i \subseteq plans(t)$, i.e., no agent believes the team is performing any plan that it is not performing.

2.5 Plan Instantiation Rules

In distributed plan instantiation, an agent can create a plan when all preconditions have been fulfilled and the plan matches a template in a library. However, since this may increase the total number of plans created, agents can only create a plan using one of three rules for instantiating plans. These rules differ in terms of the information needed to compute whether the instantiation conditions apply. The first rule, the *always instantiate rule*, is used as a baseline for the other instantiation rules. An agent is allowed to create a plan when it knows of all the preconditions necessary for the plan.

The second rule, the *probabilistic instantiation rule*, requires no knowledge of other team members. This method requires that team members wait a random amount of time before creating the plan. If during that time, it has not been informed by an informed acquaintance that another teammate is creating the same plan, it will proceed and create the plan. Thus plans will only be created during the time it takes for all team members to hear of the plan. The advantage of this rule is that no information is required of other team members. There are two disadvantages. First, there may be conflicting plans which must be later resolved. Second, there may be a significant delay between detection of the preconditions and the instantiation of the plan. These disadvantages can be traded off in the following manner. By increasing the length of time a team member can wait, the number of conflicts will be reduced, but the delay will be increased.

We can use information about who locally senses information to define another rule. This rule, which we refer to as the *local information rule*, requires that a team member detect some of the plan's preconditions locally in order to instantiate the plan. Although this will lead to conflicting plans when multiple agents locally sense preconditions, it is easier to determine where the conflicts might occur and resolve them quickly. The major disadvantage of this rule is that when a plan has many preconditions, the team members that may detect specific preconditions may never get to know all the preconditions and thus the plan will never be created.

3 Toward Efficient Communication in Large Scale Teams

Information is important in coordinating large scale multi-agent teams because each team member has to adjust its activity according to the changes in its team, teammates, and the environments. Communication is difficult because the members only have a partial views of the environment and a team member may have a piece of valuable information but not know who needs the information [31]. In this section, we explain our objective of efficient communication in terms of providing high quality information with targeted information delivery.

3.1 Information fusion

Each of the agents, when working in physical working plate, can be deemed as mobile sensors and the team can be deemed as a sensor network. We first look at the problem of information fusion in large scale teams, which not only observe physical phenomena, but also conduct high-level information processing tasks, e.g., attacking a target in a battlefield. In large teams, the sensor data generated by a single agent usually has low confidence. The low confidence sensor data cannot be used directly for coordinating plans and actions and needs to be fused with other relevant data in the team [25]. Many power-aware protocols and algorithms have been developed for static sensor networks, but very limited research has been done for the design of routing algorithms for information fusion [1, 35]. For example, in directed diffusion and geographic routing [9, 15], each source agent does not send the data back to the sink until it receives a query from the sink. For this reason, these routing protocols are called *reactive protocols*.

Reactive protocols are mainly designed for static sensor networks and are not appropriate for large scale teams, which are mobile sensor networks. Specifically, there are two key reasons. 1. The location of the data is not correlated with existing positions of mobile sensors., i.e., agent b previously knew agent a has the data in one location, but when his query comes, agent a has moved to another location. 2.

Sinks agents usually do not know when source agents will have the data, so they have always sent out volume of query.

In this section we present a *proactive protocol* for information fusion in large scale team based on our acquaintance network model. In proactive protocols, there is no querying process and each source agent, when sensing a piece of data, can proactively deliver the data to other nodes in the network. Without the querying process, the source agent has to reason about who might have other relevant data and can fuse its sensor data. In order to minimize the traffic and redundant data in the network, each node forwards the sensor data to only one of its neighbors. Without centralized control, the agent has to intelligently deliver data for fusion solely based on itself and its neighbors. The challenge, with various decisions being made by the individual agents, is how to maximize the probability that relevant data will be fused in the network, e.g., fused by at least one node in the network.

Random walks are a simple algorithm for information fusion. In random walks, when an agent receivessensor data it randomly choses a neighbor to send to. Once the neighbor receives the data, it repeats the same process until the events are successfully fused or the data reaches the stop condition. However, random walks are not efficient for information delivery when more than two agents detect the same event on the ground and there is a need to fuse them together. We propose an efficient and failure-resistant localized algorithm — *path reinforcement* algorithm [34], in which each node learns routing decisions from past information delivery processes. The logic behind the algorithm is that relevant information is likely to be fused earlier if agents follow a path they have followed earlier. In the algorithm, a agent a may pass the event to neighbor b if a has passed b relevant events before.

The experiments show that controlled information flows significantly increase the probability of relevant information being fused in the network, such that the probability could be improved by 2 - 5 times for the same hops of information propagation in comparison with random walks [34]. Our experiments indicate that the probability of fusion is surprisingly high even with limited local knowledge of each node and relatively small hops.

3.2 Information Sharing

In the previous section, we showed how requiring mutual beliefs only within subteams acting on specific goals can dramatically reduce the communication required in a large team. However, individual team members will sometimes get domain level information, via local sensors, that is relevant to members of another subteam. Due to the fact that team members do not know what each other subteam is doing, they will sometimes have locally sensed information, while not knowing who requires it. In this section, we present an approach to sharing such information, leveraging the small world properties of the acquaintance network. The basic idea is to forward information to the acquaintance in the acquaintance network who is most likely to either need the information or have a neighbor who does.

The key to the algorithm is the model that the agent maintains of its acquaintances. P_a is a matrix where $P_a[i,b] \rightarrow [0,1], b \in N(a), i \in I$ represents the probability that acquaintance b is the best to send information i to. To obey the rules of probability, we require $\forall i \in I, \sum_{b \in N(a)} P_a^t[i,b] = 1$. For example, if $P_a[i,b] = 0.7$, then a will usually forward i to agent b as b is very likely the best of its neighbors to send to. This situation is illustrated in Figure 4. The more accurate the model of P_a, the more efficient the information sharing because the agent will send information to agents that need it more often and more quickly. P_a is inferred from incoming messages and thus the key to our algorithm is for the agents to build the best possible model of P_a.

Information is encapsulated in *messages*, with some supporting information which is helpful for information sharing. Specifically, a message consists of two parts, $M = <i, path>$. $i \in I$ is the information being communicated. *path* records the track over which the message has been taken in the network. *last(path)* denotes the last agent to which the message was sent previous to current agent recipient, via acquaintance network. To ensure that messages do not travel indefinitely around the network, we stop the message when $|path| \geq$ MAX_STEPS.

When a message arrives, the agent state, S_a, is updated by the transition function, δ, which has three parts, δ_H, δ_K, δ_P. First, the message is appended to the history, $\delta_H(m, H_a) = H_a \cup m$. Secondly, the information contained in the message is added to the agent's local information knowledge K_a, $\delta_H(m, K_a) = K_a \cup m.i$.[4] Finally, and most critically for the purpose of the algorithm, δ_P is used to update agent's probability matrix, to help route future message. (We described δ_P in the next section.)

Each agent in the team runs the following algorithm when receiving message m:
Algorithm 1: Information Share (S_a)
(1) $While(true)$
(2) $m \leftarrow getMsg$
(3) $S_a \leftarrow \delta(m, S_a)$
(4) $if\ m.|path| < MAX\_STEPS$
(5) $APPEND(self, m.path)$
(6) $next \leftarrow CHOOSE(P[i, m.j])$
(7) $SEND(next, m)$

In Algorithm 1, when an agent gets a message, it updates its state according to function δ. If an agent finds that the message does not meet the stop condition (line 4), then the function CHOOSE (line 6) selects an acquaintance, according to the probabilities in matrix to pass the message to. Notice, CHOOSE can select any acquaintance, with the likelihood of choosing a particular acquaintance being proportional to their probability of being the best to send to.

The key to our algorithm is for the agent to often pass information to an acquaintance who either needs it or knows who does. These models are created based on previously received information. This requires us making use of the relationship between pieces of information and then mapping it into a mathematic description, i.e. via Bayes Rule. We define the relationships between pieces of information as $rel(i,j) \rightarrow [0,1], i,j \in I$, where $rel(i,j) > 0.5$ indicates that an agent interested in i will also be interested in j, while $rel(i,j) < 0.5$ indicates that an agent interested in i

---

[4] In this paper, we ignore difficult issues related to contradictory information.

is unlikely to be interested in j. If $rel(i,j) = 0.5$ then nothing can be inferred. Since rel relates two pieces of domain level information, we assume that it is given (or can be easily inferred from the domain).

Our information sharing algorithm defined an action of δ_P for each piece of relative information i when a received message containing j can be described as follows: assuming information j arrives to agent a from b, then agent a will first decrease the probability of sending this information back to b because clearly b already knows that information. Then H_a should be searched for to find any relevant former information. For each piece of relevant information i, j should be additional evidence for a to make a decision about sending i, and the probability of sending i to b should be strengthened.

The update of agent a's P_a based on an incoming message m containing j which is received from c can be achieved by leveraging Bayes Rule as follows:

$$\forall i,j \in I, b \in N(a) \quad \delta_P^I(P_a[i,b], m = < j, path >, d =$$
$$first(N(a), m.path))$$
$$= \begin{cases} P_a[i,b] \times rel(i,j) \times \frac{2}{|N|} & \text{if } i \neq j, b = d \\ P_a[i,b] \times \frac{1}{|N|} & \text{if } i \neq j, b \neq d \\ \varepsilon & \text{if } i = j, b \in m.path \cap N(a) \end{cases}$$

Then P must be normalized to ensure $\forall i \in I, \sum_{b \in N(a)} P_a^I[i,b] = 1$. The first case in our equation is the most interesting. It updates the probability that the agent that just sent some information is the best to send other information to, based on the relationships of other pieces of information to the one just sent. Please note, to avoid potential path detours, the message path is determined not according to who directly sent the message, but rather according to the fact that it was a's acquaintance who first got the message. The latter condition changes the probability of sending that information to agents other than the sender in a way that ensures the normalization works. Finally, the third case encodes the idea that you typically would not want to send a piece of information to an agent that sent it to you.

To see how δ_P works, consider the following example at some point doing execution:

$$P_a = \begin{array}{c} i \\ j \\ k \end{array} \begin{array}{cccc} b & c & d & e \\ \left[\begin{array}{cccc} 0.6 & 0.1 & 0.2 & 0.1 \\ 0.4 & 0.2 & 0.3 & 0.1 \\ 0.4 & 0.4 & 0.1 & 0.1 \end{array} \right] \end{array}$$

The first row of the matrix shows that if a gets information i it will likely send it to agent b, since $P[i,b] = 0.6$. We assume that agents wanting information i also probably want information j but those wanting k definitely do not want j. That is, $rel(i,j) = 0.6$ and $rel(k,j) = 0.2$. Then a message $m = < j, \{,,d,,b\} >$ with information j arrives from agent b. Applying δ_P^I to P_a we get the following result:

$$\begin{array}{cccc} b & c & d & e \end{array}$$

$$P_a = \begin{matrix} i \\ j \\ k \end{matrix} \begin{bmatrix} 0.5769 & 0.096 & 0.2308 & 0.096 \\ \varepsilon & 0.67 & \varepsilon & 033 \\ 0.4255 & 0.4255 & 0.0426 & 0.1064 \end{bmatrix}$$

The effects on P can be inferred as follows: (i) j will likely not be sent back to d and b who previously have gotten j, i.e., $P_a[i,b] = \varepsilon$; (ii) the probability of sending i to d is increased because agents wanting j probably also want i; (iii) the probability of sending k to d is decreased, since agents wanting j probably do not want k. Notice a knows nothing of the network topology *beyond* its acquaintances $n(a)$.

3.3 Effects of Network Topology on Sharing Efficiency

As noted by social scientists, information sharing efficiency will be impacted by network topology. We have found that in order to share information among large-scale teams, agents adopt the same manners as exhibited by humans operating in social groups.

The properties of social network structures have been comprehensively studied [2, 17]. According to such research, there are several parameters that are important for helping us to understand or predict the behavior of information sharing in large-scale teams. Key factors include the small-world effect, degree distributions, clustering, network correlations, random graph models, models of network growth and preferential attachment, and dynamical processes taking place on networks [11]. Most of them are interrelated. For the purpose of this paper, we specifically focus on only three properties: average distance, degree distribution and average acquaintance.

- Average distance: (commonly studied as "small world effect" [30]. The average distance $l = \frac{1}{\frac{1}{2}n(n+1)} \sum_{a_i, a_j \in A, i > j} distance(a_i, a_j)$, where $n = |A|$ and $distance(a_i, a_j)$ represents the minimum number of agents a_i, a_j that a message must pass through one agent to another via acquaintance network. For example, if agent a_1 and a_2 are not acquaintances but share an acquaintance, $distance(a_1, a_2) = 1$.
- Degree distribution: (Commonly studied as "scale free effect") The frequency of agents having different number of acquaintances. The distribution can be represented as a histogram where the bins represent a given number of acquaintances and the size of a bin is how many agents have such number of acquaintances [2].
- Average acquaintances: is the average number of acquaintances that agents have in the teams. Its value can be used to infer how many choices agents may have when delivering a message.

Well-known types of social networks can be described using these properties. For example, a *random network* has the "flat" degree distribution. While *grid network* is distinct in that all nodes have the same degree (e.g, four is the only degree in a two dimension grid network). *Small World Network* and *Scale Free Network* [2] are two important types of social network topologies and research has shown that each of them possesses some interesting properties. Small world networks have much shorter average distances as compared with regular grid networks. We hypothesize that the low average distance will improve information sharing efficiency because information can potentially take less "hops" to reach a defined destination. A scale-free network is a specific kind of network in which the degree distribution forms a power-law, i.e, some nodes are very connected hubs and connect to other nodes much more than ordinary nodes. The hubs in scale-free networks give the advantages of centralized networks, in which the distribution provides the advantages of centralized approaches.

4 Machinetta

A number of algorithms work together to achieve the teamwork, given the framework described above. There are algorithms for allocation roles[6], instantiating plans[16], sharing information[31], human interaction[20] and resource allocation. To avoid requiring a reimplementation of the algorithms for each new domain, the coordination algorithms are encapsulated in a *proxy*[10, 29, 21, 24]. Proxies are becoming a standard mechanism for building heterogeneous teams. Each team member works closely with a single proxy that coordinates with the other proxies to implement the teamwork. The basic architecture is shown in Figure 2. The proxy communicates via a high-level, domain-specific protocol with the robot, agent or person it is representing in the team. Most of the proxy code is domain-independent and can be readily used in a variety of domains requiring distributed control. Our current proxy code, known as Machinetta, is a substantially extended and updated version of the TEAMCORE proxy code[29]. Machinetta proxies are in the public domain and can be downloaded from http://teamcore.usc.edu/doc/Machinetta.

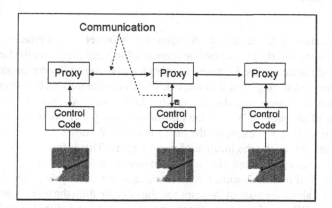

Fig. 2. The basic system architecture showing proxies, control code and Unmanned Aerial Vehicles (UAVs) being controlled.

In a dynamic, distributed system, protocols for performing coordination need to be extremely robust. When we scale the size of a team to hundreds of agents, this becomes more of an issue than simply writing bug-free code. Instead we need abstractions and designs that promote robustness. Towards this end, we are encapsulating "chunks" of coordination in *coordination agents*. Each coordination agent manages one specific piece of the overall coordination. When control over that piece of coordination moves from one proxy to another proxy, the coordination agent moves from proxy to proxy, taking with it any relevant state information. We have coordination agents for each plan or subplan (PlanAgents), each role (RoleAgents) and each piece of information that needs to be shared (InformationAgents). For example, a RoleAgent looks after everything to do with a specific role. This encapsulation makes it far easier to build robust coordination.

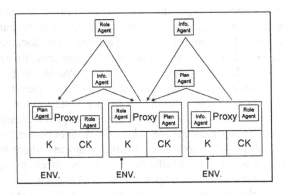

Fig. 3. High level view of the implementation, with coordination agents moving around a network of proxies.

Coordination agents manage the coordination in the network of proxies. Thus, the proxy can be viewed simply as a mobile agent platform that facilitates the functioning of the coordination agents. However, the proxies play the additional important role of providing and storing local information. We divide the information stored by the proxies into two categories, domain specific knowledge, K, and the coordination knowledge of the proxy, CK. K is the information this proxy knows about the state of the environment. For example, the proxy for a UAV knows its own location and fuel level as well as the the location of some targets. This information comes both from local sensors, reported via the domain agent, and from coordination agents (specifically InformationAgents, see below) that arrive at the proxy. CK is what the proxy knows about the state of the team and the coordination the team is involved in. For example, CK includes the known team plans, some knowledge about which team member is performing which role, and the TOP templates. At the most abstract level, the activities of the coordination agents involve moving around the proxy network, adding and changing information in C and CK for each agent. The content of K as it pertains to the local proxy, e.g., roles for the local proxy, govern the behavior of that team member. The details of how a role is executed by the control agent, i.e., the UAV, are domain- (and even team member-) dependent.

5 Experimental Results

In this section, we present empirical evidence of the above approach with a combination of high and low fidelity experiments.

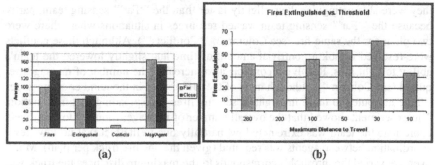

(a)   (b)

Fig. 4. Coordinating 200 agents in (a) disaster response simulation (average on y-axis extinguished, conflicts and messages per agent on x-axis); and (b) the number of fires guished by 200 fire trucks versus threshold.

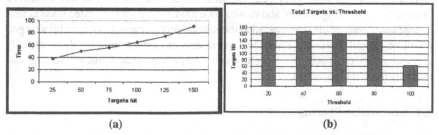

(a)   (b)

Fig. 5. Simulated coordinating 200 UAVs in a battlespace (a) time vs the number of targets hit and (b) the number of targets hit versus threshold.

5.1 Machinetta

In Figures 4 and 5, we show the results of an experiment using 200 Machinetta proxies running the coordination algorithms described in Section 3. These experiments represent high fidelity tests of the coordination algorithms and illustrate the overall effectiveness of the approach. In the first experiment, the proxies control fire trucks responding to an urban disaster. The trucks must travel around an environment, locate fires (which spread if they are not extinguished) and extinguish them. The top level goal of the team, G, was to put out all the fires. A single plan requires that an individual fire be put out. In this experiment, the plan included only one function, which was to put out the fire. We varied the sensing range of the fire trucks ("'Far'" and "'Close'") and measured some key parameters. The most critical thing to note is that the approach was successful in coordinating a very large team. The first column compares the number of fires started. The "'Close'" sensing team required more searching to find fires, and as a result, unsurprisingly, the fires spread more. However, they were able extinguish them slightly faster than the "'Far'" sensing team, partly because the "'Far'" sensing team wasted resources in situations where there were two plans for the same fire (see Column 3, "'Conflicts'"). Although these conflicts were resolved it took a nontrivial amount of time and slightly lowered the team's ability to fight fires. Resolving conflicts also increased the number of messages required (see Column 4), although most of the differences in the number of messages can be attributed to more fire fighters sensing fires and spreading that information. The experiment showed that the overall number of messages required to effectively coordinate the team was extremely low, partially due to the fact that no low- level coordination between agents was required (given the one fire truck per plan). Moreover, we varied the thresholds corresponds to the maximum distances the truck will travel to a fire and 4(b) shows increasing thresholds initially improves the number of fires extinguished, but too high a threshold results in a lack of trucks accepting tasks and a decrease in performance.

In the second domain, Figure 5(a) shows high level results from a second domain using exactly the same proxy code. The graph shows the rate at which 200 simulated UAVs, coordinated with Machinetta proxies, searched a battle space and destroyed targets. Moreover, Figure 5(b) shows while we have effectively allocated tasks across a large team, thresholds (correspond to the maximum distances UAVs can hit a target) are of no benefit. Taken together, the experiments in the two domains show not only that our approach is effective at coordinating very large teams, but it also suggests that it is reasonably general.

5.2 Information Sharing

We test our information sharing algorithm by using a team with 400 agents and each of them has, on average, four acquaintances. One agent is randomly chosen as the source of some information and another is randomly picked as the sink for that information. The sink agent first sends out 20 messages containing relative information j, each with MAX_STEPS=50. Then the source agent sends out a message with information i with $rel(i, j)$ varied. We measure how many steps or messages that it takes i to be encapsulated into message and sent to get to the sink agent. In our experiments, four different types of acquaintance network topologies are involved: two dimension grid networks, random networks, small world networks, and scale free networks. The small world network is based on the grid network with 8% links randomly changed.

The key difference between the random network and the scale free network is that the random has a "flat" degree distribution but the scale free network has a power law distribution. Each point on each graph is based on the average of 1000 runs in a simple simulation environment.

Information sharing with different information relevance

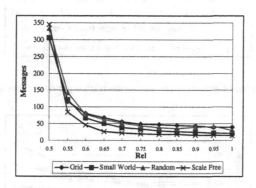

Fig. 6. The number of messages dramatically reduces as the association between information received and information to be sent increases.

We first verify our basic algorithm in different types of acquaintance network topologies. In Figure 6, we show the average number of steps taken to deliver i as we varied the strength of the relationship between the information originally sent out by the sink agent and the information i sent by the source agent from 0.5 to 1. As expected, our algorithm works on the four different acquaintance networks; further, the stronger the relationship between originally sent information and the new information the more efficient is the information delivery.

Information sharing with different number of previous messages

Next, we look in detail at exactly how many messages must be sent by the source to make the delivery from the sink efficient. We use the same settings as above except the number of messages the sink sends out is varied and the relationship between these messages and i, rel (i, j) is forced at 0.9. Notice that only a few messages are required to dramatically impact the number of messages required. This result also shows us that a few messages is enough for agents to make a "precise guess" about where to send messages.

The influence of average acquaintances

In next experiment, we looked in detail at exactly how the number of acquaintances can help to make the information sharing efficient. We run experiments with

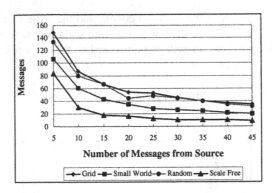

Fig. 7. The number of messages reduces as the related previous messages increased.

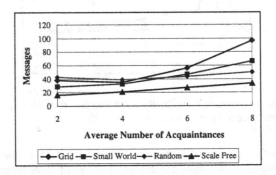

Fig. 8. The number of messages increases sligthly if each agent has more average acquaintances in acquaintance networks.

$rel(i, j) = 0.8$ and in acquaintance networks in which each agent has an average of from 2 to 8 acquaintances. The result in Figure 8 shows that the greater the number of acquaintances, the more messages that are necessary to deliver i. This means that information sharing cannot be enhanced by connecting agents with more acquaintances. Moreover, in our experiment, we don't consider the limitation of communication breadth for agent members.

Algorithm efficiency among different size teams

To investigate the influence of team scale on information sharing performance, as shown in Figure 9, we ran experiments using different sizes of agent teams, from 100 to 550 with rel(i,j)=0.7. The information sharing efficiency is measured as the percentage of agents involved for information sharing use $percentage = \frac{agents\ involved\ in\ fod\ elivery}{Total\ \#\ of\ agent\ team}$. The experiment result shows that with different team sizes,

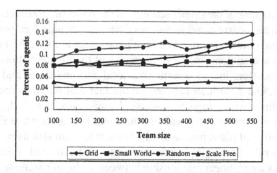

Fig. 9. Information sharing algorithm works even slightly better on large scale teams according to the measure of percentage.

the efficiency of information sharing is almost the same. This indicates that the team size is not a factor for information sharing efficiency.

5.3 Plan Deconfliction

Parameter	Minimum	Maximum	Parameter Type
Number of Team Members	10	999	Domain Dependent
Number of Plan Templates	1	20	Domain Dependent
Roles Per Team Member	1	1	Domain Dependent
Total Preconditions	20	219	Domain Dependent
Preconditions Per Plan	1	10	Domain Dependent
Roles Per Plan	1	5	Domain Dependent
Number of Capability Types	2	21	Domain Dependent
Percent Capable	0.1	1.1	Domain Dependent
Instantiate Rate	0	1	Input (Free Parameter)
New Precondition Rate	0.0020	0.5020	Domain Dependent
Precondition Detection Rate	0.0020	0.2020	Domain Dependent
Associate Network Density	2	16	Input (Free Parameter)
Information Token	1	10	Input (Free Parameter)
Instantiation Rule*	1	3	Input (Free Parameter)
Percentage Possible	0	100	Output
Reward	0.00	85.35	Output
Messages per agent	0.10	1977.38	Output

*Instantiation Type(1-Always 2-Local 3-Probabalistic)

Fig. 10. Parameter Table

We use TeamSim, a simple simulator, to analyze the effect our acquaintance model with dynamically changing subteams. TeamSim, which runs the coordination algorithm without simulating time intensive communication, quickly evaluates different combinations of parameter settings on the order of thousands. These parameters settings, which correspond to various domains, include free parameters based on our model and domain parameters. Free parameters are specific to our algorithm and include the acquaintance network density, and plan instantiation rule. A few of the domain parameters included team size, total preconditions, and roles per plan (see Figure 10). Our algorithm is based on the fact that the acquaintances network will detect conflicts with a high probability. As team size is scaled, we can assume that the number of duplicate plan will also increase. This is shown in Figure 11 where the average number of plans increases with respect to team size using the probabilistic instantiation rule. In the graph, both the actual and expected conflicts are shown. Figure 12 shows a non-linear relationship between an input parameter, team size and an output parameter, and messages per agent.

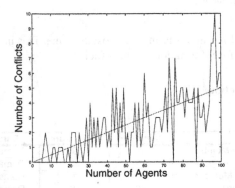

Fig. 11. The average number of plan conflicts increases with respect to team size

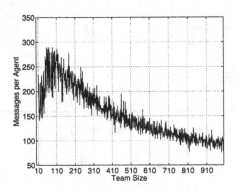

Fig. 12. Messages per Agent as Team Size is increased

6 Summary

In this paper, we have presented an approach to building large teams that has allowed us to build teams of an order of magnitude larger than those discussed in previously published work. To achieve these unprecedented scales, fundamentally new ideas were developed and new, more scalable algorithms were implemented. Specifically, we presented an approach to organizing the team based on an acquaintance network with dynamically evolving subteams. Potentially inefficient interactions between subteams were detected by sharing information across a network independent of any subteam relationships. We leveraged the social network properties of these networks to very efficiently share domain knowledge across the team. While much work remains to be done to fully understand and be able to build large teams, this work represents a significant step forward.

Acknowledgments

This research was supported by AFSOR grant F49620-01-1-0542 and AFRL/MNK grant F08630-03-1-0005.

References

1. Ian F. Akyildiz, Weilian Su, Yogesh Sankarasubramaniam, and Erdal Cayirci. A survey on sensor networks. *IEEE Communication Magazine*, 2002.
2. Albert-Laszla Barabasi and Eric Bonabeau. Scale free networks. *Scientific American*, pages 60–69, May 2003.
3. Mark H. Burstein and David E. Diller. A framework for dynamic information flow in mixed-initiative human/agent organizations. *Applied Intelligence on Agents and Process Management*, 2004. Forthcoming.
4. Hans Chalupsky, Yolanda Gil, Craig A. Knoblock, Kristina Lerman, Jean Oh, David V. Pynadath, Thomas A. Russ, and Milind Tambe. Electric Elves: Agent technology for supporting human organizations. *AI Magazine*, 23(2):11–24, 2002.
5. Eithan Ephrati, Martha Pollack, and Sigalit Ur. Deriving multi-agent communication through filtering strategies. In *Proceedings of IJCAI '95*, 1995.
6. Alessandro Farinelli, Paul Scerri, and Milind Tambe. Building large-scale robot systems: Distributed role assignment in dynamic, uncertain domains. In *Proceedings of Workshop on Representations and Approaches for Time-Critical Decentralized Resource, Role and Task Allocation*, 2003.
7. Joseph Giampapa and Katia Sycara. Coversational case-based planning for agent team coordination. In *Proceedings of the fourth International coference on Case-based Reasoning*, 2001.
8. C. V. Goldman and S. Zilberstein. Optimizing information exchange in cooperative multi-agent systems. In *Proceedings of the Second International Conference on Autonomous Agents and Multi-agent Systems*, 2003.
9. Chalermek Intanagonwiwat, Ramesh Govindan, and Deborah Estrin. Directed diffusion: a scalable and robust communication paradigm for sensor networks. In *MobiCom*, pages 56–67, 2000.

10. N. Jennings. The archon systems and its applications. Project Report, 1995.

11. N. R. Jennings. Specification and implementation of a belief-desire-joint-intention architecture for collaborative problem solving. *Intl. Journal of Intelligent and Cooperative Information Systems*, 2(3):289–318, 1993.

12. Nick Jennings. Controlling cooperative problem solving in industrial multi-agent systems using joint intentions. *Artificial Intelligence*, 75:195–240, 1995.

13. Kam-Chuen Jim and C. Lee Giles. How communication can improve the performance of multi-agent systems. In *Proceedings of the fifth international conference on Autonomous agents*, 2001.

14. Hiraoki Kitano, Minoru Asada, Yasuo Kuniyoshi, Itsuki Noda, Eiichi Osawa, and Hitoshi Matsubara. RoboCup: A challenge problem for AI. *AI Magazine*, 18(1):73–85, Spring 1997.

15. Yong-Bae Ko and Nitin H. Vaidya. Location-aided routing (LAR) in mobile ad hoc networks. In *MobiCom*, pages 66–75, 1998.

16. Elizabeth Liao, Paul Scerri, and Katia Sycara. A framework for very large teams. In *AAMAS04 Workshop on Coalitions and Teams*, 2004.

17. M.E.J.Newman. The structure and function of complex networks. SIAM Review, Vol. 45, No. 2, 2003.

18. S. Milgram. The small world problem. In *Psychology Today*, 22, 1967.

19. R. Nair, T. Ito, M. Tambe, and S. Marsella. Task allocation in robocup rescue simulation domain. In *Proceedings of the International Symposium on RoboCup*, 2002.

20. K. Sycara P. Scerri and M Tambe. Adjustable autonomy in the context of coordination. In *AIAA 3rd Unmanned Unlimited Technical Conference, Workshop and Exhibit*, 2004.

21. David Pynadath and Milind Tambe. Multiagent teamwork: Analyzing the optimality and complexity of key theories and models. In *First International Joint Conference on Autonomous Agents and Multi-Agent Systems (AAMAS'02)*, 2002.

22. David V. Pynadath and Milind Tambe. An automated teamwork infrastructure for heterogeneous software agents and humans. *Journal of Autonomous Agents and Multi-Agent Systems, Special Issue on Infrastructure and Requirements for Building Research Grade Multi-Agent Systems*, page to appear, 2002.

23. D.V. Pynadath, M. Tambe, N. Chauvat, and L. Cavedon. Toward team-oriented programming. In *Intelligent Agents VI: Agent Theories, Architectures, and Languages*, pages 233–247, 1999.

24. P. Scerri, D. V. Pynadath, L. Johnson, Rosenbloom P., N. Schurr, M Si, and M. Tambe. A prototype infrastructure for distributed robot-agent-person teams. In *The Second International Joint Conference on Autonomous Agents and Multiagent Systems*, 2003.

25. Paul Scerri, Yang Xu, Elizabeth Liao, Justin Lai, and Katia Sycara. Scaling teamwork to very large teams. In *AAMAS*, pages 888–895, 2004.

26. Katia Sycara and Micheal Lewis. Team cognition. In *Chapter Intelligent Agents into Human Teams. Erlbaum Publishers*, 2003.

27. Katia Sycara, Anandeep Pannu, Mike Williamson, and Keith Decker. Distributed intelligent agents. *IEEE Expert: Intelligent Systems and thier applications*, 11(6):36–45, December 1996.

28. Milind Tambe. Agent architectures for flexible, practical teamwork. *National Conference on AI (AAAI97)*, pages 22–28, 1997.

29. Milind Tambe, Wei-Min Shen, Maja Mataric, David Pynadath, Dani Goldberg, Pragnesh Jay Modi, Zhun Qiu, and Behnam Salemi. Teamwork in cyberspace: using TEAMCORE to make agents team-ready. In *AAAI Spring Symposium on agents in cyberspace*, 1999.

30. Duncan Watts and Steven Strogatz. Collective dynamics of small world networks. *Nature*, 393:440–442, 1998.

31. Yang Xu, Mike Lewis, Katia Sycara, and Paul Scerri. Information sharing in large scale teams. In *In AAMAS 2004 workshop on Challenges in the Coordination of Large Scale Multi Agents Systems*, 2004.

32. P. Xuan, V. Lesser, and S. Zilberstein. Communication decisions in multi-agent cooperation: Model and experiments. In *Proceedings of the Fifth International Conference on Autonomous Agents*, 2001.

33. J. Yen, J. Yin, T. R. Ioerger, M. S. Miller, D. Xu, and R. A. Volz. Cast: Collaborative agents for simulating teamwork. In *Proceedings of the International Joint Conference on Artificial Intelligence*, pages 1135–1142, 2001.

34. Bin Yu, Paul Scerri, Katia Sycara, Yang Xu, and Michael Lewis. Proactive information delivery and fusion in mobile sensor networks. In *submitted to IPSN*, 2005.

35. Feng Zhao and Leonidas Guibas. *Wireless Sensor Networks: An Information Processing Approach*. Morgan Kaufmann Publishers, 2004.

Techniques for Robust Planning in Degradable Multiagent Systems

Ping Xuan

Clark University pxuan@clarku.edu

1 Introduction

While computer systems are designed to achieve their intended purposes and attain the expected performance level when things are going as planned, there are often situations and/or scenarios that the anticipated conditions are not satisfied and therefore the intended performance level may not be attained. In some mission-critical applications (such as missile launch processes), such events are outright failures – the performance is either success or failure – and therefore the system designer's job is to make sure that there are no unexpected events, i.e. to prevent possible failures from occurring. However, in most applications, system performance is not a boolean value but could vary in a range of performance levels. In those systems, even when the anticipated conditions are not met and therefore the intended performance level cannot be achieved, the system should be able to adapt to the change and perform at a lower (i.e. *degraded*) performance level instead of simply quitting. For those degradable systems, the designer's job is to implement mechanisms for the system to detect failures/unexpected events and to adapt to the changes (by switching to a different course of action) when those events occur. Both failure prevention and failure detection/adaptation are important topics in real-time and fault-tolerant computing, where the goal is to build systems that are dependable/reliable, predictable, and fault-tolerant [22].

Evidently, multiagent systems are a type of computer systems that frequently needs to deal with the same kind of issues: the environment in which an agent is operating is changing constantly and thus the problem of uncertainty/unexpectedness is even more paramount. And in general, we can say that multiagent systems need to be a kind of degradable computing systems – the system should certainly adapt to changes and unexpected events in the environment and try its best to maintain acceptable performance levels. This would be a key element in any "intelligent" system. In fact, the development of multiagent systems presents both opportunities and challenges to fault-tolerance techniques. On one hand, a multi-agent approach to fault-tolerance can further extend the research on fault-tolerant systems, and allows the integration of performance and reliability into a unified framework. On the other hand, in a multi-agent system, the notion of fault may be different from that of traditional systems, and to enhance reliability in multi-agent systems means that we need to extend the scope of fault-tolerance and have new types of fault-tolerance techniques. We believe that a systematic study on the design of degradable multiagent systems is very urgent in order to associate words such as "reliable" and "dependable" with multiagent systems (at the moment, such associations are rare, if not nonexistent), and it is time for agent designers to explicitly consider the reliability issue of the multiagent systems.

In this article we will focus on cooperative multiagent systems and discuss the techniques that may be used to enhance the planning and coordination aspect of the agents when facing changes and unexpected events. Up to date, the research effort in this area has been largely focused on handling nondeterminism in the multiagent environment. For example in Decker and Lesser's TAEMS framework, different possible outcomes (such as duration and quality) of a task can be modeled in a probability distribution [8]. Approaches for addressing environment nondeterminism generally view it within the scope of planning under uncertainty, such as using Markov decision processes (MDPs) [4, 25, 1, 20] to model sequential decision making in stochastic environments, and using an extended model for agent commitments and applying contingency planning [24]. While these approaches provide good foundations for handling uncertainties in multiagent cooperation, due to the assumptions and limitations of the frameworks and also their complexity, they have limited applicability, especially in systems with a large number of agents. Typically, in those approaches, a system is completely specified (as some types of stochastic processes), therefore it is possible to apply the principle of maximizing expected utility (MEU) and use the expected utility as the metric. However, expected utility alone is not indicative of the reliability of the system – we not only want to achieve the best utility but also want to ensure that the system degrades gracefully when unexpected events occur. Moreover, a completely specified model is really an approximation of the actual system, with many assumptions, simplifications, and omissions – it is impossible to accurately model all aspects of systems and specify all its parameters, after all. Thus, while improving the expected utility is very important, we cannot neglect the reliability issue and need to ensure that the system implements mechanisms to enhance its robustness.

Of course, reliability issue is hardly a new issue in computer systems, as it has been studied in some classical fields such as distributed computing, fault-tolerance. There are already an abundant arsenal of techniques developed for this purpose, and much of the techniques that are going to be presented here are based on the same ideas, but applied to multiagent systems. It should be noted that because multiagent systems differs significantly from traditional distributed systems, they present some challenges to traditional fault-tolerance: while in traditional distributed systems, fault-tolerance techniques often involve the (low-level) implementation of certain FT algorithms across the network, in multiagent systems we are more concerned about the high-level decision making process toward the use of redundancy. As such, in typical FT computing, the use of FT techniques is treated as a part of the system infrastructure and low level control problem - such as task scheduling and resource allocation in the OS, but in multiagent systems, FT is really part of the agent decision making and involves planning, coordination, and cooperation.

In particular, we will discuss several techniques that could be used in degradable multiagent system to increase its robustness, with a focus on the multiagent planning aspect. First, we will present a framework for representing agent plans and try to formalize the reliability issue, and then discuss how to apply FT techniques in agent planning and coordination. We also discuss the issue of fault-tolerance for agent organizations, because failure can occur not only at agent activity level, but also at organizational level, as an agent may fail to assume its organizational role due to its failures.

2 An Integrated View of Performance and Reliability in MAS

Compared to traditional systems. multiagent systems offer a new perspective in problem solving: there are a number of characteristics of MAS that would have important impact on the ways of problem solving:

- *Autonomy.* Agents are autonomous and each agent is an independent decision maker and not mandated/controlled by external entities. Agent activities are results of its own decisions. This does not mean that agents are self-contained — agents can interact with other agents if they choose to do so. This autonomy implies that in general, an agent only has a partial knowledge of the other agents, and the agent makes decisions based on its subjective view of the system. Agent interactions expand or modify an agent's subjective view thus produces influences on its decision making, but still the decision making process is local in each agent. Also, autonomy implies that a multi-agent system is inherently decentralized, and team activities are based on coordination and cooperation rather than being implied by a distributed algorithm.
- *Explicit reasoning of utility.* Agent decision making is explicitly based on the agent's model of utility. A *rational* agent will try to maximize its utility when making a choice. This, of course, does not mean that all agents are self-interested. The utility model of an agent can indeed reflect a group/team interest, and thus making the agents cooperative. The use of a utility model implies that an agent's decision making are inherently an optimization problem rather than a satisfaction problem, and the agent's decisions have to be rationalized - they should not be bound to fixed protocols or routines, but are always changing according to the current utility assessments.
- *Uncertainty.* Agents need to deal with many sources of uncertainty in its problem solving. The partial knowledge of other agents and the rest of the system introduces uncertainty in agent decision making. The actions of the agents may produce uncertain outcomes, which require dynamic changes in agent actions, and also leads to the dynamic changes in the agent's subjective view. Hence, multi-agent problem solving is dynamic in nature, as agents need to adapt to the changes in the system from time to time. As such, agent communication, coordination, and cooperation are the key for multi-agent problem solving.

These characteristics lead to new challenges in the convergence of FT computing and multi-agent problem solving. FT mechanisms that are implemented as distributed algorithms imply some decision rules for team activities, but for autonomous agents these algorithms need to be justified, and need to be implemented via explicit coordination and cooperation. Thus, FT considerations should be an integral part in agent decision making and coordination, and we should model reliability/FT requirements as part of the utility structure.

Although reliability and performance are often regarded as two orthogonal issues, in fact they are very much inter-dependent. To evaluate a system, the most important metric is often based on an overall, stochastic performance measure, rather than the highest level of performance based on one problem solving episode. The overall performance of a system must take into account the possibility of failures and the loss of performance because of such failures. If the effect of failures can be controlled or contained, the system becomes more reliable, and this would lead to better overall performance. Thus, the effectiveness of FT techniques must reflect the changes in overall system performance.

Given that failures occur at a certain probability, a probabilistic model can be used for evaluating overall, or, *expected* performance. As such, there is no need to use separate metrics for performance and reliability, but rather we can use a combined metric that reflects the *distribution* of performance. Such a metric, called *performability*, should serve as the basis of agent utility. As such, to achieve reliability becomes an integral part for improving overall system performance (and performability), and hence the implementation of FT techniques become an integral part of the general problem solving and decision making in multi-agent systems.

From the problem solving perspective, the possible occurrence of failures is another form of the uncertainty in multi-agent problem solving, and fault-tolerance techniques offer alternative ways of achieving the goal/doing the same task, each with a different profile of uncertainty. By introducing uncertainty in problem solving, we can model failures into the agent's problem solving model, and with the introduction of performability measure, we can evaluate the impact of FT techniques on the performability, as well as the resource constraints imposed by the FT techniques. Thus, this source of uncertainty can be represented and be integrated into the agent's constraint optimization process.

A systematic research on FT in multi-agent systems, thus, must establish a framework for multi-agent problem solving that includes performability, agent utility, a model of faults in terms of uncertainty in addition to other uncertainty sources, and agent coordination and cooperation. Based on this framework we can then define the decision problem for optimizing overall performance, and provide solutions for the problem.

In the following sections we present a 3-layer approach for modeling multiagent problem solving and introducing FT techniques. Each layer corresponds to a different level of abstraction and also different level of formalness. At the bottom layer is a formal framework that describes the decision problem for multi-agent systems – a multi-agent extension to the Markov decision process (MDP) to model the multi-agent decision making problem. The middle layer studies the approximation

methods for solving the decision problems, and discuss the implication to agent coordination. The purpose of this layer is to provide theoretical foundation for agent
coordination strategies, so that we can map them in terms of agent decision making policies, and then quantitatively evaluate them. Finally in the top layer we consider various fault-tolerance techniques, integrate them into agent problem solving
by transforming them into coordination mechanisms. While going up the layers, the
problem solving becomes more and more coarse-grained, and this naturally means
the increase of the degree of approximation. In terms of the level of abstractness and
formalness, at the MDP layer we are dealing with abstract state representations of the
multi-agent systems, and then moving up in to the coordination layer we are dealing
with tasks and commitments, and finally in the FT layer we are going to deal with
structured heuristic mechanisms.

3 The Computation Model

Before describing the approach in details, however, we need to first discuss the computation model, i.e., our agent model, the nature of the agent's activities, and the
environment where the multi-agent system operates.

3.1 Agent Model

First, let's define the notion of agent used here. We view an agent as an autonomous
problem solver. As such, to specify an agent, we need to first describe the problem
solving knowledge in an agent. This knowledge base can be specified in three parts:

1. Capabilities — this is a list of the things/tasks/problems that an agent is capable
   of doing. Note that this does not mean that the agent can do it single-handedly.
   To be precise, it means that the agent has the knowledge of how to approach
   this problem, i.e., that the agent can do the task locally, or that the agent knows
   how to sub-divide the problem into sub-problems. Such a hierarchical structure
   allows the specification of complex problems/tasks. At the bottom level (leaf
   nodes) of the hierarchy are either locally capable tasks, or nodes of *inability*,
   i.e., the tasks that the agent has no knowledge how to perform or sub-divide.
   Obviously, the agent has to negotiate with other agents for the tasks it cannot do.
2. Relationships/Constraints — Often the tasks are not independent to each other.
   For example, sub-problems may have to follow a particular sequence. Or, tasks
   use the same resources and therefore may potentially be mutually exclusive.
3. Utility structure — a utility structure is defined for each task and relationship to
   specify how the agent's utility is affected. Similar to the hierarchical structure of
   the tasks, the utility structure defines the hierarchical composition of utility for
   doing a task. Again, the utility structure could involve tasks/relationships that the
   agent has no knowledge about them, but need to perform dynamic exploration
   in order to be able evaluate the utility dynamically.

Here in Figure 1 we show a task represented through agent capability structures. It shows the capability hierarchy for both agents *x* and *y*. Note that some capabilities are unique to one agent, such as B and E. In these cases they are inabilities to other agents. One *enables* relationship is shown between F and C, which means that F must finish before C can start.

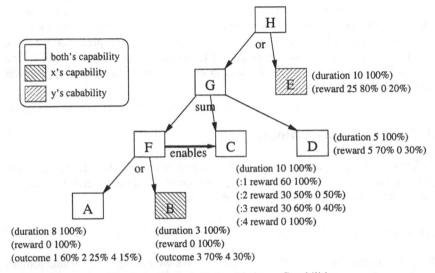

Fig. 1. An Example Task, with Agent Capabilities

A key characteristic in our agent knowledge base is uncertainty. There are several aspects of uncertainty. First, this means that tasks or relationships may have nondeterministic outcomes, and therefore the utility structure would need to define distributions rather than single value. This type of uncertainty originates from the stochastic nature of the problem solving, and the knowledge about the uncertainty is static and can be obtained offline. However, uncertainty can also originate from lack of static knowledge. For example, if an agent does not have a capability, it does not have the knowledge of how much effort or resource is needed before hand, but rather, it needs to perform dynamic exploration and discover the information it needs. Obviously, such information depends on the nature of other agents in the same system, and therefore is dynamic and cannot be specified offline.

Also, since agents are distributed and autonomous, an agent generally does not know all the events happening in other agents, and therefore it only has a partial view of the system, e.g., a partial view of the problem solving structure, a partial view of the utility structure, a partial view of the progress, i.e., runtime information about problem solving, and a partial view of the plans of the other agents.

In our definition of an agent, we hold it as a prerequisite that the agents are capable of communicating with each other, therefore be able to explore, discover, negotiate, and coordinate. The exact low level details of the underlying network, language, and format for communication among agents, although a very important part in actual implementation, are not the core subject of this study. Instead, in this research the communication is studied at the knowledge level.

We further assume that the agents are *rational*, that is, the agent would choose the actions that are of its best interest. The decisions of the choices are made to all aspects of its problem solving, including exploration of nonlocal information, local reasoning or planning, negotiation with other agents, and execution.

3.2 The Computation Model

A multi-agent system consists of several networked agents. The agents could be homogeneous or heterogeneous. As described above, each agent has its own knowledge base, and utility structure, but only has a limited view of the whole system. The agents can have streams of internal tasks to perform, i.e., internal periodic tasks, or have tasks received from outside the system, or both. There may be variations of the rate at which the tasks arrive to the system. The tasks correspond to the capabilities of one or more agents, and therefore the agents know how to perform them. In addition, there are constraints or requirements associated with each task. For example, time-critical tasks may impose deadline constraints.

When a task arrives the system, the agents would try to solve it according to its requirements, spend the necessary resources (e.g., time, money), in return for some type of reward. Note that, this assumption of per-task reward does not restrict ourselves to that kind of problems. In fact, rewards based on long-term, statistical behavior of the system (such as average throughput, annual earnings, etc.) can also be used since they can be interpreted through averaging over per-task values.

Based on how well a task is performed by the agents, there are different reward levels, therefore the problem solving is inherently a constraint optimization problem. However, we note that even when the reward is fixed regardless how the agents complete it (if they complete it at all), the problem is still an optimization problem since the agents would like to spend as little resource as possible.

According to the way utilities are received by the agents, there are two types of multi-agent systems: one that the agents are self-interested and one that the agents are cooperative. The difference between them is that for self-interested agents, each agent tries to maximize its own utility and there is no notion of global utility. But for cooperative agents, they share the same utility function — the global utility function, and their goal is to collectively maximize the global utility. In general, though, agents' utility structures can actually be very complex and there may not be a clear line between self-interested agents and cooperative agents. Thus the agents may be cooperating based on the sharing of parts of utility functions [23]. This means that coordination and cooperation becomes even more important for cooperative systems, since the agents must coordinate in order to know the impact of their local actions.

Our work will mainly focus on cooperative systems since we are interested in overall system performance, which indicates a global utility.

Given this computation model, in the following we will describe how we specify our model of agent problem solving in each of the layers in our approach, and more importantly, how to solve the problem.

4 The Bottom Layer: Decentralized Multi-agent MDP

The purpose of this layer is to provide a formal footing for cooperative multi-agent problem solving. As in any formal studies, we need a suitable mathematical representation of the problem. As such, high level representations such as capabilities and relationships have difficulty conforming to a rigorous mathematical model. To solve this problem we use a state representation, and try to model the problem solving process into a decision process. There, Markov decision processes are used as a tool for decision making under uncertainty, but to study the decision process in cooperative multi-agent systems, we need to develop an extension to the standard Markov decision process. To date, there are several flavors of such extensions [25, 1, 20, 13, 12, 14], but the DEC-MDP/POMDP model [1] is the common theoretical model used in most approaches. However, although this model is general enough, it does not distinguish agent coordination activities from agent domain actions, and thus solving a DEC-MDP/POMDP offers little insight toward developing coordination strategies. For this reason, in the following we will use the model in [25], in which the communication decisions and agent domain actions are separated. This allows us to model high level structures such as commitments and coordination mechanisms on top of this representation, and also facilitates the construction of approximation methods and heuristics.

4.1 Model Agent Meta-level Communication

In this model, an agent X's local actions and local state transitions can be modeled by a Markov process M^x: local state space S^x, local action set A^x, and local state transition probabilities $p^x(s_j^x|s_i^x, a^x)$. However, this is not a standard MDP because there is no local utility function. Instead, there is a global utility function that is based on the global states and joint actions.

The agents have partial view of the global state – the local state is really a partial observation of the global state. However, they can choose to communicate among themselves and obtain the local state information at other agents. In the more general DEC-MDP/POMDP framework, these communication actions as well as local actions can be viewed as partial observations of the global state, and it is proven that these DEC-MDP/POMDP have NEXP-complete complexity [2]. Thus, solving these problems optimally is generally very hard, although some subclass of DEC-MDP/POMDP can have a lower complexity level [12].

A solution (e.g. policy) to a DEC-MDP/POMDP consists of a set of local policies, which maps local information sets to local actions. However, the DEC-MDP/POMDP does not distinguish the agent's local outcome (something locally observable) and communication (must be done with other agents). If we treat each stage of agent problem solving as two substages, then we can separate a policy into two parts: at first substage, the agent observes local outcome of previous action and decides if communication is needed (the communication policy), and perform communication if so. Then, at the next stage, the agent decides which action is optimal given the information available (include the information just obtained through communication) – the local action policy. In this sense, communication can be viewed as an information gathering process. Figure 2 shows the sequence of the substages and the events occurring in one stage.

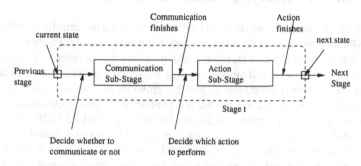

Fig. 2. Communication substage

To model communication, we use *messages* to represent the information exchange between agents. Local state information is the content of a message, and in particular, if an agent chooses not to communicate, its message will be *null*. Each agent can initiate communicate independently, we assume that the message format is mutually understood and that no message is lost/changed during communication.

Exactly how the information is shared after the communication clearly depends on the nature of communication, for example, *tell* is a type of communication in which one agent simply voluntarily tells its current local state to the other agent, i.e., information going outward; and *query* refers the type in which one agent sends a query (about other agent's local state) and receives the information back, i.e. information going inward; and another type, *sync*, is the combination of the above two, in that when an agent performs a sync communication, it reveals its own state to the other agent, and at the same time obtain the other agent's local state. As a result of sync (regardless of which agent initiates the communication), both agents now know the each other's local state, and also the knowledge that the other agent knows the same. Note that in actual implementations, more than one messages may be needed, but in our model it is sufficient to symbolize the process into one message communication.

Under this framework, we can easily establish the connection between DEC-MDP policies with agent planning and coordination strategies. Roughly speaking, the local action policy corresponds to the local planning process, which will employ a local planner to decide what domain action to perform; and the communication policy corresponds to the coordination process, which begins with establish common knowledge and uses meta-level communication to coordinate the agents' activities. Thus, this model offers a theoretical underpinning for the study of planning algorithms and coordination mechanisms: they are simply the two components in an agent's local decision-theoretic policy, and therefore they can be viewed as a way to construct agent policies. This gives us one approximation/heuristic method for solving DEC-MDP/POMDP.

5 The Middle Layer: Approximation Methods

In this layer we discuss approximation methods for solving decentralized multi-agent MDP. Although to solve the decision problem in the bottom layer exactly is computationally infeasible in most cases, the evaluation of heuristic policies is quite straightforward. This is because that since the policy tells which actions to choose at each state, we can iteratively enumerate all possible episodes and the state transition probability functions. The actual computation is similar to the policy evaluation method used in standard policy iteration algorithm for solving standard MDP, also known as backward-induction or dynamic programming. Thus, given a predefined policy, to evaluate its performance, i.e., expected total reward, is not a hard problem. However, traditionally, the research on multi-agent problem solving strategies often uses a task representation, not a low-level state-based representation. The reason is that task level representation is more intuitive and convenient for describing agent goals, intentions, and utilities than a state representation which is based on states, actions, and rewards. Therefore, in order to gain insight into the design of multi-agent problem-solving strategies, it is very important that we have a way of translating task-level strategies to state-level policies.

At task level, this representation is more coarse-grained than at state level, and this implies some approximation and simplification of the model of problem solving. At local level, the translation from task models to state models is fairly simple: each task is an action, and for each task a we can use a vector to represent all possible outcomes of the task. Then the local state space is simply a subset of all the combinations of the task outcome sequences. Such a state representation has an advantage of including the local action history information into the state model, although it does not reflect the communication history. Figure 3 shows part of the state space derived from the example task shown in Figure 1 for both agents x and y.

Next, we want to translate approximation policies, often in terms of agent coordination strategies in a task-based system. The key problem is to represent agent coordination. To achieve this we use *commitments* as the vehicle for agent coordination.

5.1 Definition of Commitments

By definition, a commitment specifies a pledge to do a certain course of action [16]. A number of commitment semantics have been proposed, for example, the "Deadline" commitment $C(T, Q, t_{dl})$ in [7], means a commitment to do (achieve quality Q

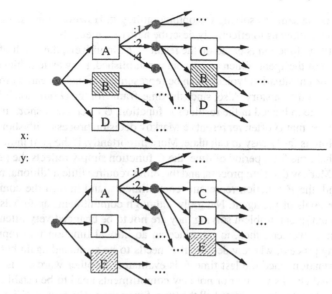

Fig. 3. State Space Representation for Tasks

or above for) a task T at a time t so that it finishes before a specified deadline, t_{dl}. When such a pledge is offered, the receiving agent can then do its own reasoning and planning based on this commitment, and thus achieves coordination between the agents. In recent years, the notion of commitment has emerged, among many research groups [5, 6, 7, 15], as the bridge for multi-agent coordination and planning. An agent's problem solving strategy, then, can be described as two parts: first, how to decide what commitments to make, and second, how to fulfill the commitments. Of course, due to the dynamic nature of problem solving, an agent also needs to monitor the problem solving and make changes to the commitments and the ways to achieve commitments when necessary, and this also part of the agent problem solving strategy.

Such a definition of commitments naturally leads to its state-level description. Specifically, a commitment reflects the agent's promise to be in a certain state (having a proper value for the outcome of a local task) at some future time. The strategy for choosing commitments can be characterized as a function F based on the agent's information. Remember in our framework the agents can choose to communicate and thus gain information during the communication sub-stage, F for agent X is defined for both $H_t^{x,m}$ and $H_t^{x,a}$. Similarly, the strategy for achieving the commitment can also be characterized as a function G, which define which actions (communication actions or task actions) is needed in order to fulfill the commitment. The G function is also defined on both $H_t^{x,m}$ and $H_t^{x,a}$. Obviously, the F and G functions are simply a different way of expressing the agent policy π, and to solve the optimal F and G

functions is the same as solving the optimal policy π. However, the use of F and G functions can allow us to effectively describe heuristic methods.

First, the G function is based on the result of F. Intuitively, the result of F represents a *goal* of the agent. When a new goal is established, the way to achieve the goal based on current situation typically can be represented through a search process, and does not depend on history. Also, since the time-frame for the G function is limited to the time-frame indicated in the result of F function, G often has a short time-frame. This indicates that G often represents a Markov decision process with short horizon, and therefore is fairly easy to calculate. More importantly, if the goal indicated by F remains the same for a period of time, the G function simply reflects the progress of the same Markov decision process, and therefore requires little additional reasoning.

Second, the F function represents commitments, and in turn the commitments reflect the goals of the agent. Naturally, although commitments and goals could be dynamic, in typical problem solving they are not to be changed very often [11, 10]. It is often convenient, then, to introduce an additional function v to represent the monitoring process, where v decides if F needs to be evaluated again based on the new information since the last time F is evaluated. In other words, v is a boolean function that checks whether or not new commitments need to be established. This way, F needs not to be evaluated all the time. Since the evaluation of F, i.e., deciding what commitments to make, is often a complex reasoning process, the use of v can significantly reduces the complexity and computational costs.

5.2 Uncertainty in Commitments

Implied in our state model for commitments is that commitments are uncertain. Due to the stochastic nature of problem solving, a promise of reaching a certain state in some future time often cannot be guaranteed. There could be several sources of uncertainty associated with a commitment. Sometimes, a task has an undesired outcome that causes the promise to be broken. This type of uncertainty can often be calculated when the commitment is made, because a stochastic process is defined by the G function, which is based on the result of F function. Another source of uncertainty is due to the possible change of commitments. Because of the dynamic nature of the system, an agent's view of the system is different from the view it had when the commitment was established. This may mean a different result of F and hence different commitments.

To deal with these uncertainties, two methods can be applied: one is to define statistical guarantee semantics to a commitment. This means that when describing a commitment, we need to also specify its reliability characteristics. This can be in the form of a distribution (often multivariate because a commitment involves potentially several uncertain parameters), or expressions regarding estimations of bounds and ranges. The description of a commitment can also include information regarding the dynamics of the reliability profile, for example when the success rate of a commitment may change and by how much. By planning ahead using these information, the agents can have a more complete picture about the future role of the commitment and thus reduce the chance of having unexpected failure events in the future that may cause ineffective coordination.

The other method is to monitor the commitment in the runtime and react to changes in the commitments. The monitoring function v is the key to this method. Based on the events occurred in the system since the F function is evaluated, i.e., the outcomes of the tasks and the communication messages the agent sent or received, v calculates the impact to the current commitments and therefore let the agents to decide if the commitments need to be changed.

5.3 System-wide Policy and Per-agent Policy

Based on the choices of F, G, and v functions (for each agent), we have an approximation to a multi-agent MDP policy. These functions are sufficient for the evaluation of this approximation policy. However, we need to make the distinction between the design of policies for *all* agents and the design of one-agent policies.

The design of policies for all agents, i.e., a system-wide policy, is based on the understanding of the global state space. In other words, the input for the this system-wide policy is the whole decision problem, including the global state space, utility function, and communication mechanisms. From an individual agent perspective, an agent can reason for a system-wide policy if knowledge about the global state space information is given, however, in that case, each agent has to follow the same system-wide policy, i.e., to assume that the other agents would reach the same system-wide policy, and therefore each agent knows the policies of other agents. This can be done, for example, by implementing the same system-wide policy produced by the system-designer in each agent. Under such a system-wide policy, the actual reasoning process does not occur within the agent. Rather, it is decided by the global state space alone.

However, if the system is an open one, or it contains heterogeneous or legacy agents, an agent cannot in general have a clear picture of the global state information necessary to reason about a system-wide policy. In some cases, even if an agent knows the global state space (thus it can reason about a system-wide policy), it cannot assume that the other agents are using the same reasoning techniques (cannot predict other agents' policies), and therefore it cannot simply derive the system-wide policy and follow that policy alone. Instead, the agent has to rely on partial knowledge of the whole system, and has a local reasoning process, and produce its own policy. This policy is not a system-wide policy but rather just for this agent only, although this policy does interact with other agents' policies. This means that, during the design of the one-agent policy, we cannot assume that we know the policy in other agents, nor assume that we can control the policy of the other agent. This is a practical assumption when designing agents for open systems. In these systems, an agent has only partial knowledge of other agents' state spaces, and also partial knowledge of other agents' policies. These partial knowledge forms the basis of the interaction among agent policies. In typical multi-agent coordination, to obtain the information about nonlocal state space and policies is a significant part of a coordination protocol. Again, commitment is the key in the interaction of the individual policies. A commitment indicates the agent's intention of reaching certain goals, thereby reveals partial information about the agent's policy. In our model, commitments are dynamic and therefore have uncertainties associated with them. To the agents who receive this commitment, dealing with these uncertainties often resembles the decision making under a partially-observable Markov process.

This distinction between a system-wide policy and a per-agent policy does not affect the evaluation of the policies, which is based on complete knowledge of the system no matter which type of policy is used. However, a system-wide policy is based on the complete view of the structure of the system, the so-called *objective view*. In comparison, a per-agent view is based on a partial view of the structure, i.e., the *subjective view*. Obviously, in many systems the subjective view does not equal the objective view. Moreover, when the system evolves during runtime, the subjective view can also evolve.

Having a subjective view means that, when designing per-agent policies, the choices of these functions are constrained, since they need to reflect the reasoning process based on a partial global view of the system, and therefore cannot use information unavailable to the agent. In particular, if an agent A only has a partial knowledge of the state space of some other agent B, to understand B's commitment, i.e., B's promise of being in a certain local state at a certain time, would be difficult. Rather, a commitment can be about some *feature* of the state rather than the state itself. This is quite natural in a task-based representation, where a state naturally contains information about the outcomes of various tasks. For example, a feature of the state may means that a certain task T is finished with a certain outcome. This is exactly the task-based semantics used in the work of Decker and Lesser [7].

Partial knowledge of some other agent's state space also leads to difficulties in understanding the other agent's policy. In particular, since commitments are uncertain, an agent needs to know not only which commitments are made, but also what can happen to these commitments. Typically, protocols often rely on explicit communication to make sure that the commitments are mutually understood among involved agents. In [26], we studied the additional information needed in order to deal with these uncertainties in commitments. This information is meant to be shared through communication. By the exchange of policy information, such as intentions, plans, schedules, actions, the agents do not need to have the global state space information needed in order to reason about other agents' policies. This can clearly make the agent's reasoning much simpler. Clearly, here the notion of communication is different from the primitive communication mechanism defined in our multi-agent decision process, which is limited to the exchange of state information. However, we note that this does not affect our evaluation of the policies (which is based on the objective view), but rather extends our definition of F, G, and v functions, such that these functions can use the policy information made available through these exchanges. In other words, such communication can be characterized as part of the dynamic expansion of the subjective view during problem-solving, so that more information is available to the agent.

5.4 Communication of Commitments

In the above discussion we indicated that communication of policy-related information can be part of the agent coordination. This is very important when agents cannot reason about other agents' policies because of the lack of knowledge about the global state space. However, note that, in our formal model, communication is limited to the sharing of nonlocal state information, and we argue that such communication may incur a cost. For policy information, though, it is often not feasible to impose a formal cost measure. One possible way to address this problem is to view policy-related information as an add-on to state information, so that the communication message contains not only state information but also some policy-related information, such as commitments, plans, and actions. Obviously, this restricts the communication of policy information to occur at the same time as the communication of state information.

Obviously, if communication is free, agents can exchange all state information at all times and thus a centralized approach (just study the optimal joint action for any global state) may be possible. In many coordination protocols, however, although communication is free, it is still prohibitive to communicate all information due to the system limitations. Thus, our decentralized model is very important even when communication is cost-free. In these systems, which information is to be communicated, and how much communication has occurred, are still important aspects of protocol design.

At the center of policy-related information is agent commitments. Commitments reveal agents' intentions, and the fulfillments of commitments is the key to successful coordination. Communication can ensure mutual understanding of the commitments, and can also specify the uncertainty in commitments. Also, communication has two roles in the dynamics of commitments. Communication is very important for the agent to decide what commitment to make since it provides the information it needs and reduces the uncertainty in agent reasoning process. At the same time, communication also allows the monitoring of the multi-agent problem solving, and therefore the agents can have the non-local information needed to decide whether or not the commitment needs to be revised. Since commitments are dynamic objects, a coordination protocol could also specify the communication for changes of commitments.

The mutual understanding of a commitment is not limited to the understanding of the promised state, but also the uncertainty associated with the commitment. The key to the handling of the uncertainty is the guarantee semantics of a commitment. Clearly, due to the stochastic nature of the system, the guarantee is a statistical one, not a 100% guarantee. Since other agents often lack the information needed in order to reason about the reliability of the commitment, communication is often also needed in order to explicitly tell what can happen to the commitment, and at what rate.

Using the same example task in Figure 1, suppose one heuristic method generates the following policy for the two agents. For x, the commitment it makes to y is that it finishes task C. The task of y is to complete task D so that task G is satisfied, and in turn task H is satisfied. However, since C may fail, y has a commitment to perform E if that happens. This covers the F function part. The G function part describes how x completes C, i.e., x shall perform A, and if the outcome is not 4, do C. Otherwise, x shall do B next, then do C. Communication is needed if C fails, in that case y start to fulfill its commitment of E. The v function here simply monitors x's commitment of C: if B fails, the commitment of C cannot be fulfilled. This policy is shown in Figure 4. It tells which action to take for both agents, and also communications between the agents (the dotted links).

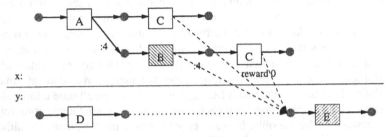

Fig. 4. An Example Policy

The key to the evaluation of this policy is the evaluation of the commitments. Obviously, the commitment about C offers only a statistical guarantee: C will succeed, i.e., obtain nonzero reward at 78.8% of the times. It is more interesting, however, to look at the dynamics of this commitment. Specifically, before A is finished, the success rate is 78.8%. After A completes, however, the rate can be 100% (if outcome is 1), 50% (outcome 2), or 42% (outcome 4, since B will be performed.) Similarly we can get updated expectations after B is completed. This information is useful for agents to dynamically adjust its policy. For example, if A finishes with outcome 1, we can see that C is now 100% guaranteed, hence y's commitment of E can be canceled if explicit communication for canceling the commitment is used, thereby improves this policy.

6 The Top Layer: Coordination Mechanisms for FT

In the two lower layers we defined the framework for multi-agent problem solving and heuristic methods. The key there is to define the underlying decision problem and to decide what information to share and what heuristic functions to use.

Through these two layers we can develop the whole agent policy from scratch. However, since a policy is often quite complex and cumbersome, we still need further approximation methods when the system scales up. To do this we need to have ways to describe a policy (or a partial policy) not at the detailed state level or task level, but at a higher level. This way, we can readily adopt many protocols and mechanisms developed previously in the context of planning and coordination. This way, we can pre-define a set of alternative mechanisms, and simplify the agent's reasoning process by selecting from these alternatives instead of using a search process. These pre-defined mechanisms are often very efficient and not computationally intensive, and at the same time provide good performance. Another important benefit of using pre-defined mechanisms is that although a detailed, low-level policy may achieve better performance, it is often not intuitive enough to give us direct insight, while the use of pre-defined mechanisms can help us understand the patterns of policy and the textures of the solution. For large, complex systems, such insight is crucial in the design of agent coordination policies.

Therefore, in this layer we shall study how to develop and use pre-defined alternatives in our framework. In this work, we focus on how fault tolerance is achieved by this approach. Fault-tolerance mechanisms have been extensively studied in the past, and we shall study how we can develop pre-defined mechanisms to adopt them into our multi-agent problem solving framework. First, we now introduce performability in terms of a measure of utility levels.

6.1 Performability

Formally, performability is based on the levels of accomplishments achieved by the system activities [19]. For finite horizon problems, problem solving is limited to a particular time interval $[T_s, T_f]$, where T_s is the start time and T_f is the finish time. Let's also assume that time is discrete.

Let Ω_f to be the set of finishing states of the system. These finishing states reflect the different levels of *accomplishments* achieved by the system activities during the problem solving period.

Let the function $d : \Omega_f \rightarrow [0,1]$ specify a probability measure of Ω_f, i.e., $\sum d(s_i | s_i \in \Omega_f) = 1$. In other words, d specifies the probability distribution on the set Ω_f. For example, if $\Omega_f =\{\text{pass,fail}\}$, then this d function: $d(\text{pass}) = 0.8$ and $d(\text{fail}) = 0.2$ means a distribution of 80% chance in state pass and 20% chance in state fail. Clearly, each d reflects an accomplishment level. Typically, system designers can have an evaluation function to compare if one distribution is better or more preferable than another distribution. Such evaluation function on the accomplishment profile is known as the *performability* measure of the system.

If a given policy π results in a finishing state distribution d, the performability of π is the same as the evaluation of d. Note that in a utility based model such as our MDP, there is a difference between d and the utility distribution resulted from π, and the performability measure is not necessarily equivalent to the evaluation of the expected utility of π. However, in many utility based models the states are distinguished by their utility values, and the utility structure can be engineered in such a way that the performability measure is simply the average expected utility. For simplicity, we will assume the equivalence of the performability measure and the utility measure in this work, and therefore finding the policy with best utility is equivalent to finding the policy with best expected utility.

Given our Markov model, under a fixed policy π, we can also evaluate the expected utility for any global state, which is simply the value of the same policy except assuming the starting state to be the current state. Clearly, under the optimal policy, the expected utility of a global state reaches its upper-bound. Notice that if a state s

has a higher upper-bound than another state s', it does not mean that s is always more preferable than s', since it often depends on the policy being used.

Using the same example task and policy illustrated by Figure 1 and Figure 4, x's policy produces a performability prospectus as such: 60% chance reward 60 and duration 18, 12.5% chance reward 30 and duration 18, 6.3% chance reward 30 and duration 21, 12.5% chance reward 0 and duration 18, 4.5% chance reward 0 and duration 11, and 4.2% chance reward 0 and duration 21. In the last three cases (21.2% chance), y need to perform E. Similarly we can calculate y's performability profile. These performability profiles allow us to calculate the performability measures, in our case expected utility values. Note that utility is not necessarily the same as reward. In our example, the utility could be the reward/duration ratio instead of the total reward, thus implies that there is cost for processing time, which is not part of the reward structure.

Like the commitments, the performability profile changes during the problem solving process, and the same for the utility expectations. Furthermore, calculations about the probabilistic outcomes of commitments can be used for performability estimations, and vice versa. In our framework, performability is the key that connects commitments with utility measures.

6.2 Fault Tolerance Mechanisms

Clearly, given our performability model, a *failure* refers to an undesirable accomplishment level. A failure can also occur during the problem solving. Intuitively, if an agent moves from a state with higher expected utility to a state with lower expected utility, that means some undesired event has occurred, and this transition can arguably be called a failure. It is arguable since these expected utility values are based on a particular policy, under another policy there could be different values, or such move cannot be made at all. In a task-based system, such a failure could be defined as a task having an undesirable outcome.

In fault-tolerance terms, the type of faults we are modeling is task fault. A task fault is transient, stochastic, and localized to this task only. It can be described through a failure probability (this corresponds to our transition probability). Historically, metrics such as MTBF (mean time between failures) and MTTF (mean time to failure) are often used to describe the reliability of an agent doing continuous tasks. By assuming that occurrence of failures follows a particular probability distribution (Poisson distribution is an often used one), these metrics can be translated as per-task failure probability as well.

To handle these faults, there are many FT techniques:

- Checkpoints: when a task spans a long duration or consists a series of subtasks, checkpoints can be inserted and the results up to these checkpoints are saved. This way, when a failure occurs, the agent only need to repeat the work (roll back) after the latest checkpoint.
- Primary-backup (PB): when a task (the primary task) is to be performed, a backup task, which is a duplication of the primary task, is also planned. If the

primary task succeeds, the backup task would be canceled. The task fails only when both primary task and the backup fails.

- Primary-exception (PE): this is essentially the same as primary-backup, except that the backup need not be a duplication, but rather a task capable of the solving the same work in a different way. Usually the backup task requires less effort but has lower performance, and hence the name.

- Triple-modular-redundancy (TMR): this technique requires parallel execution of three copies of the same task. However, unlike the techniques we listed above, here we cannot tell the result of a task is right or wrong, i.e., we can know the probability of having the right answer, but there is uncertainty regard the correctness of the result. Thus, in this technique, there is a simple *voter* procedure that compares the three results: if the majority of the three show the same result, that result is *considered* as correct, e.g., less likely to be wrong. Otherwise (all three are different from each other), a failure is concluded. This mechanism is not only a redundancy technique that improves reliability, but also a fault-detection technique.

- N-copy: here the number of copies can be N instead of 2 or 3. This can be viewed as a generalization of PB and TMR.

- Self-checked pair (SCP): this technique changes TMR a little bit: instead of performing three copies (which requires a lot of resource), two copies are performed first, followed by a comparison procedure, which decides if the two results are identical. If so, the result is considered correct and the third copy need not to be performed. Otherwise, the third copy is performed and then the voter decides if a failure has occurred. Logically it is equivalent to TMR, but it is adaptive since there is a good chance that the third copy needs not to be performed.

In an intelligent system, a key feature is that an agent often knows several ways of achieving the same task. This allows us to execute several strategies at the same time, or choose an alternative way when one strategy fails. This is a natural generalization to redundancy techniques such as primary-backup and primary-exception.

The introduction of redundancy tasks further complicates the agent problem solving. Since a task can be executed more than one times, and more than one alternative can be applied, an agent now has much more choices in its decision making. The state space can potentially grow drastically compared to the case that an agent can only execute a task once. As such, to develop pre-defined mechanisms to reduce the size of the state space and the complexity in the search for solutions becomes even more important.

Such pre-defined mechanisms are not only used in multi-agent coordination, but also in single-agent planning. For example, primary-backup technique can be used either across two agents, with one doing the primary task and the other doing the backup copy, or within a single-agent, making it completely local processing.

As an example, let us study how to translate the PE technique (a generalized one) into a pre-defined mechanism. Assuming the goal is G and two alternatives for this goal are A and B, and the two agents involved are X and Y. The mechanism PE(A, B) can be specified as:

- Agent X makes a commitment about A. The parameters to be decided include when A would finish, and a threshold to decide if A is failed.
- At the same time Y need to make a commitment about B, and decide when B should finish. Another parameter could be its start time, since B usually needs not start before A finishes.
- A communication policy to ensure that Y understands the result of A. A simple strategy would be to let X tell Y if A succeeded or not. Other communication strategy can also be used, for example, Y can assume A succeeded if it does not hear from X before some previously agreed-upon time.
- Y decommits B if it knows A has succeeded. Otherwise the commitment is kept and B will be performed.

As we can see, there are some parameters to be decided in this mechanism, and by varying these parameters there could be some variations to the PE technique. For example, Y can start B quite early, when A has not finished (or even started). Logically, there is no difference from the original PE technique, but here this mechanism can have more flexibility. In addition, X and Y could be the same agent, and in this case both commitment are local ones.

This mechanism provides a pre-defined package for the agents to understand each other's roles involving a series of activities. By using these mechanisms, agents can reduce their overhead in reasoning and communication, therefore improves efficiency. Of course, these mechanisms only defines a small part of the agent policy, and they cannot completely replace agent reasoning. For example, in PE, if B also fails, the agents then have to rely on the rest of the policy to reason and handle the failures so as to ensure a graceful degradation.

Similarly, for SCP, assuming the task is A, the mechanism SCP(A) can be defined as:

- Agents X and Y both make a commitment regarding task A.
- Agent Z also makes a commitment about A, but with a later start time and finish time.
- A communication mechanism between X and Y to compare their outcomes. Furthermore, if the results are the same, Z will be notified, otherwise both outcomes are transmitted to Z.
- Z can decommit if X and Y have the same outcome. Otherwise, A is performed, and the result is compared to X and Y's results. If one of them is the same as Z's result, Z's outcome is regarded as correct. Otherwise, all three results are distinct, a failure result is considered.

As an example, let us look at the policy illustrated in Figure 4. This policy exhibits some patterns that can be compactly represented via mechanisms, by noting that tasks A and B forms a PE mechanism for task F, and task E also serves as the exception method for task G, which consists of A, B, C, and D. Figure 5 illustrates these two cases of PE mechanism. Note that a mechanism can be applied intra-agent (like A and B) or inter-agent (like G and E), the difference is that the latter involves possible communications.

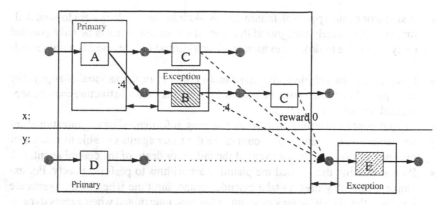

Fig. 5. Mechanisms

The use of mechanisms not only identifies common patterns in policies, but also simplifies the evaluation process. For example, the outcome profile for PE mechanism can be easily computed given the outcome profiles of both the primary and the exception tasks, even though both tasks could be complex structures on their own: if A's chance of failure outcomes is p, i.e., B is invoked at chance p, then the outcome profile of PE mechanism consists of all A's outcomes that does not result in failure, plus all B's outcomes with their chances multiplied by p.

Many more mechanisms can be defined based on a variety of existing coordination strategies. A family of mechanisms are needed, not only on fault-tolerance, but also on other aspects of problem solving, such as dealing with inter-relationships and handling uncertainties. The reason for a family of mechanisms is that mechanisms are highly situation-specific. Through the study of the mechanisms, we can gain insight into the characteristics of the problems and recognize when it is effective to apply certain mechanisms and when it is not.

7 Organization-Related Failures

So far we presented a framework in which FT mechanisms can be integrated in multiagent planning to handle tasks failures or underarchievements. However, these are not the only types of failures. While many multiagent planning research do address the issue of dealing with uncertainty and handling failures, the scope and extent of the problems that have been addressed so far is rather limited. The types of failures and events that a large scale multiagent system have to deal with not only include task failures, broken communications, violated commitments, etc. but also must include agent failures, changed agent organizations, even agent deaths. Robustness in multiagent operations must be a priority in the system design. This, however, is an immensely complex problem and has not been adequately addressed so far. It is easy to envision the kinds of problems or even catastrophes that may result if we do not address the issue of robustness:

- A single or central point-of-failure that would lead the whole system to total malfunction. It is widely recognized that even if the central point is heavily guarded (very expensive to do), the existence of such central failure point is a vulnerability.
- Fixed group control hierarchy that cannot adapt to organizational changes. For example, when agents enter or leave the group, the control structure may be segregated, broken, or disintegrated.
- Central control/planning that stores planning information or organizational information in one agent. This would cause the other agents not able to recover or resume the joint goal in the event of the failure or death of the central agent.
- Poor scalability that caused the planning algorithms to perform poorly. For example, agent may need to take extended reasoning time when many agents are involved, the algorithm may time out or become interrupted when agents dynamically enter or leave the group.

In order for existing planning frameworks (that are designed for a fixed (and often small-sized) group of agents) to work in large scale systems, we must develop mechanisms to complement them and avoid potential pitfalls. Here, we attempt to address the robustness problem by focusing on the issue of plan adaptation in the event of agent failures. We introduce several techniques to enhance the plan robustness, in particular with regard to agent deaths.

The focus here is to investigate the organizational means for piecing together the otherwise fragile and unrobust local planning frameworks to provide a level of robustness at the global level. It should be noted that the small-scale solutions (the local planning part) remain to be fragile, and the global plan (as a loose ensemble of local plans) may not be perfectly consistent at any moment. Our major concern is to contain the effects of local failures and prevent the failures from affecting the global system, by limiting the scope of the small-scale solutions and providing dynamic adaptation and organization. There is a large body of work on how to enhance plan robustness *per se* in classic literature in reliability of distributed systems and robustness in robotic systems. These and other related studies would undoubtedly benefit our approach, but at this moment they are not our main concern.

7.1 The Minesweeping Problem

To better understand the issues involved in plan adaptation, let us use the following multiagent cooperation problem as an example and focus our discussion around it:

Suppose that there is a minefield that needs to be swept. The exact number and positions of the mines are unknown. To do this, we will air-drop a batch of robotic minesweepers (hundreds or thousands of them) onto that field. Each robot is capable of roaming the field and detecting mines. A robot (i.e. an agent) can also blow itself up – by doing so it can destroy all the mines within a certain radius to itself. Each robot has some wireless communication equipment for communicating with nearby peers and they should cooperate with each other to maximize the performance – identify the existence of the mines and also destroy them as much as possible.

In addition, let's assume that all robots have positioning capability (such as GPS receivers) so that they can know their own positions. Also suppose that the map is known to all robots before the operation. For modeling purpose, we can divide the minefield into small square units and the task would be to find out if the squares contain mines and to destroy them. In practice, there will also be other constraints, such as the agent's power, range, mobility in different terrains, etc, but for simplicity let us not consider those problems for now. This problem has some resemblance to problems of swarm intelligence [3], however, our agents are not simple organisms but they do have complex planning ability and are able to communicate with each other, even at meta level. Thus, their group or organizational level behaviors are results of deliberation, rather than swarm intelligence.

Since minesweeping is inherently a dangerous operation, an agent could involuntarily step on a mine and thus be destroyed (when that happens, all mines as well other robots within a certain radius will also be destroyed.) Also, a robot could be damaged during the operation. Thus, agent deaths are quite possible – either planned or unexpected.

It is conceivable that one may pre-program the robots with a predetermined plan. For example, one could divide the region into many pieces and assign each robot to sweep a different region. However, it is easy to see that there may be drawbacks. First of all, the setup may be fairly time consuming. Second, there is little control when air-dropping the robots, so the robots would not be placed in their targeted regions. Finally, due to the uncertainties and the probabilities of failures, the plan may become rather ineffective. Thus, some form of dynamic planning would be needed.

We will not focus on the specifics of the planning approach here, rather, we are more interested at the problem of how to maintain the plan across the agent organization. Based on the characteristics of this problem, the viable planners must be able to implement some form of subgrouping coordination among the agents, so that the agents would form groups to cooperatively explore parts of the field. The following issues need to addressed to ensure robustness:

- Because of the number of agents involved, it would be infeasible for any one agent to establish/compute a global plan. Plus this would mean that if that agent dies, the plan is lost.
- It is also infeasible to allow direct negotiation among all agents, not only because of the scale of the negotiation, but also because of the limit bandwidth and possible interference in agent communication.
- Since the agents are air-dropped to a new environment, there is no external services or infrastructures that the agents can utilize. Thus, the agents need to perform self-organization and self-service.
- Thus, agents would need to form groups to cooperatively explore parts of the map. This 3-level architecture (individual agent level, group level, and the whole organization level) is the key in organizational theory and is critical in large scale multiagent systems. However there has been little work so far in the multiagent planning research society that explicitly deals with this architecture. In addition,

we need to address issues such as group formation (and division as well), agent location, and group interaction.

- Since an agent may die at any moment, this may cause problem to the group: an agent may leave the group at any moment (agent death can be seen as a special case of agent leaving.) Thus, the group status need to be constantly monitored.
- Also, if the agent leaving the group is the group leader (who is at least partially in charge of maintaining the group plan), there is a need for the group to be re-formed, and the plan need to be recovered. In some cases, when the agent voluntarily chooses to die, there could be a process for a new leader to be elected; in other cases, the group would need to discover the exit of the leader, and reconstruct a group if possible.

In the next sections we will first discuss the mechanisms for establishing groups and joint plans among the agents discuss the mechanisms for intra-group and inter-group coordination, then discuss how to maintain or monitor group status, and finally discuss how to recover plans when a group manager agent (group leader) dies.

7.2 Group Formation and Plan Composition

Although coalition formation [21, 17] is an active research subject, much of the emphasis has been put in the game-theoretic aspect rather than in the organizational aspect. In our application scenario, the agents are inherently cooperative and they share an ultimate joint goal, which is to achieve the overall minesweeping mission as a whole. In other words, this represents a top level goal. Let us define a membership relationship between a goal and any agent subscribed to this goal, i.e. **member(g)** defines the set of agents that share the intent to pursue this goal g collectively. In this sense, a goal defines a group organization. For the top level goal, its member set is simply the set of all agents.

At the bottom level, each individual agent has its own local goal, and only this agent alone subscribes to this goal. Thus, the member set for the local goal contains only the agent itself.

For a large scale system to work, there needs to be intermediate level goals, and those goals can form a goal network which specifies the goal hierarchy similar to a goal search tree [16, 18], with the top level organization goal at the root of the hierarchy and agent local goals as the bottom leaf nodes. A group can be viewed as the member set of a goal. Thus, if the agent is subscribed to a set of goals, it also has the membership to all the corresponding groups. Ideally, the goals are perfectly decomposed so lower level goals completely satisfy the high level goals. Also, the subgoals should be perfectly coordinated to maximize performance and minimize resource usage and overlap of goals. However, in reality, the goals may not be complete or even coordinated. In this minesweeping problem, we can view each goal as the intention to have all its members to cooperatively sweep a certain region. However, the goals may not cover the whole map, and there could be overlapping regions. Figure 1 shows an example of such goal hierarchy. On the top is the map of the region and the ovals and boxes show the intended sweep area for each goal (different

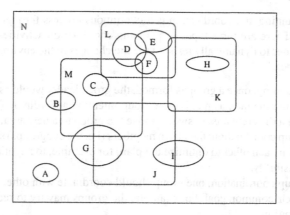

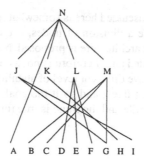

Fig. 6. Groups and the Incomplete Composition of Goals

shapes indicate different levels). On the bottom is the corresponding goal hierarchy. Clearly, the subgoals of N does not cover the whole region, and there are some overlaps between peer groups J and M. Note that although the figure shows a three level hierarchy, this does not necessarily mean that a 3-level hierarchy is sufficient. As the number of agent grows, there would certainly be more levels.

The basic group formation process for this problem can be viewed as similar to a hierarchical clustering process: we can start with each agent itself as a group, and then adjacent groups could be merged together to form larger groups. Those larger groups would also define their goals (i.e. the area the group intend to investigate.) For the mechanism to be scalable, we want to apply group size constraints so that the groups would not contain an unmanageable member size. In some cases, a large group may be divided into smaller groups, so that the groups are more manageable. The exact process of choice for this problem is not the focus of this work, but in the end we shall obtain a hierarchy like the one shown in Figure 1. Thus, for each agent, the set of goals in which this agent is a member can be decided by tracing up the goal hierarchy. The paths can be maintained in the agent and the agent thus is aware of its group memberships.

Group planning and coordination is a continuous process throughout the problem solving. There are three types of planning/coordination activities that may be involved in order to dynamically respond the the changes in the environment and the action outcomes:

1. Group planning: once a group is formed, the group leader would assume the role of the group planner, as modify the group intention accordingly (this means to decide on a different area to sweep, move the group to a new area, etc.
2. Intra-group coordination: the group members (i.e. the subgroups) should coordination with each other to optimize the plan, for example, to negotiate their areas of responsibility.
3. Inter-group coordination: one group should coordinate with other groups to optimize their common goal. For example, the groups may try to reduce the overlapping region.

This type of coordination discussed here is somewhat related to the partial global planning framework [9] where a division of nodes, acquaintances, and the whole system is made and a dynamic architecture is proposed. Note that since group membership information is distributed and therefore is not a central point of failure. The different levels of goals also have different level of stability or flexibility: at the root level the organization is almost fixed, and so it the goal; while at lower levels the groups are more and more volatile and the same is true for agents' local goals.

7.3 Group Maintenance

Each group should contain a group leader that represents the group members, manages/designs the plans for each group member, and interacts with the other groups. As such its role is quite important. The leader of the group should be able track the group members and the group members should be able to be connected with the leader. The leader of the group should be elected or decided by the members – some criteria would include to select the agent that is most convenient for the organization and optimize resource usage, as well as to select the agent that is most stable (in the sense that the agent would have a long lifetime with the group.)

Since agent failure can happen at any time, we should not implement hard constrains or commitments among the agents. Rather, the plans are inherently "best-effort" plans, with no hard guarantee semantics. Each agent can decide to enter or leave a group at any time, and the group leader can decide to remove any member as well.

A key problem for the groups is to find out if any group member has left the group. When an agent leaves a group voluntarily, it is conceivable that the agent may announce its intention before its departure (that includes blow up itself, since the agent won't be around any more). However, when an agent involuntarily leave the group, we definitely need to have a mechanism to find out. (Involuntary leaves may include being destroyed by a mine, agent internal breakdown, and also communication failures.) We propose a simple "heartbeat" mechanism to detect agent departure:

- When the group is established and the leader is identified, each member would periodically communicate with the leader, i. e. send the "heartbeat message" to indicate "I am here." If the leader does not receive the heartbeat messages for some duration, the leader can assume that the member is no long in the group.
- Similarly, the group leader periodically broadcast to other group members. If a member does not receive heartbeat message for some duration, the member can assume that the leader has left.

Of course, being able to send heartbeat messages does not mean that the agent is actually in good condition (maybe the communication component is working but other components are not). Thus, additional communications for sharing agent action outcomes may be needed (but at a less frequent rate.)

The heartbeat mechanism is often used in fault-tolerant systems for tracking the status of distributed entities and fault detection [22]. It requires a fixed amount of communication bandwidth – the larger the group is, the more bandwidth would be needed. This would impose a constraint on the size of the group. However, as we indicated before, we intentionally limit the group size so that we would not encounter a group with many members. Instead, a multi-level hierarchy can be used to deal with large scale organizations.

Note that the decision of sending a heartbeat message or not is entirely within the agent: even if the communication channel is open, the agent may decide not to send heartbeat messages – and therefore effectively disengages itself from the rest of the group (or fake death in some sense). Likewise, an agent may decide to keep membership in more than one groups at the same time. As such, this mechanism is not failure-proof, in particular when facing malicious failures (from agents that deliberately act to harm the organization.) This seems to lead to a system for establishing trust and reputation for solving this types of problems, but at present it is beyond our scope.

7.4 Plan Recovery

The loss of a non-leader member in a group would cause the group plan to be partially inconsistent, but the group leader, acting as the group planner, would be able to perform replanning and this at least partially address the problem. However, if the leader dies, the group is left without the planner, and some of plan information would be lost. For the rest of the group to continue to adapt to the environment, we need to establish a plan recovery mechanism, so that the rest of the group can reconstitute a plan and a new leader would emerge to inherit the responsibility.

One possible technique is to implement some redundancy in the group, so that the leader has a backup, or even more than one backups. Once the leader dies, the backup can take over. This way, the plan (actually, just the plan information alone) can be perfectly recoverable.

However, this adds some complexity to the organization structure and adds overhead because the backups need to be constantly synchronized with the leader. Note that the information that the backups keep is the exact copy of the leader's information, and thus the original plan would be restored when the leader dies. However, if we can relax the requirement so that it is not completely necessary to restore to the plan (or really, just to retrieve the old plan information) before the leader's death, we don't actually need backups, instead we can come up with an alternative plan based on the information in the rest of the group members - a form of imperfect recovery.

In fact, because the leader just died, the original plan before the leader's death would be somewhat obsolete anyway, so the need for keeping backups (perfect recovery) is indeed questionable.

According to the monitoring mechanisms described in the previous section, we know that when the leader dies the other members would notice the event. Thus, it is possible for any one of the other members to announce that the it is going to take over as the new maintainer of the original group goal. Other members can notice that the new announcer is announcing the same goal which the old leader maintained, and can respond with their current plans. Therefore, the new leader can collect current plan information and be able to reconstitute the old plan *except the old leader's local plan* - this part of information is lost when the old leader dies. The new leader would thus be able to replan for the new group.

8 Summary

We discussed the issue of planning in a degradable multiagent system and presented a framework in which FT techniques can be integrated into agent planning/coordination to handle uncertainty in domain problem solving as well as organizational change. Our framework starts at the decision-theoretic level to formally define performability in multiagent problem solving, then moves on to the agent planning and coordination level, and finally at the organizational level. Our ultimate goal, evidently, is to create fault-tolerant multiagent systems, and to allow simple translation or application of the many FT techniques that have been design for traditional systems in multiagent systems. The real challenge, is not about applying a few techniques that address the reliability concern of some aspects of the system, but to incorporate robustness into every aspect of the system design. At this point, a lot of work remains to be done in order to prove that those mechanisms indeed work and that the framework does allow easy integration of FT techniques in MAS.

Another important aim of this research is to enhance and extend existing planning frameworks - so that these planning frameworks can still find their applications, but with the proposed mechanisms they can implement some FT mechanisms and also form a large solution by piecing together smaller solutions. In both cases, coordination is really the key toward enhancing the robustness of the system - to handle both task failures as well as organizational failures. The FT techniques involved in the proposed mechanisms are not new - they have been used in the context of distributed systems or fault-tolerant computing, but new meanings are being developed in the context of autonomous agent systems and robust organizations.

References

1. D. Bernstein, R. Givan, N. Immerman, and S. Zilberstein. The complexity of decentralized control of markov decision processes. *Mathematics of Operations Research*, 27(4):819–840, November 2002.
2. Daniel S. Bernstein, Shlomo Zilberstein, and Neil Immerman. The complexity of decentralized control of markov decision processes. In *Proceedings of the Sixteenth Conference on Uncertainty in Artificial Intelligence (UAI-2000)*, 2000.
3. E. Bonabeau, M. Dorigo, and G. Theraulaz. *Swarm Intelligence: From Natural to Artificial Systems*. Oxford University Press, 1999.
4. C. Boutilier. Sequential optimality and coordination in multiagent systems. In *Proceedings of the Sixteenth International Joint Conferences on Artificial Intelligence (IJCAI-99)*, July 1999.
5. C. Castelfranchi. Commitments: from individual intentions to groups and organizations. In *AI and theories of groups & organizations: Conceptual and Empirical Research. Michael Prietula, editor. AAAI Workshop Working Notes.*, 1993.
6. Philip R. Cohen and Hector J. Levesque. Intention is choice with commitment. *Artificial Intelligence*, 42(3):213–261, 1990.
7. Keith S. Decker and Victor R. Lesser. Generalizing the partial global planning algorithm. *International Journal of Intelligent and Cooperative Information Systems*, 1992.
8. Keith S. Decker and Victor R. Lesser. Quantitative modeling of complex computational task environments. In *Proceedings of the Eleventh National Conference on Artificial Intelligence*, pages 214–217, 1993.
9. Edmund H. Durfee and Victor R. Lesser. Using partial global plan to coordinate distributed problem solvers. In *Proceedings of the Tenth International Conference on Artificial Intelligence*, 1987.
10. Edmund H. Durfee and Victor R. Lesser. Predictability versus responsiveness: Coordinating problem solvers in dynamic domains. In *Proceedings of the Seventh National Conference on Artificial Intelligence*, pages 66–71, 1988.
11. S. Fujita and V. Lesser. Centralized task distribution in the presence of uncertainty and time deadlines. In *Proceedings of the Second International Conference on Multi-Agent Systems*, pages 87–94, 1996.
12. C. V. Goldman and S. Zilberstein. Decentralized control of cooperative multi-agent systems: Categorization and complexity analysis. *Journal of Artificial Intelligence Research*, 2004.
13. Carlos Guestrin, Shobha Venkataraman, and Daphne Koller. Context specific multiagent coordination and planning with factored mdps. In *Proceedings of the Eighteenth National Conference on Artificial Intelligence (AAAI-2002)*, 2002.
14. Eric Hansen, Daniel Bernstein, and Shlomo Zilberstein. Dynamic programming for partially observable stochastic games. In *Proceedings of the Nineteenth National Conference on Artificial Intelligence (AAAI-04)*, pages 709–715, San Jose, California, 2004.
15. N. R. Jennings. Commitments and conventions: The foundation of coordination in multiagent systems. *The Knowledge Engineering Review*, 1993.
16. N. R. Jennings. Coordination techniques for distributed artificial intelligence. In G.M.P. O'Hare and N.R. Jennings, editors, *Foundations of Distributed Artificial Intelligence*. John Wiley, 1996.
17. K. Lerman and O. Shehory. Coalition formation for large-scale electronic markets. In *Proceedings of the International Conference on Multi-Agent Systems (ICMAS'2000)*, 2000.
18. V. R. Lesser. A retrospective view of fa/c distributed problem solving. *IEEE Transactions on Systems, Man, and Cybernetics*, 21, 1991.

19. John F. Meyer. On evaluating the performability of degradable computing systems. *IEEE Transactions on Computers*, C-29(8):720–731, 1980.
20. D. Pynadath and M. Tambe. The communicative multiagent team decision problem: Analyzing teamwork theories and models. *JAIR*, 16:389–423, 2002.
21. O. Shehory and S. Kraus. Task allocation via coalition formation among autonomous agents. In *Proceedings of the International Joint Conference on Artificial Intelligence*, 1995.
22. John A. Stankovic and Krithi Ramamritham, editors. *Advances in Real-Time Systems*. IEEE Computer Society, December, 1993.
23. Thomas Wagner and Victor Lesser. Relating quantified motivations for organizationally situated agents. In N.R. Jennings and Y. Lespérance, editors, *Intelligent Agents VI — Proceedings of the Sixth International Workshop on Agent Theories, Architectures, and Languages (ATAL-99)*, Lecture Notes in Artificial Intelligence. Springer-Verlag, Berlin, 2000.
24. Ping Xuan and Victor Lesser. Incorporating uncertainty in agent commitments. In *Intelligent Agents VI: Agents, Theories, Architectures and Languages (ATAL), Proceedings of The Sixth International Workshop on Agent Theories, Architectures, and Languages (ATAL-99), Lecture Notes in Artificial Intelligence 1757*. Springer-Verlag, 1999.
25. Ping Xuan, Victor Lesser, and Shlomo Zilberstein. Communication decisions in multi-agent cooperation: Model and experiments. In *Proceedings of the Fifth International Conference on Autonomous Agent (AGENTS 01)*, pages 616–623, Montreal, Canada, 2001.
26. Ping Xuan and Victor R. Lesser. Incorporating uncertainty in agent commitments. In N.R. Jennings and Y. Lespérance, editors, *Intelligent Agents VI — Proceedings of the Sixth International Workshop on Agent Theories, Architectures, and Languages (ATAL-99)*, Lecture Notes in Artificial Intelligence. Springer-Verlag, Berlin, 2000.

Index